Psychological Statistics

Using
SPSS® for Windows

Robert C. Gardner

Department of Psychology
The University of Western Ontario

Prentice
Hall

Upper Saddle River, New Jersey 07458

Library of Congress Cataloging-in-Publication Data

Gardner, Robert C.
  Psychological statistics using SPSS for Windows / R. C. Gardner.
    p.   cm.
  Includes bibliographical references and index.
  ISBN 0–13–028324–X
  1. Psychology—Statistical methods—Computer programs.   2. SPSS for Windows.
I. Title.
BF39.G35 2001
150′.1′5195—dc21

00–038519
CIP

VP, Editorial director: Laura Pearson
Acquisitions editor: Jayme Heffler
Assistant editor: Allison Westlake
Managing editor: Mary Rottino
Production liaison: Fran Russello
Editorial/production supervision: Bruce Hobart (Pine Tree Composition)
Prepress and manufacturing buyer: Tricia Kenny
Marketing manager: Sharon Cosgrove
Art director: Jayne Conte
Cover designer: Bruce Kenselaar

SPSS is a registered trademark of SPSS, Inc. The tables on pp. 290–93 and 296–97
from © 1963 R. A. Fisher and F. Yates. Reprinted by permission of Addison Wesley
Longman Limited. Reprinted by permission of Pearson Education Limited.

This book was set in 10/12 Times Ten by Pine Tree Composition, Inc.,
And was printed and bound by Victor Graphics, Inc.
The cover was printed by Phoenix Color Corp.

© 2001 by Prentice-Hall, Inc.
A Division of Pearson Education
Upper Saddle River, New Jersey 07458

Printed in the United States of America

10 9 8 7 6 5 4 3 2

ISBN 0-13-028324-X

Prentice-Hall International (UK) Limited, *London*
Prentice-Hall of Australia Pty, Limited, *Sydney*
Prentice-Hall Canada, Inc., *Toronto*
Prentice-Hall Hispanoamericana, S.A., *Mexico*
Prentice-Hall of India Private Limited, *New Delhi*
Prentice-Hall of Japan, Inc., *Tokyo*
Pearson Education Asia Pte. Ltd., *Singapore*
Editora Prentice-Hall do Brasil, Ltda., *Rio de Janeiro*

Contents

Chapter 5   Single-Factor Repeated Measures Designs   106

Chapter 6   Split-Plot Analysis of Variance   127

Chapter 10   Factor Analysis   236

Chapter 11   Multivariate Analysis of Variance   260

Preface

I first began writing this book seven years ago to fill a need. I had been asked to initiate a half-year course on Computer Applications in Psychological Research, and planned to place much of the emphasis on data analysis. The prerequisite was a full-course Introductory Statistics course in which students learned the basis of probability theory, t-tests, single- and two-factor completely randomized design analysis of variance, and bivariate regression. I found when I looked for a textbook that would meet our needs, that there didn't appear to be anything suitable. There were traditional statistics textbooks that dealt with some of the more complex procedures that we wanted to cover like multiple regression and factor analysis, etc., manuals that focussed primarily on communicating with computer packages, or annotated manuals that by-and-large dealt with the simpler analytic procedures such as cross-tabs, tests of means, etc. What the course needed, however, was a textbook that showed students how to interact with **SPSS,** how to understand the output and how to interpret it, and, just as importantly, one that provided the fundamentals underlying the procedures. In my view, this required a mid-level statistics book that students could read and understand, without being bogged down in computational formulae and mathematical notation. I felt, however, that the textbook should also explain the procedures so that students could see the implications of their analyses. Many computer programs are very comprehensive and versatile, but I felt that it was best to instruct readers on the basics that they needed, on the assumption that they could experiment with the extensions after they understood the fundamentals.

This book has undergone a number of revisions (the first few versions dealt with the DOS version of **SPSS**), and unpublished copies have been used as the textbook since the beginning. Initially, I also required our students to purchase a more manual-type textbook, but it soon became apparent that the students had little need for that sort of book. Once they became familiar with the system, they learned how to make use of the Help files, or simply to experiment on their own. A more important need, it appeared, was a book that explained the basic procedures in a clear and coherent fashion.

Although the book was initially intended for a third-year honors-level course, I found that graduate students and colleagues also found it helpful. Students in my graduate class in Research Design claimed that they found it useful to read the relevant chapters in my book before taking on the textbooks that I had chosen for the course. They claimed that it helped to make the textbooks more readable. Colleagues have also noted that it has served to remind them of analytic procedures that they hadn't used in some time. Some members of other faculties and other universities similarly

ix

report that the book has been useful in their courses, and one reviewer of the penultimate manuscript suggested that the book would be useful for a graduate-level textbook in some departments.

My intention in writing this book was to keep it short and simple. Many statistical concepts are relatively straightforward, and I have attempted to provide simple explanations of the concepts and principles, wherever possible. On occasions, I have had to admit that further explanation was beyond the scope of the book, but I have tried to keep this to a minimum, and to point to clear sources for further study. I have presented some formulae where I thought it would help the description, but I have refrained, in general, from showing many equations with lengthy computational exercises. It seems that with computers able to do the majority of computations, attention to computational niceties is unnecessary. The one exception to this generalization is in the discussions of post hoc tests following an analysis of variance. There I have given worked out examples, and have referred tangentially to a computer program, post hoc, that I have that will perform these computations for you.

Readers of this book will find some elements that are generally not found in other books. In addition to instructions on how to perform the major analytic procedures in both **SPSS 8.0** and **SPSS 9.0,** there are other elements that are unique. Each chapter has a brief history section on the technique and related issues. I believe this is useful to place the procedures into historical perspective. Students often miss the fact that analytic procedures are interrelated and that they evolve over time.

Chapter 1 presents a general and simple overview of different types of statistics, and uniquely, it seems presents among other things the computational formulae used in **SPSS** for measures of skewness and kurtosis. Chapter 2 reviews various forms of the t-test, showing the relation between the independent and paired t-test, and indicating how they relate to the Critical ratio. Chapter 3 presents a simplified discussion of the single-factor completely randomized design, discusses issues such as the percentage of variance accounted for, defining both ω^2 and η^2 and showing the relation between the two (a unique feature), and explains the general rationale underlying post hoc tests of means. This is extended in Chapter 4 to a discussion of two-factor completely randomized design analyses of variance and the meaning and significance of both omnibus and partial η^2, directing attention to the calculation of partial η^2 showing its relevance to the concept of power. The interpretation of results is stressed as it is in many other books, but more is made of the importance of reporting and interpreting power estimates that are associated with the F-ratios. This is continued in the subsequent chapters dealing with analysis of variance since it would seem to be as valuable to report η^2 and power estimates associated with each F-ratio as it is to report the alpha level. Chapter 5 presents the single factor repeated measures analysis of variance (and by implication the randomized blocks design). A novel feature of this chapter is that is presents both the univariate and multivariate approaches to the analysis of such data, discussing the assumptions underlying each, and their relative merits and shortcomings. Split-plot analysis of variance is considered in Chapter 6, again from both the univarirate and multivariate perspectives. Issues associated with tests of simple main effects are discussed in some detail, and differences between the **SPSS** approach to tests of means and standard textbook approaches are indicated. Chapter 7 considers the chi-square analysis of categorical data. A unique feature of this chapter is its discussion of post hoc procedures to aid in the interpretation of a significant chi-square obtained from a table that is larger than 2 x 2. Most sources are silent on this, but the present chapter describes three different methods that might be followed, and discusses the advantages and limitations associated with each of them. Chapter 8 presents bivariate regression and correlation, showing the precise meaning of each. It also presents a number of tests of significance involving correlation coefficients that are not readily available in most textbooks. Chapter 9 is the largest chapter. It discusses the general logic underlying multiple regression and multiple correlation, and outlines the generality of this analytic procedure. It distinguishes between direct and indirect procedures in building an equation, and highlights the issues involved in the use of this equation. It discusses what a "prediction" equation means, and what it doesn't mean, and considers issues concerning the "best" predictor, and the interpretation of regression coefficients, showing the direct connection between a part correlation and a regression coefficient. In addition, the chapter deals with the issue of moderator variables and nonlinear relationships. Factor analysis is discussed in Chapter 10, with emphasis on basic factor theory, the principles of rotation, and the interpretation of solutions. Chapter 11 presents multivariate analysis of variance, and discusses the use and application of **SPSS** GLM and **SPSS** MANOVA. It shows how one might proceed to interpret a canonical variate, and some of the issues involved in this interpretation. A relatively unique feature of this chapter is the presentation of the formulae (with numerical examples) for the various multivariate tests of significance and their respective degrees of freedom.

Each chapter is preceded by a Table of Contents. This is provided to help the reader to see how the chapter is organized, and to emphasize the major elements and constructs involved in that chapter. I recommend to my students that they consider the chapter outline carefully before they start reading, and to think about the organization of the material. Of course, the Table of Contents for each chapter also helps someone to look up some specific aspect.

Many individuals have provided assistance and advice in the preparation of this book. This includes the many students who have used earlier versions (as well as this one) as the textbook in our course on Computer Applications in Psychological Research for the last eight years. Many have offered suggestions, comments and criticisms that have made their way into the final form presented here. Also, many of my colleagues have given me valuable feedback for which I express my sincere appreciation. These include Professor R. W. J. (Jim) Neufeld, with whom I have discussed many statistical issues, as well as Professors Ken McRae, Sampo Paunonen, and Tom Spalding, who have used earlier versions of the book in their sections of *Computer Applications in Psychological Research*. From pointing out ambiguities to offering editorial comment, they have offered moral support, advice, and/or suggestions that I believe have been of enormous benefit to the final product. Finally, I would like to thank the following reviewers for their helpful comments on the penultimate version of this book: Gerald Gibb, Embry-Riddle Aeronautical University; Leslie Gill, Eastern New Mexico University; Charles Halcomb, Wichita State University; and Miguel Quinones, Rice University.

Robert C. Gardner

Chapter 1
Statistics, Computers, and Statistical Packages

Some of my colleagues refer to this as my manual. But I don't consider it a manual. I think of it more as a textbook that discusses the fundamentals of many frequently used analytic procedures available to psychological researchers. There is considerable reference in the following chapters to computer applications, primarily using the Windows version of the Statistical Package for the Social Sciences (**SPSS, Versions 8.0 and 9.0**), but in my opinion this is relatively incidental. My intent is to introduce students to the fundamentals of the analytic procedures so that when they use a computer package they will know how to use the information produced. I could have focused on any computer package, but I chose **SPSS** because that is the one used most frequently at our university. I have tried, however, to direct attention to the common aspects of most of the analytic procedures, so that I think that someone using another package, such as **SAS, SYSTAT,** etc., would obtain much of the same material if they were to run my examples through their package. And I think this is one of the strengths of this book. It brings standard statistical procedures face to face with the statistical packages that now produce them so that you, the student, can see how to use and understand the material both in terms of the specific example used and the underlying statistical rationale. Up until now, most books were either (a) standard statistics texts with many formulae, and exercises to do by hand, or (b) complex texts that emphasized the mathematics underlying the procedures, or (c) manuals that showed how to use a particular computer package without much attention directed to understanding fully the analytic procedure used. By writing a book that discusses the major statistical analyses in the context of a computer package that produces them, I hope to encourage you to understand the nature of every statistic they compute. In a recent issue of *American Psychologist,* the APA Task Force on Statistical Inference presented an initial discussion of the results of their deliberations (Wilkinson, 1999). This is must-reading for anyone concerned with research and data analysis. One point that is relevant to the present discussion is their admonition to users of computer programs to understand the statistics they get from their printouts. Hopefully, this book will help with that task.

A BIT OF HISTORY

In the good old days (and I mean the really old days), we didn't have computers. We didn't even have electric calculators. My first experience with a calculator was in my statistics class in second year at university. The calculator was hand-driven, with a keyboard, a series of dials on the accumulator, a lever to move the accumulator, and a crank. In order to add (and thus multiply), you turned the handle of the crank clockwise. To subtract (and thus divide), you turned the handle counterclockwise. We did critical ratios (see Chapter 2), chi-squares (see Chapter 7), and correlations (see Chapter 8) by using the calculator to compute the various sums and sums of squares needed, and then calculating the statistic of interest by inserting the relevant sums into computational formulae that we either memorized or found in handy textbooks. The length of time it took to compute the statistic of interest depended on how fast you could turn the crank and manipulate the lever, and how quickly you could perform the formulae-based calculations with a sheet of paper and a pencil (quills were no longer used in those days).

Somewhat later, these hand-driven calculators gave way to electrically driven calculators, thus eliminating the need for fast eye-hand coordination and crank turning. But they were basically the same. You still obtained various sums, and then used them in the formulae to calculate the statistics of interest. The hand-driven calculators were subject to a number of errors, largely because often we didn't turn the crank handle the requisite number of times. The electric calculator eliminated these types of errors. But often errors were made when doing the subsequent hand calculations solving the formulae, and these were probably as frequent when using the electrically driven or hand-driven calculators.

In any event, it is obvious that with these types of calculators it took a long time to perform a data analysis. Also, it was quite possible to make mistakes, so there was a lot of concern about errors and this necessitated checking one's calculations by doing most things twice (or more if discrepancies occurred). As a consequence, researchers had the opportunity to get to know both the statistical procedure and their data very well. I don't know if this was the cause, but it was also the case that many researchers tended to have their favourite analytic procedure. That is, some researchers generally did research that used t-tests as the major analytic procedure. Some did two-factor analyses of variance, others did correlations, and still others did chi-square analyses. Thus, they became specialists in that particular procedure. In those days, researchers spent much time and energy doing the data analysis, and they knew how to interpret the answers they got. They didn't rush in to do statistical analyses they didn't understand, and only the most energetic said. "I think I'll try this analysis to see what I get." Another positive feature of these "good old days" was that it took so long to perform the data analyses that statistics courses covered relatively much less material than is covered in a comparable course today.

When the computer was first introduced, things didn't change that much. To begin with, we had the computer (often it filled a large, air-conditioned room), but in order to use it you had to instruct the computer on how to do the computations required. That is, you had to write a computer program detailing in very minute terms precisely how to proceed. Not too many people were into "talking to computers," so those of us who did were often asked to write the program to do the analysis in question (often receiving payment in return—truly the good old days). It's hard to believe now, but in the initial days we often found that it took longer to write the program than it did to do the calculations by hand. We got into the habit of writing general forms of the program so that with relatively few modifications we could make the program available to someone else who had a similar need, but a slightly different data form. For example, we could write a computer program to perform a two-factor analysis of variance (see Chapter 4) but make it general so that, if needed, it could also perform a single-factor analysis of variance (see Chapter 3). The important point is that a researcher tended to get someone who knew the analysis and the computer to more or less tailor-make the program to do the task required. The chances were very good, therefore, that the answers obtained were appropriate to the problem under investigation.

In the end, it got to be a bit of a game. I know, for me at least, that was when I really began to learn that many of the different statistical tests were actually very similar, and with a bit of ingenuity, I could modify a program that did one thing so that it could do something that appeared quite different. For example, you could write a program to compute the Pearson product moment correlation (see Chapter 8) between two variables, X and Y, but with appropriate modifications, it could also be used to compute a point biserial correlation (and, thus, a t-test), a Spearman rank order correlation, a phi coefficient (and, hence, a 2x2 chi-square analysis), or even a number of other things providing the modifications were sufficiently complex. This is a very long, involved way of saying that many of the various statistical procedures that we use are very closely interrelated. In fact, Knapp (1978) wrote a fascinating article showing that many of the procedures we use, ranging from the t-test to multivariate analysis of variance, can all be shown to be special cases of one particular statistic (that we don't even discuss in the following set of chapters) called canonical correlation!

Ultimately it was realized that there was a market for general-purpose computer programs, and so began the development of what we now refer to as statistical packages. The first one that I encountered was the BMD Biomedical Computer Programs (**BMDP**). That was in the 1960s. Then I was introduced to **SPSS** (Statistical Package for the Social Sciences), and then **SAS** (Statistical Analysis System) (and since then a few other packages as well). Each of these packages came with extensive manuals, and even documents that provided the equations (algorithms) used in the programs. Often the programs were not that easy to use, and one spent a lot of time poring over the examples in the manuals to see how to run the program. As a result, you got to be relatively familiar with what a particular package could do and the type of information it provided. Over the years these packages have been refined and improved, and each has its promoters and detractors.

Personally I have found good things and bad things about most packages. What I now see as a problem with most packages, however, is that they have become too user-friendly. Particularly with the introduction of Windows versions, one need only to call up the package, click on an icon or two, input the data as requested, and have output appear on the monitor. Subsequently, this can be printed or stored in a file, again with the click of a mouse. There are Help Files available, but often it's just as easy to keep clicking on icons or options until something develops. My concern with all of this is that, if users aren't careful they can obtain output that they think is telling them one thing when in fact it is telling them something else. Also, you have to be careful because if you do keep clicking and hoping that something will develop and then print the result without checking the size of the file you have produced, you can find yourself with a rather large pile of output. The paper manufacturers might be relatively pleased with this type of occurrence, but it isn't particularly good for our forests. And if you're using a printer that belongs to someone else, such as your university, the person responsible for buying the supplies may not be too happy. User-friendly has its drawbacks!

BASIC DEFINITIONS

There is a lot of terminology associated with statistics and data analysis, and I intend to introduce much of it in the following chapters when it becomes necessary. However, some basic concepts must be dealt with before we even begin talking about any specific analytic procedure. These include the distinction between *sample* and *population, statistic* and *parameter,* and some of the more fundamental statistics.

Samples and Populations

In general terms, the distinction between sample and population is quite simple. When it comes to data analysis, a sample refers to some subset of a population, and a population is some large set of numbers. This is straightforward. Consider the population of London (be it the one in Great Britain, Canada, or the United States). The 1996 census found that the population of London, Canada, was 325,643. If we were to select one city block of individuals from this population, this could be considered a sample, though it would not be random, nor particularly representative. However, we might also consider the 325,643 individuals as a sample of the population of Canada (stated to be 28,846,761 in the 1996 census), or they could be considered a sample of North American residents, or a sample of the world, though in each of these instances it definitely couldn't be considered a random sample, and quite likely wouldn't be representative. Thus, the distinction between sample and population, although straightforward, needs a bit of elaboration.

We can distinguish between three different types of populations. A *finite population* is one which has a definite number of individuals. When we speak of the population of London as comprising 325,643 individuals, this refers to a finite population. An *infinite population* is one that has no limit on the number of individuals. We can speak of the population of Londoners, past, present, and future, and as long as time and London continue indefinitely, this would represent an infinite population—it has no upper limit. A *theoretical population* is simply an equation. We can speak of a Normal population, and by that we are referring to an equation of the form:

$$y = \frac{1}{\sigma\sqrt{2\pi}} e^{-\frac{(X-\mu)^2}{2\sigma^2}}$$

In this equation, y is the height of the ordinate for any value of X. Under appropriate circumstances, it could be used to estimate the frequency of occurrence of each value of X in the population. The values π and e are mathematical constants, while μ and σ are the mean and standard deviation of the population in question. Much of statistical inference is based on theoretical populations, many of which are normal. That is, the model underlying the tests of significance assumes that the population is as described by the equation given above.

When we discuss samples, we can differentiate between random and nonrandom samples. A random sample is one in which every observation in the population has an equal opportunity of being selected. A nonrandom sample is one in which this is not the case. The inferential statistics (tests of significance) to be discussed in the following chapters are all based on the assumption of random sampling. That is, they are concerned with estimating the probability that a certain value would be obtained if the samples were drawn at random from a Normal population that had given characteristics. We shall see, however, that many of the tests are robust with respect to violations of the assumption of Normality, though not of nonrandom sampling. That is, even if the population were not Normal, as long as all other conditions were satisfied, it has been shown that the results conform fairly well to those that would be obtained when sampling randomly from Normal populations. The justification for much of this has been demonstrated through the use of Monte Carlo techniques.

There is a distinction between how psychologists consider samples and populations and how researchers in other disciplines such as sociology view samples and populations. Often, in these other disciplines, there is interest in a specific population. Thus, a sociologist might be interested in Londoners' attitudes toward the educational system. Since she can't assess the attitudes of all Londoners, she would be interested in obtaining a sample of them. That is, the population comprises all Londoners, and the researcher wishes to estimate the attitude of all of them based on the responses made by the sample. One way of doing this would be to obtain a random sample of Londoners. Often, however, there is concern that this sample may not be representative (though there's really no reason why it shouldn't be if the sample is truly random), so what she will do is obtain a stratified random sample. That is, she will identify parameters that she believes are important in the population (such as gender, region of the city, etc.) and then obtain samples randomly from strata reflecting these characteristics. The concern is that the sample be representative of the population in question.

On the other hand, a psychologist is often interested in how differences in some treatment influence some behavior, or how two variables relate to each other. In the former case, he would simply obtain a sample of individuals (frequently from a subject pool), randomly assign them to the different treatments, and then see how they differ as a result of the treatment. In the second case, he would obtain a sample of individuals, measure them on the two variables of interest, and see how they relate. There is often no concern as to whether the sample is representative of any particular population (i.e., of Londoners, university students, or even the subject pool). It is almost as if the psychologist defines the population(s) as being that larger group of individuals from which the sample can be considered randomly obtained. Since the objective of the psychologist is often different from that of the sociologist, these different perspectives are reasonable.

Statistics and Parameters

A statistic is a number that describes a sample. If you had a sample of one number, that number would be a statistic since it describes that sample. If you had a sample of 10 numbers, the mean of the numbers would also be a statistic, as would the standard deviation, or its squared value, the variance. Any number that describes some aspect of a sample is a statistic.

A parameter, on the other hand, is a number that describes a population. We can consider, for example, the mean of the population, or the standard deviation, or the variance. In the equation for the normal population given above, it can be shown that μ is the mean, σ is the standard deviation, and σ^2 is the variance. Any number that describes some aspect of the population is a parameter.

The distinction between statistic and parameter is basic to statistical inference. Seldom are we in a position to be able to assess the population. Instead we have to make do with a sample from the population and use the information we obtain on the sample to estimate the corresponding value in the population. That is, we often have a statistic, and wish to estimate a parameter. There are two related ways in which we can proceed. If we have a sample of 10 observations, for example, and their mean is 97.3, we might want to use this information to estimate what the mean would be of the population for which this is a random sample. That is, assuming that the sample was drawn at random from a population, you might ask the question as to what is the mean of the population. In this case, the value of 97.3 is the statistic, and you want to estimate the parameter (i.e., the mean, or μ). One estimate you might make is 97.3, but of course, there is no guarantee that the parameter would be exactly 97.3. It could be a bit higher, or a bit lower. How much, as we shall see in Chapter 2, depends on a number of factors. Suffice it to say for now that the value of statistical inference is that it allows us to estimate parameters and to determine the possible error associated with our estimates. That is, it permits us to say that the parameter is such-and-such a value but that it could vary somewhere between two numbers. Thus, with our example above, we might be able to say that our best estimate of the parameter is 97.3, but that the population mean could vary from, say, 93.1 to 101.5. We would call this range of possible values the confidence interval. Using statistical inference, we could determine what we would expect to be the range of possible values that could occur 95% (or some other percentage) of the time.

Alternatively, a researcher may obtain a sample mean of 97.3, and may ask how reasonable it is to conclude that this sample could be obtained at random from a population that has a mean of 100. That is, the statistic is 97.3, and it is assumed that the parameter is 100. Inferential statistics allow us to assess how likely this is to occur. If we find that we would expect a difference as large as this less than 5% or 1% of the time if the sample were drawn randomly, we can conclude that it is unlikely that the sample was drawn from a population with that mean. We would then conclude that the sample was not drawn from a population that had a mean of 100. This is the general rationale underlying tests of significance. As can be seen, the notion of confidence intervals and tests of significance are two different ways of looking at the same phenomenon. We shall discuss this in more detail in a later section titled "Standard Error and Statistical Inference" (p. 12).

Unbiased vs. Biased Estimates

The preceding section indicates that statistics can be used to estimate parameters. That is, if we had a sample of individuals with a mean IQ of 97.3, we could use this to estimate the IQ in the population for which this could be considered a random sample. We know that if we were to obtain another random sample, the mean probably would not equal 97.3. It might be somewhat larger or smaller. That is, statistics vary from sample to sample, even though the parameter is constant, of course.

We can distinguish between biased and unbiased estimates of parameters. A statistic is said to be *unbiased* if the mean of all possible values of that statistic is equal to the parameter. The mean is a statistic that is unbiased. This is simply because the mean of the means of all possible samples from a population equals the population mean. A statistic is said to be *biased* if the mean of all possible sample values (i.e., statistics) is not equal to the population value (i.e., the parameter). Thus, for example, the variance is said to be biased because the mean of the variances of all possible samples from a population is less than the population variance.

TYPES OF STATISTICS

So far we have briefly talked about three statistics: the mean, the standard deviation, and the variance. But these are only three of a number of possible statistics. In fact, one can distinguish between four types of statistics. And for each statistic, there is, of course, the corresponding parameter. This section considers the various types of statistics (and thus the various types of parameters), and in some cases provides definitional formulae for the statistics. As indicated above, however, some statistics are biased while others are unbiased estimates of the corresponding parameter. It is thus sometimes the case that there will appear to be two different formulae for a statistic. This will occur when the statistic is a biased estimate, and one is concerned with obtaining a value for that statistic that is not biased. Thus, in the section to follow, you will find that there is one definitional formula for the mean. This is because the mean is an unbiased statistic. You will find, however, that there are two definitional formulae for the variance. This is because the variance is a biased estimate. You might think that this is an unnecessary complication—that you might as well use the unbiased estimate all the time. In fact, some writers of textbooks do just that. But this can lead to some very serious misunderstandings. The point is that the true definitional formula for a statistic is the one that shows how to compute the value that describes the sample. If that value happens to be a biased estimate of the parameter, it is nonetheless the case that it is still the best statistic to use if you want simply to describe the sample. On the other hand, if you wished to use the statistic to estimate the parameter, it would be more meaningful to use the unbiased estimate, because on average it equals the parameter. This distinction is made in a few instances in the discussion to follow.

Consider the following set of data, which represents the number of errors made on an arithmetic task by 35 students. It is in the form of a frequency distribution for various values of X. Thus, there is one X of 8, two of 10, and so on. We will use this set of data to identify each of these statistics.

X	frequency
8	1
9	1
10	2
11	7
12	5
13	5
14	4
15	3
16	2
17	2
18	1
19	1
20	1

Statistics of Location

There are many statistics of location. Each of these statistics serve to locate the sample on the number line. The number line is a concept that was probably introduced to you in elementary school. It is simply a representation of all possible numerical values ranging from minus infinity $(-\infty)$ to plus infinity $(+\infty)$, as indicated below:

$-\infty$ _____ $+\infty$

Any statistic that helps you to locate where the sample is on this line is a statistic of location. One class of such statistics are the three measures of central tendency, the median, the mode, and the mean. These are also referred to as averages.

Median.   The *median* is that value such that 50% of the values are greater than that value and 50% are less. It is the value that is at the center of all the values. It is also sometimes called the 50th percentile. In the data above, the value of the median is 13. Note in the example that 15 of the values are less than 13, five have the value of 13, and 14 are greater than 13.

Mode.   The *mode* is that value that occurs most frequently. That is, it is the most popular value. In our example, this value is 11, since there are seven values of 11 and no other value occurs more frequently. If two values had the same highest frequency, we would say that the distribution of scores is bimodal—that is, it has two modes. If a number of values have the same highest frequency, the distribution would be said to be multi-modal.

Mean.   The *mean* is that value such that the sum of the deviations of the scores from their mean add to 0. It is identified as $\bar{X}$. It can be shown that the mean is given by the following formula:

$$\bar{X} = \frac{\Sigma X}{n}$$

The formula instructs you to sum (Σ) all 35 values of X and divide by 35. In our example, the mean is equal to 13.23. Note that if you were to subtract 13.23 from each value of X, and sum these deviations they would sum to 0 (with rounding).

Note that these three statistics—the median, the mode, and the mean—are referred to as types of averages or measures of central tendency, but that they can differ quite substantially. In this case, they vary from 11 to 13.23. The important thing to note, however, is that they help you determine where the sample is located on the number line. That is, you know that it is centered somewhere in the vicinity of 11 to 13.23. If nothing else, this tells you that the number of errors was not in the vicinity of 121, or 1003, etc.

Measures of central tendency are the most commonly used measures of location, but they are not the only ones. One could think of many other such measures. For example, the *lowest value* in the sample is a measure of location, as is the *highest value*. Similarly, the various percentiles are also statistics of location. The *25th percentile* is that value for which 25% of the numbers are lower, and 75% are higher. In our example, the 25th percentile is 11. The *75th percentile* is that value higher than 75% of the numbers in the sample. In our example, the 75th percentile is 15. Other statistics of location include deciles, quartiles, etc.

Statistics of Scale

Statistics of scale describe how much differentiation there is in the sample. They are sometimes also referred to as statistics of variation or dispersion. If all the numbers are close together, the scale is small. If the values tended to be spread out and cover a wide range on the number line, the scale is large. Statistics of scale give an indication of the amount of variability in the sample. As with statistics of location, there are a number of statistics of scale.

Range.   The simplest measure of scale is that of the *range*. This is defined as the difference between the highest value and the lowest value. In our example this is $20 - 8 = 12$. When we say that the range is 12, this gives us an idea of how big the scale is. The value of 12, in and of itself, is difficult to classify as small, medium, or large, but if we knew the range for some other set of data, we would at least know whether this range is smaller or larger than that. This measure of scale is useful in a relative sense. One problem with this measure, however, is that it is based on only two values, the lowest number and the highest number, and it is desirable to involve all the measures in the definition of a statistic, if possible. Why? Because it would be more stable from a sampling point of view. If you were to obtain a number of samples and compute the range each time, you would expect the range to vary quite a bit because it is based on only the lowest and highest scores in your sample. Measures that use all of the numbers in the sample would be expected to give much more stable answers.

Semi-Interquartile Range. Another type of range statistic that uses more of the information in the distribution is the *semi-interquartile range,* also called the *quartile deviation.* This is defined as the difference between the 75th and 25th percentile divided by 2. In our example, the semi-interquartile range would be $(15 - 11)/2 = 2.0$. It is reasonable to assume that the 75th and 25th percentiles would be much more stable from a sampling point of view than the highest and lowest values in the sample simply because they are defined in part based on many of the other values in the sample. Thus, it would be expected that the semi-interquartile range would be more stable than the range.

A number of statistics of scale have been suggested that use all the deviations of each of the numbers from their mean. Obviously, it wouldn't make any sense to simply add up these deviations, since we have already seen that the mean is that number such the sum of the deviations would add to 0. However, if we could somehow get rid of the signs of the deviations, we could develop indices of scale. One way of getting rid of the sign is to simply ignore it—that is, to deal with the absolute deviations.

Mean Absolute Deviation. One such measure of scale is the *mean absolute deviation,* computed by summing the absolute deviations and dividing by the number of deviations. This mean would give an indication of the relative size of the deviations of the values from the mean. If the mean absolute deviation were 2.22 (as it is in this case), you would at least know that it is smaller or larger than that for some other set of numbers. As such, it could be useful. We shall see that this statistic is used in conjunction with some of the statistics we discuss in later chapters (see, for example, Chapters 2, 3, 4, 6, and 11) in a technique referred to as Levene's (1960) test.

Median Absolute Deviation. The *median absolute deviation* is simply the median of the absolute deviations. If you know that the median absolute deviation is 2.23 (as it is in this example), you know that roughly 50% of the values differ more than this much from the mean, while 50% of the values deviate less than this. This has a lot of intuitive value, but this statistic is not used that frequently.

Variance and Standard Deviation. One difficulty with absolute deviation scores is that disregarding the sign is not a meaningful mathematical concept. One way of handling this is to square the deviations of the values from the mean, and then calculate the mean of these squared deviations. If you do this, you obtain a statistic called the *variance,* and it is generally identified as S^2. The formula is:

$$S^2 = \frac{\Sigma(X - \bar{X})^2}{n}$$

This is the defining formula for the variance, and, as you can see, it is simply the mean of the squared deviations. For our example, the value is 7.6048. Like the mean absolute deviation, therefore, the value itself is informative, primarily in a relative sense. The square root of the variance is referred to as the *standard deviation,* and is identified as S. Thus, in our example, the standard deviation is 2.76. As above it is informative in a relative sense.

This form of the variance is often referred to as the biased estimate. The reason for this is that if you were to obtain a number of samples from the same population and calculate the variance on each one, the mean of all these variances would not equal the population variance; it would be a bit smaller than the population variance. It can be demonstrated, however, that if the formula of the variance were modified, then the mean of the variances defined that way would equal the population variance. This is referred to as the unbiased estimate of the population variance and is defined as:

$$S^2 = \frac{\Sigma(X - \overline{X})^2}{n - 1}$$

Using this definition of the variance, the value for our example is 7.8286. The square root of this value, the standard deviation, is equal to 2.80. As you can see, there is not a great difference between these biased and unbiased estimates, and obviously as sample size increases the difference between these two estimates gets smaller and smaller. Nonetheless, the distinction is important. The first expression describes the variance of the sample as simply the mean of the squared deviations. The second gives you an unbiased estimate of the parameter. Depending on your reason for calculating the variance, you would use one or the other. If you wished to describe the variance or the standard deviation of the sample, you would use the biased estimate. If you wished to use your statistic to estimate the population variance or standard deviation, you would use the unbiased estimate.

Statistics of Shape

Often we are interested in knowing not only the location of the sample on the number line, and how much of the number line is taken up by the sample, but also how the values are distributed along the line. That is, are the numbers relatively symmetrically distributed around the mean, or are they skewed to one end or the other? Are they bunched close to the mean with relatively few extreme values, or do they tend to spread out a lot? Statistics of shape provide us with this information. Although the subsequent chapters are not concerned with investigating the shape statistics, these statistics are briefly discussed here for the sake of completeness. There are two primary statistics of shape. Before discussing them, however, it is first advantageous to introduce the notion of the standard score. This is not a measure of shape, however, it is involved in the definition of the two shape statistics to be discussed. A standard score is often identified by the letter Z, and is defined as:

$$Z = \frac{X - \overline{X}}{S}$$

As discussed here, S is the biased estimate of the standard deviation. Z values are a transformation of the original X values, such that the mean of the Z is 0 and the variance is 1.0.

Skewness. *Skewness* is a measure of asymmetry of the distribution of numbers. It is identified as g_1, and is defined in most psychological statistics textbooks (cf. Ferguson, 1981, p. 72) as follows:

$$g_1 = \frac{\Sigma(X - \overline{X})^3}{nS^3} = \frac{\Sigma Z^3}{n}$$

It will be observed that a major feature of this statistic is that it is comprised of the sum of the cubed deviations of the observations from the mean. In fact, close inspection of the formula will reveal that it is really nothing more than the mean of the cubed Z scores. Thus, if there are some large positive deviations that are not offset by correspondingly large negative deviations, they will have a large influence on the sum, and g_1 will tend to be positive. On the other hand, if there are some extreme negative deviations and these are not offset by correspondingly positive ones, this value will tend to be negative. The reason for this is that cubing a large deviation yields a very large number indeed (and retains the sign of the deviation). Thus, if g_1 is positive, it indicates that there is a long tail running out to the right (the larger values); if it is negative, the tail runs out to the left (the smaller values). If g_1 is 0, it means that the distribution is symmetrical. Obviously, a normal distribution has a value of $g_1 = 0$, but so will any other symmetrical distribution. In our example, the value of g_1 is .55; as can be seen in the table, the values tend to be lumped at the lower end, but extend out slightly in decreasing frequency to the higher numbers.

Kurtosis. *Kurtosis* is a measure of the presence of extreme values in the distribution. It is defined by the notation g_2. If the distribution is relatively peaked in the middle, and has relatively high tails (i.e., also has some extreme values), kurtosis will be large. If the distribution has relatively few values at the extremes, kurtosis will be small. The formula presented below yields a value of 0 for Normal distributions. Thus, samples with a value of kurtosis equal to 0 are similar in terms of kurtosis to a Normal distribution. Those with positive values tend to have higher tails (and are said to be leptokurtic), while those with negative values have lower tails (and are said to be platykurtic). Kurtosis is not simply a matter of having high tails in the frequency distribution, however, since a rectangular distribution has a lower kurtosis than, say, a normal one. Kurtosis reflects characteristics of both the central part of the distribution and the tails. The formula for kurtosis as defined in most psychological statistics textbooks (cf. Ferguson, 1981, p. 73) is:

$$g_2 = \frac{\Sigma(X - \overline{X})^4}{nS^4} - 3 = \frac{\Sigma Z^4}{n} - 3$$

As can be seen, the major defining feature of this formula is that the deviations are raised to the fourth power, thus any large deviation will influence the magnitude of g_2. In fact, inspection of this formula will reveal that it is nothing more than the mean of the fourth power of the Z scores minus 3. In our example, g_2 is equal to $-.17$, indicating that it is fairly similar to a normal distribution in terms of kurtosis.

The formulae for skewness and kurtosis given above produce biased estimates of the corresponding parameters. Unbiased estimates are available, and in fact are used in **SPSS WINDOWS.** The formulae for the unbiased estimates are much more complex than the formulae given above though they involve a comparable logic. They will be presented later in this chapter.

Statistics of Association

Sometimes we have two sets of numbers that are paired in some way, and we are interested in obtaining a statistic that describes the degree of association between the two. There are many types of this class of statistics, generally referred to as indices of association, correlation, or regression. Since our example has only one variable, we cannot show an example of any measure of association. There are, however, many instances of statistics of association. When two variables are involved, and they are continuous variables, relevant statistics of association are the Pearson product-moment correlation and the regression coefficient (see Chapter 8). If the two variables are categorical, association is described by chi-square (see Chapter 7) and related coefficients, etc. If more than two variables are involved, measures of association include multiple correlation and multiple regression (see Chapter 9). We will defer discussion of these until Chapters 7, 8, and 9.

TYPES OF PARAMETERS

For each type of statistic, there is, of course, the corresponding parameter. Often our intent in calculating a statistic is to estimate the parameter. If we calculate the mean, or median, or median absolute deviation, or variance, or skewness, or correlation, etc., for a sample of numbers, we are often concerned with using the value to estimate the corresponding value in the population. Consider an example involving the sample mean. In our sample data, we obtained a mean of 13.23. Our best estimate of the mean of the population from which this can be considered a random sample is, therefore, 13.23. However, we wouldn't be surprised to find that, if we were to take another random sample from the same population, the mean we obtained would generally not be 13.23 again. That is, we expect that there will be a sampling distribution of the sample means (i.e., statistics) around the population mean (i.e., parameter). Statistical inference is concerned with providing us with a means of estimating what possible range of values we might expect in a parameter that would still give us the statistic we obtained (these are referred to as confidence intervals), or with a way of deciding how reasonable it is to obtain a statistic with the magnitude we did provided the parameter had some specified value. The next section, "Standard Error and Statistical Inference," will demonstrate how to do this in the simple case of using a sample mean to estimate the population mean. Much of the material in the subsequent chapters is concerned with somewhat more complex instances of statistical inference concerning location (means), scale (variances), or association (correlation and regression).

STANDARD ERROR AND STATISTICAL INFERENCE

All statistics have sampling distributions in that they vary from sample to sample, and this variability can be measured. That is, one could calculate the variance of the sampling distribution for any given statistic, and, by taking the square root of this value, one would also obtain the standard deviation of the sampling distribution. The standard deviation of the sampling distribution is referred to as the *standard error* of the statistic in question. Providing the samples are drawn at random from a population, there are formulae for the standard errors of most of the statistic discussed above. In this section, we will focus on only one, viz., the standard error of the mean. The standard error of the mean is defined as:

$$\sigma_{\bar{x}} = \frac{\sigma}{\sqrt{n}}$$

That is, the standard error of the mean is equal to the standard deviation in the population divided by the square root of the sample size. More precisely, this is the standard deviation of all possible means for a population. Moreover, the sampling distribution of the mean will be normally distributed if the population is normally distributed. Thus, if a population is normally distributed, the sampling distribution of means will also be normally distributed, and will have a mean equal to the mean in the population (μ) and a standard deviation equal to $\sigma/\sqrt{n}$. We could thus form a standard score for any sample mean using the formula:

$$Z_{\bar{X}} = \frac{\bar{X} - \mu}{\frac{\sigma}{\sqrt{n}}}$$

Note that this is exactly the same as the standard scores discussed earlier in that it is the deviation of a statistic from its mean divided by its standard deviation. The formula looks different from that given on page 10 because the present one refers to a standard score derived from the mean of a sample relative to the mean and standard deviation of the population from which it was obtained. As we saw, earlier, the mean of standard scores is 0, and the standard deviation is 1.0. Thus, the distribution of these standard scores has a mean of 0, a standard deviation of 1, and is normally distributed (since as we have already seen, the means themselves are normally distributed). That is, it has a standard Normal distribution.

The standard Normal distribution, however, has a characteristic shape. More importantly, we know much about this distribution. For example, we know that 95% of the area under the standard Normal distribution falls between −1.96 and +1.96. That is, 95% of all possible values that can be calculated fall within this range. It follows, therefore that 5% of all possible values are either more negative than −1.96, or more positive than +1.96. Similarly, we know that 99% of the area falls within the range −2.58 to +2.58; or that 1% of all possible values fall outside this range.

More detailed information about the standard normal distribution is given in Table A, Appendix B. This table gives values for the standard normal deviate (Z) varying from 0 to 4.00 in steps of .05. Associated with each of these Z values are three measures, (a) the proportion of the area between the value of 0 and that value of Z (labeled Area: m to z), (b) the proportion of the area between Z and infinity (labeled Area: q smaller), and (c) the height of the ordinate of the standard normal deviate for that value of Z (labeled Ordinate). The values of Z given in the table are all positive, but since the distribution is symmetrical around 0, these values can be used for negative values as well. The q smaller area is that which is used to determine whether or not a Z value differs significantly from 0. Note for example that a Z value of 1.95 has a corresponding value in "q smaller" of .02559. This means that the probability of obtaining a value of $Z = +1.95$ or larger is .02559. This would correspond to what is referred to as a one-tailed test, or a one-tailed probability. Of course, it is also the case that the probability of obtaining a Z of −1.95 or more negative is also .02559. Thus, if we wanted to determine the probability of obtaining a value of Z with a magnitude of 1.95 or larger, the combined probability would be .02559 + .02559 = .05118. This corresponds to what is referred to as a two-tailed test.

We can use this table, therefore, to help us make an inference about the population mean based on a sample mean. Thus, given a sample mean of 13.23 based on 35 observations, we could ask how likely it is that the sample was randomly obtained from a population with a mean of 12. If we knew the population standard deviation, we could simply solve the formula above, and compute a standard Normal deviate. We don't know the population standard deviation, of course, but we have an unbiased estimate of it in the standard deviation. This value was shown to be 2.80 (see page 10). We could thus use this information to compute the following standard Normal deviate:

$$Z_{\bar{X}} = \frac{\bar{X} - \mu}{\dfrac{\sigma}{\sqrt{n}}} = \frac{13.23 - 12}{\dfrac{2.80}{5.92}} = 2.60$$

Inspecting Table A, Appendix B, reveals that we would expect a value greater than 2.60 less than 1% of the time on the basis of chance (actually the two tailed probability from Table A is .00466 + .00466 = .00932, which rounds to .01). Since this value is so small, we would conclude that this value of 2.60 is greater than we could reasonably attribute to chance. We would thus conclude that the sample did not come from a population with a mean of 12. Of course, it could have done so 1% of the time, so that when we make this conclusion, we must recognize that we could be wrong 1% of the time. That is, our Type-I error rate is .01. This is the general logic underlying inference testing.

Earlier we noted that, rather than asking how reasonable is it that a given statistic came from a population with a given parameter, we might instead ask what parameters might be expected to yield the statistic obtained. In determining the range of possible values of the parameter, we again desire to express our level of confidence. Using the present example, then we might ask what are the 99% confidence intervals for the population mean that could yield a sample mean of 13.23 with 35 observations. The formula for the 99% confidence interval is as follows:

$$\bar{X} \pm \frac{Z_{01}\sigma}{\sqrt{n}} = 13.23 \pm \frac{(2.58)(2.80)}{5.92}$$

This formula would yield two values, 12.01 and 14.45. That is, we would expect populations that had means varying from 12.01 to 14.45 could yield a sample mean of 13.23 based on 35 cases. Thus, based on our analysis we could say that our best estimate of the population mean would be somewhere in the range of 12.01 and 14.45. Since we made these estimates using the value of 2.58 for Z, we also know that we could be wrong 1% of the time because of sampling fluctuations. Note that our confidence interval does not contain the mean of 12. This is why in the preceding analysis, we concluded that our sample was not drawn from a population with a mean of 12. As can be seen, the notion of tests of significance and confidence intervals are closely inter-related.

If we wished to make these estimates, but only with a 95% confidence interval, we would substitute the value of 1.96 for Z in our calculations. In this case, the estimates would be 12.30 to 14.16. In this case, the confidence interval is not as large, and we could be wrong 5% of the time.

In our discussion, we assumed that the sample was drawn from a Normal population, and thus that the distribution of means would also be normal. It just so happens, however, that even if the population is not normally distributed, the distribution of means still tends to be normal. The *central limit theorem* states that the distribution of means will tend to be normal regardless of the shape of the distribution in the population provided that the population variance is finite, and sample size is large. Obviously, large can mean anything, and in this context it is relative to the degree of non-normality of the population distribution. The more different the population distribution is from normal, the larger the sample size has to be for the distribution of means to be normal. For extreme departures from normality, however, Monte Carlo research suggests that sample sizes of 50 to 100 are generally sufficient. For less extreme departures, smaller sample sizes will be appropriate. For all practical purposes a sample size of 30 is often considered a reasonable compromise.

This discussion has focused on the sampling distribution of the mean. However, as indicated above, the same general rationale applies to most of the statistics we have discussed in this section. We shall return to another application of the general logic of tests of significance in a later section when we discuss statistics generated by **SPSS** to describe skewness and kurtosis (see pages 33–36).

OVERVIEW OF SPSS 8.0 AND SPSS 9.0 FOR WINDOWS

If you type data directly into the Data Editor, you will probably not notice too many differences between **SPSS 8.0** and **SPSS 9.0.** There are some, however. For example, in **SPSS 8.0,** the various programs are located on the toolbar by *clicking on* **Statistics.** This results in a drop-down menu that directs you to the various statistical programs. In **SPSS 9.0,** the programs are located on the toolbar by *clicking on* **Analyze,** and some entries in this menu are slightly different from those in **SPSS 8.0.** These are minor differences, however, and should not result in much confusion, as long as you allow for some variability in labelling, the format of some of the Windows, and some aspects of the output.

All of the output in this book were generated in **SPSS 8.0 for WINDOWS,** but most of the output from **SPSS 9.0** is identical. The **SPSS** system is a general-purpose program that permits you to perform many statistical tests and to construct graphs of the results. In both **SPSS 8.0** and **SPSS 9.0,** reference is made to three major components, a **Data Editor,** a **Syntax Editor,** and a **Viewer** (of the output). The functions of these three components are obvious from their names.

The Data Editor permits you to type in the data or to inspect it if it already exists. It is the first Window you see when entering **SPSS WINDOWS.** The Data Editor Window, with nothing entered into it, appears as follows:

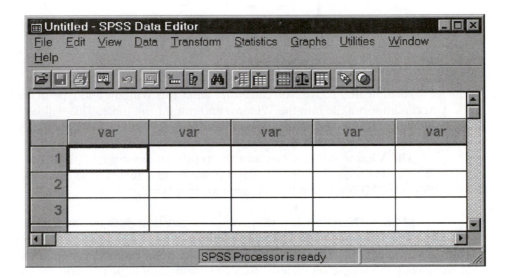

In this illustration, the line at the top containing the terms **File, Edit,** etc., is referred to as the **Menu Bar.** The line below that containing the various icons is called the **Toolbar.** The line at the bottom of the file (that here contains the notation "SPSS Processor is ready") is called the **Status Bar.** These three lines are common to most components of **SPSS WINDOWS,** and permit you to select various options. The Data Editor itself, as you can see, consists of a series of rows and columns. If you wish, you can enter data and variable names into this table directly. However, if you have already created a data file as an ASCII (or Text) file (a file that contains only the material typed, with no system control characters), you can read it into this editor for the purpose of performing an analysis. The examples used throughout the following chapters use this latter approach. Moreover, they all assume that the data are in freefield format **SPSS 8.0**) or deliminted format (**SPSS 9.0**). Other means of inputting data (e.g., from a Minitab or Excel file) are available in **SPSS WINDOWS,** however.

The Syntax Window (or Syntax Editor) is where you would enter the syntax file if you were to type it yourself, or where you would read it into if you had already prepared it as an ASCII (Text) file [see "Running Frequencies With an Existing Syntax File" on page 31 (Step 1) to see how to access this Window]. Alternatively, you could use the Windows [see the section below titled "Steps in Using **SPSS FREQUENCIES**" (p. 28)] to construct the file and then paste it into the Syntax Editor. The syntax file itself is the set of instructions that result in the computations and output you request. A blank Syntax Editor Window appears as follows:

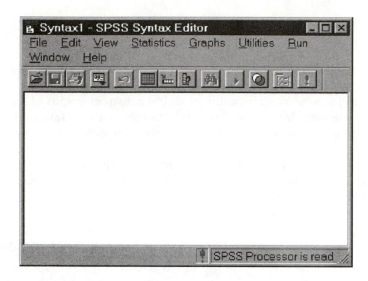

As indicated above, you can either enter this Window and type in the instructions you want, or you can import a file into the Window and run it from there. This will be discussed more fully in the section on "Running Frequencies with an Existing Syntax File" (see p. 31).

The Viewer Window contains the results of any computations the computer completes. You will be seeing many Viewer Windows (sometimes referred to as the Output Viewer) when running **SPSS WINDOWS,** so I will not reproduce that Window here.

SPSS WINDOWS is a very complex statistical package, and there are a number of ways in which it can be run. In the chapters to follow, attention is directed to the use of **WINDOWS** in what I prefer to call the *click and hope* approach (it might be abbreviated as the *clope* approach). That is, you *click* the mouse on various icons or options, *and hope* that you get what you think you have requested. Another alternative is to construct the syntax file to perform the functions you desire, and then run this file. There is much to be said for this latter approach, because to use it, you have to be relatively familiar with **SPSS WINDOWS.** With this approach, you can either construct the syntax file in some other editor and store it as an ASCII file, or enter the Syntax Window and type it there. In this chapter, we will use the program **Frequencies** to compute most of the statistics we talked about above, and we will do so using both approaches.

Setting Preferences

When you install **SPSS WINDOWS** on your computer it will have a basic setup. As you use it, you may find that some of the options chosen are not useful for you. You can change various aspects of the setup once you have entered **SPSS WINDOWS. In SPSS 8.0** and **SPSS 9.0** this is done through **SPSS Options.** You enter this from inside **SPSS WINDOWS,** by *clicking on* **Edit** in the Menu Bar. This produces a drop-down menu, and you *click on* **Options** in that menu. This presents you with the **SPSS Options** window that permits you to access ten menus controlling various things like general settings, the Viewer, etc. One option that you should ensure is operating is the one that prints your syntax file at the top of your output. It is extremely important that you do this so that you will know exactly what commands you have given the computer for any given analysis, if the question ever arises. If your version is not set up for this variation, you would make the change under Viewer, clicking the option that instructs the computer to "Display Commands in the Log."

ASCII (Text) files

The data files for all of the examples in this book are text files (ASCII) files. These files are read differently in **SPSS 8.0** and **SPSS 9.0,** and a slightly different terminology is used with the two versions. The following sections demonstrate how to read in ASCII (a term used with **SPSS 8.0**) and Text (a term used with **SPSS 9.0**) files. In each case, the procedures used to read data in freefield (Delimited) and fixed format (fixed width) are illustrated.

INPUTTING DATA INTO SPSS 8.0

Types of Files

As indicated above, there are two types of data that can be considered. In **SPSS 8.0,** these are referred to as freefield and fixed-width formats respectively. A **Freefield** (or free-format) file is one in which the data are presented separated by blanks. Consider the following data file consisting of four lines of five variables each:

```
 1   2    3  4   5
12   5  167  1  14
 1  23   4  12  6
   40   21    23   6  19
```

Note in the four lines of data, at least one space separates one variable from another, and there is no restriction on how many spaces there are between variables. Thus, in the first line the values are 1, 2, 3, 4, and 5. In the second line, they are 12, 5, 167, 1, and 14. In the third line, they are 1, 23, 4, 12, and 6. And, in the fourth line, they are 40, 21, 23, 6, and 19. In this type of file, the computer simply defines a variable as any value that is separated by a line delimiter (i.e., the beginning or end of a line) and/or spaces. It is a very useful way of preparing a file as long as there are no missing values for a variable for any one case. The computer has no way of identifying a missing value unless it is coded in some way. A space cannot signify a missing value for this type of file. As we shall see, this differs somewhat from the Delimited file in **SPSS 9.0.**

A *fixed variable* (or fixed-format) file contains the numbers in given fields. Assume, for example, that an individual had typed the above text file in a series of three column fields so that the first variable was in columns 1 to 3, the next in columns 4 to 6, etc. The same values as shown above would appear as:

```
 1  2  3  4   5
12  5167  1  14
 1 23   4 12   6
40 21 23   6  19
```

Note that in this file, the data appear in columns. They are right justified in that each value ends on the column to the right of the specification indicated, and it isn't even necessary to have a space between the variables. The values line up on the right-hand side. (As a minor point, it should be noted that although the example had all the variables in 3 column fields, it is not necessary to have the field widths identical. What is important is that the values be right justified in their fields.)

Inputting a Freefield File

Assume that you had entered **SPSS 8.0,** and you are presented with the Data Editor (See page 15). To input the freefield file shown above (see page 17), you would *click on* **File** in the menu bar. This will present you with a drop-down menu with a series of choices. *Move to* **Read ASCII data** *and click on* **Freefield** *in the pop-up menu to the right.* This presents the Window, **Define Freefield Variables** (see figure below):

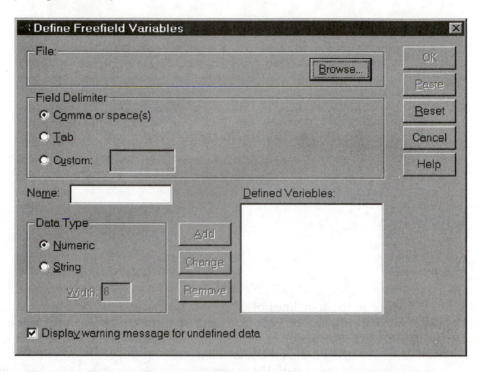

There are many choices. *To obtain the data file, click on* **Browse.** This presents an Open File Window like the following:

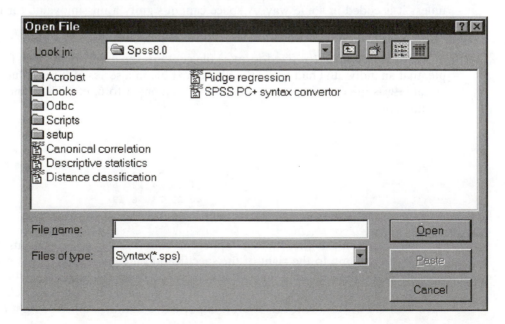

*Move your cursor to the down arrow to the right of the **Look In** white pane and click.* This presents a drop-down menu with many choices. Assuming that your data are on the A Drive, *move the cursor to 3½ floppy (A:)* and click on it. This presents a list of all ASCII(*.dat) files on the A Drive as shown in the following Window:

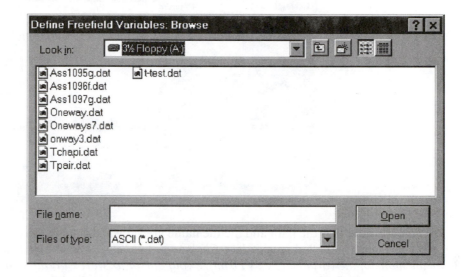

*Select the one of your choice, click on it, and then click on **Open.** If your file doesn't have the **.dat** extension, it will not show in this list. To list all files, change the Type of Files in the Window to **All Files (*.*)**. Once you have all files listed, choose the one you want and proceed as described above.*

This returns you to the Window, **Define Freefield Variables.** *Click on the white pane immediately to the right of **Name**, type in the name for the variable (e.g., **V1**), and click on **Add.** Repeat this process for all of the variables* (there are five in this example), *then click on **OK.** You are now ready to analyze the data (see relevant sections in the chapters in this book).*

Inputting a Fixed-Variable (ASCII) File

Assume that you had entered **SPSS 8.0,** and you are presented with the Data Editor (see page 15). To input the file shown above as a fixed-variable ASCII file, you would *click on **File*** in the menu bar. This will present you with a drop-down menu with a series of choices. *Move to **Read ASCII data** and click on **Fixed columns** in the pop-up menu to the right.* This presents the Window, **Define Fixed Variables.** This particular Window is not shown here, but it is similar to the **Define Freefield Variables** Window presented earlier. The procedure is comparable to the initial phase for inputting a Freefield file (see page 18) in that you must first identify the Data file, and as before there are many choices. Thus, to obtain the data file, *click on **Browse.*** This presents the **Open File** Window (not shown here, but it is comparable to the one shown above). *Move your cursor to the down arrow to the right of the **Look In** white pane and click.* This presents a drop-down menu with many choices. Assuming that your data are on the A Drive, *move the cursor to **3½ floppy (A:)** and click on it.* This presents a list of all ASCII(*.dat) files on the A Drive (comparable to the Window shown above, except this one is called **Define Fixed Variables: Browse**). *Select the one of your choice, click on it, and then click on **Open.*** If your file doesn't have the **.dat** extension, it will not show in this list. *To list all files, change the Type of Files in the Window to **All Files (*.*)**. Once you have all files listed, choose the one you want and proceed as described above.*

This returns you to the Window, **Define Fixed Variables.** This Window is shown below:

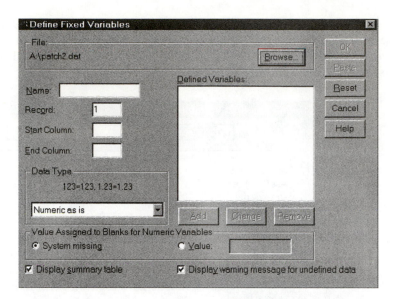

You will note that the path and the file name are shown in the File box (in this case, the file is on the A drive and is labelled patch2.dat). *Click on the white pane immediately to the right of **Name**, type in the name of the variable (e.g., V1), move your cursor to **Start Column** and type in the column number that starts the field* (1 in our example), *move the cursor to **End Column** and type in the column that ends the field (3 in our example), then click on **Add**.* This will result in the variable identification being shown in the **Defined Variables** pane. *Continue this process until all five variables and their column identifications (i.e., 4–6, 7–9, etc.) are entered.* This will show in the **Defined Variables** pane as the record number, the start and end column numbers, and the variable name. *Then click on **OK** (which will be visible now).* Note that the record "1" in the window indicates that the data for a case is on the first line. If there were multiple lines of data for each case, you would have to change this value also when you refer to a line other than the first one for each case. You are now ready to analyze the data (see relevant sections in the chapters in this book).

INPUTTING DATA INTO SPSS 9.0

There are a few more windows involved in reading a Text (ASCII) file into **SPSS 9.0,** though once you beome used to it, it is a relatively simple task. **SPSS 9.0** uses a **Text Import Wizard** which involves using six Windows. The following description shows how to use the Text Input Wizard for either Delimited (comparable to Freefield files) or Fixed-width files. If one were to use text files as input to **SPSS 9.0,** therefore, it is necessary to use the input routines described here rather than those described above.

Types of Files

A *Delimited* file is one that separates the data by some form of delimiter. In **SPSS 9.0,** you are provided with a number of options such as tab, space, etc . . . (See below). An example of a *Delimited* file involving five variables would be the following. Note in the four lines of data, one space separates one variable from another:

```
1  2  3  4  5
12  5  167  1  14
1  23  4  12  6
40  21  23  6  19
```

Thus, in the first line the values are 1, 2, 3, 4, and 5, and so on. The Delimited file in **SPSS 9.0** differs slightly from the Freefield format in **SPSS 8.0.** In Freefield, you could have any number (and even a varying number) of spaces between variables. In the Delimited file you can have only one space (or other delimiter) between variables. There is an advantage to this limitation, however. In the **SPSS 8.0** freefield model, you could not have missing data. If you did, the variables would be read out of line, with much confusion. With the Delimited file in **SPSS 9.0,** however, you can have missing data. Simply leave a blank space for the missing variable. It will be interpreted by the computer as a system-missing value (sysmis) and will appear in the Data Editor as a **.** (period). Thus, if the value 12 was missing in line 3 of the example, you would simply type the number preceding it (i.e., the 4) followed by a space to indicate that variable is finished, and then one space in place of the 12. This would be followed by the next number 6. (For complex data files, this is initially a bit confusing, so it is wise to check the data in the preview files, and in the data editor if you are using the Delimited option with missing data.) Actually, its always a wise move to check your data in the Data Editor in any event.

A *Fixed-width* file contains the numbers in given fields. Assume, for example, that an individual had typed the above text file in a series of three column fields so that the first variable was in columns 1 to 3, the next in columns 4 to 6, etc. The same values as shown above would appear as:

```
 1   2   3   4   5
12   5167   1  14
 1  23   4  12   6
40  21  23   6  19
```

Note that this file is identical to the Fixed Variable file in **SPSS 8.0** and that the data appear in columns. They are right justified in that each value ends on the column to the right of the specification indicated, and it isn't even necessary to have a space between the variables. The values line up on the right-hand side. (As a minor point, it should be noted that although the example had all the variables in 3 column fields, it is not necessary to have the field widths identical. What is important is that the values be right justified in their fields.)

Inputting a *Delimited* File

Assume that you had entered **SPSS 9.0,** and you are presented with the Data Editor Screen (see page 15). This is the standard screen that is presented when entering **SPSS 9.0,** but see Step 1 on page 28 for comments about a slightly different screen you might see the first time you enter **SPSS 9.0,** and subsequently if you don't cancel it. To input the Delimited file shown above, you would *click on* **File** *in the menu bar.* This will present you with a drop-down menu with a series of choices. *Move to* **Read Text Data** *and click on it.* This presents you with a Window like that on page 18 except that **9.0** is given as the file in the **Look In** pane, and a series of files shown below this. *Move your cursor to the down arrow to the right of the* **Look In** *white pane and click.* This presents a drop-down menu with many choices. Assuming that your data are on the A Drive, move the cursor to **3½ floppy (A:)** and click on it. This presents a list of all Text (*.dat) files on the A Drive as shown in the Window on page 19. *Select the one of your choice, click on it, and then click on* **Open.** *If your file doesn't have the* **.dat** *extension, it will not show in this list. To list all files, change the* **Type of Files** *in the Window to* **All Files (*.*).** *Once you have all files listed, choose the one you want and proceed as described above.* Once you have selected your file, you are presented with the first Window of the Text Import Wizard.

The following example shows how to input a *Delimited* file. Close inspection of the example will show that we will use the simplest procedure possible for a *Delimited* file (i.e., the various Defaults) and, in fact, will simply click on **Next** in the first five Windows, and **Finish** in the sixth. Nonetheless, I describe some of the options available.

The Window for Step 1 is shown below.

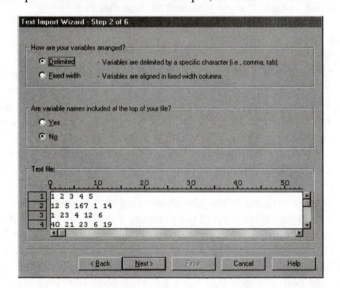

Step 1. If you had used this file before and had prepared a predefined format for it, you could select the *Yes* option. If you selected *Yes,* this would mean that you had already defined a format suitable to this file (see Step 6, below), and you would type in the path and name of the format file (not the data file) in the small white window that opens up next to *Yes*. If not, you would leave the selection in the Default position (*No*) as indicated in this Window. Note that the first four lines of data are presented in the Window at the bottom. Note too, that these values are not right justified. *To continue, click on Next*. This presents the Window for Step 2, as shown below:

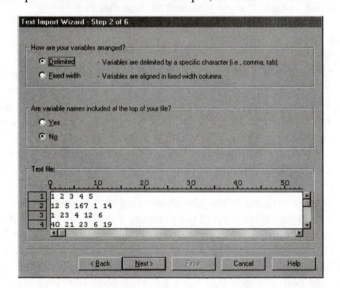

Step 2. In this window, the default option for "How are your variables arranged?" is Delimited. Since we wish to consider the data delimited, this is the appropriate option. It also asks "Are variable names included in the top of your file?" The default setting is *No*. Since we do not have variable names in our file, we shall not change this. *To continue, click on Next.* This presents the Window for Step 3, as shown below:

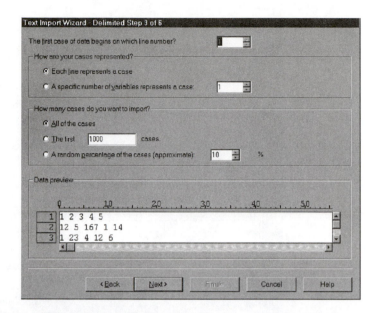

Step 3. This Window asks about the general nature of the data. In our example, the first case begins on line 1, each line corresponds to the data for a case, and we want to import all the cases, so there is no need to make any changes. Note that the first three lines of data are shown in what is now referred to as **Data Preview.** *To continue, click on Next.* This presents the Window for Step 4, as shown below:

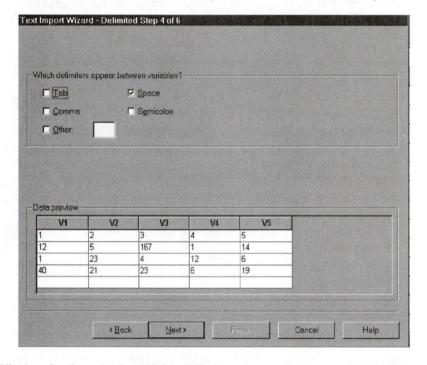

Step 4. The Window for Step 4 asks "Which delimiters appear between variables?" and provides the four **SPSS 9.0** options plus one that allows the researcher to specify a customized one. In this Window, **Space** is indicated as the Delimiter, so the computer will consider one space to define the separation between one variable and another. This means that more than one space between variables will result in the file not being read properly. It will be noted in this Window that the data are now shown in columnar form, left justified. *To continue, click on Next.* This presents the Window for Step 5, as shown below:

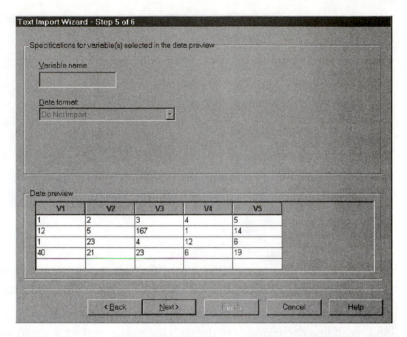

<u>Step 5</u>. The Window for Step 5 allows you to provide variable names and to indicate the nature of the data format. We shall use the defaults here, however, if you wished to change the variable names (i.e., V1, V2, . . . V5, in the Window) and/or the format of the data, you could do so. This is discussed in Step 5 of the example for inputting Fixed width data (see page 27). *To continue, click on* **Next**. This presents the Window for Step 6, as shown below:

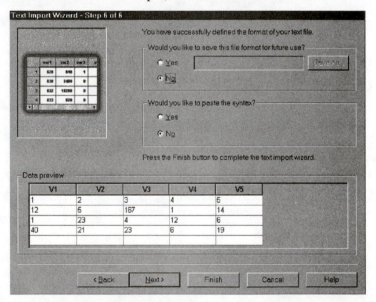

<u>Step 6</u>. The Window for Step 6 asks "Would you like to save this file format for future use?" We will use the Default option *No*, but if you were planning to read in this file again, you might select *Yes*. If you did, the Area next to *Yes* would open to allow you to type the name of the format file. You would enter this file name at Step 1 on your next use of this data file when asked "Does your text file match a predefined format?" The Window for Step 6 also asks "Would you like to paste the syntax?" We shall stay with the Default option *No*, but if you select *Yes*, it would paste the syntax for the input format into the Syntax Editor (see page 14). You would then have to execute the Syntax file by clicking on **Run** in the **Menu Bar** of the Syntax Editor Window.

If you do not paste the syntax, but instead *click on Finish* at the bottom of this Window, the computer will input your data into the Data Editor (see page 15). If your monitor displays the output file at this time, you can switch to the **Data Editor** by clicking on the appropriate selection (often identified as Untitled . . .) in the Status Bar (at the bottom of the screen). The Data Editor would then appear as follows:

You are now ready to analyze the data (see relevant sections in the chapters in this book).

Inputting a *Fixed-Width* File

Assume that you had entered **SPSS 9.0,** and you are presented with the Data Editor (see page 15). To input the Fixed-width file shown on page 21, you would *click on* **File** in the menu bar. This will present you with a drop-down menu with a series of choices. *Move to* ***Read Text Data*** *and click on it.* This presents you with a Window like that on page 18 except that **9.0** is given as the file in the **Look In** pane, and a series of files shown below this. *Move your cursor to the down arrow to the right of the* ***Look In*** *white pane and click.* This presents a drop-down menu with many choices. Assuming that your data are on the A Drive, move the cursor to **3½ floppy (A:)** and click on it. This presents a list of all Text (*.dat) files on the A Drive as shown in the Window on page 19. *Select the one of your choice, click on it, and then click on* ***Open.*** *If your file doesn't have the* ***.dat*** *extension, it will not show in this list. To list all files, change the* ***Type of Files*** *in the Window to* ***All Files (*.*).*** *Once you have all files listed, choose the one you want and proceed as described above.* Once you have selected your file, you are presented with the first Window of the Text Import Wizard.

The following example shows how to input a *Fixed-Width* file. The data used in this example are those shown on page 21 in the definition of a fixed-width file, so the data in the Text file Window will be right justified. The Window for Step 1 is identical to the last example so that window will not be illustrated here. Similarly, the Window for Step 2 is the same as in the example with the Delimited file, but in this case you would *click on* ***Fixed width.*** *Clicking on* ***Next*** would produce the Window for Step 3 which, except for the appearance of the data in the Data Preview Window, will be the same as the third window in the last example. *Clicking on* ***Next*** produces the Window for Step 4, which is different, and is shown below:

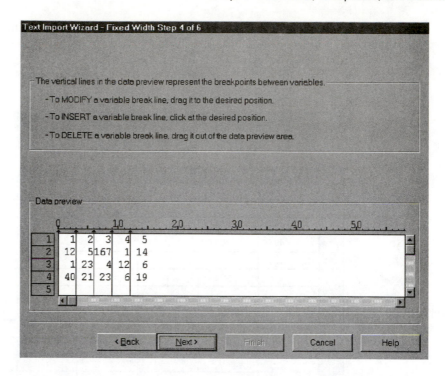

Step 4. As can be seen this Window is different from the Window for Step 4 in the example with the Delimited file. This Window permits you to check the alignment of the data to ensure that it is correct. Note, that there are variable breaks (the arrows) separating the fields in the **Data preview.** If there are more than four lines of data in your file (which will likely be the case), you can scroll down the entire file to ensure that the data are lined up properly. Once you are satisfied that this is correct, you can *click on Next* to produce the Window for Step 5. For this example, the Window appears as follows:

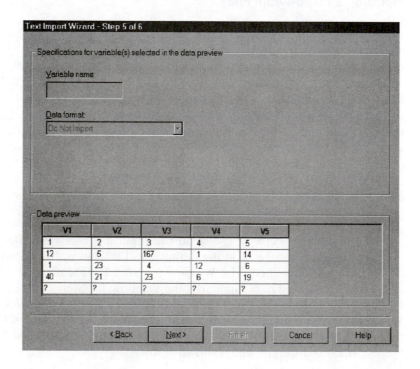

<u>Step 5</u>. This Window is comparable to Window 5 in the previous example. It differs, however, in that the data are currently considered as alphanumeric (String) variables by **SPSS 9.0,** and thus cannot be used in any numeric analyses. To change the variables to numeric, you would click on the **Variable name** (i.e., V1). This would open up the two small windows at the top of Window 5, permitting you to change the variable name and the data format. This is shown in the next figure (see below) which was produced by clicking on V1 in the **Data preview.**

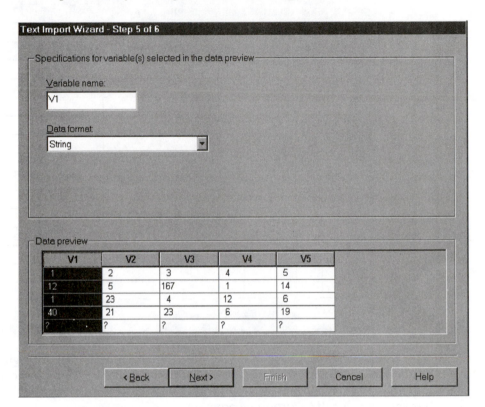

Note that the format must be changed for each variable. The Window above shows the configuration with these windows open. You can see that variable 1 (V1) has been clicked (V1 is depressed, and the column is black), and that the **Variable name** is given as V1 while the **Data format** is given as **String.** To change the variable name (this isn't necessary, but I did it to change many of the variable names in the examples in the chapters to follow), you would click on the **Variable name** window, delete the V1, and type in the new name. To change the format (this is necessary if you want to do any computations with this variable, because **SPSS 9.0** does not do calculations on a string variable), you would *click on the arrow to the right of the **Data format** window, then scroll up to find numeric. Click on numeric to change the variable to numeric.* To continue with the second variable, *click on V2 and proceed as above.* Once you have finished changing all the data formats, *click on **Next** to produce the Window for Step 6.* This Window is the same as that for Window 6 in the previous example, except for the appearance of the data in the Data preview. To terminate this table, *click on **Finish.*** This will produce the data in the **Data Editor** as shown in the next figure.

Sometimes it happens that, although you follow the above instructions, you find (when you leave the Import Wizard) that the variable is still in "string" format. You will know this because the Data list statement will show the variable in **A** (Alphabetic) format, and **SPSS** will not perform the computations you request. If this happens, return to the Data Editor and change the format of the variable there. This is done by *double-clicking on the variable name of the variable in question.* This will produce a window labeled **Define Variable,** which permits you to change the variable name, the format etc. . . . Change the format by *clicking on **Type** under **Change Settings.*** This produces another Window, labeled **Define Variable Type.** *Click on **Numeric** and then click on **Continue.*** This returns you to the **Define Variable** Window. *Click on **Scale under Measurement,** and then on **OK.*** This will return you to the Data Editor.

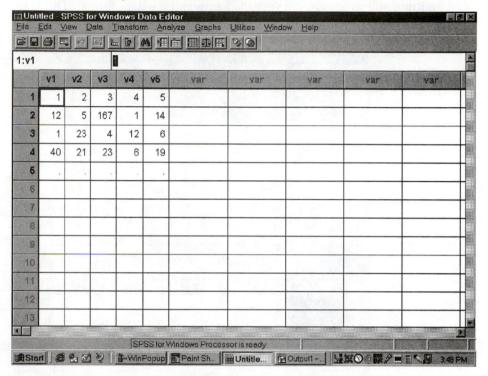

Note that the data appear in the data field as integers that are right justified. Thus the Data Editor looks different from that in the previous example. This has no implications for the data analysis, however, and you can now proceed to analyze the data by *clicking on **Analyze*** in the Menu Bar and selecting the appropriate program.

There are undoubtedly other differences between **SPSS 8.0** and **SPSS 9.0** that you will encounter. All of the examples in this book were run on **SPSS 8.0,** so if your input Windows and/or output are not identical in form to that presented herein, it means simply that there are changes. They should be minor, however, and the important point is that the explanations of the output apply nonetheless.

STEPS IN USING SPSS FREQUENCIES

Many of the statistics we discussed earlier can be computed using the **SPSS WINDOWS FREQUENCIES** program. This can be run using **SPSS** as follows:

1. *Enter SPSS WIN.* It is possible, particularly if you are using **SPSS 8.0 or SPSS 9.0 for Windows** for the first time, that you will be presented with a window labelled SPSS for Windows, offering a number of choices such as "Open an Existing File," "Type in Data," etc. If you click on **Type in Data,** this will take you to the **Data Editor;** we will use that procedure here. If you wish to go directly to the data editor every time you use **SPSS,** you can click on "Don't show this dialog in the future." If you were to follow the procedure suggested, this presents you with an empty **SPSS** Data Editor (see page 15). At this point, you could begin to type in the data. However, we will assume here that you already have the data in an ASCII file on the A Drive

in a file labelled **chap1.dat**. For each participant there would be the one value, referred to as X in this example.

2. Use one of the options described for **SPSS 8.0** (pages 17–20) or **SPSS 9.0** (pages 20–28) as appropriate, to input the one variable in the file. It will be necessary to name it X to have your output appear as in this example, otherwise it will appear as V1.

3. *Click on the **Statistics** (in **SPSS 8.0**) or **Analyze** (in **SPSS 9.0**) option on the menu bar. This presents you with a drop-down menu. Move your cursor to **Summarize** (in **SPSS 8.0**) or **Descriptive Statistics** (in **SPSS 9.0**), and you are presented with another menu to the right with a number of choices.*

4. *Click on **Frequencies**.* This presents you with the following Window, **Frequencies:**

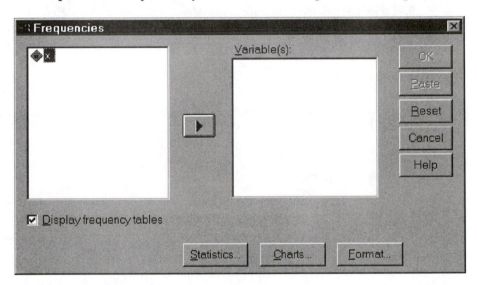

   The variable, X, appears in the white pane to the left and is highlighted. Define it as the variable by clicking on the arrow to the left of the Variable(s) pane.

5. *Then click on **Statistics** at the bottom of the Window.* This produces another Window, **Frequencies: Statistics:**

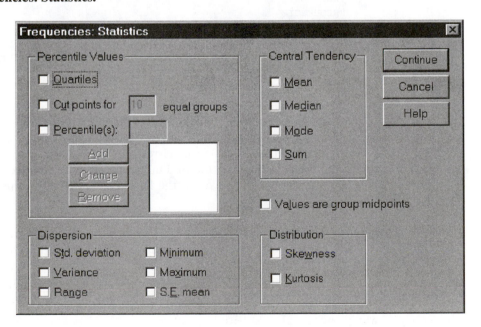

6. This Window presents a listing of all possible statistics that this program will produce. *Move your cursor to* **Mean** *and click the mouse. A checkmark will appear in the pane to the left. Do the same thing for each of* **Median, Mode, Skewness, Kurtosis, Std. Deviation, Variance,** *and* **Range.** *Then move your cursor to* **Percentiles** *and click. Type 25 in the white pane to the right, then click on* **Add.** *Then type 75 in the white pane and again click on* **Add.** *Then click on* **Continue.**

7. This takes you back to the Window, **Frequencies.** *Click on* **OK** *to run the analysis.*

8. This runs the **Frequencies** program, and the answers are returned to the **SPSS** Viewer, as well as to your monitor. At this point, you can print your answers, save them in a file, or transfer them to some other editor.

9. To exit **SPSS,** *click on* **File** *in the Menu Bar, and click on* **Exit** *on the drop-down menu. Before you can exit, however, the program will ask if you wish to save the contents of the* **SPSS** *Viewer as well as those of the Data Editor.* If you have already saved them, you need not do so again.

The Syntax File

If you were to follow the instructions given above, you would produce the following Syntax File in **SPSS 8.0**:

```
DATA LIST FILE='A:\Chap1.dat' FREE/ x * .
EXECUTE.
FREQUENCIES
        VARIABLES=x
        /PERCENTILES= 25 75
        /STATISTICS=STANDARD DEVIATION VARIANCE RANGE MEAN MEDIAN
        MODE SKEWNESS SESKEW KURTOSIS SEKURT
        /ORDER ANALYSIS .
```

Or the following one in **SPSS 9.0**:

```
DATA LIST list() file='A:\Chap1.dat' / X(f8.2).
EXECUTE .
FREQUENCIES
        VARIABLES= X
        /PERCENTILES= 25 75
        /STATISTICS=STANDARD DEVIATION VARIANCE RANGE MEAN MEDIAN
        MODE SKEWNESS SESKEW KURTOSIS SEKURT
        /ORDER ANALYSIS .
```

You will note that except for the Data List lines the two files are the same. These were run with the Freefield and Delimited formats respectively, and would appear slightly different for the Fixed Variable and Fixed width formats respectively. In the chapters that follow, the Data List and associated Execute lines are omitted in the examples of Syntax files to eliminate the need to show the file twice. Obviously, however, the Data List and Execute lines are a necessary part of the file.

This file runs the program. The Data List line instructs the computer that the data are in a file called chap1.dat, that it is located on the A Drive, that the data are in free format (in **SPSS 8.0**, or in f8.3 format in **SPSS 9.0**) and that there is one value, identified as X on each line. The line Execute causes **SPSS** to input the data. The line Frequencies instructs the computer to calculate the Frequency distribution for the variable(s), X. The Percentiles line tells it to compute the values for the

25th and 75th percentiles, and the Statistics line has it compute the standard deviation, variance, range, mean, median, mode, skewness, standard error of skewness, kurtosis, and standard error of kurtosis.

Pasting the Syntax File

When using the click-and-hope method, it is often desirable to save the Syntax File that it creates. One advantage of doing this is that it gives you a record of the job. In future runs, then you can simply execute the Syntax File without having to create it all over. [This way of running **SPSS WINDOWS** jobs is discussed in the following section titled "Running Frequencies With an Existing Syntax File" (p. 31)]. Also in running the same job with different data sets, it might be easier to modify the Syntax file than to create a new one.

When using the click-and-hope method, you can paste the file into the Syntax Editor as follows:

1. *Begin by using the click-and-hope method as described in the section titled "Steps in Using **SPSS FREQUENCIES**" (p. 28). Follow steps 1 to 6, but at Step 7, click on **Paste** instead of clicking on **OK.***

2. This will produce the Window labelled **Syntax1-SPSS Syntax Editor** (see figure, p. 16). The only difference between the figure shown on page 16 and the one you will see at this step is that the syntax for the **Frequencies** run will be listed in the Window. That is, that part of the Syntax file shown above, beginning with **Frequencies** and ending with **Analysis,** will be shown in the Window. Note, the part of the Syntax File referring to inputting the data (i.e., the lines beginning Data List and Execute) is not pasted at this stage. *If you wish to add these statements to the file (which you would have to do, if you wished to run the job without entering the data into the data editor), you would move your cursor to the beginning of the first line (i.e., to the F in Frequencies), and type in the statements, so that the file appears as above.*

3. *To save this file, click on **File** in the menu bar of this Window. This will produce a drop-down menu. Select either **Save** or **Save As,** and click on it.* This will result in a **Save** or **Save As** window with a filename (e.g., Syntax1) indicated in the Filename pane. *(If you want to change the name, click on the pane and type in the name you want.) To save the file, click on **Save.*** If you do not give the filename an extension, **SPSS** will give it the extension **.sps.**

4. This will save the Syntax file as an ASCII (Text) file. *If you now wanted to run the file, you could click on **Run** on the menu bar for this window.* This will produce a drop-down menu. *Click on **All,** and this will also run the job.*

Running Frequencies with an Existing Syntax File

If you already had typed the Syntax file as it exists in the section titled "The Syntax File" (p. 30) and had stored it as an ASCII (Text) file on the A drive, in a file labelled **FREQ.SPS,** you could run this job without using the click-and-hope method. To run this program, you would still need to access **SPSS WINDOWS.** Once presented with the Data Editor, however, you would proceed as follows:

1. *Click on **File** in the Menu Bar.* This produces a drop-down menu. *Move the cursor to **New.*** A side menu will then be presented. *Click on **Syntax,*** and this produces a blank Syntax Window.

2. *Click on **File** in the Menu Bar for this Window. This again produces the drop-down menu, but this time click on **Open.*** This produces the following **Open File** Window (though the files listed may not be as shown in the example).

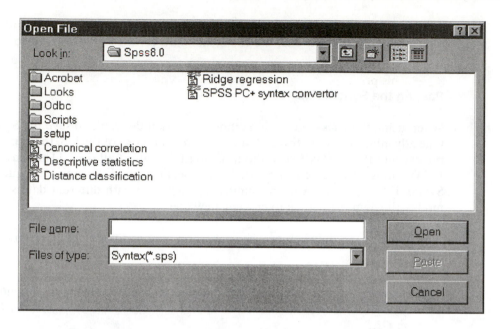

3. *Click on the down arrow to the right of the* **Look In** *pane, and click on the drive where the Syntax file is located (e.g., the A:\Drive).* This will cause the computer to list all files with the extension *.sps, though the extension is not shown. *If your file is not listed, click on the down arrow at the right of the* **Files of Type** *pane, and click on* **All files** *(*.*), in the drop-down pane.*

4. *Click on your file.* It will appear in the "Filename" pane. *Click on* **Open.** The file will then appear in the Syntax Window.

5. *Click on* **Run.** This presents a drop-down menu. *Click on* **All** *to run the program.* You will note that the entire set of instructions (i.e., the Syntax file) is highlighted briefly.

6. The answers are presented in the **SPSS** Viewer, from which they can be printed, or stored in a file.

Obtaining a Listing of the Command Syntax for a Program

It is obvious that you must know the relevant instructions and syntax in order to type your own Syntax file. You can obtain this information while inside **SPSS WINDOWS,** by performing the following steps. I shall use the example of obtaining the instructions for the **Frequencies** program. The steps are as follows:

1. *Click on* **Help** *on the Menu Bar.* This produces a drop-down menu. *Click on* **Topics** *in this menu.* This produces the Window, Help Topics: SPSS for Windows. This Window presents a number of topics you can search. You are told here to *"Click a book, and then click* **Open.** *Or click another Tab such as Index."* We shall *click on* **Statistical Analysis,** one of the books listed. When this is highlighted, we will then *click on* **Open.**

2. This presents a number of choices and we will *click on* **Summarize,** the first in the list, and then *click on* **Open.**

3. This presents more choices. We will *click on **Frequencies Procedure,*** and then *click on **Display.*** This presents a side Window with information on the Frequencies subcommand. *Click on **Syntax.***

4. This presents another Window, **Topics Found,** with **Command Syntax** highlighted. *Move cursor to **Frequencies Command Syntax,** and click on **Display**.* This presents a list of Syntax commands, but you may have to *click on the large square in the upper-right of the tool bar* to see them.

If you followed these instructions, you would obtain the following information:

```
Frequencies Command Syntax


FREQUENCIES [VARIABLES=]varlist
[/FORMAT=[{DVALUE}] [{NOTABLE }]]
        {AFREQ } {LIMIT(n)}
        {DFREQ }
[/MISSING=INCLUDE]
[/BARCHART=[MIN(n)][MAX(n)][{FREQ(n) }]]
              {PERCENT(n)}
[/PIECHART=[MIN(n)][MAX(n)][{FREQ }]
              {PERCENT}
        [{MISSING }]]
         {NONMISSING}
[/HISTOGRAM=[MIN(n)][MAX(n)][{FREQ(n) }]
               {PERCENT(n)}
        [{NONORMAL}][INCREMENT(n)]]
         {NORMAL }
[/NTILES=n]
[/PERCENTILES=value list]
[/STATISTICS=[DEFAULT][MEAN][STDDEV][SUM]
        [MINIMUM][MAXIMUM][RANGE]
        [SEMEAN][VARIANCE][SKEWNESS][SESKEW]
        [MODE][KURTOSIS][SEKURT][MEDIAN]
        [ALL][NONE]]
[/GROUPED=varlist [{(width) }]]
         {(boundary list)}
[/ORDER = [{ANALYSIS}]
[{VARIABLE}]
```

As you can see, the program **Frequencies** can do many more things than simply produce the frequency distribution, and compute a few statistics. Like all the programs in **SPSS** it is a very general one, and we have simply selected a few of the possible functions. The same can be said for our discussion of all the other programs in the following chapters.

The Output

Whether you had run the program using the click and hope method or had prepared the Syntax File by typing it into an ASCII file, or even if you had typed the file while in the **SPSS** Syntax Editor, you would have obtained the following output with the data presented earlier. One aspect of this output is the Frequency Distribution, as follows:

X

		Frequency	Percent	Valid Percent	Cumulative Percent
Valid	8.00	1	2.9	2.9	2.9
	9.00	1	2.9	2.9	5.7
	10.00	2	5.7	5.7	11.4
	11.00	7	20.0	20.0	31.4
	12.00	5	14.3	14.3	45.7
	13.00	5	14.3	14.3	60.0
	14.00	4	11.4	11.4	71.4
	15.00	3	8.6	8.6	80.0
	16.00	2	5.7	5.7	85.7
	17.00	2	5.7	5.7	91.4
	18.00	1	2.9	2.9	94.3
	19.00	1	2.9	2.9	97.1
	20.00	1	2.9	2.9	100.0
	Total	35	100.0	100.0	

This output presents a frequency distribution of the values, as well as the percentage of cases and the cumulative percentage. The distinction between percent and valid percent allows for an accounting of missing values if there are any in the data set. Since we did not have any missing observations, the two sets of numbers are identical.

The output labelled **Statistics** presents the variable X, an indication of the number of valid cases and the number of missing cases, followed by the various statistics. You will note that in most cases these values agree (within rounding) with the values that were presented in our discussion of the various statistics.

X	Statistics	
N	Valid	35
	Missing	0
Mean		13.2286
Median		13.0000
Mode		11.00
Std. Deviation		2.7980
Variance		7.8286
Skewness		.580
Std. Error of Skewness		.398
Kurtosis		.010
Std. Error of Kurtosis		.778
Range		12.00
Percentiles	25	11.0000
	75	15.0000

The two exceptions to this are the statistics for skewness and kurtosis. The values are similar, but not identical to those presented earlier. The reason for this is that **SPSS WINDOWS** calculates unbiased estimates of these values rather than the biased estimates that are presented in many psychological statistics textbooks, and were presented above. The formulae used in **SPSS** are attributed by SPSS Inc. Reports (1986) to Bliss (1967). For the sake of completeness, the formulae are reproduced here, however, it should be noted that they are conceptually the same as the earlier ones, and the description given earlier applies equally to these. The formula for skewness is:

$$g_1 = \frac{n\Sigma(X - \bar{X})^3}{(n-1)(n-2)S^3}$$

The formula for the standard error is:

$$SE_{g_1} = \sqrt{\frac{6N(N-1)}{(N-2)(N+1)(N+3)}}$$

According to the output, these two formulae yielded values of .580 and .398, respectively. We could use this information, therefore to test whether it is reasonable to assume that the sample was obtained from a population that was symmetrical (i.e., had a parameter of 0). To do this, we would form a standard normal deviate as the ratio of the statistic minus the parameter divided by the standard error, as follows:

$$Z = \frac{.580 - 0}{.398} = 1.46$$

Note, this value is not greater than 1.96 (the value of Z required for significance at the .05 level), thus we have no evidence to conclude that our population is skewed.

The formula for kurtosis is:

$$g_2 = \frac{n^2\left[\dfrac{(n+1)\Sigma(X-\bar{X})^4}{n} - \dfrac{3(n-1)[\Sigma(X-\bar{X})^2]}{n^2}\right]}{(n-1)(n-2)(n-3)S^4}$$

The formula for the standard error is:

$$SE_{g_2} = \sqrt{\frac{(4N^2-1)(SE_{g_1})^2}{(n-3)(N+5)}}$$

The output indicates that the values of these two statistics are .010 and .778, respectively. We can use these two values to determine whether our population has a higher or lower kurtosis than a normal population (0). The test is:

$$Z = \frac{.010 - 0}{.778} = .01$$

The value of Z is not greater than 1.96, therefore, we can conclude that we have no evidence to assume that our population distribution is different from normal in kurtosis. Taking the two tests, together, we have no evidence to suggest that our population is not normally distributed.

Obviously these formulae are a bit more complex than the ones presented earlier, but they are similar and they do assess the same characteristics using the same general idea. Presenting these formulae, however, does allow me to make the point that to some extent the user is at the mercy of the computer package. There is no easy way of knowing what formulae the programmers of a particular package are using unless you can obtain a copy of a book that presents the algorithms used. The manuals that are readily available do not give information about the algorithms used, and books containing the algorithms are not easy to find.

In the present instance, the formulae given earlier for skewness and kurtosis are typically the ones researchers would find if they were to look in psychological statistics textbooks, and one might reasonably expect that the computer program would be based on these formulae. The simple truth is, however, that you can't always assume that the computer is using the formula you know. There are other instances in **SPSS** where the computations or logic do not agree with that found in most psychological statistics textbooks. When this occurs (and I have spotted it), I have noted it in the appropriate section. But unless you actually run an example of everything for which you know the answers, you never really know for sure. This is another case where user friendly can have its drawbacks.

CONCLUDING COMMENTS

This chapter has provided an overview of the majority of basic statistics that are discussed in the following chapters, some concepts that are fundamental to statistical inference, and ways of accessing **SPSS WINDOWS.** Although attention is directed to the click and hope method in the subsequent chapters, it was also indicated here that all programs in **SPSS WINDOWS** can be run from the Syntax Editor, either prepared beforehand as an ASCII file, or in **SPSS WINDOWS** at the time of execution. Personally I prefer to use the Syntax file because that way I know what I have asked the computer to do. At a minimum, I feel that it is imperative that one always knows the syntax file, and I have recommended that researchers always include it with their output so that when reviewing their output at a later date, they will know exactly what requests were made of the computer.

The example used in this chapter involved only one variable. In most research, however, a researcher would be interested in a number of variables. Clearly more than one variable can be investigated in any given analysis simply by having them in the data file, and defining them in the run. Attention was directed to only one variable in this chapter in order to keep the example simple. The same strategy is followed in the remaining chapters. The simplest form of analysis is followed in all instances, but often multiple analysis can be performed in any one run.

Chapter 2
The t-Test

Often in research we have information concerning the means of two samples and we are interested in determining whether they are truly different from each other. Thus, we may have tested two samples of students, one under some experimental condition, and the other under a control condition. We really want to conclude that the two groups are different; that the mean for the experimental group is really higher or lower than that for the control group. If we look in a statistics book, we are told that we can make use of the *t*-statistic in order to test this difference. To do this, however, we are told that we must assume a null hypothesis, and use the *t*-statistic to determine how reasonable it is to conclude that the null hypothesis is true. If the probability is quite low (e.g., less than .05, written as $p < .05$), we will conclude that the null hypothesis is not true. This seems like a rather circuitous route, but as we shall see it is really very straightforward. In the following sections we will discuss the basic rationale in some detail, and give a brief history underlying this procedure. We will then go on to discuss how the *t*-test is applied to two different types of situations involving tests of means, one in which the means are obtained from independent samples, and the other where the means are based on the same individuals or individuals paired in some way.

GENERAL RATIONALE

The general rationale underlying tests of means began with generalizations based on the Normal Distribution, and was concerned with one of two inferential questions. One asked how reasonable it was to assume that a sample originated from a population with a given mean. It thus involved inferences about a single sample mean. The other question asked how reasonable it was that two samples came from populations with identical means. That is, it involved inferences about two means. Answers to both of these questions were based on knowledge about the standard Normal Population.

As we saw in Chapter 1, the Standard Normal Distribution is such that 95% of the area lies between -1.96 and $+1.96$. Thus, if we obtained a value of Z that was less than -1.96 (e.g., -2.11) or greater than $+1.96$ (e.g., $+2.34$), we would consider this quite a rare event. We might conclude that since we would expect a value between -1.96 and $+1.96$ to occur 95% of the time, the fact that our value (e.g., -2.11 or 2.34) was outside that range indicates that it would occur less than 5% of the time on the basis of chance. We would conclude therefore that the Z was "significant at the .05 level." Similarly, the Standard Normal Distribution is such that 99% of the area lies between -2.58 and $+2.58$, thus if our value of Z was outside that range, we would conclude that the difference was significant at the .01 level. The probability of a Type I error in this case is .01. Although some individuals loosely say that this is more significant than something significant at the .05 level, this misrepresents what has been determined. Before the event, a researcher decides what Type I error he/she is willing to make, and any value of the test statistic (i.e., Z) that has a probability less than this is considered significant. With Table A, Appendix B, researchers can determine the Type I error that they feel is most appropriate. The only reason for stating the probability level of a statistic (i.e., $<.05$, $<.01$, $<.001$, etc.) is to permit readers with their own concept of what constitutes significance to consider a reported finding in terms of this preference. In common practice, however, $p < .05$ is generally considered to indicate significance.

Inferences Involving a Single Sample Mean

One of the earliest interests of inferential statistics was determining how likely it was that a sample with a given mean (statistic) could originate from a population with a given mean (parameter). Thus, let us assume that you had determined that the mean weight of a sample of $n = 100$ individuals was $\overline{X} = 127$ pounds, and you wondered how likely it was that this sample could have been randomly obtained from a population with a mean weight (μ) of 120 pounds, and a standard deviation

(σ) of 40. You could determine this by recourse to the Standard Normal Distribution. Assuming an underlying normal population, the statistic:

$$Z = \frac{\bar{X} - \mu}{\frac{\sigma}{\sqrt{n}}}$$

is normally distributed. Even if the underlying population is not normally distributed, the statistic will still be normally distributed assuming large sample size because of the Central Limit Theorem. The Z value for our example is:

$$Z = \frac{127 - 120}{\frac{40}{\sqrt{100}}} = 1.75$$

The value of 1.75 is not greater than 1.96, thus we have no reason to conclude that our sample did not come from a population with a mean of 120 (i.e., we do not reject the null hypothesis). We could, if we wished, use Table A, Appendix B, to determine the probability level associated with this statistic, but generally a probability level of .05 (corresponding to $Z = \pm 1.96$) is taken as a meaningful cut-off value.

In the above example, it was assumed that the researcher knew both the population mean and standard deviation. However, it was often the case that a researcher would not know the population standard deviation, but wanted to determine whether or not a sample with a given mean could be considered representative of a population with a given mean. Under these conditions, the researcher would simply estimate the population standard deviation by using the value of the standard deviation computed from the sample data. This standard deviation is what has been referred to as the biased estimate, and is defined by the equation:

$$S = \sqrt{\frac{\Sigma (X - \bar{X})^2}{n}}$$

Inferences Involving Two Sample Means

Sometimes a researcher wanted to evaluate whether the difference between two sample means was sufficiently large as to suggest that the two samples were drawn from populations with different means. This test is a direct extension of the preceding single sample test. In the single sample test, one simply divides the difference between the sample mean and the assumed population mean by the standard error of the mean. As applied to a contrast between two independent sample means, one simply contrasts the difference between the difference of two sample means from their population means, as:

$$(\bar{X}_1 - \mu_1) - (\bar{X}_2 - \mu_2)$$

and divides this by the standard error of the difference between two independent means. This standard error can be shown to be equal to the square root of the sum of the variances of the two means, σ_1^2/n_1 and σ_2^2/n_2, estimated by S_1^2/n_1 and S_2^2/n_2 respectively if the population variances (σ_1^2 and σ_2^2) are not known. If one further assumes that the two population means are equal (i.e., the null hypothesis), then $\mu_1 = \mu_2 = \mu$, and the equation is:

$$\frac{\bar{X}_1 - \bar{X}_2}{\sqrt{\dfrac{S_1^2}{n_1} + \dfrac{S_2^2}{n_2}}}$$

This is the equation for what was often called the Critical Ratio (see, for example, Shen, 1940).

Suppose a researcher had two samples, one with a mean of 11.8000, a sample variance of 1.7594, and a sample size of 5, and the other with a mean of 14.8571, a sample variance of 11.5511, and a sample size of 7, this Critical Ratio would be equal to:

$$C.R. = \frac{11.8000 - 14.8571}{\sqrt{\dfrac{1.7594}{5} + \dfrac{11.5511}{7}}} = -2.16$$

This value is greater in magnitude than 1.96, thus the researcher would conclude that in fact the two means were more different than one would expect on the basis of chance, and would therefore conclude that they were significantly different from each other at the .05 level.

A BIT OF HISTORY

One problem with the application of the single sample Z statistic is that it assumes that the researcher knows the values of the population mean (μ) and standard deviation (σ), and that the population is either normally distributed or the sample size is large enough (often considered to be around $n = 100$ or greater) to offset the effects of non-normality. As indicated above, this was generally achieved by assuming the population mean to be some value, and then estimating the population standard deviation (σ) by using the sample value (S), where S was computed using the biased estimate.

This was reasonable as long as sample size was large, but at least one researcher was concerned that it was not reasonable when sample size was small. W. S. Gosset (Student[1], 1908a) realized that both the sample mean and standard deviation varied from one sample to another, even though the formula for the single sample Z was based on the notion that only the sample mean varied. He felt too that the effects of the variability of the variance estimate would be greater the smaller the sample size. Gosset often was forced to use small numbers of samples, and was concerned that tests of significance that were applicable to large samples may not be appropriate to small samples. In fact, he published an article on the sampling distribution of the correlation coefficient for small samples (Student, 1908b).

With respect to the single sample Z statistic, Gosset reasoned that since the standard deviation was also varying, it was likely that there would be relatively more extreme values of Z with small samples than one would expect based on the Standard Normal Distribution. This was because with a small sample size, one might expect that on some occasions a sample mean that was somewhat removed from the population mean would also have a particularly small variance, thus producing a relatively larger Z score. He investigated this by performing a series of what we would now call Monte Carlo studies. He had access to a set of measurements made by Macdonell (1901) of 3,000

---

[1] "Student" was a *nom de plume* that W. S. Gosset used in his publications. Gosset worked for the Guinness Breweries, which had a policy against publication by their scientist-employees.

criminals, so he obtained a series of samples of $n = 4$, computed the values of both S and Z, and studied their sampling distributions. His results confirmed his expectations!

As a result of his research, Gosset published an article concerned with the probable error of the mean (Student, 1908a), in which he presented his major observations about the sampling distribution of Z when the value of the population standard deviation is expressed in terms of the sample value, and made the distinction between statistic and parameter which is so basic today. Cowles (1989) notes that despite the enormity of his findings, Gosset's research was largely ignored for many years, though ultimately, it did achieve the recognition it deserved. It wasn't until 1925, however, that the *t*-test, as we know it today, was used to test the significance of the difference between two sample means. Fisher (1925a) introduced this application, but even then the procedure did not receive much attention from researchers. Rucci and Tweney (1980) show how the proportion of published articles using the *t*-test or the Critical Ratio procedures changed from 1935 to 1952. In 1935, use of the *t*-test was virtually non-existent while the Critical Ratio accounted for about 27% of the articles, by 1941, the values were about 5% for the *t*-test and 31% for the Critical Ratio, while in 1952 the *t*-test was used in approximately 30% of the articles while use of the Critical Ratio dropped to around 5%. The Critical Ratio is not used any more!

THE DENSITY FUNCTION FOR *t*

The shape of any sampling distribution is given by its density function. The density function is simply an equation that describes the shape of the distribution, but once this equation is known, it can be used to determine the area under the curve between any two points (e.g., values of the statistic in question). This is done by using the technique of integration from Calculus, a procedure that is beyond the scope of this discussion.

The density function for the standard Normal Distribution is:

$$y = \frac{1}{\sqrt{2\pi}} e^{-\frac{z^2}{2}}$$

The value of y is the value of the ordinate given in Table A, Appendix B. More importantly, Calculus can be used to integrate this function, and in this way one can determine the area between any two values. This is how the values for the areas presented in Table A, Appendix B were obtained. It is this analysis that permits us to say that 95% of the area lies between the values of -1.96 and $+1.96$, or that 34.134 % of the area lies between 0 and 1.0 etc.

The density function for the *t*-distribution is:

$$y = \left(1 + \frac{t^2}{df}\right)^{\frac{-(df+1)}{2}}$$

It will be noted in this equation that there are two variables, df and t, thus the nature of this function changes as a function of df. For this reason, there are in fact a family of curves, one for each value of df. The figure below presents curves for this function for df = 2, as well as that for Z, the Normal Distribution. The horizontal axis represents the various values of t or Z as appropriate, while the height of the curves refer to the values of y in the two equations just presented. Note that the *t*-distribution is more peaked in the middle and higher at the tails than the normal curve, particularly for small degrees of freedom.

By using Calculus, the area under the curve can be determined for the values of t for each df. The probability values given in tables of t are the results of such calculations applied to this family of curves. Thus, when $df = 2$, it can be shown that 5% of the area is outside the limits of −4.30 and +4.30. We thus say, for $df = 2$, that any value of t that exceeds the value of 4.30 is significant at the .05 level. Similarly, for $df = 15$, 5% of the area lies beyond the values of −2.13 and +2.13,

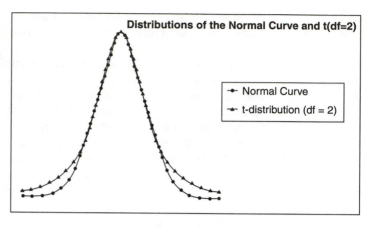

and thus for $df = 15$ any value of t with an absolute value greater than 2.13 is significant at the .05 level. Examination of any table of probability values for the t-distribution will show that as df increases, the value of t required for significance at the .05 level gets closer and closer to the value of 1.96 (the value required for significance for the normal curve). That is, as would be expected, as df increases, the t distribution gets more and more like the Standard Normal Distribution.

More detailed information about the t-distribution is presented in Table B, Appendix B. This table presents values of df in steps of 1 from 1 to 30, and then for four selected higher values. Associated with each df are the corresponding t-values for two-tailed probabilities of .1, .05, .02, .01, and .001. Thus, for $df = 15$, a t-value of 2.131 has a two-tailed probability of .05. That is, 5% of the time one would expect to obtain a t-value as extreme as 2.131 (positive or negative) or larger on the basis of chance. Since this is a relatively rare event, one is thus likely to conclude that the result is not due to chance.

THE t-TEST AND COMPARISONS OF INDEPENDENT MEANS

As indicated earlier, Gosset argued that researchers should use the t-statistic when evaluating sample means rather than statistics based on the Normal Distribution. For the single sample test, this t-statistic would be defined as:

$$t = \frac{\bar{X} - \mu}{\sqrt{\dfrac{S^2}{n}}}$$

where S^2 is defined as the unbiased estimate of the population variance. The equation for this unbiased estimate is:

$$S^2 = \frac{\Sigma(X - \bar{X})^2}{(n - 1)}$$

and the df would be equal to $(n - 1)$.

For the two sample test, this t-statistic would be defined as:

$$t = \frac{\bar{X}_1 - \bar{X}_2}{\sqrt{\dfrac{S_1^2}{n_1} + \dfrac{S_2^2}{n_2}}}$$

Although this equation appears identical to that for the Critical Ratio (see p. 40), it differs in that the S^2 values are defined as the unbiased estimates of the population variances in this form, whereas they are biased estimates for the Critical Ratio.

In this equation, separate estimates are made for each of the population variances, and this requires one to also estimate the df associated with the sum of these two estimates. Welch (1938) found, however, that if the population variances were unequal, this would influence the magnitude of the df. He also showed that a reasonable estimate of the resulting df was:

$$df = \frac{\left(\dfrac{S_1^2}{n_1} + \dfrac{S_2^2}{n_2}\right)^2}{\dfrac{S_1^4}{n_1^2(n_1 - 1)} + \dfrac{S_2^4}{n_2^2(n_2 - 1)}}$$

Thus, when a t-test is performed to compare two independent means, and it is found that the two sample variances are themselves more variable than reasonably can be attributed to chance, it is necessary to compute the Welch (1938) estimate of the df instead of simply summing the df for the two estimates [i.e., $(n_1 - 1) + (n_2 - 1)$]. We shall discuss two different ways of determining whether the variances differ significantly in the next section, labelled "Determining if Variances are Heterogeneous or Homogeneous."

If, however, one can assume that the variances in the two populations are equal to each other (i.e., the assumption of homogeneity of variance), it is reasonable to estimate this variance by computing a pooled estimate as follows:

$$S^2 = \frac{\Sigma(X_1 - \bar{X}_1)^2 + \Sigma(X_2 - \bar{X}_2)^2}{n_1 + n_2 - 2}$$

and the formula for the t-statistic becomes:

$$t = \frac{\bar{X}_1 - \bar{X}_2}{\sqrt{\dfrac{S^2}{n_1} + \dfrac{S^2}{n_2}}}$$

where $df = n_1 + n_2 - 2$.

Thus, when comparing two independent samples, one uses a slightly different equation and estimate of degrees of freedom depending upon whether or not the population variances can be considered homogeneous.

Determining if Variances Are Heterogeneous or Homogeneous

In order to determine whether or not the variances in the underlying populations are heterogeneous (i.e., different) or homogeneous (i.e., the same), one conducts a test of the difference between the variability in the two samples. There are at least two procedures one can use to make this test, and both of these use a sampling distribution referred to as the F-distribution.

More detailed information about the F-distribution is presented in Table C, Appendix B. This table describes the distribution of the ratio of two variances, which is often referred to as an F-ratio, or F-value. This table presents F-values for probabilities of .05, .01, and .001 for combinations of two sets of degrees of freedom (df). The degrees of freedom ($df\,1$) for the numerator of the F-ratio are given along the top of the table for the values of 1, 2, 3, 4, 5, 6, 8, 12, 24, and infinity (∞). Those for the degrees of freedom ($df2$) for the denominator are given along the side of the table and vary from 1 to 30 in steps of 1, and then for the values of 40, 60, 120, and infinity (∞). Thus, if the variance in the numerator had 3 degrees of freedom associated with it, and that in the denominator had 30 degrees of freedom, then from the table, one would see that the probability is .05 of obtaining a ratio as large or larger than 2.92. That is, on the basis of chance, one might obtain a ratio that large or larger less than 5% of the time. Similarly, there is a probability of .01 associated with an F-ratio of 4.51, and a probability of .001 associated with an F-ratio of 7.05.

Note that all of the F-ratios presented in Table C are greater than 1.0. When constructing the table, it was decided to focus the table on large F-ratios, thus in some instances these probabilities can be considered one-tailed probabilities. That is, if there is no *a priori* reason for placing one of the variance estimates in the numerator, the probabilities can be considered one-tailed. Under these conditions, the probability should be doubled. If, however, there is an *a priori* basis for the formation of the F-ratio, then the values are two-tailed probabilities.

One procedure used to test for heterogeneity of variance is to compute an F-ratio by dividing the largest variance by the smaller variance. Note in this case that there is no *a priori* reason for determining which variance should be in the numerator, thus the largest one was used. In this case, the F-table should be considered as describing a one-tailed test, and the obtained probabilities should be doubled. Thus, if we had two variances, 2.20 and 13.48 with 4 and 6 degrees of freedom respectively, the resulting F-ratio would be:

$$\frac{13.48}{2.20} = 6.127 \text{ at 6 and 4 degrees of freedom respectively.}$$

Inspection of Table C, Appendix B would reveal that a value of 6.16 is significant at the .05 level one-tailed, or .10 two-tailed. Since our value of 6.127 is not significant at the .05 level two-tailed, we would conclude that we have no reason for concluding that our two variances differ in the population. We use a two-tailed test here, because we arbitrarily put the largest variance in the numerator of the F-ratio. We will not discuss this procedure any further since **SPSS WINDOWS** does not use this procedure in conjunction with the t-test.

The procedure used by **SPSS WINDOWS** is that proposed by Levene (1960). This procedure involves comparing the size of the deviations of each observation from the mean of the group in which it appears. The procedure involves doing an analysis of variance of the absolute deviations of each observation from its mean. An F-ratio is formed where the numerator is a measure of the variance of the means of the absolute deviations while the denominator is the variance of the absolute deviations within the groups. This is true, regardless of which variance is largest. The result is an F-ratio which has 1 degree of freedom in the numerator and $(n_1 + n_2 - 2)$ degrees of freedom in the denominator. Since this F-ratio has an *a priori* form, the probability levels in the table are two-tailed by definition. That is, the probability refers to the chances of getting an F-ratio of this form on the basis of chance. If this F-ratio is significant it indicates that the variability in one group is greater than that in another. If this is the case, we conclude that the variances are heterogeneous. If this F-ratio is not significant, we conclude that the variances are homogeneous (i.e., we assume that the variances are equal).

An Example Using SPSS for WINDOWS

Consider the following data from two independent samples of individuals. Assume that the five individuals in Group 1 constituted the control (i.e., no treatment) group, and that the seven individuals in Group 2 were in the experimental group (i.e., they were given a pill 20 minutes before the experiment began). Assume further, that the dependent measure is the number of correct responses made by individuals in a learning task administered to the two groups.

The data might look as follows:

Group 1	Group 2
10	18
12	10
14	11
12	13
11	16
	20
	16

In order to run these through the **SPSS WINDOWS** program, we could create a file, referred to below as "tchapi.dat" and store it on disk. Each line in this file would involve the group number (i.e., 1 or 2) and the score. Thus, the file would look as follows:

1 10
1 12
1 14
1 12
1 11
2 18
2 10
2 11
2 13
2 16
2 20
2 16

It is also necessary to create a syntax file, that is a file that instructs the computer how to perform the analysis. This can be done using the following steps.

Steps in Using SPSS WINDOWS *t*-TEST

The following steps are applicable to **SPSS 8.0** and **SPSS 9.0** except for the input of the ASCII or Text data file. In the example to follow you are instructed at Step 3 to input your data following the procedures described in Chapter 1. The output for this example was obtained by using the freefield format in **SPSS 8.0,** and depending upon the input procedure you use, the format may be somewhat different. The answers are the same, however. Using the **WINDOWS** version of the program, you could simply type the Syntax file [the set of instructions required to run the procedure, including the relevant Data List and Execute statements (see page 30)], and then execute the job from inside the Syntax Editor (not discussed here), or use the program itself to create the syntax file. This latter procedure involves using the mouse to bring up a number of windows, and then selecting the appropriate options or typing in the required information.

1. *It is first necessary to enter **SPSS WIN**.* How you do this will depend on the system you are using, however, once you have entered, you are presented with the first window, the SPSS Data Editor (see figure below).

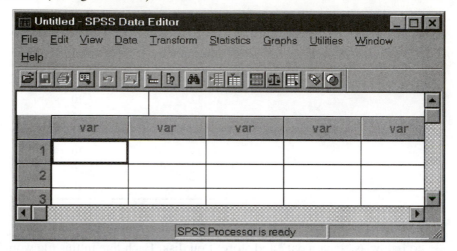

At this point, you could begin to type in the data. However, we will assume here that you already have the data in a file on the A Drive, and that this file is labelled **tchapi.dat.**

2. *Click on **File** in the menu bar.*

3. Enter your ASCII (**SPSS 8.0**) or Text (**SPSS 9.0**) data file by following the steps on pages 17 to 20 for **SPSS 8.0,** or pages 20 to 28 for **SPSS 9.0.** For this example, the file will consist of two variables labelled **a** and **data** respectively.

4. *Click on the **Statistics (SPSS 8.0)** or **Analyze (SPSS 9.0)** option in the menu bar.* This presents you with a drop-down menu. *Move your cursor to **Compare Means,** and you are presented with another menu to the right with a choice of the following:*

   Means . . .
   One-Sample T Test . . .
   Independent-Samples T Test . . .
   Paired-Samples T Test . . .
   One Way Anova . . .

5. *Click on **Independent-Samples T Test.*** This presents you with the Window, Independent Samples T Test (see below), and the variable **a** (see 3 above) is highlighted.

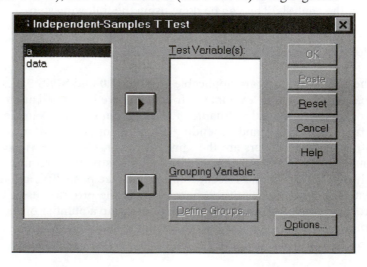

*Add this to the Grouping Variable by clicking on the appropriate arrow. Then click on **Define Groups.*** This will present you with the **Define Groups** window (see below), with the cursor flashing in the window to the right of Group 1. *Type the value for the first group (e.g., 1 in our example), move the cursor to the right of Group 2, and do the same for the second group (e.g., 2 in our example). Then click **Continue.***

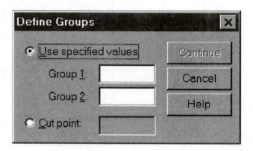

6. This takes you back to the Window, Independent Samples T-Test. *Click on **data** (see 5 above), and then click on the arrow for **Test Variables(s)**. Click **OK** to indicate that you are finished.*

7. This runs the *t*-test program, and the answers are returned to the SPSS Viewer, as well as to your monitor. At this point, you can print your answers, save them in a file, or transfer them to some other editor.

8. To exit SPSS, *click on **File** in the Menu Bar, and click on **Exit.** Before you can exit, however, the program will ask if you wish to save the contents of the Output Navigator as well as those of the Data Editor. If you have already saved them you will not have to do so again.*

The Syntax File

If you follow the preceding steps, you will create the following syntax file [note that the Data List and associated Execute statement are not shown (see Chapter 1, p. 30)]:

```
T-TEST GROUPS=GP(1,2)
/MISSING=ANALYSIS
/VARIABLES = X
/CRITERIA=CIN(.95).
```

Consideration of the syntax file is informative. The *T*-Test line instructs the computer to perform a *t*-test with the two conditions defined by the variable gp which can take one of two values, 1 or 2. The MISSING line informs the computer to include in the analysis any value that is not a missing value, and the VARIABLES line identifies the variables to be considered as the dependent variables in this analysis (in the present case, this is only one variable, *x*). Finally, the CRITERIA line indicates that the 95% confidence limits should be computed for the mean difference of the means.

The following two tables present the output from the basic **SPSS WINDOWS** run of these data.

	A	**N**	**Mean**	**Std. Deviation**	**Std. Error Mean**
Group Statistics					
DATA	1.00	5	11.8000	1.4832	.6633
	2.00	7	14.8571	3.6710	1.3875

Independent Samples Test									
	Levene's Test for Equality of Variances		t-test for Equality of Means						
								95% Confidence Interval of the Difference	
	F	Sig.	t	df	Sig. (2-tailed)	Mean Difference	Std. Error Difference	Lower	Upper
DATA Equal variances assumed	5.610	.039	−1.744	10	.112	−3.0571	1.7533	−6.9637	.8494
Equal variances not assumed			−1.988	8.398	.080	−3.0571	1.5379	−6.5745	.4602

Examination of this output reveals a considerable amount of information. To begin, the output presents a table labelled **Group Statistics.** This table provides information about the subjects in the two groups defined by A = 1, and A = 2. For each level of the independent variable, it then gives the sample size (N), the mean for the dependent variable, the standard deviation and the standard error of the mean. The standard deviation is the square root of the unbiased estimate of the population variance. It is a measure of how much variability there is among the data that make up any one group. Thus, in our example, there is more variability in group 2 (where the standard deviation = 3.6710) than there is in group 1 (standard deviation = 1.4832).

The standard error of the mean refers to the standard deviation of the sampling distribution of the mean. It is directly related to the standard deviation of the sample and is given by the equation:

$$S.E. = \frac{S}{\sqrt{n}}$$

Thus, the standard error of the mean for group 1 is equal to:

$$S.E. = \frac{1.483}{\sqrt{5}} = .663$$

The second table labelled **Independent Samples Test** presents two sets of results, one for the situation in which it is appropriate to use the pooled estimate of the population variance when computing the t-statistic, and the other when the separate variance estimate should be used.

As we saw earlier, whether you use a pooled or separate variance estimate for the population variance is dependent upon whether or not it is reasonable to assume that the population variances are homogeneous. **SPSS WINDOWS** assesses the validity of this assumption by conducting the Levene (1960) test. As indicated earlier, this test makes use of an analysis of variance procedure to compare the mean absolute deviations of the observations in each group from their mean. If one group has a significantly larger mean absolute deviation than another, we conclude that the groups come from populations with different (i.e., heterogeneous) variances. In the present example, this F-ratio has a value of 5.610, and is evaluated at 1 and 10 (i.e., $n_1 + n_2 - 2$) degrees of freedom. The output shows that this F-ratio is significant at the .039 level. Since this value is less than .05, we would conclude that the variances are heterogeneous, and would report the test statistic as (Levene's $F(1,10) = 5.610, p < .05$)).

Independent *t*-Test Using a Pooled Variance Estimate

Since the F-ratio is significant, we *should not* use the t-statistic based on the pooled variance estimate of the population variance. However, we do so here just to show how it would be presented if the Levene F-ratio were not significant. If this F-ratio were not significant, we would have concluded that there is no reason to assume that the populations have different variances, thus it is meaningful to simply estimate the population variance by computing a weighted average of the sample variation. In the **SPSS WINDOWS** output, we would thus use the information associated with Equal Variances Assumed. Thus, when determining whether or not the two means differ, we would consider the t-statistic based on the pooled variance estimate, viz., $t = -1.74$ at 10 df. The probability level shown for this value is .112, and since this value is not less than .05, we would conclude that the t-statistic is not significant.

Interpretation. In interpreting these results, we would note that the means of the Control (11.80) and Experimental (14.86) groups did not differ significantly [$t(10) = -1.74$, ns]. That is, we failed to reject the null hypothesis.

Independent *t*-Test Using Separate Variance Estimates

When the Levene F-ratio is significant as it is in this example, this indicates that the variances are not both estimates of the same population variance, and therefore the t-test should make use of different variance estimates. In the table on page 48, this is indicated in the section identified Equal Variances Not Assumed, and we find that the t-statistic is -1.99, the df are 8.40, and the probability of obtaining such a value of the t-statistic under these conditions is less than .080. Since this value is not less than .05, we would thus conclude that the means do not differ significantly. Generally, df are considered to be whole numbers, and when reporting this t-statistic, we would indicate the result as ($t(9) = -1.99$, ns). Some might question rounding the df of 8.40 to 9 rather than 8, but the rationale here is that since the value is greater than 8, it is acceptable to round up to indicate that more than 8 df are involved in the determination of the probability level. Using this logic, even if df had been 8.01 or even 8.001, etc., we would round the estimate to 9. This logic eliminates any confusion if the df were found to be less than 0.5, since they would round to 1, as opposed to 0 if regular rounding conventions were followed.

Interpretation. Since the F-ratio was significant, we would state that these results demonstrated that the means for the Control (11.80) and Experimental (14.86) groups did not differ significantly [$t(9) = -1.99$, ns]. That is, we failed to reject the null hypothesis, and would thus conclude that there was no evidence to indicate that the pill had any overall effect on learning. We would probably note, however, that ingesting the pill did result in individuals being more variable in their learning scores (since the standard deviation was greater for the experimental than the control group, and Levene's F-ratio was significant). This suggests that the pill did in fact influence individuals' learning performances, though it didn't influence the mean. We might, as a consequence, conduct further research to determine whether we could identify some individual difference characteristic responsible for it.

Earlier (p. 40), we computed the Critical Ratio on these data. The value was -2.16, which is significant at the .05 level when evaluated in terms of the Normal Distribution. Thus, if we had used the Critical Ratio, we would have concluded that the difference between the means was significant. This is an indication of the inappropriateness discussed by Gosset of using the Critical Ratio with small samples.

Probability Values and One- and Two-Tailed Tests

In our discussion, we have considered the *two-tailed probability*. That is, we have expressed the probability in terms of the chances of obtaining a value of the t-statistic as large in *magnitude* as 1.74 (in the case of the pooled variance estimate) or 1.99 (in the case of the separate variance estimate). In our case, the t-statistics were negative, simply because the mean for Group 1 (11.8000) was less than that for Group 2 (14.8571). In adopting the two-tailed strategy, we have allowed for the possibility that they might have been positive. That is, we have tested the null hypothesis that the population means were equal. This is expressed as:

$$H_0: \mu_1 = \mu_2 = \mu$$

and our experimental alternative hypothesis was that μ_1 was not equal to μ_2. That is:

$$H_1: \mu_1 \neq \mu_2$$

We might have been interested, however, in determining how reasonable it was to conclude that the means were different only if the mean of population 1 was less than that for population 2. In this case, we would be concerned only with the case of a negative t-statistic, and thus would be interested in making a *one-tailed* test. Our null hypothesis is still as before, but our experimental alternative hypothesis is that μ_1 is less than μ_2. That is:

$$H_1: \mu_1 < \mu_2$$

Under these conditions, we would be concerned only with the probability of obtaining a t-statistic less (i.e., more negative) than the value required for significance. In this case, any positive t-value, regardless of its magnitude, is evidence that the null hypothesis has not been rejected. Since we are concerned with only negative values in this case, this is referred to as a *one-tailed* test, and since the sampling distribution of the t-statistic is symmetrical, this means that this probability would be equal to half of that indicated on the output. Under these conditions, therefore, the t-statistic for the pooled variance estimate would still not be significant, while that for the separate variance estimate would be significant, written as, $[t(9) = -1.99, p < .04,$ one tailed$]$.

This may sound like an easy way to make some results significant in that after the fact, one could simply declare that they were doing a one-tailed test. Such decisions should not be taken lightly, however, and should be made *a priori* (i.e., made before the statistics are calculated, or, even better, before the data are collected) and based on solid prior empirical or theoretical considerations. If the decision is not justified, you are in essence simply increasing the probability of making a Type I error. Be warned, furthermore, that many researchers reading your results might simply double the probability anyhow, and disregard your claim of significance.

THE t-TEST AND COMPARISONS OF CORRELATED MEANS

The situation discussed thus far involved the case where the means were based on independent samples. That is, the observations producing the first mean were independent of those producing the second. Sometimes, however, the observations are not independent. Thus, if a researcher were to test the same individuals under two conditions, the observations would be paired (i.e., correlated), and not independent. Since the observations are paired one could, if one wanted to, compute a correlation between the two sets of observations. Even if it were the case that this correlation was 0, the observations are none-the-less paired, and this correlation must be considered when performing the t-test. Note too, that obtaining repeated measures on the same individuals is not the only way to obtain paired (correlated) observations. The following also represent situations in which the observations are correlated:

(a) Sampling siblings and randomly assigning one to one group and one to the other. That is, a researcher may wish to account for familial/genetic factors by obtaining samples of pairs of family members and randomly assigning one to one group and one to the other. In this case, the observations are paired, not independent, and the correlation between the pairs of observations must be taken into account.

(b) Matching individuals on some variable, and then assigning one to one group and the other to the other. Again, the interest here is to control for the effects of some other variable (e.g., intelligence or anxiety or height, etc.), thus individuals are sampled in pairs to be equal on this other variable. One member of each pair is then assigned to one group, and one to the other. Again, the possible correlation between the pairs of observations must be taken into account.

(c) Testing two individuals at the same time with one in one group and one in the other. On some occasions, individuals will be tested in pairs, sometimes because the nature of the study demands it, and sometimes for convenience. Regardless of the reasons, the individuals are sampled in pairs, and thus the possible correlation must be taken into account, even if the actual correlation is essentially zero, which it may well be given that there is no attempt to equate the individuals on any other variable.

It will be noted that, in each of these cases, the manner in which the samples were obtained means that the observations are paired, and thus a correlation can be computed between them. It is the nature of the sampling, not the magnitude of the correlation, that determines that the *t*-test for paired or correlated observations should be used instead of the independent *t*-test. Obviously, it is also the case under any of these conditions that the number of observations in group 1 will be equal to the number in group 2, and thus sample size can now be identified simply as n, the number of *paired* observations.

Under these considerations, the magnitude of the correlation must be taken into account in computing the *t*-statistic. The resulting equation is:

$$t = \frac{\bar{X}_1 - \bar{X}_2}{\sqrt{\dfrac{S_1^2}{n} + \dfrac{S_2^2}{n} - \dfrac{2r_{12}S_1S_2}{n}}}$$

Examining the equation will indicate that the nature and magnitude of the correlation plays an important role in the magnitude of this *t*-statistic. If the correlation is 0, this equation would reduce to the equation for the *t*-statistic presented on page 42. If the correlation is positive, the denominator would be less than, and therefore the magnitude of the *t*-statistic would be larger than that for the equation presented on page 42, and the size of the *t*-statistic would increase as the correlation increases. On the other hand, if the correlation were negative, the denominator would be larger, and thus, the *t*-statistic smaller, than that for the equation given on page 42, and the value of the *t*-statistic would get even smaller as the magnitude of the correlation increases.

There is one other difference between these two forms of the *t*-statistic. For the correlated *t*-statistic, observations are sampled in pairs. Thus, the *df* are equal to the number of pairs of observations minus 1 (i.e., $df = n - 1$).

A bit of algebra provides a formula that is slightly less complicated than that presented above, though both are equivalent. Thus, since the observations are presented in pairs, one could compute a difference score for each pair of observations (taking into account the sign of this difference). One could then compute the mean and variance of these difference scores. The *t*-test would then be computed in which the mean difference score is tested by determining whether it is significantly larger or smaller than 0, by dividing this mean difference by the standard error of this difference. The equation is as follows:

$$ t = \frac{\overline{d}}{\sqrt{\dfrac{S_d^2}{n}}} $$

An Example Using SPSS for WINDOWS

Consider the following data from a sample of individuals who were tested under two conditions. Assume that the scores are the number of correct responses made in a learning task when the same individuals were tested twice, once under a control condition (X_1) and once under an experimental condition (X_2) where they were given a pill twenty minutes before learning the material. For the purpose of completeness, assume that the two learning tasks had been shown to be equivalent in previous research (to control for any task effects), but that even so, one half of the individuals were given one task first while the other half received the other task first. In addition, assume that half the subjects received the control condition first (to control for any possible order effects), and that two weeks intervened between the first and second testing (to control for any carryover effects).

X_1	X_2
23	20
20	20
17	15
23	22
24	21
20	17
22	20
21	20
23	18
21	21

If these data were to be typed into a data file, this file would appear as 10 lines of data with the values of X_1 and X_2 for each individual appearing on each line, as follows:

```
23 20
20 20
17 15
23 22
24 21
20 17
22 20
21 20
23 18
21 21
```

Using **SPSS WINDOWS** to analyse these data, we would make use of a *t*-test for correlated data. Following are the steps needed to produce the syntax file.

Steps in Using SPSS WINDOWS Paired *t*-Test

The following steps are applicable to **SPSS 8.0** and **SPSS 9.0** except for the input of the ASCII or Text data file. In the example to follow, you are instructed at Step 3 to input your data following the procedures described in Chapter 1. The output for this example was obtained by using the freefield format in **SPSS 8.0,** and depending upon the input procedure you use, the format may be somewhat different. The answers are the same, however. Using the **WINDOWS** version of the program, you could simply type the Syntax file [the set of instructions required to run the procedure, including the relevant Data List and Execute statements (see page 30)], and then execute the job from inside the Syntax Editor (not discussed here), or use the program itself to create the syntax file. This latter procedure involves using the mouse to bring up a number of windows, and then selecting the appropriate options or typing in the required information.

1. *Double-click on the **SPSS** icon to enter **SPSS WIN**.* This presents you with the **SPSS Data Editor.** At this point, you could begin to type in the data. However, we will assume here that you already have the data in a file on the A Drive, that this file is labeled **tpair.dat.**

2. *Click on **File** in the Menu Bar.*

3. Enter your ASCII (**SPSS 8.0**) or Text (**SPSS 9.0**) data file by following the steps on pages 17 to 20 for **SPSS 8.0,** or pages 20 to 28 for **SPSS 9.0.** For this example, the file will consist of two variables labelled **X1** and **X2,** respectively.

4. *Click on the **Statistics** (or **Analyze**) option in the Menu Bar.* This presents you with a drop-down menu. *Move your cursor to **Compare Means,** and you are presented with another menu to the right with a choice of the following:*

   Means . . .
   One-Sample T Test . . .
   Independent-Samples T Test . . .
   Paired-Samples T Test . . .
   One Way Anova . . .

5. *Click on **Paired-Samples T Test.*** This presents you with the Window, **Paired-Samples T Test** as follows:

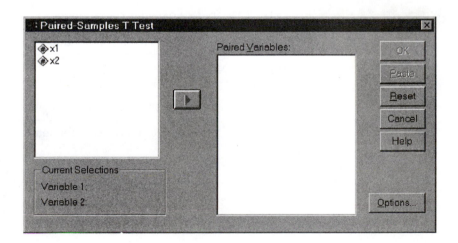

Variables, X1 and X2 (see 3, above) are listed in a window. *Move your cursor to X1 and click. Then move the cursor to X2 and click.* Note that the two variables are now listed as Variables 1 and 2 in the Current Selections. *Add these variables to the Paired Variables by clicking on the arrow beside the Paired Variables white pane. To run this analysis, click on OK.*

6. This runs the *t*-test program, and the answers are returned to the **SPSS Viewer,** as well as to your monitor. At this point, you can print your answers, save them in a file, or transfer them to some other editor.

7. To exit **SPSS,** *click on File in the Menu Bar, and click on Exit. Before you can exit, however, the program will ask if you wish to save the contents of the SPSS Output Viewer as well as those of the Data Editor . If you have already saved them you will not have to do so again.*

The Syntax File

The syntax for this run would take the following form (omitting the Data List and Execute statements, see p. 30):

```
T-TEST /PAIRS X1 WITH X2 (PAIRED)
/CRITERIA = CIN(.95)
/MISSING = ANALYSIS.
```

Note that this file identifies the program as T-TEST, indicates that the PAIRS to be compared are X1 and X2, and that the CRITERIA for the Confidence Intervals are the 95% ranges. The statement MISSING = ANALYSIS indicates that data will be included for each pair providing there are non-missing values for each member of the pair. This is the default option. If more than one pair had been indicated in the analysis, this could mean that some subjects might contribute to some analyses, but not others if they were missing only some data.

Following are the output for this run:

Paired Samples Statistics

		Mean	N	Std. Deviation	Std. Error Mean
Pair 1	X1	21.4000	10	2.0656	.6532
	X2	19.4000	10	2.1187	.6700

Paired Samples Correlations

		N	Correlation	Sig.
Pair 1	X1 & X2	10	.721	.019

Paired Samples Test

		Paired Differences					
					95% Confidence Interval of the Difference		
		Mean	Std. Deviation	Std. Error Mean	Lower	Upper	t
Pair 1	X1–X2	2.0000	1.5635	.4944	.8816	3.1184	4.045

Paired Samples Test

		df	Sig. (2-tailed)
Pair 1	X1–X2	9	.003

This output consists of three tables (the last one is shown in two sections). The first presents the *Paired Samples Statistics*, identifying the variable name for each member of the pair, as well as the mean, sample size (N), standard deviation and standard error of the mean for each. This is followed by a second table of *Paired Samples Correlations*, which presents the members of the pair (X1 and X2), the number of paired observations ($N = 10$), the correlation and the level of significance of the correlation (i.e., the two-tailed probability of obtaining a correlation this large in magnitude based on chance alone). This correlation of .721 is thus significant ($p < .05$), and though it is not shown, the *df* for this test is equal to ($n - 2 = 8$). Since this correlation is positive and significant, it suggests that high values of X_2 are associated with high values of X_1 while low values of X_2 are associated with low values of X_1. If the correlation were significantly negative (which seldom occurs with repeated measures on the same variable), it would suggest the opposite (i.e., high values of one of the variables were associated with low values of the other and vice versa). If the correlation were not significant, this would suggest that there is no linear relationship between the two variables.

The final part of the output presents *Paired Samples Test*. This consists of an identification of the pair being compared, the mean of the differences (2.0000), the standard deviation of the differences (1.563), and the standard error of the differences (.494). That is, if you were to compute the difference score for each individual, you could compute these values on the difference scores. Note that the mean of the difference scores is equal to the difference between the two means (i.e., 21.4 – 19.4 = 2.00). This table also presents the 95% confidence interval of the difference, which indicates that 95% of the time one would expect this difference to be as low as .882 or as high as 3.118, based on the results of this study. Finally, the table indicates the value of the *t*-test (4.045), the degrees of freedom associated with this value ($n - 1 = 9$), and the two-tailed probability (<.003) associated with obtaining a value this large based on chance if the null hypothesis was true.

Interpretation.   We would interpret these results by indicating that the mean for the control condition (21.4) was significantly larger [$t(9) = 4.045, p < .01$] than that for the experimental condition (19.4), and would conclude that the pill did effect learning. We make this statement, even though we appreciate that we would be wrong approximately 1% of the time. Oftentimes researchers would not mention the fact that they found that the correlation between scores on the two occasions was .721 and that it was significant ($p < .05$), but there is value in providing this information in that it suggests that not only did the pill result in improved learning, but also the effects were relatively consistent for all individuals (i.e, individuals with high scores in the control condition tended to also have high scores in the experimental condition, etc.). If the correlation were not significant, it would suggest that although the pill had the effect of improving performance on the learning task overall, it also tended to influence the relative ordering of individuals on the task. This itself, might lead to further research to determine why.

Possible Confounds with Paired *t*-Tests

In the introduction of the paired *t*-test, we noted that the two tasks were equivalent, that they had nonetheless been counterbalanced across time and condition, and that in addition we had counterbalanced the order of presentation of the two conditions, and had allowed a large period of time to elapse between the first testing and the second. These various cautions were necessary to permit a relatively unequivocal interpretation of the results.

Using equivalent tasks removed any effect that might have occurred by giving the same learning task twice. It is reasonable to expect that if subjects were given the same learning task on two occasions, their performance might improve simply because they were experiencing the same task twice. To some extent, the effect of this on inferences about the effects of the pill could be countered by counterbalancing control and experimental conditions but even so it would be anticipated that the means would tend to be elevated because in each instance the second testing might be expected to result in higher scores than otherwise expected. In the present example, it was indicated that even the order of the two tasks was counterbalanced to counter any possibility of order effects on the task.

It was also noted that the order of the conditions was counterbalanced, with half the subjects getting the control condition first, and the other getting the experimental condition first. This is necessary to rule out order effects. That is, if the experimental condition always appeared second, it might be expected that the scores would be higher just because individuals had performed a similar task before. That is, by using a fixed order we would be confounding any obtained differences due to treatment with possible order effects, which might enhance or depress the difference between the control and experimental conditions. Note, even if different tasks are used, there is still the experiential factor that must be considered. That is, just performing one learning task might influence performance on another learning task (regardless of whether or not it is similar or different). Also note that this counterbalancing is not completely fool-proof. If it were the case that experiencing the control condition first had a greater effect on a second testing than experiencing the experimental condition first, counterbalancing would reduce the influence of this on the means obtained, but it wouldn't completely eliminate it.

It was also noted that a lengthy interval intervened between administration of the two conditions. It is necessary to provide such an interval to permit the effect of one treatment to wear off before administering another. Thus, assume that the pill tended to make individuals drowsy. If you were to test them under the control condition immediately following the experimental condition, it is possible that the pill would not have worn off, and thus individuals would also tend to be drowsy in the following control condition. That is, the control condition is contaminated by the experimental condition. By letting time intervene between the administration of the two conditions, this effect will be reduced. But, how long is "lengthy"? Many drugs have relatively long half-lives (i.e., the length of time it takes for one-half of the effects of the drug to leave the system) so with drugs this interval can be relatively long. But one can ask about the "half-lives" of any treatment. The effects of experiences can also remain in one's system a long time too. Intervals can possibly dull the effects but any test/retest situation, regardless of the length of the duration, carries with it possible carry-over effects. (Note, the one situation in which this isn't a problem is where the focus of attention is the change resulting from prior experience—as in a learning task, where one wants to determine whether performance on Trial 2 is better than on Trial 1).

Taken altogether, you might question whether you would ever perform a paired t-test on repeated measures. They are not easy to interpret, and researchers often take great pains when using this procedure. In fact, more times than not, they make use of other analytic procedures (such as analyses of variance making use of split plot factorial and/or repeated measure factorial designs, or simply an independent t-test). It should be noted, finally, that the other types of situations making use of paired data that were mentioned at the beginning of this chapter do not have these possible confounds.

OTHER FORMS OF THE t-TEST

The t-distribution is used to evaluate significance in other contexts as well. As we saw earlier, the t-distribution is used to determine the significance of the correlation coefficient. The equation for this form is:

$$t = \frac{r}{\sqrt{\frac{(1 - r^2)}{(n-2)}}}$$

where the degrees of freedom are $(n - 2)$. As applied to the data analysed for the paired *t*-test, $r =$ .721, $n = 10$, and this formula would yield a value of $t = 2.94$ with 8 *df*. In fact, this is the test used in the paired *t*-test program of **SPSS WINDOWS,** though the program indicates only the significance level and does not output the corresponding *t*-value.

The *t*-distribution can also be used to evaluate the difference between two correlated variances, and will provide the same result for both biased and unbiased estimates of the population variances. The equation for this test is:

$$t = \frac{(S_1^2 - S_2^2)\sqrt{n - 2}}{\sqrt{4S_1^2 S_2^2 (1 - r_{12}^2)}}$$

where the degrees of freedom are $(n - 2)$. This test is not reported in the paired *t*-test program of **SPSS WINDOWS,** though it could be useful in indicating whether or not the two conditions also resulted in differences in variability for paired observations. (It will be noted that the *F*-ratio that was used in the independent *t*-test cannot be used with the paired *t*-test since the variances are not based on independent samples.) Applying this equation to the data analysed for the paired *t*-test yields a value of $t = -.10$ with 8 *df*, which, of course, is not significant. However, if the standard deviation for the experimental group was significantly less than that for the control group, this would suggest that the pill had the effect of making everyone more similar than ordinarily. Or, alternatively, if the variance of the experimental group was significantly more than that for the control group, it would indicate that the pill had the effect of making individuals more variable than expected. In either event, this might be worthy of further investigation.

Chapter 3
Single-Factor Analysis
of Variance Designs

Suppose you were interested in comparing a number of groups on how they performed on some test. For example, you might have three groups of students, majors in arts, social science, and science, and you may wonder if there are any differences on scores on an intelligence test. Or you may be interested in the effects of alcohol on a learning task. To investigate this, you could randomly assign students to one of four levels of alcohol consumption (e.g., 2 ml, 5 ml, 10 ml, and 15 ml), administer a learning task to them, and determine the total number of errors they make in 6 trials. In each instance, your question would be simply whether or not the mean scores of the groups differ. To conduct such investigations, you would probably make use of the single-factor analysis of variance procedure.

Considerable research is concerned with investigating differences between groups of subjects. As indicated above, this research generally focuses on the means of the groups concerned, and asks whether or not the means of the samples are sufficiently different from each other to suggest that they are representative of different populations. Thus, if a researcher had formed three different groups of individuals and had administered one treatment to the subjects in one group, another treatment to those in the second group, and yet another to the third group, she/he would quite probably obtain different means on the three groups. A meaningful question then would be whether the three means differ more than one would reasonably expect on the basis of chance. If they did, the researcher could conclude that one of more of the treatments did have an influence on the behavior in question. If they did not, the researcher could conclude that there was no evidence to suggest that the treatments did influence the behavior under investigation. You will note that this is very much like the t-test, where there are two groups and the researcher is concerned with testing the hypothesis that the two groups are representative of the same or different populations. The single-factor analysis of variance is comparable, except that there are more than two groups, and rather than computing a t-test, a different test is performed. It can be shown, however, that the t-test is a special case of the single-factor analysis of variance with two groups.

SOME BASIC TERMINOLOGY

There are many different types of analysis of variance procedures, of which the most basic procedure is the single factor design, and there are a number of terms associated with analysis of variance. One such term is the name of the basic procedure. It has been variously referred to as the single-factor design, the completely randomized single-factor analysis of variance design, and the oneway design. Regardless of its name, the major characteristics of this design are that:

(a) There is one *independent variable*. This variable forms the basis of classification of subjects into different groups. Thus in the two examples given above, the independent variables were Academic Major and Amount of Alcohol consumed, respectively. The independent variable is often referred to as the *factor* of interest, or the factor under investigation.

(b) There are a number of different groups of subjects formed by the independent variable. These different groupings are referred to as the *levels* of the factor. Thus, in the above two examples, the levels of Academic Major are Arts, Social Science, and Science; the levels of Amount of Alcohol consumed are 2, 5, 10, and 15 ml.

(c) Subjects are *randomly* assigned to the levels of the factor of interest, or are random representatives of the group in question. Any given subject can be a member of only one group.

(d) There is only one *dependent variable*. This is the variable that yields the scores that are analysed. In the above examples, the dependent variables are intelligence, and number of errors made in the learning task, respectively.

There are a number of different types of independent variables. In some cases, the independent variable is not the result of a treatment manipulation, but instead is defined in terms of an *individual difference* variable. In the Academic Major example, the independent variable is based on individual differences. Subjects are not randomly *assigned* to their Academic Major. This is a characteristic of them as individuals. Other examples of individual difference independent variables would be Sex, Height (e.g., less than 4 feet, 4–5 feet, 5–6 feet, greater than 6 feet), Trait Anxiety (defined as low, average, high), Socio-economic Status (lower, lower-middle, upper-middle, and upper class), Ethno-linguistic Background (English, French, German, Chinese, etc.). Obviously, with these types of independent variables, subjects cannot be randomly assigned to conditions. It is nonetheless the case that subjects can be considered a random (or at least representative) sample of individuals in that particular category.

In other cases, the independent variable is defined in terms of a treatment variable, that is, one that the experimenter manipulates. In the example concerned with the Amount of Alcohol Consumed, the levels of the independent variable were determined by the experimenter, and subjects were randomly assigned to the conditions. Other examples of independent variables defined in terms of treatments would include any in which the levels were defined by the experimenter, and subjects were randomly assigned to one level, and then that level administered by the experimenter. Examples might include Type of Reinforcement (positive, negative, none), Level of Electric Shock (5 volts, 10 volts, 15 volts, 20 volts), Anxiety Condition (a treatment in which subjects are asked to perform in front of a friend (low anxiety), in front of a TV camera (medium anxiety), or in front of a large audience (high anxiety)). As you can see, the possibilities are limitless!

You will note in the various examples that independent variables can vary in other ways as well. Independent variables can refer to groupings that could appear in any order, as in the example of Ethno-linguistic Background. Or independent variables can involve levels that are ordered, but the intervals between them are not particularly equal—as in the two Anxiety examples. Or independent variables can involve quantitative differences in levels—as in the Level of Electric Shock example. The single-factor analysis of variance procedure is applied in exactly the same way, regardless of the nature of the independent variable, but the nature of the generalizations that can be made can differ depending on the nature of the factor (see the section entitled "A Note on Random Assignment and Random Samples" on page 62). Furthermore, if the independent variable is an ordered quantitative factor with equal intervals, other additional procedures such as Trend Analysis can be applied (see Myers & Well, 1991).

AN EXAMPLE OF A SINGLE-FACTOR ANALYSIS OF VARIANCE

Consider the situation in which a researcher is interested in investigating the effects of three drugs on behavior, and assume further that he/she wants to contrast these three drugs with a no drug condition. This experiment could be conducted in a number of different ways, but one procedure the researcher might use is to form four random groups of individuals, and administer one treatment (i.e., No Drug, Drug I, Drug II, or Drug III) to each subject individually in each of the different groups. If the research were conducted in this way, you can appreciate that there are two possible sources of variation involved in each subject's score. One is the treatment group to which the subject was randomly assigned, and the other is the individual himself/herself. There are no other sources of variation that could be isolated in this study as described that could not be attributed to one of these two classes. Thus, a researcher could attempt to estimate the extent to which these two sources influenced each subject's score.

You might say that there are other possible sources of variation that haven't been mentioned. Two that come readily to mind are any characteristics of the experimenter that might influence the subject's behavior, and any characteristics of the experimental setting (e.g., apparatus, testing room, etc.). These are possible influences on the subject's scores, but to the extent that they are constant in the study, they are not sources of variation that can be estimated in this analysis. This would require another type of design. Note that if these sorts of influences were not held constant in this study (i.e., if different testing rooms were used for different subjects) they would be attributed to what we will see is called error.

Assume that such an experiment was conducted, and the data are as presented in Table 1 below. You will note that there are 15 subjects in each of the four groups. If you were to compute the means for each group, you would find that they are 65.00, 63.60, 70.60, and 73.87. The mean of the entire table is 68.27. The variances for each of the groups are 69.4286, 67.8286, 52.1143, and 60.5524. In the definitional formulae to follow, each observation is referred to as an X_{ai}, where the X refers to an observation, the a defines the group in which it appears, and the i indicates which observation it is in the group. Thus, X_{35} refers to the fifth observation in the third group, which in our example has a value of 64. The mean of each group is referred to as an $\overline{X}_a$. Thus, the mean for group 4 is $\overline{X}_4$, and it equals 73.87. The mean for the entire table is referred to as $\overline{G}$, and it has a value of 68.27.

Table 1   Fictitious Data for the Experiment

	Levels of A		
1	2	3	4
50	72	60	68
54	75	60	65
55	65	70	76
68	60	72	74
66	69	64	75
76	64	79	83
75	56	73	82
63	57	75	76
62	55	72	85
61	63	77	75
75	54	67	63
63	63	83	64
62	51	60	77
77	72	77	62
68	78	70	83

ASSUMPTIONS UNDERLYING THE SINGLE-FACTOR DESIGN

There are four assumptions underlying the single-factor analysis of variance. They are:

Independent Random Sampling

The assumption of independent random sampling means that it is assumed that the subjects in any one group or treatment condition are a representative sample of that condition. This is normally achieved by randomly assigning subjects to conditions. For some type of factors (e.g., individual difference ones), random assignment to groups is not possible, but it can be assumed that the subjects are representative of that group, or more precisely, there exists a population for which this sample can be considered representative. As long as the appearance of an individual in any group is not dependent upon the membership of any other individual in that group or any other group, the necessary conditions exist to perform the analysis of variance. If this assumption is violated, the results of the analysis are invalidated [see Glass, Peckham, & Sanders (1972) for a thorough discussion].

Normality

The assumption of Normality means that the populations from which the samples were obtained are normally distributed. This assumption is important because, unless this is true, the means and variances are not independent (unrelated) of one another, and this is a necessary precondition underlying the F-distribution. It has been shown, however, that the single factor analysis of variance is robust with respect to violations of this assumption (Glass, Peckham, & Sanders, 1972). That is, if the assumption is violated, it does not appreciably influence Type I or Type II error, particularly if sample sizes are equal.

Homogeneity of Variance

The assumption of homogeneity of variance means that the populations from which each of the groups are obtained have the same variance. This assumption is important, because the variances within each of the groups are averaged to obtain the $MS_{S/A}$, and it would not be meaningful to average numbers that were not all estimates of the same population value. It has been shown, however, that as long as the sample sizes are equal, even relatively large violations of this assumption do not materially influence Type I and Type II error (Glass, Peckham & Sanders, 1972).

The Null Hypothesis

The null hypothesis means that the means of the populations from which the groups were obtained are the same. This is generally written as:

$$H_0: \mu_1 = \mu_2 = \cdots = \mu$$

where μ_1, μ_2, etc. refer to the means of the respective populations estimated by the means $\bar{X}_1$, $\bar{X}_2$, etc.

A NOTE ON RANDOM ASSIGNMENT AND RANDOM SAMPLES

Earlier it was indicated that, in an analysis of variance, subjects should be randomly assigned to the levels of the factor. In such cases, providing the other assumptions have been met (with the provisions indicated above) any significant effects due to A can be attributed to the treatment factor. It is true that the "significant" effect might be due to chance fluctuation, but this is reflected in the Type I error. Thus, in this type of investigation, any effects can be interpreted in terms of causation. That is, within the limitations of Type I error, a significant effect for factor A would be interpreted as meaning that the A factor had a *causal* effect on the dependent variable.

There are other cases in which analysis of variance is used. These are as meaningful as the example above, except that the "causal" conclusions are not strong ones. For example, assume that a researcher was interested in the effects of Academic Major on intelligence, and performed a single factor analysis of variance. In this case the assignment of subjects to conditions is not random. Arts students cannot appear in the Science group and vice versa. Nonetheless, assuming the subjects can be considered representative samples of the Academic Major conditions, we can still perform the same analysis as before, in that we can determine whether or not there are effects due to A. To the extent, however, that there are significant effects due to A, we cannot say that these are caused by A.

Clearly A plays a role in the results, but the best that can be said is that there is covariation in Academic Major and Intelligence. Although a researcher might say that such results indicate that Academic Major influenced intelligence, the nature of this influence is correlational at best. Since subjects were not randomly assigned to the Academic Major condition, there are many non-random factors that could vary with Academic Major, and any of them might be responsible for the effect noted. That is, Academic Major did not *cause* the effect noted. Instead, differences in Academic Major are associated with differences in intelligence. (Incidentally, this is true regardless of the dependent variable. Even if the dependent variable were knowledge about current events, or salary five years after graduation, or whatever, the absence of random assignment to conditions means that any causal interpretation of the results is weak at best.) You may, if you wish, interpret this correlation causally, but it is a weak causal statement, not a strong one like that which can be made when subjects are randomly assigned to treatment conditions.

DEFINITIONAL FORMULAE AND EXAMPLE OF COMPUTATIONS

The definitional formulae for the single factor analysis of variance are as follows:

Source	Sum of Squares	df
Between Groups	$n\sum\limits^{a}(\bar{X}_a - \bar{G})^2$	$(a-1)$
Within Groups	$\sum\limits^{a}\sum\limits^{i}(X_{ai} - \bar{X}_a)^2$	$a(n-1)$
Total	$\sum\limits^{a}\sum\limits^{i}(X_{ai} - \bar{G})^2$	$an-1$

I have used the terms Between Groups and Within Groups in this table because this is fairly common practice (see, for example, Myers & Well, 1991) when referring to the completely randomized single-factor analysis of variance design, and this is the terminology used in **SPSS WINDOWS ONEWAY,** the program emphasized in this chapter. The Between Groups source, however, is a measure of the effects of Treatment A, so often it is also labelled A. In much the same way, the Within Groups source is a measure of the variability between subjects in each group, so it is often labelled S/A (to mean the variability among Subjects within each A group). We will use these two terms in the equations to follow.

Examining the formulae above will indicate that they are really very straightforward. The Sum of Squares Between Groups for example is simply a measure of the extent to which the sample means differ from the grand mean. The larger this number, the more the means differ among themselves. The sum of the squared deviations is multiplied by the sample size. In much the same way, the Sum of Squares Within Groups is a measure of how much subjects in a group differ among themselves, and this is summed over all the groups. The more subjects differ among themselves within any one group, the larger the squared deviations of their scores from the mean of the group and the larger the sum of these squared deviations over all groups. The Sum of Squares Total is a measure of how much the individuals differ from the grand mean. The Sum of Squares Total will equal the sum of the Sum of Squares Between plus the Sum of Squares Within.

The degrees of freedom (df) refer to the number of values that are free to vary, given any restrictions imposed. We stated earlier that the mean of the means will equal the grand mean, thus, if we knew the value of the grand mean, the means of all but one of the groups could take any value, but the mean of that last group would have to be such that the mean of the means equalled the grand mean. Therefore, given a groups, $(a-1)$ of the means are free to vary. Stated another way, the degrees of freedom associated with the Between Groups Mean Square are $(a-1)$. In much the same way, when we consider the degrees of freedom for the Within Groups, we must know the mean for each group. Given that the mean for a group is the sum of the n scores in that group divided by n, it is obvious that within each group $(n - 1)$ of the scores are free to take any value, but one must be such that the mean of all n of them is equal to the mean for that group. Thus, in any one group, there are $(n - 1)$ degrees of freedom. Given a groups, there are, therefore, $a(n - 1)$ degrees of freedom associated with the Within Groups Mean Square. Finally, the degrees of freedom for the Total Sum of Squares is $(an - 1)$ since given that the grand mean is known, all but one of the an observations would be free to vary and we would still have the same grand mean.

If we divide each of the Sums of Squares by their Degrees of Freedom, we compute what are called Mean Squares. These Mean Squares are simply variances, hence the name of the procedure, Analysis of Variance. The Mean Square Between Groups is:

$$MS_A = \frac{SS_A}{df_A} = \frac{n\sum_{}^{a}(\bar{X}_a - \bar{G})^2}{(a - 1)}$$

Examination of MS_A will reveal that it is nothing more than n times the unbiased estimate of the variance of the means around the grand mean. The more the sample means differ among themselves, the larger this number. This value can be shown to be an estimate of the population variance, σ^2.

The Mean Square Within Groups is:

$$MS_{S/A} = \frac{SS_{S/A}}{df_{S/A}} = \frac{\sum^{a}\sum^{i}(X_{ai} - \bar{X}_a)^2}{a(n - 1)}$$

Examination of this formula will reveal that the $MS_{S/A}$ is nothing more than the mean of the sample variances [calculated using the unbiased estimate (see p. 10)]. If each of the sample variances are all estimates of the same population variance, then this number can be seen to be an estimate of the common population variance, σ^2. If the variances in each group are relatively small, this value will also be relatively small. As the sample variances get larger, this value will get larger.

Given these two Mean Squares, we can compute the ratio of MS_A to $MS_{S/A}$ to form an F-ratio, thus:

$$F = \frac{MS_A}{MS_{S/A}}$$

with $(a - 1)$ degrees of freedom in the numerator, and $a(n - 1)$ degrees of freedom in the denominator. We form the F-ratio this way so that if MS_A (which is n times the variance of the A means) is greater than $MS_{S/A}$ (which is the mean of the treatment variances), this value will be greater than 1.0. If it is sufficiently larger than 1.0, we can conclude that the means differ more among themselves than would be expected based on the average variance among the subjects in each treatment group. As indicated before, if the assumptions have been met, both MS_A and $MS_{S/A}$ are estimates of σ^2. If MS_A proves to be an overestimate of σ^2, it indicates that the null hypothesis is not true.

These formulae can be applied to the data in Table 1. Thus:

$$SS_A = (15)[(65.00 - 68.27)^2 + \ldots + (73.87 - 68.27)^2] \qquad = 1038.80$$
$$SS_{S/A} = (50 - 65.00)^2 + \ldots + (68 - 65.00)^2 + \ldots + (83 - 73.87)^2 \quad = 3498.93$$
$$SS_{Total} = (50 - 68.27)^2 + \ldots + (83 - 68.27)^2 \qquad = 4537.73$$

The corresponding Mean Squares are:

$$MS_A = \frac{1038.80}{3} = 346.27 \quad MS_{S/A} = \frac{3498.93}{56} = 62.48$$

and:

$$F = \frac{346.37}{62.48} = 5.54 \text{ @ 3 and 56 degrees of freedom.}$$

Inspection of Table C, Appendix B will reveal that at 3 and 60 degrees of freedom, one requires an F-ratio of 4.13 for significance at the .01 level. Since our obtained F-ratio = 5.54 exceeds this value, we can conclude that it is significant at the .01 level. Our degrees of freedom for the denominator was only 56, so a conservative estimate might use 3 and 40 (the next lowest df in the table). Even using this criterion, the F-ratio is still significant at the .01 level.

A BIT OF HISTORY

The completely randomized single-factor analysis of variance is a technique originally introduced by Fisher (1925) in a book entitled *Statistical Methods for Research Workers,* though it is much different in form now than it was when Fisher introduced it. To begin with, he didn't use the F-ratio to evaluate the significance of effects. It hadn't been discovered yet! In his 1925 book, he used a test based on a Z statistic. This statistic was evaluated in a way much like the F-ratio (in fact, there is a direct mathematical relation between the two) but it involved the difference between the logarithms of two standard deviations. Values required for significance were a function of the degrees of freedom associated with each standard deviation. Fisher presented a table of these values in which the degrees of freedom associated with one of the standard deviations formed the columns of the table, and the degrees of freedom associated with the other standard deviation formed the rows.

Although the analysis of variance procedure was introduced by Fisher in 1925, two articles were published in 1923 that involved the use of analysis of variance. Both of these articles were concerned with agricultural research, and both investigated two factors. (This type of design will be discussed in Chapter 4.) One of these articles was by Fisher and Mackenzie (1923). It was concerned with the effects of different potato varieties on response to manure. It investigated 12 different varieties of potatoes and six manurial treatments, and found effects of both. The other article was by Student (1923), and involved a discussion of the effects of variety and trials on the yield of corn. The first article making use of a single-factor analysis of variance and involving a dependent variable with a more psychological focus was published by Reitz (1934). It investigated the variability in mean scores on a measure of intelligence (the American Council Psychological Examination) over a number of years, separately for two different institutions.

Although we credit Fisher with developing analysis of variance, according to historians (e.g., Cowles, 1989; Lovie, 1979; Rucci & Tweney, 1980) it was actually Snedecor (1934) who demonstrated that the ratio of two independent estimates of the population variance will have a characteristic distribution, if the populations are themselves normally distributed. He suggested that this distribution should be referred to as the F-distribution (after Fisher), and the ratio of the two estimates has come to be known as the F-ratio. The distribution itself varies as a function of the degrees of freedom in the numerator and denominator. Rucci and Tweney (1980) point out that although

Fisher published many editions of his 1925 text (the last one appearing in 1970), he never did include F-tables in any of them.

ANALYZING THESE DATA USING SPSS WINDOWS ONEWAY

The analysis of a completely randomized single-factor analysis of variance experiment can be performed in **SPSS WINDOWS** using the program **ONEWAY.** The following section shows how to access the **ONEWAY** program. It is also possible to use the program **GENERAL FACTORIAL** in the GLM section, and obtain other information such as estimates of power that are not available in **ONEWAY.** However, this chapter directs attention to the use of **ONEWAY.**

Steps for Using SPSS WINDOWS ONEWAY

The following steps are applicable to **SPSS 8.0** and **SPSS 9.0** except for the input of the ASCII or Text data file. In the example to follow you are instructed at Step 3 to input your data following the procedures described in Chapter 1. The output for this example was obtained by using the freefield format in **SPSS 8.0,** and depending upon the input procedure you use, the output may be somewhat different. The answers are the same, however. Using the **WINDOWS** version of the program, you could simply type the Syntax file [the set of instructions required to run the procedure, including the relevant Data List and Execute statements (see page 30)], and then execute the job from inside the Syntax Editor (not discussed here), or use the program itself to create the syntax file. This latter procedure involves using the mouse to bring up a number of windows, and then selecting the appropriate options or typing in the required information (the **clope** procedure). In the example to follow, it is assumed that one has already created the data file, that it consists of one line for each subject, and that there are two numbers on each line separated by at least one blank (i.e., in free format). The first number is the group in which the subject belongs (1 to 4 in the example); the second number is the subject's score on the dependent variable. It is further assumed that the file is labelled **oneway.dat,** and that it is located on the A Drive.

1. *Enter SPSS WIN.* This presents you with the SPSS Data Editor (figure shown on page 15). At this point, you could begin to type in the data. However, we will assume here that you already have the data in a file on the A Drive, and that this file is labelled **oneway.dat.**

2. *Click on File in the menu bar.* This will present you with a drop-down menu with a series of choices.

3. Enter your ASCII (**SPSS 8.0**) or Text (**SPSS 9.0**) data file by following the steps on pages 17 to 20 for **SPSS 8.0,** or pages 20 to 28 for **SPSS 9.0.** For this example, the file will consist of two variables labelled **a** and **x,** respectively.

4. *Click on the **Statistics** (SPSS 8.0) or **Analyze** (SPSS 9.0) option on the menu bar.* This presents you with a drop-down menu. *Move your cursor to **Compare Means,** and you are presented with another menu to the right with a choice of the following:*

   Means . . .
   One-Sample T Test . . .
   Independent-Samples T Test . . .
   Paired-Samples T Test . . .
   One-Way ANOVA . . .

5. *Click on **One-Way ANOVA.*** This presents you with the Window, **One-Way Anova,** and the variable **a** is highlighted (see figure below).

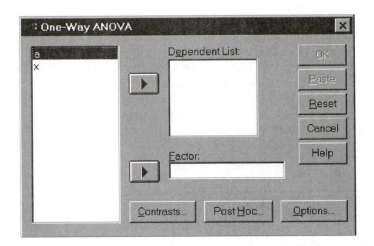

*Add this (i.e., **a**) to the **Factor Variable** by clicking on the appropriate arrow. Then move the cursor to **X** and click. This highlights the X. Add this to the **Dependent List** by clicking on the appropriate arrow.*

6. *Then click on **Post Hoc**.* This produces the following Window, **One-Way ANOVA: Post Hoc Multiple Comparisons:**

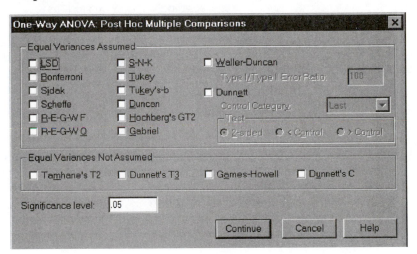

Many options are available, but we will focus attention on the Tukey HSD procedure. *Move the cursor to the box preceding Tukey, and click. Then click on **Continue**.*

7. This returns you to the Window, **One-Way ANOVA.** *Click on **Options**, and this will produce another Window (see figure below).*

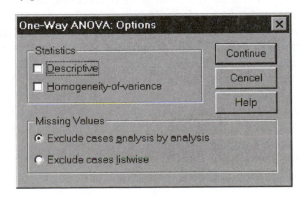

This figure is slightly different in **SPSS 9.0** where it adds the option to draw a graph of the means, but we will ignore that option here. *Move your cursor to the box preceding **Descriptive**, and click. Then move your cursor to the box preceding **Homogeneity-of-Variance**, and click. Then click on **Continue**.* This returns you to the Window, **One-Way Anova**. *To perform the analysis, click on **OK**.* This runs the One-Way program, and the answers are returned to the SPSS VIEWER, as well as to your monitor. At this point, you can print your answers, save them in a file, or transfer them to some other editor.

8. To exit **SPSS,** *click on **File** (upper row of operations), and click on **Exit**. Before you can exit, however, the program will ask if you wish to save the contents of the SPSS Output Viewer as well as those of the Data Editor.* If you have already saved them you will not have to do so again.

The Syntax File

If you used the procedure described above, you would produce the following Syntax File (omitting the Data List and Execute statement, see page 30):

```
ONEWAY X BY A
      /STATISTICS DESCRIPTIVES HOMOGENEITY
      /MISSING ANALYSIS
      /POSTHOC = TUKEY ALPHA(.05).
```

The statement "ONEWAY X BY A" causes the computer to perform the single-factor analysis of variance on the data. It instructs the computer that X is the dependent variable and A is the independent variable, and the computer determines the number of levels of the A factor based on the number of different values of A in the data file. This statement yields the following analysis of variance summary table:

ANOVA

		Sum of Squares	df	Mean Square	F	Sig.
X	Between Groups	1038.80	3	346.267	5.542	.002
	Within Groups	3498.93	56	62.481		
	Total	4537.73	59			

Interpreting the Analysis of Variance Summary Table

When we did these computations by hand (see pp. 64–65) we made use of the table of the F-distribution (Table C, Appendix B) to determine whether or not our obtained F-ratio was significant. We determined that with 3 and 56 degrees of freedom, we required an F-ratio of approximately 2.84 for significance at the .05 level, and 4.31 for significance at the .01 level. [Note, I say approximately because the F tables I have do not give values for 3 and 56 degrees of freedom, so I took the nearest (conservative) value for 3 and 40 degrees of freedom.] Since our value of $F = 5.54$ is larger than the value required for significance at the .01 level, we would conclude that our four means are more variable than we would expect on the basis of chance. And the probability of this being due to a Type I error is less than .01. This means that there is at least one contrast between means that is probably not due to chance—though whether or not this involves a simple contrast between just two of the means we obtained remains to be seen (see the section on Tests of Means, below).

Since we analysed our data using **SPSS WINDOWS ONEWAY,** we don't have to look up the value of the F-ratio required for significance in any tables. **ONEWAY** provides the probability level associated with the F-ratio. The value in the "Sig" column is the probability of a Type I error. Thus, when referring to this F-ratio, you could use the format $[F(3,56) = 5.54, p < .002]$ if you wish. Some researchers (correctly, I believe) feel that this might be giving too much precision to the experiment, and would prefer to use only the .05, .01, or .001 designation. Under these conditions, they would indicate their results using the notation $[F(3,56) = 5.54, p < .01]$.

Proportion of Variance Accounted for. Having obtained a significant F-ratio, researchers and consumers of the research are often interested in knowing whether or not the effect is large or small in terms of the proportion of variance that it explains. There are two different ways of defining this proportion. One involves a class of statistics defined as ω^2 (omega-squared) and ρ_I (the intraclass correlation). The definition of these statistics is beyond the scope of this chapter. The other involves the statistic η^2 (eta-squared), and its definition is much simpler. It is simply the ratio of the Sum of Squares of the Effect to the Total Sum of Squares. That is:

$$\eta^2 = \frac{SS_A}{SS_{TOTAL}}$$

In our example:

$$\eta^2 = \frac{1038.80}{4537.73} = .23$$

The finding that $\eta^2 = .23$ indicates that 23% of the total variance is accounted for by the variation in drug levels. This is a rather strong effect. In his analysis of power, Cohen (1988) discusses the calculation of a statistic measuring effect size, and distinguishes between small, medium, and strong effects. We will not discuss the statistic for effect size here, except to say that it is based on the conceptually similar, but computationally different ω^2. For Cohen (1988), small effects correspond to $\omega^2 = .01$, medium effects to $\omega^2 = .059$, and strong effects to $\omega^2 = .138$. Although conceptually similar, η^2 yields slightly larger values than ω^2. It is possible, however, to calculate ω^2 from η^2. The formula is:

$$\omega^2 = \frac{\eta^2(df_1 + df_2) - df_1}{\eta^2(df_1 + df_2) - df_1 + N(1 - \eta^2)}$$

For our example, $df_1 = 3$, $df_2 = 56$, $N = 60$, and $\eta^2 = .23$. Therefore:

$$\omega^2 = \frac{.23(3 + 56) - 3}{.23(3 + 56) - 3 + 60(1 - .23)} = \frac{10.57}{10.57 + 46.2} = .19$$

Thus, our value of $\eta^2 = .23$ yields an $\omega^2 = .19$ which would be characterized as a strong effect in Cohen's (1988) terms. The above example wasn't meant to suggest that one should compute ω^2 values from η^2. It is presented to demonstrate only that the two ways of defining the proportion of variance accounted for yield different estimates, and one simply can't equate the two. As indicated above, SPSS Windows uses η^2 in its other analysis of variance programs, and also computes power estimates for that statistic. Thus, transforming η^2 to ω^2 isn't needed that frequently.

Summary Statistics Produced by the Statistics Line

The addition of the Command "/STATISTICS DESCRIPTIVES HOMOGENEITY" resulted in the computer giving two additional sets of output. Because of the "DESCRIPTIVES" command, it output the following information about each of the groups:

Descriptives

				Std.	Std.	Lower	Upper		
			N	Mean	Deviation	Error	Bound	Bound	Minimum	Maximum

Columns header: 95%Confidence Interval for Mean (spanning Lower Bound / Upper Bound)

			N	Mean	Std. Deviation	Std. Error	Lower Bound	Upper Bound	Minimum	Maximum
X	A	1.00	15	65.0000	8.3324	2.1514	60.3857	69.6143	50.00	77.00
		2.00	15	63.6000	8.2358	2.1265	59.0392	68.1608	51.00	78.00
		3.00	15	70.6000	7.2190	1.8639	66.6022	74.5978	60.00	83.00
		4.00	15	73.8667	7.7815	2.0092	69.5574	78.1759	62.00	85.00
		Total	60	68.2667	8.7699	1.1322	66.0012	70.5322	50.00	85.00

Much of this information is fairly straightforward. The X at the left of the table identifies the dependent variable as X, the A identifies the level of the factor, and the information following to the right is as labelled. Thus, the number of observations (N) in group $A = 1$ is 15, the mean is 65.0, and the standard deviation is 8.3324. It will be noted that these standard deviations are the square roots of the variances presented earlier on page 61. The value labelled "std. error" refers to the standard deviation of the mean. This is defined as the ratio of the standard deviation to the square root of the sample size. Thus, the standard error for group $A = 1$ is:

$$SE_1 = \frac{8.3324}{\sqrt{15}} = 2.1514$$

Confidence Intervals. The above table also provides information about the 95% Confidence Interval for each of the means. This information appears under the heading "95% Confidence Interval for Mean." These values are computed as follows:

$$\bar{X} - SE * t(df = 14, p < .05) \text{ and } \bar{X} + SE * t(df = 14, p < .05).$$

The t-value required for significance at the .05 level for 14 degrees of freedom is 2.145.

Thus, for Group 1 the lower limit for the confidence interval is:

$$65.00 - 2.1514 * 2.145 = 60.3857$$

and the upper limit is:

$$65.00 + 2.1514 * 2.145 = 69.6143$$

The confidence interval provides useful information though few researchers have yet to avail themselves of it. The 95% confidence interval is defined as the range in which you would expect to find the population mean 95% of the time. Given a sample with a mean of 65.00, and a standard error of 2.1514, 95% of the time we would expect to find the population from which such a sample was drawn to have a mean anywhere from 60.3857 to 69.6143. That is, once we know the sample statistics, we can make some estimate of what the population value might be, or at least the range of possible values. Note, this does not mean to imply that the population mean varies. The population mean is a fixed value. It is the fact that sample means vary that requires us to estimate the possible range of population means that could produce such a sample value.

One way of using this information is to investigate the confidence intervals for two population means. Note, for example, the 95% confidence interval for the mean for Group 1 is 60.39 to 69.61, while that for Group 2 is 59.04 to 68.16. Since there is overlap in these two sets of confidence intervals, it is possible that the two populations have the same mean—i.e., the population means do not differ. If we consider the 95% confidence intervals for group 2 (59.04 to 68.16) and that for group 4 (69.56 to 78.18), we note that they do not overlap. That is, 95% of the time in both cases we would not expect the population means to be from overlapping ranges. From this, we might conclude that the two populations do indeed differ. Note that this procedure is a bit different from straightforward hypothesis testing. It permits an examination of the hypothesis of whether or not two sample means are representative of the same population mean (in much the same way as the t-test does), but it goes beyond that to give the researcher some idea of how similar or different the population means might be. That is, in this example, the population means could be as similar as 68.16 and 69.56, or as different as 59.04 and 78.18, though, these would be relatively rare events. It is more likely that the differences lie somewhere in between these extreme values, but even these extreme values are possible within the 95% confidence range.

A final point concerning the information derived from the confidence interval data: It is possible that the generalizations derived from this information could be a bit different from that derived from the analysis of variance itself. This is because the confidence intervals depend upon the standard errors calculated for each group separately. The analysis of variance procedure uses the Mean Squares within groups as the basis of its tests of the equality of the treatment means. As such, generalizations can be a bit different—but not that much, unless the assumption of homogeneity of variance is violated quite severely.

The table also gives the minimum and maximum values in each group. It is a good idea to always check these values to ensure that no obvious gross errors have been made in the data file.

Test of Homogeneity of Variance

The Statistics command Homogeneity causes **SPSS WINDOWS ONEWAY** to output the following table providing the results of the Levene (1960) test of the homogeneity of variance assumption:

Test of Homogeneity of Variances

	Levene Statistic	$df1$	$df2$	Sig.
X	.139	3	56	.936

As indicated in the previous chapter, the Levene (1960) test of homogeneity of variance is simply an analysis of variance of the absolute deviations of each observation from the mean of the group in which it occurs. In our sample data, the first observation in group 1 was 50, and the mean for group 1 was 65.0, thus the absolute deviation is $50 - 65 = 15$ (in the absolute deviation, the sign is ignored). Similarly, the last observation in group 4 is 83, the mean is 73.87, and the absolute deviation is $83 - 73.87 = 9.13$. You can see that if one group had large absolute deviations, this would indicate that it has a large variance. And, if another group had small absolute deviations, this would indicate that it has a small variance. By comparing the mean absolute deviations, then, you have a test of the extent to which the variances differ from one another. The Levene statistic (.139) in the above table is, therefore, simply the F-ratio for an analysis of the absolute deviations. The degrees of freedom for this F-ratio are the same as they were for the analysis of the original data (i.e., 3 and 56). As can be seen, this F-ratio is not significant (i.e., $p < .936$), so we would conclude that we have not violated the assumption of homogeneity of variance. If we wished to indicate the statistic in a report, we would use the notation, $[F(3,56)= .139, ns]$, having specified that we are referring to the Levene statistic.

As indicated earlier, if sample sizes are unequal, violation of the assumption of Homogeneity of Variance can influence the results. And it can influence the results in two ways. It can either result in an underestimate of the Type I error or an overestimate depending on the relationship of the sample sizes to the sample variances. If larger sample sizes tend to be associated with larger variances, this will result in an overestimate of the value of $MS_{S/A}$, thus making the F-ratio smaller than expected, and therefore decreasing the probability of a Type I error. If, on the other hand, larger sample sizes tend to be associated with smaller sample variances, the $MS_{S/A}$ will be smaller than expected, making the F-ratio larger, and increasing the probability of a Type I error. All this assumes, of course, that the Null Hypothesis is true. If you want to guard against Type I error, you might consider being a bit more conservative (i.e., adopting a more stringent alpha level such as .01 instead of .05) when larger sample sizes are associated with smaller variances. Another strategy might to be to perform a transformation on the data to eliminate the heterogeneity of variance. Kirk (1995, pp. 103–107) discusses the type of transformations that might be performed and their relative advantages and disadvantages.

TESTS OF MEANS

Many tests can be performed to determine which, if any, means differ significantly from each other, but there are two broad classes of such tests. One involves the use of *planned comparisons* (i.e., comparisons that are planned before the experiment is even conducted). These are also called *a priori contrasts*. These contrasts may involve comparisons between pairs of means, or between combinations of means; they can be performed in **SPSS WINDOWS ONEWAY** using the **Contrasts** option. Such contrasts are beyond the scope of this chapter, but are discussed in many textbooks (see, for example, Kirk, 1995). The other makes use of *a posteriori tests*. In this chapter, we focus attention on these tests. **SPSS WINDOWS ONEWAY** presents 18 *a posteriori* tests, but we will focus on only one of them, Tukey's **Honestly Significant Difference (HSD)** test.

A Posteriori Tests

As indicated earlier, the significant F-ratio in the analysis of variance indicates that there is at least one contrast among the means that is significant, but it doesn't say which. If the F-ratio is significant, *a posteriori* (sometimes referred to as post hoc or data snooping) procedures can be performed; otherwise it is inappropriate to do so, because any "significant" results would reflect Type I error. Following a significant F-ratio, researchers generally are interested in determining which of the pairwise comparisons are significant. **SPSS WINDOWS ONEWAY** provides 14 different tests of the differences between pairs of means that are applicable when the assumption of homogeneity of variance is true, and four that are applicable when the variances are heterogeneous.

Each of these tests have their own proponents, and it is beyond the scope of this chapter to discuss each of the tests. The 18 tests are really quite comparable, differing in the underlying statistic they use (t, F, or q), how they characterize Type I error in any particular contrast, and in the validity of the homogeneity of variance assumption. As indicated above, we will direct attention to the Tukey **HSD** procedure.

The Tukey **HSD** procedure defines Type I error in terms of a sampling distribution (referred to as q or the Studentized range statistic) involving the difference between the largest and smallest mean in a set of r means. In our example, $r = 4$. This distribution is conceptually like the t-distribution, except the t-distribution concerns two means drawn at random from the same population, whereas q concerns the sampling distribution of the highest versus lowest mean in a set of means. This distribution was developed based on work by Tippett (1925), Student (1927) and Newman (1939), but according to secondary sources (e.g., Kirk, 1995), the **HSD** procedure was first proposed by Tukey (1953) in an unpublished manuscript. The Tukey **HSD** procedure compares all possible pairs of means in a set (there are six such comparisons in a set of four means) by evaluating them in terms of the q sampling distribution. Because of this, the Type I error is set at alpha for the collection of all possible pairwise tests.

The formula for the q-statistic is:

$$ q = \frac{\overline{X}_i - \overline{X}_j}{\sqrt{\dfrac{MS_{S/A}}{n}}} $$

The value of q could be compared with tabled values of q (see, Appendix B, Table D) to determine whether or not it is significant.

The statement "POSTHOC = TUKEY ALPHA(.05)" in the Syntax File presented on page 68 results in the computer performing the Tukey **HSD** test among all possible pairs of means. The results are presented in two different formats. Neither format actually reports the q-value, but they do give all other information. In the first format, rather than reporting the value of a q-test for all possible pairs of means, **SPSS WINDOWS ONEWAY** reports the difference between all possible pairs of means (with a significant difference indicated by an *), the standard error of the difference, the significance of each difference, and the 95% confidence interval for each difference (contrast).

The first format is as follows:

Multiple Comparisons

Dependent Variable: X
Tukey HSD

					95% Confidence Interval	
(I)A	(J)A	Mean Difference (I – J)	Std. Error	Sig.	Lower Bound	Upper Bound
1.00	2.00	1.4000	2.886	.962	−6.2427	9.0427
	3.00	−5.6000	2.886	.223	−13.2427	2.0427
	4.00	−8.8667*	2.886	.017	−16.5093	−1.2240
2.00	1.00	−1.4000	2.886	.962	−9.0427	6.2427
	3.00	−7.0000	2.886	.084	−14.6427	.6427
	4.00	−10.2667*	2.886	.004	−17.9093	−2.6240
3.00	1.00	5.6000	2.886	.223	−2.0427	13.2427
	2.00	7.0000	2.886	.084	−.6427	14.6427
	4.00	−3.2667	2.886	.672	−10.9093	4.3760
4.00	1.00	8.8667*	2.886	.017	1.2240	16.5093
	2.00	10.2667*	2.886	.004	2.6240	17.9093
	3.00	3.2667	2.886	.672	−4.3760	10.9093

*The mean difference is significant at the .05 level.

In this format, the contrasts are presented comparing each level of A with every other level of A. Thus, the first line shows the levels of A (1 vs 2), and the mean difference (1.4000) which is the difference between means 1 and 2 (i.e., $65.00 - 63.60 = 1.40$). The standard error of the difference is 2.886. This is computed using the following formula:

$$\sqrt{\frac{2\,MS_{S/A}}{n}}$$

$$\sqrt{\frac{2(62.4810)}{15}} = 2.886$$

It will be noted that this value is not identical to the denominator of the q statistic as defined on page 73. It is the square root of 2 larger. Therefore, if you wanted to compute the q-value to report in a manuscript, you would divide this value by the square root of 2 (i.e., 1.4142) to obtain the denominator for q. In our example, then, the denominator of the q-statistic would be:

$$\frac{2.886}{\sqrt{2}} = \frac{2.886}{1.4142} = 2.0407$$

and the value of q would be computed by dividing the mean difference by this value. That is, to compute the q-value for the first contrast, you would compute:

$$q = \frac{1.400}{2.0407} = .69$$

If you wished to report this value in an article, you would use the notation, $[q(4,56) = .69,$ ns]. This is because the Tukey **HSD** statistic is dependent on the total number of means being compared (i.e., 4 in our example), and the degrees of freedom associated with the Mean Square for error.

The 95% confidence interval requires the computation of the following:

$$\psi_{q*} = q*\sqrt{\frac{MS_{S/A}}{n}} = 3.74\sqrt{\frac{62.481}{15}} = 7.6427$$

where the value for $q* = 3.74$ is obtained from the sampling distribution for the q-statistic for 4 steps and degrees of freedom for error = 60 (see Appendix B, Table D).

This formula can be used to compute the confidence interval for the difference. Thus, the lower limit would be ($1.4 - 7.6427 = -6.2427$) and the upper limit would be ($1.4 + 7.6427 = 9.0427$). Since these two values differ in sign, this means that one value that would be expected is 0. This is why the difference is not indicated as significant. Note, however, that the difference between the means for groups 1 and 4 both have the same signs associated with both confidence limits (that is, the confidence interval does not include 0 as one possible value), and that the mean difference is shown as significant.

The second format for the Tukey **HSD** test presents the means in two groups and ordered in increasing magnitude, as follows:

X

Tukey HSD[a]

		Subset for alpha = .05	
A	**N**	**1**	**2**
2.00	15	63.6000	
1.00	15	65.0000	
3.00	15	70.6000	70.6000
4.00	15		73.8667
Sig.		.084	.672

Means for groups in homogeneous subsets are displayed.

[a]Uses Harmonic Mean Sample Size = 15.000

This format is intended as a summary showing which means do not differ significantly from one another. It will be noted that the mean for $A = 3$ is in both groups. This table also presents significance levels for each subset (.084 for subset 1 and .672 for subset 2). These significance values refer simply to the significance of the difference between the largest and smallest mean in each set. For the HSD procedure, these values will always be greater that the alpha required for significance (i.e., .05 in our example), and has no particular relevance for interpretation. That is, the value of "Sig." equal to .084 is simply the level of significance reported for the contrast between Mean 2 (63.6) and Mean 3 (70.6) as reported in the previous table, and our decision rule was to keep all ordered means in a group that did not differ significantly from each other at the .05 level. Finally, note the reference to the harmonic mean of the sample sizes at the bottom of the table. Since our sample sizes are equal, this value is equal to this value. However, if the sample sizes were unequal, this value would be equal to:

$$\frac{a}{\dfrac{1}{n_1} + \dfrac{1}{n_2} + \cdots + \dfrac{1}{n_a}}$$

where a = the number of groups (levels of A), and the n's refer to the sample sizes in the various groups.

Interpreting the HSD Results

Researchers differ in which type of output they prefer. In the first format in this example, **ONEWAY** shows that two differences are significant, one involving groups 1 and 4, and the other groups 2 and 4. That is, group 4 differs significantly from groups 2 and 1 (as indicated by the *'s in the table). Note that all contrasts are presented twice, so that there are in fact four significant comparisons indicated in the first format. In interpreting these results, a researcher would probably note that significantly more errors were made in the learning Task by subjects who had taken Drug III (group 4) than by subjects in the Control condition (group 1), or by subjects who had taken Drug I (group 2). No other differences were significant. In discussing the results, the researcher would probably focus attention on the nature of Drug III, and the processes that might be responsible for the differences obtained. She/he might comment too on the apparent similarity in effects for Drugs I and II, and the Control condition, though strictly speaking failure to reject the null hypothesis does not indicate similarity of effects—only the absence of detecting differences. Similar comments might also be made about the apparent similarity of Drugs II and III, but the same caveat applies.

In the second format in this example, **ONEWAY** presents a summary in terms of relatively homogeneous subsets of means. Thus, it shows two partially overlapping sets of means as follows:

Group 2	Group 1	Group 3	Group 4
63.60	65.00	70.60	
		70.60	73.87

In interpreting these results, the researcher would probably focus attention on the fact that the four treatment conditions form two overlapping groups. There is a tendency for groups 1, 2, and 3 to form one grouping, and groups 3 and 4 to form another, as shown by the underlining above. In discussing the results, he/she would probably discuss why the two groupings occurred. The first subset of means suggests that Drugs I and II (groups 2 and 3) are sufficiently benign to produce very little difference from a No Drug condition (group 1). The second subset suggests, however, that Drug III (group 4) does result in behavior that is different from the No Drug condition and Drug I (groups 1 and 2), but not from Drug II (group 3). Clearly, in terms of potency, Drug II is somewhere between Drug I and Drug III.

Obviously, there is a lot of similarity in the interpretations one draws from the two different ways of considering the results. This is only sensible since the two sets of results do refer to the same tests. The only difference in the presentation of the results is in the nature of the language that is used.

ANALYSIS OF VARIANCE AND UNEQUAL SAMPLE SIZES

Thus far we have limited discussion of the analysis of variance and the related tests of means to the, situation where the sample sizes are equal. There are many good reasons for having equal sample sizes, and when the experiment involves treatment manipulations, researchers should strive for equal sample sizes. If sample sizes are unequal under these conditions, it has some meaning with respect to the nature of the treatment, over and above that reflected in the dependent measure. That is, if one condition has a smaller n than others it could suggest that treatment causes subject attrition, and this may or may not be reflected in the dependent measure.

When sample sizes are unequal, it is possible to perform two different types of single-factor analysis of variance, and these can produce different answers. One type is like that described above, except that the n's are unequal. This requires some modification of the definitional formulae on pages 63 to 65 (which we will not discuss here). The other involves an unweighted means analysis of variance (for a discussion, see Edwards, 1985, pp. 96-100). In general, most researchers make use of the first type, and this is the one performed by **SPSS WINDOWS ONEWAY.** If you do make use of a single-factor analysis of variance with unequal sample sizes, you should at a minimum investigate very carefully the validity of the assumption of homogeneity of variance.

Chapter 4
Completely Randomized Factorial Designs

Sometimes researchers want to investigate the effects of more than one independent variable on a dependent variable. For example, a researcher may be interested in studying the effects that both drugs and sleep deprivation have on learning. One approach to this task would be to do two different studies, each employing a single-factor analysis of variance. However, the researcher may feel that there is sufficient overlap in these two phenomena to investigate them together, and thus to combine the two studies into one. If this approach is followed, the result is a two-factor analysis of variance.

The completely randomized factorial design is a form of analysis of variance that permits a researcher to investigate the effects of two or more factors, and to assess any possible interactions between these factors. The primary characteristic of this type of design is that each cell in the design is made up of a random sample of observations. Thus, in a two factor (AB) design, there are axb groups of observations, and the researcher can assess the effects of the A factor, the B factor, and the combination of the A and B factors (i.e., the AB interaction). In a three factor design, there are $axbxc$ random samples of observations, and the researcher can investigate the effects of A, B, and C by themselves, the two-way interactions of AB, AC, and BC, and the three-way interaction, ABC. In theory, this can be extended to any number of factors, but the **SPSS WINDOWS GLM** program (the analysis of variance program we will feature in this chapter) is limited to five-way interactions.

This type of design is, therefore, slightly more complex than the single-factor analysis of variance. The completely randomized factorial design is sometimes described as two or more single-factor designs in the same study, but it is more than that. It permits the researcher to determine whether or not differences that can be attributed to one of the factors are consistent at all levels of the other factor(s)—i.e., whether or not the two (or more) factors interact with one another to produce effects that could not be determined if the factors were investigated one at a time.

SOME BASIC TERMINOLOGY

As you have already seen, there are a number of terms used in conjunction with analysis of variance. We will define and illustrate some of the ones used in the factorial design analysis of variance with the help of an example that we will follow throughout this chapter. In this example, there are two *factors,* or two independent variables. Factor A is Type of Drug, and Factor B is amount of Sleep Deprivation. Each of these factors is made up of different *Levels*. Thus, in our example, Factor A consists of four levels (No Drug, Drug I, Drug II, and Drug III), and Factor B has three levels (No Sleep Deprivation, 24 hours of Sleep Deprivation, and 36 hours of Sleep Deprivation). It will be noted in this example that each factor has a Control Condition (i.e., a No Treatment Condition). This is not a requirement of the factorial design, though there are very good reasons for including Control conditions to provide a type of baseline. In this study we are interested in the effects the factors have on the total number of errors made in a paired associates learning experiment (an experiment in which subjects learn pairs of words). The *dependent variable* then is the total number of errors.

There are a number of things to note in this description. To begin with, since there are four levels of the A factor, and three levels of the B factor, this would often be referred to as a 4×3 (or $a \times b$) factorial design. Second, in a factorial design, each level of one factor (e.g., A) appears in combination with each level of the other factor (e.g., B), thus the two factors are said to be *crossed*. Third, subjects are randomly assigned to one of the Drug conditions and one of the Sleep Deprivation conditions. That is, any one subject has an equal opportunity of being assigned to any one condition—and his or her appearance in any one condition is due to chance. In this instance, then, Subjects are said to be *nested* in AB. Subjects are said to be nested in AB because each subject appears in only one combination of the AB factors. This is often written as S/AB. In our example, you might consider that there are $4 \times 3 = 12$ nests, and that any one subject appears in only one nest!

This chapter will devote most of its coverage to a two factor design in which the number of observations in each of the AB cells are equal. Later, there will a brief discussion of more than two factors, as well as the problems that can arise when cell frequencies are not equal. Most computer programs deal with designs that have more than two factors, and also those with unequal sample sizes, but as we shall see there are a number of issues that must be considered before performing these analyses willy-nilly.

A BIT OF HISTORY

As we indicated in the previous chapter, Fisher developed much of the rationale underlying analysis of variance (for an interesting review of many of these and related developments, see Cowles, 1989). We noted also that the first textbook that referred to analysis of variance was published by Fisher in 1925, even though there were two publications before that time that made use of analysis of variance (Fisher & MacKenzie, 1923; Student, 1923). Both of these publications were concerned with the analysis of agricultural data, and both involved two independent variables (i.e., two factors).

It wasn't until the appearance of Fisher's (1935) textbook *The Design of Experiments,* however, that there was a comprehensive discussion of the factorial design analysis of variance and its implications for research. It was also shortly after this that the first publication in psychology appeared using a factorial design analysis of variance. In this article, Grace Rubin-Rabson (1937) investigated the effects of three major factors (Compositions, Methods and Order) on three different dependent measures, the time taken to memorize piano music, relearning time, and relearning repetitions. Interestingly, the analysis of variance was directed only to a consideration of the main effects of the three factors, as well as subjects. All other variation was referred to as residual, and no attempt was made to investigate any of the interactions among the factors (which was just as well since all of the factors were not crossed).

AN EXAMPLE OF A TWO-FACTOR DESIGN

Table 1 on page 80 presents fictitious data for our example. In the table, it will be noted that the number of levels of A is $a = 4$, the number of levels of B is $b = 3$, and the number of subjects per cell is $n = 5$. There are consequently $4 \times 3 \times 5 = 60$ observations. The algebraic notation for each score in this table is written as X_{abi}.

Table 2 on page 80 presents the means for A (the row means) and B (the column means) as well as the cell means and variances. Since the cell sizes are equal, the row means are simply the means of the means of the cells in that row, and thus are confounded by any column differences. That is, when referring to the row means, the data are collapsed across B. Similarly, the column means are simply the means of the means of the cells in that column, and thus are confounded by any row differences. The grand mean (68.27) is the mean of the cells, which of course is also the mean of the row means (or the mean of the column means). The algebraic notation for the row means is $\bar{X}_a$, that for the column means is $\bar{X}_b$, and that for the grand mean is $\bar{G}$.

The term *effects* is used very frequently in analysis of variance. This term has a very precise meaning, and it is well to get used to it. In analysis of variance, the effect of a level of a factor is defined as the deviation of the mean of that level from the grand mean, and is referred to as a *main*

Table 1   Fictitious Data for the Example

	Levels of B		
Levels of A	1	2	3
1	50	76	75
	54	75	63
	55	63	62
	68	62	77
	66	61	68
2	72	64	54
	75	56	63
	65	57	51
	60	55	72
	69	63	78
3	60	79	67
	60	73	83
	70	75	60
	72	72	77
	64	77	70
4	68	83	63
	65	82	64
	76	76	77
	74	85	62
	75	75	83

effect. Thus, the estimate of the main effect of A_1 is equal to $(\bar{X}_1 - \bar{G})$ which, in our example, is equal to $65.00 - 68.27 = -3.27$. The main effect of B_3 is $(\bar{X}_3 - \bar{G})$, or $68.45 - 68.27 = .18$.

The concept of an *interaction effect* refers to deviations of cell means from the grand mean once deviations due to other possible sources are removed. Thus, a two-factor interaction effect

Table 2   Row Means, Column Means, Cell Means, and Variances

	Levels of B			
Levels of A	1	2	3	Row Means
1	58.6	67.4	69.0	65.00
	(62.80)	(55.30)	(46.50)	
2	68.2	59.0	63.6	63.60
	(34.70)	(17.50)	(132.30)	
3	65.2	75.2	71.4	70.60
	(31.20)	(8.20)	(79.30)	
4	71.6	80.2	69.8	73.87
	(23.30)	(19.70)	(91.70)	
Column Means	65.90	70.45	68.45	68.27

refers to the deviation of a cell mean from the grand mean once deviations attributable to the two main effects are removed. That is, the interaction effect of A_2B_1 is:

$$(\bar{X}_{21} - \bar{G}) - (\bar{X}_2 - \bar{G}) - (\bar{X}_1 - \bar{G})$$

which, in our example, is equal to:

$$(68.2 - 68.27) - (63.60 - 68.27) - (65.90 - 68.27) = 6.97$$

or its algebraic equivalent

$$(\bar{X}_{21} - \bar{X}_2 - \bar{X}_1 + \bar{G}) = (68.2 - 63.60 - 65.90 + 68.27) = 6.97$$

The factorial design analysis of variance procedure is therefore concerned with isolating the variance of these main effects and interaction effects. It will be noticed in the formulae that follow that the various sums of squares are, in fact, nothing more than the sums of squares of these effects.

DEFINITIONAL FORMULAE AND EXAMPLE OF COMPUTATIONS

The definitional formulae for the completely randomized design analysis of variance are very straightforward, and are as follows:

Source	Sum of Squares	df
A	$nb\sum\limits^{a}(\bar{X}_a - \bar{G})^2$	$(a-1)$
B	$na\sum\limits^{b}(\bar{X}_b - \bar{G})^2$	$(b-1)$
AB	$n\sum\limits^{a}\sum\limits^{b}((\bar{X}_{ab} - \bar{G}) - (\bar{X}_a - \bar{G}) - (\bar{X}_b - \bar{G}))^2$	$(a-1)(b-1)$
S/AB	$\sum\limits^{a}\sum\limits^{b}\sum\limits^{i}(X_{abi} - \bar{X}_{ab})^2$	$ab(n-1)$
$TOTAL$	$\sum\limits^{a}\sum\limits^{b}\sum\limits^{i}(X_{abi} - \bar{G})^2$	$abn-1$

Examining the definitional formulae will reveal that the computations for the various sums of squares are very simple. The Sum of Squares for A, for example, simply assesses the extent to which the A means vary from each other. Obviously, if the A means were all the same, the grand mean $(\bar{G})$ would take the same value, and the Sum of Squares for A would equal 0. As the A means differ from each other, the Sum of Squares for A will increase. The same could be said for the Sum of Squares for B. The Sum of Squares for AB looks a bit more complex, but it still represents a simple measure of variation. In this case, it describes the variation of the cell means from the grand mean, once any of this variation that can be attributed to the variation of the A means from the grand mean, and the variation of the B means from the grand mean is removed. Similarly, the Sum of Squares for Within Cells (S/AB) is simply a measure of how much the scores in each cell differ from each other. Finally, the Total Sum of Squares indicates the extent to which the scores differ from the grand mean.

In much the same way, the degrees of freedom can be shown to reflect simple notions. The degrees of freedom for A are the number of A means minus 1. If one recalls that the grand mean is the mean of the A means, it will be noted that if one knows the value of the grand mean, it would be possible for $(a-1)$ of the A means to take any value, but that the value of the a_{th} mean would have to be such that their mean was equal to the grand mean. That is, $(a-1)$ of the A means are *free to vary;* the degrees of freedom for A are $(a-1)$. The same argument can be made for the degrees of freedom for B, i.e., the degrees of freedom are $(b-1)$.

To determine the number of degrees of freedom for the AB interaction, one could simply look at the table of means given earlier, and consider the situation where one knew the values of the grand mean, the A means, and the B means. You could then ask, how many of the cell means are free to take any value without changing any of the values of these means that are already known. You can see that, in row 1, two means could take any value, but the third mean would have to be such that the mean of the three means equals the mean of the first row. That is, $(b - 1) = (3 - 1)$ of these means are free to vary. The same could be said for the second row, as well as for the third row. When it comes to the fourth row, however, none of these means are free to vary since the mean of each column is already known, and, given that the previous three means in each column are free to take any value, the fourth one is not. That is, only $(a - 1)$ of the means in each column are free to vary. Considering the entire table, therefore, we can say that $(a - 1)(b - 1) = (4 - 1)(3 - 1) = 6$ of the means are free to vary. The degrees of freedom for the interaction are then $(a - 1)(b - 1) = 6$.

The same general logic applies to the degrees of freedom for the Within Cells (S/AB) and Total components. For the within cells term, there are $(n - 1)$ degrees of freedom in each cell (since given the mean of the cell, $(n - 1)$ of the means are free to vary, but the last one is not). And given that there are ab cells, the degrees of freedom for the within cells term is equal to $ab(n - 1) = (4)(3)(5 - 1) = 48$. For the Total Degrees of Freedom, the only restriction that we have is that the mean of all the observations ($\overline{G}$) is known, so that $(abn - 1)$ of the scores could vary, but the last must be such that the grand mean retains its value.

These formulae can be applied to the sample data to compute the various Sums of Squares and Degrees of Freedom. Thus:

$$SS_A = (5)(3)[(65.00 - 68.27)^2 + \ldots + (73.87 - 68.27)^2] \qquad = 1038.80$$

$$SS_B = (5)(4)[(65.90 - 68.27)^2 + \ldots + (68.45 - 68.27)^2] \qquad = 208.03$$

$$SS_{AB} = (5)[\{(58.6 - 68.27) - (65.00 - 68.27) - (65.90 - 68.27)\}^2 + \ldots$$
$$+ \{(69.8 - 68.27) - (73.87 - 68.27) - (68.45 - 68.27)\}^2] \qquad = 880.90$$

$$SS_{S/AB} = (50 - 58.6)^2 + \ldots (66 - 58.6)^2 + \ldots + (83 - 69.8)^2 \qquad = 2410.00$$

$$SS_{TOTAL} = (50 - 68.27)^2 + \ldots + (83 - 68.27)^2 \qquad = 4537.73$$

Similarly, the degrees of freedom and Mean Squares are:

$$DF_A = (4 - 1) = 3 \qquad MS_A = 1038.80/3 \qquad = 346.267$$

$$DF_B = (3 - 1) = 2 \qquad MS_B = 208.03/2 \qquad = 104.017$$

$$DF_{AB} = (4 - 1)(3 - 1) = 6 \qquad MS_{AB} = 880.90/6 \qquad = 146.817$$

$$DF_{S/AB} = (4)(3)(5 - 1) = 48 \qquad MS_{S/AB} = 2410.00/48 \qquad = 50.208$$

$$DF_{TOTAL} = (4)(3)(5) - 1 = 59$$

The F-ratios are:

$$F_A = 346.267/50.208 = 6.897 @ df_1 = 3, df_2 = 48$$

$$F_B = 104.017/50.208 = 2.072 @ df_1 = 2, df_2 = 48$$

$$F_{AB} = 146.817/50.208 = 2.924 @ df_1 = 6, df_2 = 48$$

To determine whether or not these F-ratios are significant, you could examine the table of F, Table C, Appendix B. Since Table C does not have information for $df_2 = 48$, we will use $df_2 = 40$ (the closest lower value). For 3 and 40 df, $F = 6.60$ is significant at the .001 level, thus we would conclude that F_A is significant at the .001 level. Similarly, for 2 and 40 df, $F = 3.23$ is significant at the .05 level. Since F_B is less than this value, we would conclude that F_B is not significant. Finally, for 6 and 40 df, $F = 2.34$ is significant at the .05 level, thus we would conclude that F_{AB} is significant at the .05 level.

Proportion of Variance Accounted For

In addition to the F-ratios that you compute in an analysis of variance, we have seen that you can also ask questions about the proportion of variance accounted for by the effects. Also, you recall from Chapter 3 that there are two different classes of such indices. One class involves the measures of ω^2 (omega-squared) and ρ_I (the intraclass correlation), while the other makes use of η^2 (eta-squared). These different indices give slightly different answers, even though they are conceptually very similar. The simplest one to compute is η^2, which is defined as the ratio of two Sums of Squares. Within each of these classes of proportions, we can further distinguish between two further classes, **Omnibus proportions** and **Partial proportions.**

Omnibus η^2. In the context of η^2, Omnibus proportions refer to the ratio in which the Sum of Squares for the source of interest forms the numerator and the denominator is the Total Sum of Squares. Thus, for our example:

$$\eta_A^2 = \frac{SS_A}{SS_{TOTAL}} = \frac{1038.80}{4537.73} = .23$$

Similar computations would yield $\eta_B^2 = .05$ and $\eta_{AB}^2 = .19$. (Note, however, that since the F-ratio for B is not significant, we have no evidence to conclude that there is any variance due to B in the population, thus it is probably best to consider the best estimate of η_B^2 to be 0, by definition, regardless of what value is estimated.) The results of these calculations indicate, therefore, that Factor A (Drugs) accounts for 23% of the variance in learning scores in this type of task, and the interaction between Drugs and Sleep Deprivation (AB) accounts for 19%. And taken together, the effects for A and AB account for 42% of the variance while 58% of the variance is accounted for by error. It will be noted that these proportions, therefore, give the proportion of the effects for the experiment as a total.

Partial η^2. Often in factorial analyses, attention is directed toward partial proportions rather than omnibus ones. Partial proportions are defined in terms of the ratio of the Sum of Squares of Interest to the sum of the Sum of Squares of Interest plus the Sum of Squares of Error. Thus, in our example:

$$\eta_A^2 = \frac{SS_A}{SS_A + SS_{S/AB}} = \frac{1038.80}{1038.80 + 2410.00} = .301$$

$$\eta_B^2 = \frac{SS_B}{SS_B + SS_{S/AB}} = \frac{208.03}{208.03 + 2410.00} = .079$$

and

$$\eta_{AB}^2 = \frac{SS_{AB}}{SS_{AB} + SS_{S/AB}} = \frac{880.90}{880.90 + 2410.00} = .268$$

Note that these are referred to as partial η^2s because they contrast the variability of the source in question with the variability of itself plus the estimate of error variability. Note too that, although the computed value of η_B^2 is .079, the best estimate we have of η_B^2 is 0, since the F-ratio for B was not significant.

The values of partial η^2 can be computed directly from the values of the F-ratios and the associated degrees of freedom. The formula for these calculations is very useful and reproduced in general terms below:

$$\eta^2 = \frac{df_1 F}{df_1 F + df_2}$$

where:

df_1 = the degrees of freedom associated with the numerator of the F-ratio
df_2 = the degrees of freedom associated with the denominator of the F-ratio.

Applying this formula to these data yields the following:

$$\eta_A^2 = \frac{3(6.897)}{3(6.897) + 48} = .301 \quad \eta_B^2 = \frac{2(2.072)}{2(2.072) + 48} = .079 \quad \eta_{AB}^2 = \frac{6(2.924)}{6(2.924) + 48} = .268$$

As stated in the previous chapter, Cohen (1988) distinguishes between what he terms small, medium, and large effects, characterizing them in terms of ω^2 of .01 (small), .059 (medium), and .138 (large). Also as indicated in the previous chapter, these η^2 could be transformed to ω^2 values using the formula on page 69. Applying that formula here yields values of $\omega_A^2 = .227$, $\omega_B^2 = .034$ (which nonetheless must be considered as 0 since the F-ratio for B was not significant), and $\omega_{AB}^2 = .162$. In this study, therefore, we would characterize the Effects of Drugs (Factor A), and the Drug X Sleep Deprivation interaction (AB) as large. To reiterate, a note of caution should be made about the meaning of a value of η^2 (or ω^2) when the corresponding F-ratio is not significant. That is, $\eta_B^2 = .079$, but since the corresponding F-ratio is not significant, we have no reason to conclude that the variance in the population due to B is anything other than 0. It would not, therefore, be meaningful to conclude that Factor B has even a small effect because $\omega_B^2 = .034$, since it is best considered to be 0. Our best estimate of the variance accounted for by B, therefore, is 0%!

Estimates of Power. The partial η^2 values are used to estimate power in factorial designs. Power refers to the probability of rejecting the null hypothesis when it is false, and it can be calculated once the values of the partial η^2 are known. The computations for these calculations are beyond the scope of this chapter. Individuals interested in investigating the concept of power more fully are directed to Kirk (1995) for a general textbook dealing with the issues involved, or Cohen (1988) for a textbook that deals with the concept in various contexts. It is becoming more common to report these values. It should be noted, however, that they are based on considering the estimates obtained in the study as the population values.

ASSUMPTIONS UNDERLYING THE FACTORIAL DESIGN

Four assumptions underly the factorial design analysis of variance. They are:

Independent Random Sampling

It is assumed that subjects are randomly assigned to conditions. This means that each subject has an equal probability of belonging to any cell in the experiment. As long as subjects are randomly assigned to conditions by the researcher, this condition is satisfied (even if the researcher must restrict this so that there are an equal number of observations in each cell). This is a basic requirement, and the analysis is *not* robust to violations of this assumption. Sometimes, when an individual difference attribute such as Gender, Hair Color, or Level of Intelligence (grouped in some way) is used as one of the factors, researchers argue that sampling is random within this condition. This satisfies the basic requirement with respect to that condition; however, as noted below in the section labelled "Note on random assignment and random sampling," any findings involving that factor represent correlations of that factor with the dependent variable, and not strong causal relationships that follow from true random assignment for all conditions.

Normality

The assumption of Normality holds that the observations in the populations represented by each of the cells in the experiment are distributed normally. This does not mean to say that the sample values must be normally distributed, only that is meaningful to assume that the samples were drawn from normally distributed populations. Sometimes visual inspection might help to determine whether this is probably the case, but, as might be expected, such tests are open to interpretation. There are also tests of normality available, but generally these are more applicable to larger samples than those that characterize most analysis of variance investigations.

This assumption is important because, with underlying Normality, it can be shown that the means and variances are independent of one another (see Lindquist, 1953, pp. 31–35 for the proof). This means that the Mean Square for the source of interest (i.e., A, for example) which is defined in terms of the means, is independent of the Mean Square for the S/AB, which is defined in terms of the cell variances. And this independence is required for the ratio of the two Mean Squares to be distributed as F. Luckily, however, the factorial design analysis of variance is robust to violations of this assumption providing sample sizes are equal.

Homogeneity of Variance

The assumption of homogeneity of variance means that the variances in the populations represented by the cells in the experiment are all equal to one another. This assumption is important because the error term (i.e., $MS_{S/AB}$, the denominator for the F-ratios) is simply the average of the cell variances. Obviously if some of these variances are based on observations from populations with large variances, and some from populations with small variances, it is not meaningful to argue that the average is representative of any particular population. Thus, it is not meaningful to average them. Luckily, as long as sample sizes are equal and the variances are not too disparate, the factorial design analysis of variance is robust with respect to violations of this assumption.

Null Hypotheses

There are three sets of null hypotheses in the two factor analysis of variance. For the case of the A treatment factor, the hypothesis is that the means in the populations corresponding to each level of A are identical. In this case, the levels of B are ignored, and the means are based simply on a consideration of the levels of A. The sample values corresponding to these population means are the row means shown in Table 2, and obviously we would expect them to vary somewhat in the sample represented in this experiment. The formal statement of this hypothesis for Factor A is:

$$H_0: \mu_1 = \mu_2 = \cdots = \mu_4 = \mu$$

or: $(\mu_a - \mu) = 0$ for all levels of A. Note that the expression $(\mu_a - \mu)$ is the effect in the population for treatment level a, and is often written α_a (not to be confused with α when it is used to refer to Type I error).

In similar fashion, the null hypothesis for factor B can be expressed as:

$$H_0: \mu_1 = \mu_2 = \cdots = \mu$$

or: $(\mu_b - \mu) = 0$ for all levels of B. In this case, $(\mu_b - \mu)$ is the effect for level b, and is often written as β_b.

The null hypothesis concerning the AB interaction concerns the variability of the cell means relative to the main effect means for A and B. That is, it is possible to have interaction effects in the presence or absence of main effects. For the AB interaction, the null hypothesis is:

$H_0: (\mu_{ab} - \mu) - (\mu_a - \mu) - (\mu_b - \mu) = 0$ for all combinations of AB. This is the interaction effect for the ab mean, and is often written as $\alpha\beta_{ab}$.

If we obtain a significant F-ratio in an analysis of variance, we conclude that one of our assumptions is wrong, and generally we focus on the appropriate null hypothesis. It is possible that violations of one of the other hypotheses might be responsible, however. This is particularly true for the first assumption. If the assumption of random sampling is violated, it will seriously distort the F-statistic obtained. This assumption is under the direct control of the experimenter, however, so to the extent that the researcher claims to have sampled subjects randomly, we can be assured that this assumption has not been violated. The other two assumptions are less problematic, assuming sample sizes are equal. Monte Carlo studies (see, for example, Glass, Peckham, and Sanders, 1972) have demonstrated that violations of either of these assumptions when sample sizes are equal can have an effect on the sampling distribution of the F-ratio, but the effects are generally minimal unless the assumptions have been violated to a very large extent. Violations of these assumptions are much more serious when sample sizes are unequal, and in fact Milligan, Wong, and Thompson (1987) have demonstrated that violations of either assumption in the presence of unequal sample sizes can inflate *and* deflate the Type I error of the F-ratios in the same analysis. The effects were much more pronounced for violations of homogeneity of variance than they were for violations of normality. Based on their study, Milligan, Wong, and Thompson (1987) recommend against using a factorial design analysis of variance if cell sizes are unequal *and* variances are heterogeneous. They suggest five alternative approaches under such conditions, but none of them are particularly satisfactory for different reasons. The moral to be drawn from their study is beware of unequal sample sizes in a factorial design!

A NOTE ON RANDOM ASSIGNMENT AND RANDOM SAMPLES

Earlier it was indicated that in an analysis of variance, subjects should be randomly assigned to treatment conditions (i.e., the levels of A and B). In such cases, providing the other assumptions have been met (with the provisions indicated above) any significant effects due to A, B, or AB can be attributed to the factor or interaction in question. It is true that the "significant" effect might be due to some chance fluctuation, but this is reflected in the Type I error. Thus, in this type of investigation, any effects can be interpreted in terms of causation. That is, within the limitations of Type I error, a significant effect for factor A would be interpreted as meaning that the differences in Drugs *caused* whatever differences were found in paired associate learning.

There are other cases in which such factorial designs are used. These are as meaningful as the example above, except that the "causal" conclusions are not strong ones. For example, assume that the researcher above was interested in the four levels of Drugs, but rather than also studying Time of Testing, the researcher was more interested in the effects of the Sex of the Subject. In this case, the AB design is a 4×2, with the factors, Drug Condition and Sex of Subject. Lindquist (1953) referred to such designs as Treatment by Level designs. Subjects are still nested in AB, but in this case the assignment of subjects to conditions is not completely random. Male subjects cannot be assigned to the Female condition and vice versa. Nonetheless, assuming the subjects can be considered representative samples of the Sex conditions, we can still perform the same analysis as before, in that we can determine whether or not there are effects due to A, B, and/or the interaction of A and B. To the extent, however, that there are significant effects due to B or the AB interaction, we cannot say that these are caused by B (i.e., Sex of Subject). Clearly B plays a role in the results, but the best that can be said is that there is covariation in Sex of Subject and Paired Associate Error scores. Although it is often said, for example, that a significant effect due to B indicates that Sex of Subject influenced the results, the nature of this influence is correlational at best. Since subjects were not randomly assigned to the Sex of Subject condition, there are many non-random factors that could vary with Sex of Subject, and any of them might be responsible for the effect noted. That is, Sex of Subject did not *cause* the effect noted. Instead, differences correlated with Sex are associated with the reported differences in the dependent variable. One may, if he or she wishes, interpret this correlation causally, but it is a weak causal statement, not a strong one like that which can be made when subjects are randomly assigned to treatment conditions.

ANALYZING THESE DATA USING SPSS WINDOWS GLM

These data are analysed using the **GLM** General Factorial program of **SPSS 8.0** or the **GLM** Univariate in **SPSS 9.0.** This chapter will focus on the **GLM** General Factorial program. The following instructions assume that the data were typed into an ASCII (text) file with the level of A, the level of B, and the score on each line, and that the file was on the A Drive in a file called **FAC.DAT.**

Steps for Using SPSS WINDOWS GLM General Factorial (Univariate)

The following steps are applicable to **SPSS 8.0** and **SPSS 9.0** except for the input of the ASCII or Text data file. In the example to follow you are instructed at Step 3 to input your data following the procedures described in Chapter 1. The output for this example was obtained by using the freefield format in **SPSS 8.0,** and depending upon the input procedure you use, the output may be somewhat different. The answers are the same, however. Using the **WINDOWS** version of the program, you could simply type the Syntax file [the set of instructions required to run the procedure, including the relevant Data List and Execute statements (see page 30)], and then execute the job from inside the Syntax Editor (not discussed here), or use the program itself to create the syntax file. This latter procedure involves using the mouse to bring up a number of windows, and then selecting the appropriate options or typing in the required information (the **clope** procedure).

1. *Enter **SPSS WIN.*** This presents you with the **SPSS** Data Editor (see figure in Chapter 2, p. 15). At this point, you could begin to type in the data. However, we will assume here that you already have the data in a file on the A Drive, and that this file is labelled **fac.dat.**

2. *Click on **File** in the upper row of selections.* This will present you with a Window with a series of choices.

3. *Enter your ASCII (**SPSS 8.0**) or Text (**SPSS 9.0**) data file by following the steps on pages 17 to 20 for **SPSS 8.0**, or pages 20 to 28 for **SPSS 9.0.*** For this example, the file will consist of three variables labelled **a, b,** and **x,** respectively.

4. *Click on the **Statistics (SPSS 8.0)** or **Analyze (SPSS 9.0)** option on the top row.* This presents you with a drop-down menu. *Move your cursor to **General Linear Model**, and you are presented with another menu to the right with a choice of the following:*

SPSS 8.0	**SPSS 9.0**
GLM—General Factorial . . .	Univariate
GLM—Multivariate . . .	Multivariate
GLM—Repeated Measures . . .	Repeated Measures
Variance Components . . .	Variance Components

5. *Click on **GLM—General Factorial (SPSS 8.0) or Univariate (SPSS 9.0)*** This presents you with the Window, GLM General Factorial, and the variable **a** is highlighted (see figure below).

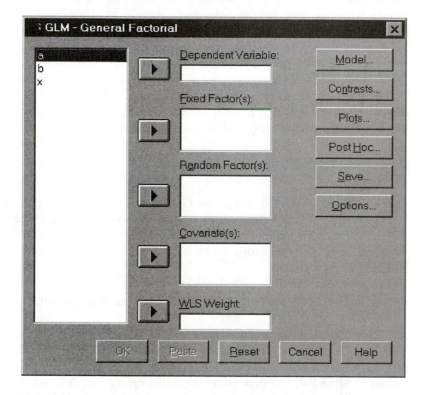

*Add this (i.e., **a**) to the **Fixed Factors** by clicking on the appropriate arrow. Then move your cursor to **b** and click. Add this to the **Fixed Factors** by clicking on the appropriate arrow. Then move the cursor to **x** and click. Add this to the **Dependent Variable** by clicking on the appropriate arrow.* [Note, you could have added variables **a** and/or **b** to the Random Factors, if either factor had been random. The example (and most problems) involve Fixed factors. There is a brief discussion of the distinction between Fixed and Random factors and the implications of such a distinction at the end of this chapter.] *Once you have identified the nature of the variables, click on* **OK.**

6. At this point, you have a number of choices, **Model, Contrasts, Plots, Post Hoc, Save,** and **Options.** If you were to click on **Model** (but don't do it), this would provide a Window which allows you to choose between different models. Where sample sizes are equal, this will have no effect on the analysis. Hence, we will not discuss it here. The default model is SSTYPE3, which corresponds to the Unique Sums of Squares Model (Overall & Spiegel, 1969, Model I), which is often considered the most appropriate when you have unequal sample sizes (but see the discussion of the different models at the end of this chapter).

7. The only choice we will use here is **Options.** Click on **Options.** This presents the **GLM General Factorial Options** Window (labelled **Univariate Options** in **SPSS 9.0**).

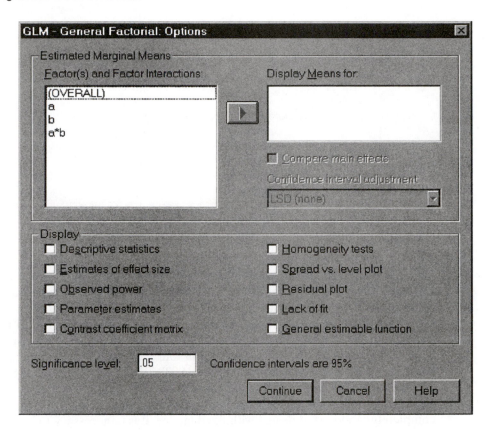

*Click on **Overall**, and add to **Display Means** by clicking on the appropriate arrow. Then click on **a**, and add to **Display Means** by clicking on the appropriate arrow. Then click on **b**, and add to **Display Means** by clicking on the appropriate arrow.* If we wished, we could click a*b as well, but with equal sample sizes the means are the same as those yielded by descriptive statistics (see below).

8. *Move the cursor to the **Display** section and select the following options by clicking on the small white pane preceding each*:

    Descriptive Statistics
    Estimates of Effect Size
    Observed Power
    Homogeneity Tests

*Then click on **Continue**.*

9. This takes you back to the Window, **GLM General Factorial (SPSS 8.0)** or **Univariate Options (SPSS 9.0).** *Click on **OK** to run the analysis of variance.*

10. This runs the analysis of variance program, and the answers are returned to the SPSS Output Viewer, as well as to your monitor. At this point, you can print your answers, save them in a file, or transfer them to some other editor.

11. To exit **SPSS,** *click on **File** (upper row of operations), and click on **Exit**. Before you can exit, however, the program will ask if you wish to save the contents of the SPSS Output Viewer as well as those of the Data Editor. If you have already saved them you will not have to do so again.*

The Syntax File

If you were to follow the instructions given above, you would produce the following Syntax File (omitting the Data List and Execute lines):

```
UNIANOVA X BY A B
       /METHOD = SSTYPE(3)
       /INTERCEPT INCLUDE
       /EMMEANS = TABLES(OVERALL)
       /EMMEANS = TABLES(a)
       /EMMEANS = TABLES(b)
       /PRINT = DESCRIPTIVE ETASQ OPOWER HOMOGENEITY
       /CRITERIA = ALPHA(.05)
       /DESIGN = A B A*B .
```

This set-up reads the levels of A and B and the observation for each subject, and performs the calculations for the factorial design analysis of variance. As indicated above, we made use of the **SPSS WINDOWS GLM General Factorial** option. This is indicated in the Syntax file by the line UNIANOVA X BY A B. The following line /METHOD=SSTYPE(3) indicates which method is used in making the calculations (The program does not use the formulae that were presented earlier). In this program, use is made of one of four methods for calculating the analysis of variance results. These are referred to as SSTYPE(1), SSTYPE(2), SSTYPE(3), or SSTYPE(4). If sample sizes are equal, all four methods give the same answers (and identical to those shown in our example), so which is chosen is irrelevant. The default method is SSTYPE(3), so with equal sample sizes and a completely randomized design with fixed factors, it is unnecessary to even enter the Model window. If sample sizes are unequal, however, the various methods give different results that have different implications for interpretation. Many authors [see, for example, Kirk (1995)] recommend SSTYPE(3), but if you do have unequal sample sizes in your analysis you should consult a textbook like Kirk (1995) to ensure that you are using the correct method for your purposes.

The statement /INTERCEPT = INCLUDE is the default approach in **GLM General Factorial** and, although it is seldom used by psychological researchers, it was retained in this example. It can, however, be omitted by changing this option in the Model Window. It provides a test to determine whether the grand mean of all the observations is greater than 0, and has little interpretative significance in most studies.

The statement /PRINT = DESCRIPTIVES ETASQ HOMOGENEITY results because of the three choices made in the Options window (see Step 10 above). It results in the computer providing information about the cell means as well as the main effect means, the estimates of effect size and power, and the test of homogeneity of variance. Each of these are discussed in the sections to follow when the corresponding results are presented.

The statement /DESIGN is required as the last statement in the Syntax File. It is simply an indication to the computer to perform the completely randomized factorial design analysis of variance in the present case

The Output

The first section of output presents a listing of the Factors and the various levels that are included in this analysis. If Value Labels had been given for each level, they would also be indicated in this table. Since we did not make use of Value Labels in this run, these are not indicated as in this table.

Note that this table is labelled Between Subjects Factors; this is because we indicated this in our instructions and in our choice of **GLM General Factorial.**

Between-Subjects Factors

		N
A	1.00	15
	2.00	15
	3.00	15
	4.00	15
B	1.00	20
	2.00	20
	3.00	20

The second section of output is the Descriptive Statistics. This consists of the means, standard deviations, and sample sizes for each of the cells as well as the main effect means for the first factor listed (i.e., A in our example). It is important to inspect this table to assure yourself that the sample sizes are correct, and that the means and standard deviations are meaningful given the nature of your data.

Descriptive Statistics

Dependent Variable: X

A	B	Mean	Std. Deviation	N
1.00	1.00	58.6000	7.9246	5
	2.00	67.4000	7.4364	5
	3.00	69.0000	6.8191	5
	Total	65.0000	8.3324	15
2.00	1.00	68.2000	5.8907	5
	2.00	59.0000	4.1833	5
	3.00	63.6000	11.5022	5
	Total	63.6000	8.2358	15
3.00	1.00	65.2000	5.5857	5
	2.00	75.2000	2.8636	5
	3.00	71.4000	8.9051	5
	Total	70.6000	7.2190	15
4.00	1.00	71.6000	4.8270	5
	2.00	80.2000	4.4385	5
	3.00	69.8000	9.5760	5
	Total	73.8667	7.7815	15
Total	1.00	65.9000	7.4896	20
	2.00	70.4500	9.4394	20
	3.00	68.4500	9.0929	20
	Total	68.2667	8.7699	60

A third section of output for this example gives three sets of results: (a) the Grand Mean and Standard Error for the entire table, (b) the means and standard errors for the main effects of A, and (c) the means and standard errors for the main effects of B. This output is provided because of the option we chose in Step 7 above. These results are as follows:

1. Grand Mean

Dependent Variable: X

		95% Confidence Interval	
Mean	Std. Error	Lower Bound	Upper Bound
68.267	.915	66.427	70.106

2. A

Dependent Variable: X

A	Mean	Std. Error	95% Confidence Interval	
			Lower Bound	Upper Bound
1.00	65.000	1.830	61.321	68.679
2.00	63.600	1.830	59.921	67.279
3.00	70.600	1.830	66.921	74.279
4.00	73.867	1.830	70.188	77.545

3. B

Dependent Variable: X

B	Mean	Std. Error	95% Confidence Interval	
			Lower Bound	Upper Bound
1.00	65.900	1.584	62.714	69.086
2.00	70.450	1.584	67.264	73.636
3.00	68.450	1.584	65.264	71.636

Another section of output (not necessarily the third one in the output) is the analysis of variance summary table. This table contains considerable information in addition to the basic analysis of variance summary table (most notably the last three columns in the table, which were generated because we chose the option "Estimates of Effect Size" in step 8, page 89).

Tests of Between-Subjects Effects

Dependent Variable: X

Source	Type III Sum of Squares	df	Mean Square	F	Sig.	Eta-Squared	Noncent. Parameter	Observed Power[a]
Corrected Model	2127.733[b]	11	193.430	3.853	.001	.469	42.378	.993
Intercept	279620.27	1	279620.27	5569.200	.000	.991	5569.200	1.000
A	1038.800	3	346.267	6.897	.001	.301	20.690	.968
B	208.033	2	104.017	2.072	.137	.079	4.143	.406
$A * B$	880.900	6	146.817	2.924	.016	.268	17.545	.855
Error	2410.000	48	50.208					
Total	284158.00	60						
Corrected Total	4537.733	59						

[a] Computed using alpha = .05

[b] R Squared = .469 (Adjusted R Squared = .347)

You will note that the analysis of variance summary table presents values for most lines for Sum of Squares, df, Mean Square, F, and "Sig," as well as for Eta-Squared, Noncentral Parameter, and Observed Power. The definitional formulae for most of these values are presented on page 81, with the actual computations shown on pages 82. The values under "Sig" are the probability values associated with the F-ratio in question given the degrees of freedom (df) for the numerator and denominator. When calculating the F-ratios by hand, it is necessary to determine the significance by evaluating the F-ratio in terms of tabled values of F, given in many textbooks (see, for example, Kirk, 1995, pp. 800–805). In **GLM General Factorial, SPSS WINDOWS** evaluates the significance for you. You will note, too, that there are three more lines of results in this table than there are in the table of definitional formulae presented on page 81. This is because **SPSS WINDOWS GLM General Factorial** presents additional results which were not discussed in the earlier presentation.

The additional lines in the above table are labelled Corrected Model, Intercept, and Total, respectively. The Sums of Squares and df for the line labelled Corrected Model are aggregates of the corresponding values for A, B and AB. Thus, the Sum of Squares for Corrected Model is 1038.80 + 208.03 + 880.90 = 2127.73. The value for the sum of squares on the line labelled Intercept is the square of the grand mean (68.266667) times the total number of subjects (60). That is:

$$NG^2 = 60(68.26667)^2 = 279620.3$$

To the extent that the grand mean is seldom very close to 0, this value will generally be quite large, and thus the other numbers given on this line are seldom of interest. Finally, the value of the sum of squares on the line labelled "TOTAL" is the sum of the sums of squares for all sources, including that for "Intercept." The corrected total below this omits the value for the Intercept, and corresponds to the Total Sum of Squares presented on page 82.

In the formulae presented on pages 81 and 82, the label for the error term was given as S/AB. In this table, it is referred to as Error. It should be emphasized, however, regardless of the label used, that the mean square associated with this source describes the variation among subjects nested in each group. In fact, a simple computation will reveal that the Mean Square for S/AB (or Error) = 50.208) is simply the mean of the variances for the cells (since cell sizes are equal). That is, using the values for the cell variances presented in Table 2 on page 80:

$$MS_{S/AB} = (62.80 + \cdots + 46.50 + \cdots + 91.70)/12 = 50.208$$

The analysis of variance summary table presents three additional columns, Eta-Squared, Noncentral Parameter, and Observed Power. Discussion of the Noncentral Parameter is beyond the scope of this chapter. The others, however, deserve comment. The values of eta-squared for A, B, and AB are, as can be seen, the values of the partial eta-squared (η^2) as discussed on page 84. The value for eta-squared for the Corrected Model (.469) is the "R Squared" shown as a footnote to the table, and it is calculated as the ratio of Sums of Squares Corrected Model divided by Sum of Squares Corrected Total (2127.73/4537.73 = .469). (The adjusted R Squared has no interpretative value.) The eta-squared for the Intercept is similarly of little interpretative value, but like the others it too is a partial eta-squared. In this example, therefore, attention would be directed primarily to the eta-squared values for A and AB since these were the two effects that were significant.

The values under Observed Power are the probabilities of obtaining significant values if these eta-squared values were in fact population values. Thus, it will be noted that the power for the A effect is .968. This means that 96.8% of the time we would expect to obtain significant ($p < .05$) results if we were to replicate the study. Similarly, 85.5% of the time, we would expect to obtain a significant AB interaction. It is also the case, that if the obtained estimates were in fact population values, 40.6% of the time we would expect to obtain a significant effect for B (but note, B was not significant in this analysis, therefore a more meaningful estimate of power is 0).

There is a growing movement to report power estimates because they provide useful information about the probability of obtaining significant results on replication. However, it must be kept in mind that these power values are estimates, and thus are susceptible to considerable variation from study to study. Clearly, the power estimates depend on the magnitude of the effects, so that if the F-ratio is significant, power will tend to be greater than if it is not significant, other things being equal. The values can be informative because they do give some measure of the confidence in your findings, however, they should be treated with caution, particularly in cases where the F-ratio is not significant. In such cases, as we have seen, we have no evidence to conclude that eta-squared is not 0 in the population. Using the estimated value to compute power, therefore, can be misleading. Sometimes it is the case that the power is low because the sample sizes are too small, and it is always possible that by increasing sample size, power will be increased and significance obtained. On the other hand, it must be remembered that the eta-squared values are only estimates, and if the null hypothesis is true, no amount of increased sample size will improve the chance of finding significance.

A final section presents the results for Levene's (1960) test of homogeneity of variance. This output is as follows:

Levene's Test of Equality of Error Variances[a]

Dependent Variable: X

F	$df1$	$df2$	Sig.
2.633	11	48	.010

Tests the null hypothesis that the error variance of the dependent variable is equal across groups.
[a] Design: Intercept $+ A + B + A * B$

The Levene (1960) test consists of an analysis of variance of the absolute deviations of each observation from the mean of the cell to which it belongs. If the Levene F-ratio is significant, this indicates that the assumption of homogeneity of variance has been violated. In this analysis there were $3 \times 4 = 12$ cells, with 5 observations per cell, thus the degrees of freedom for the F-ratio is $(12 - 1) = 11$ and $12(5 - 1) = 48$. To report Levene's F-ratio, then one would use the notation $[F(11,48) = 2.6333, p < .01]$, and conclude that the variances in the cells are heterogeneous. Inspection of the table of Descriptive Statistics (p. 91) will reveal that the standard deviation for group A_2B_3 is very large while that for group A_3B_2 is very small. In an actual experiment, it might be the case that the particular combination of A and B levels results in increased or decreased individual differences, and the researcher should consider whether or not this is the case. It could have interpretative value. In any event, as we have seen, as long as sample sizes are equal, violations of the homogeneity of variance assumption have little effect on the results and will not compromise interpretation. If sample sizes are unequal, on the other hand, the consequences can be severe and unpredictable (see, Milligan, Wong, & Thompson, 1987).

INTERPRETING RESULTS FROM AN ANALYSIS OF VARIANCE

Typically, it is the case that a researcher will interpret the results of an analysis of variance by considering the F-ratios one at a time. It is most often the case, moreover, that attention is directed only to the primary effects of interest, i.e., F_A, F_B, and F_{AB} in a two factor design. The F-ratios for A and B are referred to as tests of main effects, because they are concerned with the variability in the marginal means (i.e., the row and column means respectively). The F-ratio for AB is referred to as a test of an interaction effect.

Main Effects

The F-ratio for A is significant $[F(3,48) = 6.897, p < .001]$. This suggests that the four means for A (65.00, 63.60, 70.60, and 73.87) are more variable than would be expected on the basis of chance. This is the only information the significant F-ratio gives. You cannot say on the basis of this that the means all differ from each other, nor that any one mean necessarily differs significantly from any other. If one wishes to determine which of the means differ significantly from which other means, it is necessary to perform further tests. This is discussed below in the section labelled "Tests of Means." SPSS GLM does give one additional bit of information that is informative, and I suspect we will be seeing more of this in research articles in the future. This information is the estimate of power for each effect. In the analysis of variance summary table (p. 93), it is indicated that the power associated with the test of A is .968, and in a footnote to the table it is indicated that this estimate was computed using alpha = .05. This means that the probability of obtaining results significant at the .05 level on replication of your study is .968. Stated another way, if 100 other researchers were to do this study, the expectation is that 97 (you can't have 96.8 researchers) researchers would obtain results significant at the .05 level. That is, it is very likely that your results would replicate. This could be very informative in a research article, virtually as informative as the report that the results were significant.

The F-ratio for B is not significant $(F(2,48) = 2.072, ns)$. This suggests that the means for B (65.90, 70.45, and 68.45) are no more variable than you would expect by chance. Since this F-ratio is not significant, one would ordinarily not proceed to perform any tests of these means. Note that the estimate of power associated with this test is .406 (see the analysis of variance summary table on page 93). Some researchers might argue that since power is so low, this is why the results are not significant. That is, if the null hypothesis were false, you would expect to obtain significance at the .05 level, only 40.6% of the time. So that this study is one of the 59.4% of the studies that failed to obtain significant results. Perhaps larger sample sizes would yield significant results! This is always possible, of course, but it begs the question. If one adopts this line of reasoning, the research process loses all meaning. The most sensible solution would seem to be to conduct an investigation with the number of participants deemed necessary to detect an effect if it is there. If the F-ratio is not significant, conclude that there is no evidence to suggest that there is an effect. The power calculations are based on the η^2 values, and as indicated above, if the corresponding F-ratio is not significant, the best estimate of the variance accounted for is 0, hence the best estimate of η^2 is 0. In its calculations, however, SPSS used the value of .079.

Interaction Effects

The F-ratio for AB is significant [$F(6,48) = 2.924, p < .05$]. This suggests that the means in the cells do not act consistently across B (Sleep Deprivation) for each level of A, and/or they do not act consistently across A (Drugs) for each level of B, given the results from the tests of Main Effects. To elaborate, consider the meaning of the significant AB interaction in the light of the main effects described above. Above, it was noted that the A means were more variable than you could reasonably attribute to chance, while the B means were not. Other things being equal, we would expect, therefore, that allowing for sampling fluctuations, at each level of B, the A means would be more variable than might be attributed to chance (and display the same pattern as the main effect means for A), while at each level of A, the B means would not be any more variable than we would expect. The significant interaction indicates, however, that this is not the case. The means in the cells act differently from what you would expect given the results of the Main Effects.

The power estimate for this interaction is .855 (see the analysis of variance summary table on page 93). That is, the probability is .855 that researchers would obtain interaction effects significant at the .05 level if they were to replicate this study. This indicates that the results are quite stable, and that a researcher could have confidence in them.

Significant interactions are often demonstrated by plotting the cell means on a graph, much like that in Figure 1 below.

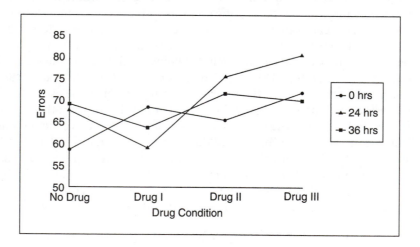

Figure 1. Errors as a Function of Drugs and Hours of Sleep Deprivation

One could plot Figure 1 in one of two ways, and the choice is up to the researcher. In Figure 1, I have indicated the four levels of the A factor on the X axis, and have drawn three plots, one for each level of B. In general, I recommend that, if there are different numbers of levels of A and B and there is no substantive reason to do otherwise, you should use the X axis for the factor with the greatest number of levels. The rationale for this is that you have fewer lines on the graph. Really, however, which you do is up to you, and some researchers find that one way of plotting the means may be easier to describe than another. Often, too, researchers interpret the interaction simply by describing the graph. There is much to be said for this approach because such verbal descriptions can refer to the entire figure which is, of course, presenting the entire interaction. The problem with this approach is that often "beauty is in the eye of the beholder," and one researcher's description may not be acceptable to another. It is often the case that researchers may wish to perform tests of the cell means to explain the interaction. These tests are often referred to as tests of simple main effects (see section on "Tests of Means," below). I recommend this approach, though as we shall see in that section these tests are not, strictly speaking, tests of the interaction (see also Kirk, 1995, pp. 377–383).

We could attempt a verbal description of Figure 1 as follows:

Inspection of Figure 1 suggests that, in general, errors tend to be higher under Drugs II and III than the other conditions, and there is a slight indication that fewer errors tend to made under the Control conditions (No Drug, No Sleep Deprivation) than the other conditions (with the possible exception of Drug I under 24 hours of sleep deprivation). If attention is directed toward the differences attributable to the hours of sleep deprivation for each drug condition, the following summary statements might be made:

(a) for the No Drug condition, learning appears to be much poorer (i.e., more errors) at 24 and 36 hours of sleep deprivation than at 0 hours;

(b) for Drug I, no sleep deprivation seems to result in poorer learning than 36 hours which, in turn, is poorer than at 24 hours;

(c) for Drug II, 24 hours results in poorer learning than 36 hours which, in turn, is poorer than for no sleep deprivation; and

(d) for Drug III, learning is poorer after 24 hours than it is after either 0 or 36 hours of sleep deprivation.

Alternatively, we might make similar observations concerning the differences between the drugs at each of the three periods of sleep deprivation. The problem with either of these types of verbal description is that the researcher makes somewhat arbitrary decisions about when a particular difference is large enough to be considered worth mentioning. For this reason, researchers often resort to post hoc tests of simple main effects when interpreting interactions, even though such tests confound interaction and main effects. We shall return to this later (see pp. 99–101).

TESTS OF MEANS

It is possible to distinguish between two different classes of tests of means in analysis of variance investigations. One class refers to *a priori* or planned comparisons, and the other refers to *a posteriori* or post hoc (also sometimes called data snooping) comparisons. Within each of these classifications, one can also distinguish between tests of main effect means and tests of cell means.

The major distinction between *a priori* and *a posteriori* tests lies in the definition of Type I error; another distinction is that *a priori* tests most often make use of some form of the t-test, while *a posteriori* tests make use of t, q, or F. The major distinction between *a priori* and *a posteriori* tests, however, lies in the definition of Type I error, and some of the *a posteriori* tests can be used for *a priori* tests by simply changing how one defines Type I error. Such considerations are beyond the scope of this chapter; see Kirk (1995) for further details.

In this chapter, we will consider the basic formulae used in such tests (t, q, and F), for tests of both main effects and simple main effects, and we will provide examples of Tukey's **HSD** q-statistic in each instance. These examples will focus on the actual value of q obtained, and procedures used to assess the significance of the q statistic.[1]

---

[1]These calculations would have to be conducted by hand. The author has an interactive program, Posthoc, designed for Window's application that will perform such calculations, and made use of it for all computations shown in this text. It was not possible, however, to include a copy of that program with this book.

It should be noted that **SPSS WINDOWS GLM General Factorial** provides two ways of conducting tests of main effect means, however, as in the application in the program **Oneway,** no summary statistics (i.e., t, q, or F) are given. One way involves clicking on the **Posthoc** button at Step 6, page 88. This procedure permits the use of any one of 18 procedures that are also used in the **Oneway** program. The other way involves clicking on **Options** at Step 6, page 88, and having moved the factors of interest over to the **Displays Means for** pane, clicking on the **Compare main effects** pane (see Step 7, pp. 88–89). This provides for the use of three tests using the t-distribution, but again the t-statistics are not given, only an indication of whether or not the difference is significant. There does not appear to be a way of performing tests of simple main effects using the **clope** approach, but it is possible to perform such tests of simple main effects using these three t-test procedures if you patch the job into the Syntax file. Thus, if you have transferred a*b to the **Display Means for** pane, and then paste your job to the Syntax Editor, you can edit the job. One line in the Syntax file will read /EMMEANS = TABLES(A*B). If you edit this line and add COMPARE (A), and run the job from the Syntax editor, it will perform the test of the simple main effects of A at B. Obviously, if you added COMPARE (B) instead, it would perform the tests of the simple main effects of B at A. These applications are not discussed in this chapter.

Tests of Main Effects

If the interaction is not significant, it is meaningful to test the differences between main effect means, providing the corresponding F-ratio is significant. The form of the tests is the same for the main effects of both A and B); however, in the present example, the F-ratio for B is not significant, so we will consider only the test statistics for the main effects of A. The formulae for the t, q, and F statistics for comparing level A_1 with A_2 are as follows, where nb refers to the number of observations making up each A mean.

$$t = \frac{\overline{X}_1 - \overline{X}_2}{\sqrt{\frac{2MS_{S/AB}}{nb}}}$$

$$q = \frac{\overline{X}_1 - \overline{X}_2}{\sqrt{\frac{MS_{S/AB}}{nb}}}$$

$$F = \frac{(\overline{X}_1 - \overline{X}_2)^2}{\frac{2MS_{S/AB}}{nb}}$$

Applying the formula for the q-statistic for Tukey's **HSD** for the comparison of the mean for A_1 with that for A_2 yields:

$$q = \frac{65.00 - 63.60}{\sqrt{\frac{50.208}{15}}}$$

$$= .765$$

There are four A means involved in the main effects of A, thus in terms of the Tukey **HSD** test, the maximum number of steps (r) is 4. To determine whether this q is significant, therefore, we would compare the obtained q with the value in the table for the Studentized range statistic for $r = 4$ steps, and $df_{S/AB} = 48$ (see Table D, the Appendix). Since our obtained q (.765) is not greater than the tabled q (3.79), we would conclude that the difference is not significant. (Note: since $df = 48$ does not occur in the table, we use the nearest df less than that, which is 40.) Similar tests could be made on the other contrasts of A means.

Tests of Simple Main Effects

When the AB interaction is significant, there is generally very little interest in the test of main effects since the interaction indicates that the variability in the cell means does not mirror that in the row (A) and/or column (B) means. Thus, one might turn one's attention to the cell means. In this case, one might perform tests of the simple main effects of A, or the simple main effects of B (but not both). There are a number of considerations that come into play when considering which simple main effects to investigate. An important one is the interest of the researcher. In our example, for instance, a researcher may be primarily interested in how learning is affected by sleep deprivation within each drug condition. The question would be "Do the differing periods of sleep deprivation influence learning under this drug?" In this case, one would conduct a test of the simple main effects of B (Sleep Deprivation) at A (Drugs). That is, for each set of contrasts, A is held constant and comparisons are made of the B means. On the other hand, the researcher might be interested more in whether at any given period of sleep deprivation, one or more drugs has a greater of lesser effect on learning than another. In this case, the researcher would be making a test of the simple main effects of A—holding B constant, and determining how the A means differ among themselves.

A second consideration might rest on the total variation involved. A test of simple main effects is not a test of the interaction, but rather a test of the combination of the interaction and the corresponding main effects. It can be shown (see, for example, Kirk 1995, pp. 377–380) that the sum of the sums of squares of the orthogonal[2] simple effect contrasts of a factor is equal to the sum of the Sums of Squares for the interaction and those for the corresponding main effect. Thus, the sum of squares for the orthogonal simple effects for A is:

$$1038.80 + 880.90 = 1919.70$$

while that for B is:

$$208.03 + 880.90 = 1088.93$$

One might anticipate, therefore, that she/he might find more significant contrasts by investigating the simple main effects of A rather than B, simply because there is more possible variability involved. Note, however, that these estimates are based on orthogonal contrasts and, in many post hoc tests, at least, many of the contrasts are not orthogonal.

A third consideration that often drives the decision of which set of simple main effects to investigate is a consideration of whether corresponding main effect F-ratios were significant as well as inspection of the graph of the means, like that shown in Figure 1. Inspection of the graph might indicate which contrasts may be the most interesting and the most profitable in terms of number of significant contrasts and interpretability. If one attempts a description of the figure like that made on

---

[2] Two contrasts are said to be orthogonal when they are nonredundant or uncorrelated. By this is meant that there is no overlap in the information provided by the two contrasts. A simple example of two orthogonal contrasts would be the contrast of the A_1 mean minus the A_2 mean and the contrast of the A_3 mean minus the A_4 mean. These two contrasts are said to be orthogonal because there is no overlapping information contained in them. A simple example of two non-orthogonal contrasts would be the contrast of the A_1 minus A_2 means, and the A_1 minus the A_3 mean. These two contrasts are non-orthogonal because they involve overlapping information in that the mean for A_1 is involved in both. Procedures for determining whether or not contrasts are orthogonal are discussed by Kirk (1995, pp. 115–118).

page 97, this also helps one decide which set of simple main effects to conduct. The one point that should be remembered in all of this is that having decided to make one set of simple main effect contrasts, one should stick with that, and not perform the others as well—since these will be redundant with the first set.

The formulae for the t, q, and F statistics for the simple main effects of A_1 minus A_2 at B_1 are:

$$t = \frac{\overline{X}_{11} - \overline{X}_{21}}{\sqrt{\dfrac{2MS_{S/AB}}{n}}}$$

$$q = \frac{\overline{X}_{11} - \overline{X}_{21}}{\sqrt{\dfrac{MS_{S/AB}}{n}}}$$

$$F = \frac{(\overline{X}_{11} - \overline{X}_{21})^2}{\dfrac{2MS_{S/AB}}{n}}$$

Application of the Tukey **HSD** test produces the following result:

$$q = \frac{58.6 - 68.2}{\sqrt{\dfrac{50.208}{5}}}$$

$$q = -3.029$$

As before, this would be evaluated at $r = 4$ steps, and $df = 48$. Since the obtained q (−3.029) is not larger in absolute value than the tabled value of q (3.79), we would conclude that this difference is not significant. We could perform Tukey **HSD** tests between the Sleep Deprivation levels at each level of Drug, or between the Drug Levels at each level of Sleep Deprivation. If we were doing tests of the simple main effects of B at each level of A, we would consider the differences between the B means at each level of A, and reorder the means from lowest to highest. With these data, we would find that none of the contrasts involving simple main effects of B at each level of A were significant using the Tukey **HSD** procedure. If, however, we performed tests of the simple main effects of A at each level of B, some significant effects would be obtained. If we computed all six of the q-statistics comparing the four means two at a time, and identified those that were significant, and those that were not, we could summarize the pattern of results by ordering the means from lowest to highest, and then drawing lines under means that did not differ significantly from one another. Following is one way to present the results. In the presentation, means sharing a common underlining do not differ significantly from one another. Thus, for no sleep deprivation, the results were:

Drug Condition	1	3	2	4
	58.6	65.2	68.2	71.6

In interpreting these results, we might conclude that under the "No Sleep Deprivation" condition, only the difference between Drug Condition 4 and Drug Condition 1 differs significantly ($p < .05$). That is, Drug 4 results in significantly more errors than the No Drug condition. None of the other differences were significant.

The results for the 24-hour sleep deprivation condition were:

Drug Condition   2   1   3   4
                   59.0 67.4 75.2 80.2

These results indicate that there are three sets of overlapping groups of means. Drug Condition 4 differs significantly from Drug Conditions 1 and 2, while Drug Condition 3 differs significantly from Drug Condition 2.

The post hoc analysis for the 36-hour sleep deprivation condition found no significant differences between pairs of means. The results were:

Drug Condition   2   1   4   3
                   63.6 69.0 69.8 71.4

The common line indicates that none of the differences between pairs of means were significant at the .05 level using the Tukey **HSD** procedure.

Taking these results together, clearly there are different patterns of the relative effects of the drugs under the different sleep deprivation conditions. Under no sleep deprivation, the means form two overlapping groupings, under 24 hours, they form three overlapping groups; and under 36 hours, they form one grouping. The most consistent finding appears to be that Drug 4 differs significantly from the No Drug condition under 0 and 24 hours of sleep deprivation, but not under 36 hours of sleep deprivation. That is, when stress on the body is relatively low, Drug 4 appears to impair learning in comparison with no drug. There is also the suggestion that Drug 4 differs from Drug 2, and Drug 3 differs from Drug 2 under 24 hours of sleep deprivation. Future research might focus attention on the relative effects of the drugs under conditions of mild stress (like the 24-hour sleep deprivation condition). It might also be meaningful to consider attempting to replicate the present study with larger sample sizes to improve the power of the tests of the differences. The patterns of means for the 0- and 24-hour sleep deprivation conditions are suggestive of possible effects of the other drugs, but the sample size may have been too low in this study to detect them.

EXPECTED MEAN SQUARES

An important concept in analysis of variance is that of the expected mean square. We have seen above that the mean square is a form of variance and that it takes a numerical value. Thus, the mean square for A, (MS_A), is the sum of squares for A divided by its degrees of freedom, and, in our example, it had the value 346.267. The *expected mean square* refers to the population values estimated by this number. That is, the expected mean square indicates what population variances are estimated by the value obtained in any given study.

There are two types of factors that are possible when conducting an analysis of variance. One, and by far the most common, is a *fixed factor*. A fixed factor is one for which each level of the factor in the population is included in the experiment. When the results of the experiment are interpreted, they apply only to the levels of the factor in the experiment. Thus, if we have an experiment where one factor is Sex of Subject, there are only two levels of that factor and we make conclusions about the differences between these two levels. The other type of factor is a *random factor*. A random factor is one in which it is assumed that there are a number of levels of the factor in the population, but only a random sample of them are included in the experiment. Any generalizations made about a random factor apply to all possible levels of that factor, not merely those included in the experiment. The best example of a random factor is Subjects. We include only a (random) sample of all possible subjects in any one experiment, but we generalize our results to all subjects.

These definitions are fairly straightforward, however, sometimes the decision of whether or not a factor is fixed or random appears somewhat arbitrary even though it is not. Consider the two factors in our example, Type of Drug, and Hours of Sleep Deprivation. At first glance, they would appear to be examples of random factors. There are many possible drugs that might be considered in an experiment, and many possible hours of sleep deprivation, and we have included only four and three of them, respectively. However, we have considered them as fixed factors because we are interested in making generalizations only about these particular levels. We do not want to generalize about all possible drugs, only a No Drug condition and the effects of Drugs I, II, and III. Similarly, in terms of sleep deprivation, we are concerned only with what happens at 0, 24 and 36 hours of sleep deprivation. Since our focus is on only the four drug conditions as described here and the three sleep deprivation conditions, the two factors are considered fixed.

If it were the case that the four drug conditions were obtained randomly, and/or the three sleep deprivation conditions were determined randomly, then the factor(s) in question would be considered random. We then would be interested only in whether or not there was significant variation in the results, but we would not be interested in determining how any one level differed from any other. Thus, we would not, for example, be interested in doing any tests of the difference between any two means, because to do so would indicate an interest in the specific level of the factor(s) concerned—which is not an interest with random factors.

The distinction between fixed and random factors is important in analysis of variance because it influences which mean squares will be involved in constructing F-ratios. In the **SPSS WINDOWS GLM General Factorial** program, factors can be defined as fixed or random (see Step 5, p. 88). I recommend caution in using this option, however. At the time of writing this chapter, the models used by SPSS are not the same as those discussed in most statistics books. That is, the rationale used in generating the expected mean squares is non-standard. At least, for a two-factor analysis, for which one factor is fixed and the other random, the F-ratio for the random factor is incorrect, given common conceptualizations of fixed and random factors in standard textbooks dealing with psychological statistics (e.g., Kirk, 1995) and briefly presented in the next paragraphs. It is true that alternative conceptualizations are possible (see, for example, Montgomery, 1984, pp. 218–223) but they are non-standard, and do not appear applicable to most psychological research.

The following table indicates the general form of the Expected Mean Squares for a two-factor analysis of variance. Three forms are shown, one where both factors A and B are fixed, one where A is fixed and B is random, and one where both A and B are random.

	A FIXED B FIXED	A FIXED B RANDOM	A RANDOM B RANDOM
A	$\dfrac{bn\sum\limits_{a}^{a}\alpha_a^2}{a-1} + \sigma_\epsilon^2$	$\dfrac{bn\sum\limits_{a}^{a}\alpha_a^2}{a-1} + n\sigma_{AB}^2 + \sigma_\epsilon^2$	$bn\sigma_A^2 + n\sigma_{AB}^2 + \sigma_\epsilon^2$
B	$\dfrac{n\sum\limits_{b}^{b}\beta_b^2}{(b-1)} + \sigma_\epsilon^2$	$an\sigma_B^2 + \sigma_\epsilon^2$	$an\sigma_B^2 + n\sigma_{AB}^2 + \sigma_\epsilon^2$
AB	$\dfrac{n\sum\limits_{a}^{a}\sum\limits_{b}^{b}\alpha\beta_{ab}^2}{(a-1)(b-1)} + \sigma_\epsilon^2$	$n\sigma_{AB}^2 + \sigma_\epsilon^2$	$n\sigma_{AB}^2 + \sigma_\epsilon^2$
S/AB	σ_ϵ^2	σ_ϵ^2	σ_ϵ^2

This table of expected means squares indicates the population values that are included in each mean square estimated in a two factor analysis of variance. It is beyond the scope of this chapter to explain how the table is determined; however, it is presented to indicate how the correct F-ratios are calculated for the different models. The one model that isn't shown is for when A is random, and B is fixed. This is left as an exercise for the student.

The rationale for constructing F-ratios is to determine a ratio that has one more element in the numerator than in the denominator, and have this element to be the measure of variability of the effect in question. Thus, for the situation where both A and B are fixed, the expected mean square for A is shown to have two components, $bn\sum_a \alpha_a^2/(a-1)$ and σ_ϵ^2. Dividing this by a mean square that estimates only σ_ϵ^2 (i.e., $MS_{S/AB}$) would yield an F-ratio that estimates $bn\sum_a \alpha_a^2/(a-1)$. If the F-ratio is significant, this would indicate that this value is not 0, and that there is, therefore, an effect due to A. If the F-ratio were not significant, this would suggest that this value is 0, and that, therefore, there was no effect due to A. In much the same way, it can be determined whether there are effects due to B, and due to AB.

The same rationale can be used on the other models. It will be noted, for example, that when A is fixed and B is random, the appropriate F-ratio for A would have the mean square for AB in the denominator, while the appropriate F-ratio for B would have the mean square for S/AB in the denominator. **SPSS WINDOWS GLM General Factorial,** however, also uses the mean square for the interaction as the denominator (this is the non-standard solution referred to earlier). As can be seen in this table, the presence of a random factor influences what will be the error term (i.e., denominator of the F-ratio) for the other factor.

UNEQUAL SAMPLE SIZES

To now, we have focussed attention on the factorial design analysis of variance when sample sizes are equal. Under such conditions the analysis is said to be *balanced* (or orthogonal). If sample sizes are not equal, however, the analysis is said to be unbalanced (or non-orthogonal). There are many good reasons for always making sure that the design is balanced, one of which concerns the difficulties one encounters when sample sizes are unequal and the assumption of homogeneity of variance is not met. A second reason concerns the fact that there are a number of different models that might be used when sample sizes are not equal, and that these different models can yield different results. Four such models are the unweighted means analysis, and three least-squares estimates models, referred to as Model I (SSTYPE3) (Regression), Model II (SSTYPE2) (Classic Experimental), and Model III (SSTYPE1) (Hierarchical).[3] A third reason concerns the question of just what means are being referred to when attempting to perform tests of means following a significant F-ratio.

It is beyond the scope of this chapter to discuss the different models in detail. Suffice it to say that the unweighted means analysis focuses attention on the means in the cells of the table (in the case of a three factor analysis, this would be the ABC cell), calculates the $MS_{S/ABC}$ as a weighted average of the cell variances, estimates the $A, B, C, AB, AC, BC,$ and G means by averaging the means of the ABC cells (hence, the name unweighted means analysis), and estimating the average cell size using the harmonic mean of the cell ns. The analysis then proceeds using the definitional formulae (as modified) presented earlier. Kirk (1995) recommends against the use of this type of analysis, given the availability of the least squares procedures, but one advantage of it is that you

---

[3]A note on notation is in order. The terms Model I, II, and III were used by Overall and Spiegel (1969) to refer to the three different procedures. In **SPSS** and other sources, they have since been referred to as SSTYPE 3, 2, and 1, respectively. The transposition of the numbers 1, 2, and 3 is not a typographical error.

know precisely what means are being considered in the various F-ratios that are computed when it comes to perform follow-up tests of means.

The three least-squares procedures are best understood in terms of multiple regression procedures, and again will not be discussed in any detail here. Spinner and Gabriel (1981), however, present an excellent and very clear discussion of these models. In essence, all three models involve the construction of a number of codes (referred to as effect codes) representing the various main effects and interaction effects. These are then used in a series of multiple regression procedures, and tests of the differences between squared multiple correlations are performed using F-ratios. If sample sizes are equal, these F-ratios are identical to those used following the procedures discussed above. If, however, there are unequal sample sizes, different F-ratios (and thus, Mean Squares, etc.) will be obtained. The different models (Model I, Model II, and Model III or SSTYPE3, SSTYPE2, and SSTYPE1) result because of different squared multiple correlations that are considered in the computations, based on what terms (i.e., Effect Codes) are omitted from the multiple correlations that are calculated. The following table makes use of a three-factor analysis of variance to indicate just what adjustments are made.

Effects Removed in Computing the R^2 for Each Source in the Three Models

Effect	Model I SSTYPE3 (Regression) (SPSS WINDOWS DEFAULT)	Model II SSTYPE2 (Classic Experimental)	Model III SSTYPE1 (Hierarchical)
A	B,C,AB,AC,BC,ABC	B,C	none
B	A,C,AB,AC,BC,ABC	A,C	A
C	A,B,AB,AC,BC,ABC	A,B	A,B
AB	A,B,C,AC,BC,ABC	A,B,C,AC,BC	A,B,C,AC,BC
AC	A,B,C,AB,BC,ABC	A,B,C,AB,BC	A,B,C,AB,BC
BC	A,B,C,AB,AC,ABC	A,B,C,AB,AC	A,B,C,AB,AC
ABC	A,B,C,AB,AC,BC	A,B,C,AB,AC,BC	A,B,C,AB,AC,BC

To illustrate, consider Model I and the R^2 for the A effect. This would be computed as follows:

$$R'^2_A = R^2_{A,B,C,AB,AC,BC,ABC} - R^2_{B,C,AB,AC,BC,ABC}$$

The R^2 for A for Model II would be:

$$R'^2_A = R^2_{A,B,C} - R^2_{B,C}$$

The R^2 for A for Model III would be:

$$R'^2_A = R^2_A$$

Model I is often referred to as the Unique Sum of Squares approach because all other sources of variation are removed when estimating the variance of each effect. As you might imagine, each of these procedures have their supporters, and the rationale for deciding which is the most appropriate involves decisions that are beyond the scope of this chapter. The current choice in psychology appears to be Model I (see, for example, Kirk, 1995, p. 422–426; Myers & Well, 1991, p. 559), while Myers and Well (1991, p. 563) refer to situations where Model III might be appropriate.

One difficulty with all three of these approaches is that each of them are concerned with estimating sources of variance when the analysis is not balanced. They are not strictly concerned with describing the variability in specific means. Thus, having performed any one of these analyses, if one wishes to proceed to a contrast of means, one might well ask what means? If the focus is the highest order interaction, this is not a problem since the obtained means are the means of interest. But for any other source, the issue of which means to consider is not clear. To the extent that Model I refers to the unique sources of variation, a case can be made for focussing attention on the unweighted means when proceeding with tests of means. In fact, Horst and Edwards (1982) have demonstrated that for the case of completely randomized factorial designs in which all factors have only two levels, the results for Model I and the Unweighted means analysis are identical, even though they are not for factors having more than two levels.

Chapter 5
Single-Factor Repeated Measures Designs

This chapter is concerned with the use of analysis of variance with data based on repeated observations of the same subjects. The simplest form of a repeated measures design is one in which there is only one treatment factor. For example, consider the situation in which you wished to investigate the effects of four levels of alcohol consumption (0, 2, 4, and 6 ounces) on memory for a list of 100 words read once. If this study were conducted as a completely randomized single factor design (see Chapter 3), subjects would be randomly sampled and assigned independently to one of the four treatment conditions. In this study then, you might, for example, have individuals read the list of words, then in the next 10 minutes have them drink the allotted liquid and then test them for their memory. To conduct it as a repeated measures design, however, we would proceed slightly differently. Thus, in our example, we would obtain a random sample of subjects, and test them under each of the four alcohol conditions. We might, for example have them read the list of words, then have them drink the allotted amount of liquid in the 10-minute period, and then test them for their memory. We could then have them read the list again, drink the allotted liquid, and test them again etc., until the four treatment conditions are finished. As you can see this second approach is not without its problems, and no one would recommend it as a meaningful way to approach the problem. The example is useful, however, in that it does highlight some of the non-numerical problems that one must consider when using repeated measures designs. We shall return to this again in the section on Design Issues (see below). The point emphasized here is that the purpose of a completely randomized single factor design and the single factor repeated measures design can be exactly the same, only the nature of the sampling and some logistical considerations are different. But these differences can have far-reaching implications.

There are two analytic approaches that can be employed with repeated measure designs. One uses a univariate approach where the factor (e.g., B) is treated as an independent variable. It can be viewed as a single factor analysis of variance not unlike the completely randomized single factor design, except that the observations in the various treatments are not independent. Or it can be viewed as a two factor design (B and S) with only one observation per cell. Regardless of which conceptualization one prefers, the arithmetic is identical. The second approach considers the problem in multivariate terms, and treats the data as being comprised of a number of measures obtained on a single group of individuals. We shall consider each approach separately, the first in what I will refer to as the *Univariate Approach,* and the second that I will discuss as the *Multivariate Approach*. Unfortunately, when you analyze data using SPSS, it presents the output in a mixed form so it is necessary for you to identify which output is appropriate to the approach you have decided to follow. To confound the issue, the two approaches sometimes lead to different conclusions—one yielding significant results, and the other not. To confound things even further, you will find that some researchers insist that you should use the multivariate approach, but you will find too that many of the better known textbooks on analysis of variance (e.g., Kirk, 1995; Myers & Well, 1991) focus most attention on the univariate approach, sometimes to the exclusion of the multivariate approach. Most journal articles also seem to favor the univariate approach, at least among the journals I read.

Although some researchers prefer one approach over the other, neither is uniformly the best. O'Brien and Kaiser (1985) comment that , as long as adjustments are made to counteract the effects of violations of assumptions in the univariate approach, both approaches control the Type I error rate quite well. Moreover, neither demonstrates greater power than the other. O'Brien and Kaiser (1985) perhaps sum it up best when they state "Because no clear-cut power differences exist, the best strategy is to choose a single method and seek to master it, We believe that method should be the MANOVA (i.e., multivariate) approach" (parenthetical comment added) (p. 319).

DESIGN ISSUES

There are a number of factors to be considered when making use of a repeated measures design. These can be made clearest, I believe, by considering a single factor repeated measures design like that discussed in this chapter. The observations apply, however, to any type of design that involves repeated measures. Examples of such more complex designs are the split-plot factorial design to be considered in Chapter 6, or repeated measures factorial designs. The latter are not considered in this book, but the extension should be very clear.

The issues are highlighted in the experiment described earlier when we were interested in studying the effects of alcohol consumption on the memory of a word list. It is fairly obvious that if you were interested in conducting the experiment described above, you would be far better off using the completely randomized single factor design instead of the repeated measures design for three reasons. First, with the repeated measures design, there would be general *memory and/or fatigue effects*. That is, to do the study as described, you would have to in essence run the subject through the sequence of events four times. Since the individual would thus see the list four times, it is likely that subjects would remember some of the words on subsequent presentations even if no treatments were applied. Moreover, they might become somewhat fatigued over time. An individual's second experience in a study is not the same as the first, and one must be aware of this in repeated measure designs. The mere act of testing more than once will have an influence on scores obtained. There is no way of combatting this effect. Second, if you were to conduct the study all in one testing session, there would be *carryover effects* of the alcohol. Carryover effects refer simply to the cumulative effects of the treatment. The alcohol would accumulate in the bloodstream, so that in the 4-ounce condition, for example, the subjects would actually have something in the neighborhood of 6 ounces of alcohol in their system if it followed the 2-ounce condition, and 10 ounces if it followed the 6-ounce condition. By the time the individuals had taken part in all conditions, they would have consumed 12 ounces of alcohol, and it is quite possible that they wouldn't even remember the earlier conditions, or at least they probably wouldn't be able to discuss them very coherently! The consequences of carryover effects are obvious with treatments like levels of alcohol consumed, but they exist with all repeated measure factors. Carryover effects can be minimized by having a large inter-treatment interval. Thus, if you were to conduct this study over a four-week period, administering one alcohol condition each week, the alcohol would have dissipated in the interim, and would no longer be in the system. It is still the case, however, that the individual might have some recollection of the earlier experience, which could be considered one aspect of the carryover effect.

The third reason why repeated measure designs can be problematic is because of *order effects*. These can be seen as similar to carry over effects, but they are different in that they refer more to the order in which the treatments are administered. Consider again, our example of the repeated measure experiment where all testing is done in the same session. You can imagine the behavior of an individual who received the treatments in the order 0, 2, 4, and 6 ounces and compare that with the individual who received them in the order of 6, 4, 2, and 0 ounces. The results of the two individuals would be much different under, for example, the 0-ounce condition for a couple of reasons. For the first individual, the 0-ounce condition is the first experience with the experiment. For the second individual, it is the fourth. Moreover, for the first individual, no alcohol had been consumed prior to the 0-ounce condition, while for the second, 12 ounces had. Similar observations could be made for the other conditions. Simply, the order in which the treatment levels are administered can influence the results obtained in a way over and above the treatment condition itself. Often different orders are used in repeated measure experiments to "eliminate" order effects. It doesn't really eliminate the effects, however. It simply confounds the effects of order by averaging them out. Carryover effects are still present, and the means for the treatments could be much different than they would be if subjects were tested only once, instead of repeatedly.

You can see, therefore, that there can be some very serious logistical difficulties with repeated measures designs, and one shouldn't be surprised to find that the same study conducted as a completely randomized single factor design and as a repeated measures design, might well yield different results. In the completely randomized single factor design, each participant is tested only once; in the repeated measures design each participant is tested more than once, so that on subsequent testings not only the treatment condition is changing, but so is the participant's experience with the materials and the situation. The effects of these extraneous factors are exaggerated in the alcohol experiment described here, making this a very poor experiment indeed. It does, however, highlight potential problems with repeated measure designs, and these exist, regardless of the nature of the treatment. This is not to say that one should not use repeated measure designs. One should, however, be aware of the implications of such designs.

One of the advantages of the repeated measures design is that each subject serves as his or her own control, and thus the effects of individual differences are minimized. This is a definite asset, and the repeated measures design is much more efficient as a result. As indicated above, however, this efficiency is not without it problems. An alternative approach to this problem which would be appropriate to our experiment is what has been referred to as a randomized blocks design. This design is numerically equivalent to the single factor repeated measures design, but lacks some of the problems. It is described in a later section on "Randomized Block Designs" (p. 125).

BASIC ARITHMETIC AND SAMPLE DATA

Let us assume that despite our misgivings we had conducted the study described above, with a large inter-treatment interval to reduce carry over and memory effects, and by using different random orders of presentation to minimize order effects. In this study we tested 6 participants, each under the four treatment conditions. Assume that in the following table, $B1$ refers to the 0 ounces of alcohol condition, $B2$ refers to the 2-ounce condition, $B3$ refers to the 4-ounce condition, and $B4$ refers to the 6-ounce condition.

Subject	$B1$	$B2$	$B3$	$B4$	$\bar{P_i}$
1	80	70	40	29	54.75
2	70	54	47	31	50.50
3	50	62	38	31	45.25
4	50	43	41	29	40.75
5	40	34	20	17	27.75
6	23	27	21	14	21.25
Mean	52.17	48.33	34.50	25.17	40.04

THE UNIVARIATE APPROACH

The univariate approach treats the above data as a series of four observations obtained from six individuals in four different treatment conditions. As can be seen the table looks very similar to that presented in Chapter 3 on the completely randomized single factor design, except that each subject contributes to each treatment condition. Because of this it would be possible to calculate the correlation between each pair of treatment conditions. In the completely randomized single factor design these correlations would all be 0, by definition. The table also looks like the table in Chapter 4 for the completely randomized factorial design. The table above could be considered as referring to a 6×4 design with one observation per cell.

Each observation (e.g., 80) in the table refers to an X_{ib}, the means for each treatment are referred to as $\bar{X_b}$, the mean for each participant is identified as $\bar{P_i}$, and the grand mean is coded as $\bar{G}$. The formulae for the Sums of Squares, and Degrees of Freedom for this analysis are as follows:

Source	Sum of Squares	df
Between Subjects	$\overset{i}{\Sigma}(\bar{P}_i - G)^2$	$(n-1)$
Within Subjects		
B	$n\overset{b}{\Sigma}(\bar{X}_b - \bar{G})^2$	$(b-1)$
BS	$\overset{b}{\Sigma}\overset{i}{\Sigma}(X_{ib} - \bar{P}_i - \bar{X}_b + \bar{G})^2$	$(b-1)(n-1)$

Note in this breakdown that B is considered as a Within Subjects effect because of the repeated measures on B. The application of these formulae are shown below:

BETWEEN SUBJECT VARIATION

$$SS_S = 4[(54.75 - 40.04)^2 + ... + (21.25 - 40.04)^2] \qquad = 3430.21$$

$$DF_S = (6-1) = 5 \qquad\qquad MS_S = 3430.21/5 = 686.04$$

WITHIN SUBJECT VARIATION

$$SS_B = (6)[(52.17 - 40.04)^2 = ... + (25.17 - 40.04)^2] \qquad = 2806.46$$

$$SS_{BS} = (80 - 54.75 - 52.17 + 40.04)^2 + ...$$

$$+ (14 - 21.25 - 25.17 + 40.04)^2 \qquad = 970.29$$

$$DF_B = (4-1) = 3 \qquad\qquad MS_B = 2806.46/3 = 935.49$$

$$DF_{BS} = (4-1)(6-1) = 15 \qquad\qquad MS_{BS} = 970.29/15 = 64.69$$

$$F_B = 935.49/64.69 = 14.46$$

If all assumptions (see below) were met, this F-ratio could be evaluated for significance using the table of the F-distribution (Table C, Appendix). The degrees of freedom for the F-ratio would be 3 and 15 in this example.

This information can be summarized in a table as follows:

Source	Sum of Squares	df	Mean Square	F-ratio
Between Ss (S)	3430.21	5	686.04	
Within Ss				
B	2806.46	3	935.49	14.46
BS	970.29	15	64.69	
Total		23		

Since the data are correlated, we could compute a variance/covariance matrix showing the variation in the various cells and the relationships between them. We have already seen that the definition of the variance is:

$$s^2 = \frac{\Sigma(X_i - \bar{X})^2}{n-1}$$

The formula for a covariance is:

$$cov = \frac{\Sigma(X_i - \overline{X})(Y_i - \overline{Y})}{n - 1}$$

Using these formulae, we could compute the following variance/covariance matrix:

	B1	B2	B3	B4
$B1$	420.168	296.533	184.900	122.967
$B2$	296.533	275.467	139.800	106.133
$B3$	184.900	139.800	126.700	81.700
$B4$	122.967	106.133	81.700	57.767

The diagonal values in the above table are the variances, the off-diagonal values are the co-variances. Note that the table is symmetrical in that the values above the diagonal are the same as those below the diagonal (i.e., the $B1B2$ value is identical to the $B2B1$ value). If you were to compute the mean of the variances and also the mean of the covariances, you could compute the difference between the two. If you did, you would obtain the value of the Mean Square for BS as:

$$\overline{s^2} - \overline{cov} = 220.03 - 154.34 = 64.69$$

This is an important observation. The Mean Square for BS is equal to the mean of the variances for the treatments minus the mean of the covariances. You will recall from our discussion of the completely randomized single-factor design (Chapter 3) that the Mean Squares within groups was simply the mean of the sample variances. Thus, it would generally be larger than the Mean Squares for BS. All that is required is that the mean of the covariances be positive, and this is generally the case. As we saw, the Mean Square for BS is used as the denominator for the F-ratio to evaluate the effects of B, thus, other things being equal the F-ratio for the repeated-measures design would tend to be larger than that for the completely randomized single-factor design. The value of the degrees of freedom associated with the Mean Square for BS, however, is smaller than that for the Mean Square within groups.

Assumptions

There are four assumptions underlying the single-factor repeated measures design analysis of variance. They are:

1. *Independent Random Sampling.* Like all statistical analyses, it is assumed that the subjects are randomly obtained, or at least can be considered a random sample of the population of interest. Random sampling means that any one observation in the sample is independent of any other observation in the sample, and this is a necessary precondition to determine the underlying sampling distribution. Note that this requirement of independence does not mean that the observations in one treatment condition are unrelated to those in another condition. In fact, one of the strengths of the repeated measures design is that the observations are generally positively correlated, and this results in a smaller estimate of the variance due to error than what would be obtained if the observations were uncorrelated, or negatively correlated, for that matter! The point is that the various replications (i.e., subjects) must be independent.

2. *Normality.* As with the completely randomized single factor design, it is assumed that the distributions in the sub-populations are normally distributed. Unlike the completely randomized design, however, it cannot be assumed that the observations in one treatment condition are independent of those in another, and this has implications for the analysis.

3. *Circularity of the Variance/Covariance Matrix.* The assumption of circularity of the variance/covariance matrix means that the variance of the difference between any two treatment subpopulations is equal to the variance of the difference between any other two. Thus, you could form a difference score of the form $B1 - B2$, and calculate the variance of this difference. You could then calculate the difference $B1 - B3$, and compute the variance of the resulting numbers, and do this for all possible pairs. In our example, there would be six such differences, and their variances can be shown to be 102.57, 177.07, 232.00, 122.57, 120.97, and 21.07 for $B1 - B2$, $B1 - B3$, ..., $B3 - B4$ respectively. Incidentally, you need not compute the variances of the differences this way. They could be computed directly from the variance/covariance matrix as follows:

$$S^2_{B1\text{-}B2} = S^2_{B1} + S^2_{B2} - 2\text{cov}_{B1B2} = 420.17 + 275.47 - 2(296.53) = 102.57$$

As can be seen from the values of the variances given in the previous paragraph, they are generally very similar with the exception of that for $B3 - B4$, which is considerably smaller. There are a number of tests that can be used to determine whether they differ sufficiently to suggest that the underlying populations of differences differ in variance. The procedure used by SPSS GLM is the Mauchly (1940) test of Sphericity.

4. *Null Hypothesis.* The null hypothesis for the single-factor repeated measures design is the same as that for the completely randomized single-factor design. That is:

$$H_0: \mu_1 = \mu_2 = \mu_3 = \mu_4 = \mu$$

This states that the means of the treatment subpopulations are equal, and thus equal to their mean. If all of the assumptions are true, the F-ratio MS_B / MS_{BS} is distributed as F with $(b - 1)$ and $(b - 1)(n - 1)$ degrees of freedom. If these assumptions are not satisfied, particularly the assumption of circularity, the F-ratio has a positive bias. That is, the F-ratio will be inflated, and the Type I error rate will be larger than the tabled value (often considerably so!). It is because of this positive bias that it is recommended that some adjustments be made when evaluating the F-ratio for significance, regardless of the results of the Mauchly test. We shall discuss this in a later section.

THE MULTIVARIATE APPROACH

In the multivariate approach, the data are treated as a single-group design with b-dependent variables. Lewis (1993) states that this approach was first introduced by Rao (1952) who proposed that since the b measures are all measured on the same scale (i.e., the measure is the same, it is simply made at different times under different conditions), new variables could be formed consisting of differences between the pairs of variables. These new variables could then be analyzed using Hotelling's T^2, which is a special case of multivariate analysis of variance. This logic is used in **SPSS GLM** for repeated measures.

Assumptions

Three assumptions underly this test. It will be noted that none of these assumptions refer to circularity of the variance/covariance matrix. This is because this assumption is not necessary for the multivariate approach. This is one major reason why researchers such as O'Brien and Kaiser (1985) and Lewis (1993) recommend its use. The assumptions underlying this test are:

1. *Independent Random Samples.* As with the univariate approach, it is assumed that the observations are randomly obtained from the population of interest. As stated earlier, this means simply that the various replications are independent.

2. *Multivariate Normality* The assumption of multivariate normality means that not only must the variables individually be normally distributed, but that their conjoint distributions must also be normal. Although this is a necessary assumption, it has been demonstrated that the multivariate analysis of variance is robust with respect to violations of this assumption. That is, even if this assumption is not satisfied, the Type I error rate is not materially affected. This is just as well! Since tests of multivariate normality are somewhat complex, researchers seldom even concern themselves with evaluating the validity of the assumption.

3. *Null Hypothesis.* The null hypothesis could be stated in univariate terms as:

$$H_0: \mu_1 - \mu_4 = \mu_2 - \mu_4 = \mu_3 - \mu_4 = 0$$

That is, the difference between the means of population 1 and 4 is equal to the difference between populations 2 and 4 is equal to the difference between populations 3 and 4 is equal to 0. This is often expressed in matrix form as:

$$\begin{vmatrix} \mu_1 - \mu_4 \\ \mu_2 - \mu_4 \\ \mu_3 - \mu_4 \end{vmatrix} = 0$$

It will be noted that this multivariate null hypothesis is equivalent to the univariate null hypothesis given above that:

$$H_0: \mu_1 = \mu_2 = \mu_3 = \mu_4 = \mu$$

Note that any form of the difference score can be used as long as the net effect is that setting the difference scores all to zero indicates that the means are identical. Using **SPSS GLM** to test this null hypothesis results in a multivariate analysis of variance. This procedure produces four different test statistics, Pillai's Trace, Wilks' Lambda, Hotelling's Trace, and Roy's Largest Root. Although the four procedures yield three different values, the corresponding F-ratios are identical. The degrees of freedom associated with these F-ratios are $(b - 1)$ and $(N - b + 1)$ respectively. As indicated above, moreover these F-ratios are identical to the Hotelling's T^2.

A BIT OF HISTORY

The most extensive review of repeated measures designs appears to be that of Lovie (1981). In it, he identifies the major publications in the history of this technique, and reviews substantive articles as well as other review articles (such as Kogan, 1953) on the topic. In his review, he lumps together a number of designs that involve repeated measures, including the single-factor repeated measures design which is the focus of this chapter, but also other designs such as the split-plot design (see Chapter 6), and multifactor-repeated measure designs that are not discussed in this book.

It is generally agreed that L. G. Humphreys provided the initial formulations of repeated measures designs. Rucci and Tweney (1980) state for example that "Gilliland and D. W. Humphreys (1943) acknowledged L. Humphreys for providing the computational formulas for the repeated measures analysis used in their study" (p. 173). Edwards (1950) also cites articles by L. G. Humphreys (1943) and Gilliland and D. W. Humphreys (1943) as the first presentations of repeated measures designs, but Lovie (1981) claims that analyses of repeated measures originated as early as 1926. Like many statistical procedures, however, there are often antecedents that can be identified. Statistical techniques are continuously developing, even though we like to think that the techniques we have are relatively permanent, with clear rationale and applications, and free of any difficulties or questions.

It is clear from reading reviews like that of Lovie (1981) that there was considerable concern about the issue of repeated measures designs and that they were distinct in a number of ways from completely randomized designs. In his presentation, Lovie (1981) identifies Garrett (1940) as the one who suggested that the interaction between Treatments and Subjects should be used as the estimate of error instead of within treatment variation, and Garrett and Zubin (1943) as the first to differentiate between Within Subject and Between Subject variation. He also identifies Edwards (1950) as a major source in the introduction of repeated measure designs to psychological researchers. This is particularly meaningful to me since this is one of the first statistics books I had as a text (in a third-year honor's course).

In addition to the purely arithmetical developments, there were also a number of discussions of the logistical and conceptual difficulties associated with the use of repeated measures designs. Lovie (1981) refers to a series of articles by Baxter (see, for example, Baxter, 1942) who proposed more complex designs to deal with some of the design issues discussed earlier in this Chapter. Similarly, Babington-Smith (1950) questioned the use of repeated measure designs because of issues such as memory effects, fatigue, and the like.

There was also considerable concern about the positive bias in repeated measure designs, much of which is reviewed by Lewis (1993). In 1954, Box showed that the F-ratio for repeated measures designs approximated the F-distribution but with degrees of freedom reduced to take into account the pattern of correlations among the treatments. Geisser and Greenhouse (1958) produced lower-bound estimates of these degrees of freedom, resulting in a conservative test (i.e., Type I error was generally too low), and in 1959, Greenhouse and Geisser developed another estimate based on Box's (1954) model, which was less conservative than their lower bound estimate. Huynh and Feldt (1976) produced yet another estimate which was even less conservative than the Greenhouse and Geisser (1959) estimate. All of these estimates can be arrived at by multiplying the nominal degrees of freedom by a coefficient, ϵ, which is defined in accordance with the approach in question. Thus we speak of the lower bound, the Greenhouse-Geisser, and the Huynh-Feldt ϵ estimates.

There is another approach to the analysis of repeated measures designs that uses a different logic. Hotelling (1931) introduced a generalization of student's t-statistic appropriate to the case where there is more than one dependent variable. This was Hotelling's T^2 statistic. Rao (1952) made use of this statistic to show how a different approach could be taken to the repeated measures problem without having to consider the issue of circularity of the variance/covariance matrix. He proposed that if you had, for example, four repeated measures, you could form three difference scores, and then use Hotelling's T^2 to evaluate the hypothesis that the means of these difference scores were all 0 in the population. Any form of a difference score could be used, as long as they resulted in a complete set of contrasts involving all the means. An example of this type of contrast is discussed in the section on the null hypothesis under the Multivariate Approach (see page 113).

ANALYZING THESE DATA USING SPSS WINDOWS

These data are analysed using the **GLM Repeated Measures** program. The following instructions assume that the data were typed into an ASCII file with scores for each level of a repeated measures factor on a line for each subject. In our example, there are four levels of the repeated measures factor. It is assumed, further, that the file is on the A Drive in a file called **REPEAT.DAT.**

Steps in Using SPSS WINDOWS GLM Repeated Measures

The following steps are applicable to **SPSS 8.0** and **SPSS 9.0** except for the input of the ASCII or Text data file. In the example to follow you are instructed at Step 3 to input your data following the procedures described in Chapter 1. The output for this example was obtained by using the freefield format in **SPSS 8.0,** and depending upon the input procedure you use, the output may be somewhat different. The answers are the same, however. Using the **WINDOWS** version of the program, you could simply type the Syntax file [the set of instructions required to run the procedure, including the relevant Data List and Execute statements (see page 30)], and then execute the job from inside the Syntax Editor (not discussed here), or use the program itself to create the syntax file. This latter procedure involves using the mouse to bring up a number of windows, and then selecting the appropriate options or typing in the required information (the **clope** procedure).

1. *Enter **SPSS WIN**.* This presents you with the SPSS Data Editor (see figure in Chapter 2, p. 46). At this point, you could begin to type in the data. However, we will assume here that you already have the data in a file on the A Drive, and that this file is labelled **repeat.dat.** For each participant, there would be the four repeated-measure scores.

2. *Click on **File** in the upper row of selections.* This will present you with a drop-down menu with a series of choices.

3. *Enter your ASCII (**SPSS 8.0**) or Text (**SPSS 9.0**) data file by following the steps on pages 17 to 20 for **SPSS 8.0,** or pages 20 to 28 for **SPSS 9.0**.* For this example, the file will consist of four variables labelled **b1, b2, b3,** and **b4,** respectively.

4. *Click on the **Statistics (SPSS 8.0)** or **Analyze (SPSS 9.0)** option on the menu bar.* This presents you with a drop-down menu. *Move your cursor to **General Linear Model,** and you are presented with another menu to the right with a choice of the following:*

SPSS 8.0	SPSS 9.0
GLM - General Factorial . . .	Univariate
GLM - Multivariate . . .	Multivariate
GLM - Repeated Measures . . .	Repeated Measures
Variance Components . . .	Variance Components

5. *Click on **GLM-Repeated Measures**.* This presents you with the Window, **GLM Repeated Measures Define Factor(s)** (see figure below).

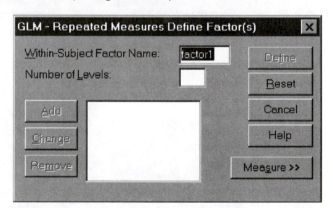

*There is a name (**factor1**) in the panel labelled **Within-Subject Factor Name**. If you wish to change it (as I did), you would click on the panel, delete factor1 and type in the name you wish (**b** in our example), then move the cursor to the pane for **Number of Levels,** and type in the number (**4** in our example). Otherwise the cursor would already be in this pane and you would simply type in the number of levels (**4**). Then click on **Add.***

6. *Then click on **Define** (it will be darker and accessible at that point).* This produces another Window, **GLM-Repeated Measures** (see figure below).

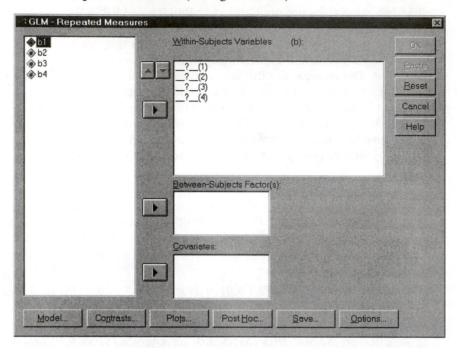

In this window, the first level of the repeated measures factor (i.e., **b1**) is highlighted. *Click on the arrow for the **Within-Subjects** Variables. This adds **b1** as the defining variable for the first level of the within subjects variable. Click on **b2**, and repeat this process until you have entered all variables.*

7. There are many choices available in this Window, but we will consider only one of them, **Options.** *Click on **Options.*** This produces another window (see figure below).

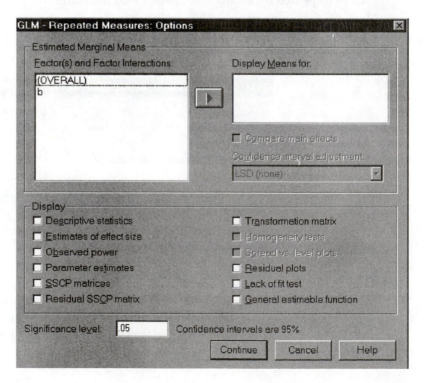

*Click on **Overall** in the white pane at the top left of the Window, and add to **Display Means** by clicking on the arrow to the left of the **Display Means for:** pane. Then click on **b**, and add to **Display Means** by clicking on the arrow.* This will result in two sets of tables for (1) the grand mean, and (2) the B means.

8. *Select the following options by clicking on the small white pane preceding each:*
   Descriptive Statistics
   Estimates of Effect Size
   Observed Power
   *Then click on **Continue.***

9. This takes you back to the Window, **GLM Repeated Measures.** *Click on **OK** to run the analysis of variance.*

10. This runs the analysis of variance program, and the answers are returned to the SPSS Viewer, as well as to your monitor. At this point, you can print your answers, save them in a file, or transfer them to some other editor.

11. To exit **SPSS,** *click on **File** (upper row of operations), and click on **Exit.*** Before you can exit, however, the program will ask if you wish to save the contents of the SPSS Viewer as well as those of the Data Editor. If you have already saved them you will not have to do so again.

The Syntax File

If you were to follow the instructions given above, you would produce the following Syntax File (omitting the Data List and Execute lines):

```
GLM
    b1 b2 b3 b4
    /WSFACTOR = b 4 Polynomial
    /METHOD = SSTYPE(3)
    /EMMEANS = TABLES(OVERALL)
    /EMMEANS = TABLES(b)
    /PRINT = DESCRIPTIVE ETASQ OPOWER
    /CRITERIA = ALPHA(.05)
    /WSDESIGN = b .
```

The first line of the syntax file calls up the program **GLM,** which is a very general program. It can perform both multivariate analysis of variance procedures and related analyses as well as univariate analyses of variance. We have already used it to perform a factorial design analysis of variance in the last chapter. We will use it again in the next chapter to perform a split-plot analysis of variance. And we will use it again in Chapter 11 to perform a multivariate analysis of variance. The second line indicates simply that there are the four variables $b1$, $b2$, $b3$, and $b4$. The next line, /WSFACTOR instructs the computer to consider the four measures as observations in a repeated measures (or within subjects) factor (B). It also instructs the computer to perform trend analyses (Polynomial) (though in all probability you will not be interested in these analyses).

The following line, /METHOD=SSTYPE(3), indicates which method is used in making the calculations. (The program does not use the formulae that were presented earlier.) In this program, use is made of one of four methods for calculating the analysis of variance results. These are referred to as SSTYPE(1), SSTYPE(2), SSTYPE(3), or SSTYPE(4). If sample sizes are equal, all four methods give the same answers. Since there is only one group of subjects in this design and all subjects must have all data, that will always be the case, so which is chosen is irrelevant. The statements defined by the keyword EMMEANS identifies the two tables of means we requested, viz., the grand mean (Overall), and the means for the repeated measures factor, B. The statement, /PRINT = DESCRIPTIVES ETASQ OPOWER results because of the three choices made in the OPTIONS window (see, Step 8, above). It results in the computer providing information about the treatment means and the estimates of effect size and power.

Basic Output

Two tables provided by **SPSS WINDOWS GLM** are appropriate to both the univariate and multivariate approaches. The first is just a description of the variables and is as follows:

Within-Subjects Factors

Measure: MEASURE_1

B	Dependent Variable
1	B1
2	B2
3	B3
4	B4

The second is provided because we clicked on **Descriptive Statistics** in Step 8, page 117. It is as follows:

Descriptive Studies

	Mean	Std. Deviation	N
$B1$	52.1667	20.4980	6
$B2$	48.3333	16.5972	6
$B3$	34.5000	11.2561	6
$B4$	25.1667	7.6004	6

This table is redundant with that provided by requesting Display Means for b on Step 7, page 117. The advantage of that option is that it provides confidence intervals for the means, which the above table does not, if that information is of interest to you. Otherwise, one might save paper by choosing only one of the two options.

Statistics Appropriate for the Univariate Approach

SPSS GLM presents three analysis of variance summary tables. One is labelled Tests of Between Subjects Effects, but in the present situation, the table does not contain any information relevant to differences between subjects. This table is presented below.

Tests of Between-Subject Effects

Measure: MEASURE_1
Transformed Variable: Average

Source	Type III Sum of Squares	df	Mean Square	F	Sig.	Eta Squared	Noncent. Parameter	Observed Power[a]
Intercept	38480.042	1	38480.042	56.090	.001	.918	56.090	1.000
Error	3430.208	5	686.042					

[a]Computed using alpha = .05

Examination of this table will reveal that it is a test of the hypothesis that the grand mean is 0. As has been noted in other chapters, this information is generally of little value if all the data consist of positive values. The F-ratio of 56.090 with 1 and 5 degrees of freedom is significant, and permits us to conclude that the grand mean is not 0 in the population. As such, it doesn't give us any information about Between Subject differences, unless you consider the value of the Mean Square Error = 686.042 to be informative. This is the variance of the mean scores for subjects, and thus the larger the value, the more individual differences in the data. I suspect that the labelling derives from the use of this table in other types of designs [see, for example, a comparable table in the next chapter (Chapter 6) on split-plot designs].

The second analysis of variance summary table is labelled Tests of Within-Subjects Effects. It is as follows:

Tests of Within-Subjects Effects

Measure: MEASURE_1

Source		Type III Sum of Squares	df	Mean Square	F	Sig.	Eta Squared	Noncent. Parameter	Observed Power[a]
B	Sphericity Assumed	2806.458	3	935.486	14.462	.000	.743	43.386	.999
	Greenhouse-Geisser	2806.458	1.672	1678.172	14.462	.002	.743	24.185	.972
	Huynh-Feldt	2806.458	2.414	1162.432	14.462	.000	.743	34.915	.996
	Lower-bound	2806.458	1.000	2806.458	14.462	.013	.743	14.462	.856
Error(B)	Sphericity Assumed	970.292	15	64.686					
	Greenhouse-Geisser	970.292	8.362	116.041					
	Huynh-Feldt	970.292	12.071	80.379					
	Lower-bound	970.292	5.000	194.058					

[a]Computed using alpha = .05

This analysis provides four lines of information for each source of variance. These lines are labelled Sphericity Assumed, Greenhouse-Geisser, Huynh-Feldt, and Lower Bound. Some statistics (Type III Sum Of Squares, F, and Eta-Squared) are identical within the set while others (df, Mean Square, Sig., Noncentral Parameter, and Observed Power) can vary. This will be discussed in more detail below. For now, we will focus attention on the first row in each set, since these statistics are based on the definitional formulae presented earlier.

The F-ratio for B is computed as:

$$\frac{MS_B}{MS_{BS}} \quad \frac{935.486}{64.686} = 14.462$$

with 3 degrees of freedom for the numerator and 15 for the denominator. It will be noted in the table that the Mean Square for the denominator of this F-ratio is referred to as Error(B). I prefer to use the label MS_{BS} because this labelling indicates that the variation is due to the interaction of treatment B and Subjects. We will use this label from now on. At any rate, this F-ratio is significant indicating that the four B means vary more than you could reasonably attribute to chance. In this case, the four means are 52.17, 48.33, 34.50, and 25.17 [see the Table of Descriptive Statistics (p. 118) or Table 2.B, page 124)]. *A posteriori* tests of means could be performed to identify which means differ significantly from each other. These will be discussed in a later section, labelled Tests of Means (p. 123).

The eta-squared associated with the F-ratio for B is reported in the table as .743. This value is computed as the ratio of 2806.458 / (2806.458 + 970.292). Alternatively, it could be computed as:

$$\eta^2 = \frac{df_1 F}{df_1 F + df_2} = \frac{3(14.462)}{3(14.462) + 15} = .743$$

where:

df_1 = the degrees of freedom associated with the numerator of the F-ratio
df_2 = the degrees of freedom associated with the denominator of the F-ratio.

The power associated with this value of eta-squared is .999. That is, it would be expected that if this study were replicated, 99.9 % of the time it could be expected that the results would be significant at the .05 level.

The third analysis of variance summary table is generally of little value in my opinion. It is presented here with the Statistics Appropriate to the Univariate Approach because the statistics are univariate in nature. The table is equally appropriate as a follow-up analysis of the multivariate analysis of variance, and could have equally been presented under Statistics Appropriate to the Multivariate Approach. It is as follows:

Tests of Within-Subjects Contrasts

Measure: MEASURE_1

Source	B	Type III Sum of Squares	df	Mean Square	F	Sig.	Eta Squared	Noncent. Parameter	Observed Power[a]
B	Linear	2698.008	1	2698.008	19.738	.007	.798	19.738	.939
	Quadratic	45.375	1	45.375	2.705	.161	.351	2.705	.268
	Cubic	63.075	1	63.075	1.554	.268	.237	1.554	.175
Error(B)	Linear	683.442	5	136.688					
	Quadratic	83.875	5	16.775					
	Cubic	202.975	5	40.595					

[a]Computed using alpha = .05

SPSS WINDOWS GLM Repeated Measures routinely outputs this Table of Within Subjects Contrasts. It consists of a series of contrasts using orthogonal polynomials, describing trend components. These trend components refer to the relationship of the means to the ordered levels of the treatment factor. If this trend is in the form of a straight line with the means either increasing or decreasing in a relatively straight line, the linear trend would be significant. If the relationship is in the shape of a U function or an inverted U function, the quadratic trend would be significant, and so on. And of course, you could have a mixture of linear and quadratic trends, which would show as significant in both. Personally, I recommend that you ignore this table unless you are particularly interested in the nature of the trend in the pattern of means. In any event, the results should never be interpreted if the corresponding F-ratio from the Tests of Within-Subjects Effects (see page 119) is not significant, or the multivariate F-ratio on page 123 if you had decided to adopt that approach. Note that the sums of squares for these three contrasts add to the sum of squares for B presented in that table. That is, 2698.008 + 45.375 + 63.075 = 2806.458. It is therefore possible that the univariate or multivariate F-ratio for B may not be significant, but that one of the trend components could be significant. This would not make sense. The omnibus test would indicate that you have no reason to assume the means differ in the population, while the test of trend suggests there is some type of trend.

Even so, the information provided by this analysis is incomplete. In our example, the F-ratio for B was significant, thus we might be interested in considering the nature of the trend in the data. The analysis of the trend components indicates that there is evidence of a linear trend. That is, the results indicate that there is a linear trend in the means as we move from 0 to 2 to 4 to 6 ounces of alcohol. However, no equation is given showing the nature of this trend. An unsuspecting researcher might assume that this trend is positive. However, a consideration of the means indicates that the trend is negative. That is, in order of increasing levels of alcohol consumption, the means are 52.17, 48.33, 34.5, and 25.17. Of course, the observant researcher would notice this, but if one of the higher trend components were significant, the pattern might be less clear.

Mauchly's Test of Sphericity and the Epsilon Multipliers

As indicated earlier, one problem with F-ratios of Within Subject effects is that they tend to have a positive bias if the assumption of circularity is violated. That is, violation of the assumption influences the magnitude of the Mean Squares in such a way that the F-ratios will tend to be inflated, increasing the chance to committing a Type I error. The assumption of circularity is simply that the variance of the differences among the repeated measures is equal in the population for all pairs of differences. In this case, there are 4 repeated measures, and therefore there are (4)(3)/2 or 6 such differences that could be computed (i.e., $B_1 - B_2, \ldots B_3 - B_4$). Mauchly's (1940) test of sphericity, computed by **SPSS WINDOWS GLM** provides a test of the assumption of circularity of the pooled variance/covariance matrix. The mathematics underlying this test are quite complex. Suffice it to say that it is performed on a transformation of the variance/covariance matrix, to determine whether this transformed matrix satisfies the assumption of sphericity (equal diagonals, and off-diagonal values of 0). Mauchly's test makes use of a statistic, W, that has associated with it an approximate chi-square test of significance. If the test is not significant, it indicates that there is no evidence to suggest that the matrix violates the assumption of sphericity, and thus it is concluded that the original variance/covariance matrix satisfies the assumption of circularity. This is a rather roundabout procedure, to be sure. Moreover, the test itself is influenced by violations of assumptions of normality. Often, researchers ignore the test, and make modifications to their analysis of variance to counteract any violations of circularity. In any event, it is generally recommended that you make the modifications described below.

The **SPSS WINDOWS GLM** output for this example is as follows:

Mauchly's Test of Sphericity[b]

Measure: MEASURE_1

Within Subjects Effect	Mauchly's W	Approx. Chi-Square	df	Sig.	Epsilon[a]		
					Greenhouse-Geisser	Huynh-Feldt	Lower-bound
B	.145	7.188	5	.221	.557	.805	.333

Tests the null hypothesis that the error covariance matrix of the orthonormalized transformed dependent variables is proportional to an identity matrix.

[a]May be used to adjust the degrees of freedom for the averaged tests of significance. Corrected tests are displayed in the layers (by default) of the Tests of Within Subjects Effects table.

[b]Design: Intercept
Within Subjects Design: B

As applied to these data, the lack of significance of the test (x^2 (5) = 7.188, ns) suggests that there is little reason to assume that the assumption of circularity has been violated. Many statisticians (e.g., Kirk, 1995; Myers & Well, 1991), however, recommend another procedure that routinely adjusts the degrees of freedom of both numerator and denominator of all tests of Within Subject effects. This adjustment is based on research by Box (1954), who demonstrated that an F-ratio based on Within Subject effects follows the F-distribution with the degrees of freedom reduced to reflect the degree of violation of circularity. This procedure reduces the degrees of freedom for both the numerator and denominator of the F-ratio for the repeated measure factor by multiplying them by a correction factor. Three such correction factors have been suggested, and **SPSS WINDOWS GLM** provides each of these *epsilon* multipliers in the preceding table.

SPSS WINDOWS GLM also gives adjustments to the Mean Squares by dividing the Sums of Squares by the adjusted degrees of freedom [see the table for tests of Within-Subjects Effects (page 119)]. These adjustments also result in changes to Sig., Noncentral Parameter, and Observed Power.

Various textbooks (see, for example, Kirk, 1995) suggest a three step procedure for making adjustments to the degrees of freedom for the Within-Subject Effects. In the good old days, the epsilon multipliers had to be calculated by hand, and this procedure was rather laborious for all but the lower-bound epsilon. In *Step 1*, you first determine whether or not the F-ratio is significant without any modification of the degrees of freedom (i.e., the first line in each step, identified as Sphericity Assumed, in the table of Tests of Within-Subjects Effects on page 119. If it is not, there is no need to use the epsilon multipliers. If it is, however, you could use the epsilon multipliers to adjust the degrees of freedom and conduct more conservative tests. The multipliers vary in terms of their conservativeness.

Step 2 used the most conservative estimate, the *lower-bound epsilon*. This value is simply the reciprocal of the degrees of freedom for the repeated measures factor. If the F-ratio was significant using this value, then one could conclude that it was significant, even taking into account maximum violation of the assumption of circularity. This test was conservative, however, so if the F-ratio was not significant, it was recommended that you repeat the procedure using an epsilon multiplier based on the degree of non-circularity present in the sample data.

For *Step 3*, two estimates are available, one described by Greenhouse and Geisser (1959) (see also, Collier, Baker, Mandeville, and Hayes, 1967), and one proposed by Huynh & Feldt (1976). The Greenhouse and Geisser estimate is the more conservative of the two. Which you use is a matter of preference. Kirk (1995) recommends using the Greenhouse-Geisser estimate, while Myers and Well (1991) opt for the Huynh-Feldt one. Some researchers would do the computations with the next most conservative epsilon multiplier (i.e., the Greenhouse-Geisser), and if this was not significant, proceed with the least conservative (the Huynh-Feldt epsilon). Since **SPSS WINDOWS GLM** presents all three epsilon values (see table, p. 121) as well as the results of the actual calculations (see table, p. 119), researchers can choose the one they prefer so the three step procedure is not necessary. We will illustrate the use of the *Greenhouse-Geisser epsilon*.

Multiply the degrees of freedom for both the numerator and denominator of the F-ratio for **B** by the Greenhouse-Geisser epsilon as follows: (Note the Greenhouse-Geisser epsilon is given as .557 in the table on page 121, but it is actually .55746. This value is used in the following calculations, so that the answers agree with those given in the table on page 119.)

$$\text{Numerator} = (.55746)(3) = 1.672$$

$$\text{Denominator} = (.55746)(15) = 8.362$$

Generally when reporting degrees of freedom in a manuscript, values are given in whole numbers. It is thus customary to round these values. I recommend always rounding up. Thus, the adjusted degrees of freedom in this example would be 2 for the numerator and 9 for the denominator. The alpha level presented in the table on page 119, however, evaluates significance for the actual degrees of freedom calculated above. If it were necessary for you to evaluate significance using the table of the F-distribution (Table C, Appendix), you would use 2 and 9 degrees of freedom, which could result in slightly different values. In any event, the F-ratio is significant in this case so you could proceed to conduct tests of significance between the B means, if such tests were meaningful.

Statistics Appropriate for the Multivariate Approach

Hotelling's T^2 statistic is given as the equivalent F-statistic by **SPSS GLM.** Also, because of the nature of the output, four different statistics are provided, corresponding to Pillai's Trace, Wilks' Lambda, Hotelling's Trace, and Roy's Largest Root. The only value needed for this presentation, however, is the corresponding F-ratio. The relevant output is reproduced below:

Multivariate Tests[c]

Effect		Value	F	Hypothesis df	Error df	Sig.	Eta Squared	Noncent. Parameter	Observed Power[a]
B	Pillai's Trace	.906	9.614[b]	3.000	3.000	.048	.906	28.841	.640
	Wilks' Lambda	.094	9.614[b]	3.000	3.000	.048	.906	28.841	.640
	Hotelling's Trace	9.614	9.614[b]	3.000	3.000	.048	.906	28.841	.640
	Roy's Largest Root	9.614	9.614[b]	3.000	3.000	.048	.906	28.841	.640

[a]Computed using alpha = .05

[b]Exact statistic

[c]Design: Intercept

Within Subjects Design: B

When reporting the results from this analysis, one should present the test statistic along with the degrees of freedom, as Hotelling's T^2 (3,3) = 9.614, $p<.05$), or if one prefers, Multivariate $F(3,3)$ = 9.614, $p<.05$). Note, as indicated earlier that the degrees of freedom for this test are given as $(b-1) = (4-1) = 3$, and $(N-b+1) = (6-4+1) = 3$. We shall see in Chapter 11 that in other multivariate analyses, the different types of statistics (i.e., Pillai's Trace, etc.) can take on different values, and the corresponding degrees of freedom and F-ratios can vary from one statistic to the next. This is not the case in this type of analysis, however.

TESTS OF MEANS

Tests of means can be performed following a significant F-ratio for Treatments in ways that are similar to those discussed in the context of the single factor completely randomized design. Only the formulae are different. This is because the means are not independent. Because of the lack of independence, the estimate of error must take the correlation into account, and this is done by using the Mean Squares for BS as the error term. This presentation will direct attention to *a posteriori* (post hoc) tests.

Generally, when a significant *effect* is obtained, a researcher is interested in making comparisons of the means. This is true whether one makes use of the univariate or multivariate approach. And the tests of means are identical regardless of which omnibus test was used. As indicated previously, *a posteriori* comparisons of means make use of one of three basic statistics, referred to here as q, t, and F, and a number of sampling distributions based on one of these statistics. Tests such as the Tukey Honestly Significant Difference, the Newman-Keuls test, and Duncan's New Multiple Range test make use of a statistic that takes the form of q (see below). Tests such as the Least Significant Difference, the Dunn Bonferroni t, and Dunnett's comparison with a control condition are based on the t-statistic, while Scheffé's S-statistic makes use of an F-ratio.

SPSS WINDOWS GLM Repeated Measures outputs tables of means and standard errors as requested in Step 7, pages 116–117. The table output by the request for OVERALL is for the grand mean and is as follows:

1. Grand Mean

Measure: MEASURE_1

		95% Confidence Interval	
Mean	**Std. Error**	**Lower Bound**	**Upper Bound**
40.042	5.347	26.298	53.785

The F-ratio for the Intercept shown in the table of Tests of Between-Subjects Effects on page 118 is a test that this mean (40.042) is significantly greater than 0.

A second table that is output is the table of the means for the main effect of B. The F-ratio for B in the table of Tests of Within-Subjects Effects on page 119, as well as the F-ratio associated with Pillai's Trace, etc., on page 123, is a test that these four means are more variable than would be expected on the basis of chance.

2. B

Measure: MEASURE_1

			95% Confidence Interval	
B	**Mean**	**Std. Error**	**Lower Bound**	**Upper Bound**
1	52.167	8.368	30.655	73.678
2	48.333	6.776	30.916	65.751
3	34.500	4.595	22.687	46.313
4	25.167	3.103	17.190	33.143

The form of the tests of means are as follows for the three sampling distributions:

$$q = \frac{\bar{X}_{b1} - \bar{X}_{b2}}{\sqrt{\dfrac{MS_{BS}}{n}}}$$

$$t = \frac{\bar{X}_{b1} - \bar{X}_{b2}}{\sqrt{\dfrac{2MS_{BS}}{n}}}$$

$$F = \frac{(\bar{X}_{b1} - \bar{X}_{b2})^2}{\dfrac{2MS_{BS}}{n}}$$

For each test, the results of the computations will be compared with values in the appropriate table corresponding to a particular sampling distribution. The following example makes use of the q-statistic as applied to the Tukey Honestly Significant Test (HSD), and compares the first and fourth means.

$$q = \frac{52.17 - 25.17}{\sqrt{\dfrac{64.69}{6}}} = \frac{27.00}{3.28} = 8.23$$

For the Tukey HSD test, we would compare the value of 8.23 against the value in the table of the Studentized Range (see Table D, Appendix) for four steps (the number of B means), and degrees of freedom for the error term of 15. This value is 4.08 ($p < .05$), and 5.25 ($p < .01$), thus we would conclude that this difference is significant at the .01 level. Of course, it is generally the case that a researcher would be interested in testing all possible pairs of means. It is possible to perform such posthoc tests using **SPSS WINDOWS GLM** Repeated Measures using an option available in the set-up. These tests do not use the error term for the analysis of variance, but instead consist of a series of paired t-tests using only the data from the two levels of interest, hence the appropriate degrees of freedom would be $(n - 1)$. Moreover, the output allows only for one of three types of posthoc tests [Least Significant Difference (LSD), Bonferroni, and Sidak], and generally, the LSD procedure is not recommended because the Type I error rate tends to be high. Moreover, since the t-values are not given, this approach seems of limited value. As a consequence, this option was not discussed in this chapter.[1]

RANDOMIZED BLOCKS DESIGNS

Randomized blocks designs are those in which subjects are sampled in blocks (hence the block is random) and then different treatments are applied to different members of the block. For example, consider our experiment on the effects of the four levels of alcohol consumption on memory for words in a list. We could obtain a sample of four individuals, and then randomly assign one of them to each of the four alcohol conditions. The main point to emphasize here is that since blocks are sampled as a unit, the observations in any one block are linked together, and this linking has implications. Randomized blocks designs are most often employed when we want to control for variation in some other variable. Thus, in our example, let us assume that we were concerned that intelligence might have some influence on the memory for words, and we wanted to make sure that our results were not influenced by any differences in intelligence between subjects in the different conditions of levels of alcohol. And we weren't content to assume that random sampling, as done in the simple randomized design, would even things out. In such a situation, we could use the randomized blocks design, but add the requirement that all the subjects in any given block had the same IQ (this measure being taken obviously before subjects receive the treatment). That is, the subjects in any one block are individually matched on IQ. Note, we don't care what the IQ in any given block is (we may not even record it), only that the subjects in any one block have the same IQ. We still have randomized blocks, except now we have eliminated any differences in IQ from the different levels of the treatment. If this were important to us, then we would use a randomized blocks design (thus removing any possible contamination of IQ with treatment differences). On the other hand if we were content to trust to the luck of sampling to eliminate any possible IQ confound, we would use the completely randomized single-factor design.

---

[1] I use the program, **POSTHOC**, for tests of means referred to in a footnote in the previous chapter.

Note that by using this design, the researcher accomplishes a number of goals. If intelligence is an important element in the memory of the words, equating subjects in each block on intelligence removes a considerable amount of variance that would normally be attributed to error (in the completely randomized single factor design). Moreover, if memory for words is related to IQ, then to the extent that there are differences in IQ between the various blocks, the treatments would tend to be positively correlated. And since the individuals in each block are linked, this correlation can be assessed. The result is that this design satisfies all the characteristics of the repeated measures design, and hence would be analyzed in exactly the same way. If one wished to distinguish between the repeated measures design and the randomized blocks design, one could substitute the term Block for Subject in the definitional formulae given on page 110, but otherwise the arithmetic is identical.

There is, however, one important difference. Since different subjects receive the various treatments, although the treatments are correlated (because of the common IQ effect), there is no opportunity for carry over or order effects. Thus, the randomized blocks design has all the strengths of the repeated measures design and none of the weaknesses. One would even expect that there would be less problems with circularity of the variance/covariance matrix, especially if the relation between IQ and memory for the words was linear.

In summary, a randomized block design refers generally to any single factor design where observations are sampled in a block. Randomized block designs are applicable when:

a. Subjects are sampled randomly in blocks matched on some other variable (e.g., IQ).

b. Subjects are linked together in some way. Thus, if subjects were sampled because of some biological link (e.g., all from the same family, or litter, to control for genetic and experiential factors).

c. Subjects are randomly sampled in a block and tested under different conditions. That is, in our alcohol study, if the experimenter wanted to test four subjects at a time to save time, etc., and had a different one in each treatment condition, the appropriate analysis would be a randomized blocks design. Some students might argue that if the subjects were tested in different rooms, etc., that it would be just as appropriate to use a simple randomized design, but such a strategy belies the nature of the sampling, and doesn't take into account that all members of a block share common variance with respect to testing time, and all other factors that they have in common. It is certainly the case, however, that this may not be a good way to use the randomized block design, largely because it is very likely that the correlations between treatment conditions would probably not be very large (in fact, they could even be negative), so that the Mean Square for *BS* might not be smaller than that for the Mean Square Within groups that would be calculated in a completely randomized single-factor design (see Chapter 3).

Chapter 6
Split-Plot Analysis
of Variance

The split-plot analysis of variance is a factorial design analysis of variance in which at least one of the factors is based on independent observations and at least one is based on correlated observations. When a factor is based on independent observations, it makes use of between-group comparisons, as in single-factor analysis of variance. When it is based on correlated observations, it makes use of within-subject or within-block comparisons, as in a repeated measures or randomized blocks design.

There are many instances in psychology where one would use a split-plot design. A common one is in learning research, where for example, a researcher might be interested in the effects of three different treatments on learning over trials. The treatment factor would be formed by randomly assigning subjects to one of the three treatment conditions. If observations were obtained on each of, say, five trials, and the data were analysed with the two factors, Treatment and Trials, the resulting analysis would be a split-plot analysis of variance. The observations in the Treatment factor are based on independent groups, while those in the Trials factor constitute repeated observations on the same subjects.

Other examples could be given that involve repeated measures over one of the factors. Thus, research might be concerned with the effects of *Therapeutic Intervention* on depression, with observations being taken over *Time* (i.e., before, immediately after treatment, and post follow-up). Alternatively, one might study the effects of *Gender* on the speed of recognizing male and female stimuli in a *Perception Task*. Or one could investigate the effects of different levels of *Alcohol Consumed* on the ability to pronounce different *Classes of Words* (English vs. Nonsense Words). In each of these examples, the first factor listed would involve different groups of subjects, and the second one, repeated measures on the same subjects.

Split-plot factorial designs can also be used when subjects are formed into homogeneous blocks, and then randomly assigned to a treatment condition. Consider, for example, a study concerned with investigating the effects of three different *Vitamins* on the weight of rats raised in four different *Home Environments*. One might do this study with, say, three different rats from each of twenty different litters. Five litters could be randomly assigned to one of four home environments, and each rat from the litter given one of the vitamins. Since the rats from the same litter are matched, the observations across vitamins are correlated, but since litters are randomly assigned to home environments, observations across home environments are independent. This then is an example of a split-plot analysis of variance involving matched subjects as opposed to repeated measures (see the discussion of randomized blocks in Chapter 5). The nature of the analysis is, however, the same in both cases.

Split-plot factorial designs can involve more than two factors, provided that there is at least one between subjects (or between blocks) comparison and at least one within subjects (or within blocks) comparison. Thus, a three-factor experiment (ABC) in which Factor A was based on different subjects, and Factors B and C were based on repeated measures (correlated observations) would be an example of a split-plot design. Similarly, it would be a split plot factorial design if Factors A and C were based on between subject contrasts and Factor B was based on correlated observations.

A major feature of the split-plot factorial design is that there are different error terms (denominators for the F-ratios) for the factors based on between subject comparisons and those based on within subject comparisons. Moreover, the F-ratios for interactions that involve combinations of between subject and within subject factors make use of error terms involving the within-subject factor(s).

A BIT OF HISTORY

We have already seen most of the history of the split-plot analysis of variance in Chapter 5 in our discussion of repeated measure designs, largely because this is a variant of a repeated measure design. The term "split-plot" derives from agricultural research, where many of the concepts of analysis of variance originate (see, for example, Snedecor, 1946). In this research, different plots of land were assigned randomly to different levels of a Treatment factor (A). Each plot of land was then subdivided into smaller sections, and the conditions of another Treatment factor (B) were randomly assigned to each of the sections. In this way, the characteristics of each plot of land were kept relatively constant across the levels of the B treatment associated with any given plot. Some of the original studies that employed analysis of variance (see, for example, Fisher & MacKenzie, 1923) made use of aspects of the split-plot in the execution of the experiment, but the analysis didn't capitalize on some of the analytic advantages of the split-plot design.

In psychology, the split-plot factorial design came to be associated with those experiments in which at least one (but not all) of the factors was based on repeated measures on the same individuals. (That is, the individual was analogous to the plot). According to Lovie (1979; 1981), there were many articles published that made use of analysis of variance for experiments in which there were repeated measures, but the analyses did not take cognisance of the fact that the sources of error should be different for those effects based on between subject factors, and those based on repeated measures. The first article to make use of repeated measures in this way *and* to analyze the data with different error terms for between and within subject components was published by A. R. Gilliland and D. W. Humphreys (1943). They studied the effects of Sex, Age, Approach, Method of Judgement, and Time Interval on time estimation. Time Interval was the repeated measures factor. In 1943, L. G. Humphreys also proposed that the form of analysis should be different for the two different types of factors. This type of design was soon used quite frequently in educational research because of the influence of Lindquist (1953), who introduced it into his well known textbook, referring to it as a mixed design.

As we have seen, other developments in this area were, concerned with the issue of the positive bias in the F-ratio for within subject effects when the variance/covariance matrix does not have a particular form. First, there was research by Mauchly (1940), providing a test of significance that came to be used to determine whether a variance/covariance matrix violated the assumption of circularity. Then there was research by Box (1954), Geisser and Greenhouse (1958), Greenhouse and Geisser (1959), and Huynh and Feldt (1976) providing the rationale for making adjustments to the degrees of freedom, and statistics for making these adjustments.

Many statistical procedures undergo developments over time, however, and there is now another way to analyze data based on repeated observations of the same respondents. This procedure, which is a multivariate approach, is at least as old as the procedure described above (which reflects a univariate approach), but it is now only beginning to be used with any frequency. Its application to designs having repeated measures was proposed by Rao (1954). It makes use of a procedure called multivariate analysis of variance where the repeated observations are considered different dependent measures. This procedure was discussed in some detail in Chapter 5 as it applies to repeated measures designs. It has been recommended by a number of writers since then, but is not discussed in much detail by most statistics books concerned primarily with analysis of variance (see, for example, Kirk, 1995; Myers and Well, 1991). A very readable description of its application is provided by O'Brien and Kaiser (1985), who show how it can be used in a number of different analytic situations, including the one that is discussed in this chapter.

BASIC ARITHMETIC AND SAMPLE DATA

As indicated above, the split-plot factorial design can be viewed from a univariate or a multivariate perspective. This section presents the basic data and focusses on the univariate perspective; the multivariate perspective will be discussed subsequently. In the present section, the split-plot factorial design will be discussed in terms of a two-factor model. Consider an experiment in which a researcher assigned subjects to one of three treatment conditions: (A) low, medium or high levels of anxiety. Suppose then, that she/he had each subject learn four (B) lists of 20 words each. Assume that the lists varied in difficulty (being comprised of words four, six, eight or ten letters in length), and that the dependent measure was the number of trials needed to recite a list twice correctly with no errors. The researcher might have three hypotheses of interest:

(a) That increases in anxiety would interfere with learning.

(b) That lists made up of longer words would be harder to learn than lists of shorter words.

(c) That level of anxiety would interact with list difficulty such that at higher levels of anxiety, increases in list difficulty would have increasingly greater effects on the ability to learn the words, while at lower levels of anxiety, the effects of list difficulty on learning would be less pronounced.

An example of the data that might be obtained from five subjects in each of the three anxiety conditions is:

	B_1	B_2	B_3	B_4	$P_{i/a}$
	3	5	7	6	5.25
	6	6	7	7	6.50
A_1	4	8	9	7	7.00
	5	6	7	8	6.50
	5	7	8	9	7.25
	4	4	5	8	5.25
	8	7	9	7	7.75
A_2	7	9	9	9	8.50
	7	8	6	8	7.25
	5	7	7	9	7.00
	7	8	9	11	8.75
	6	8	10	11	8.75
A_3	6	9	11	13	9.75
	5	7	10	13	8.75
	7	8	9	10	8.50

In this table, A refers to the three levels of anxiety, B refers to the four levels of list difficulty, and $P_{i/a}$ (read P_i nested in A) is the individual's mean across the four word lists. The four values in each line are the number of trials that each subject needed to learn each of the four lists. Different subjects make up the three groups of A.

For this analysis, one could compute means for factor A, factor B, and the AB interaction. These means are as follows:

		B				
		1	2	3	4	A-Means
	1	4.60	6.40	7.60	7.40	6.500
A	2	6.20	7.00	7.20	8.20	7.150
	3	6.20	8.00	9.80	11.60	8.900
	B-Means	5.667	7.133	8.200	9.067	7.517

In order to perform an analysis of variance on these data, it is necessary to make a distinction between Between-Subject and Within-Subject sources. The formulae for the Sums of Squares, and Degrees of Freedom for this analysis are as follows:

Source	Sum of Squares	df
Between Subjects		
A	$nb\sum^{a}(\bar{X}_a - \bar{G})^2$	$(a-1)$
S/A	$b\sum^{a}\sum^{i}(\bar{P}_{i/a} - \bar{X}_a)^2$	$a(n-1)$
Within Subjects		
B	$na\sum^{b}(\bar{X}_b - \bar{G})^2$	$(b-1)$
AB	$n\sum^{a}\sum^{b}(\bar{X}_{ab} - \bar{X}_a - \bar{X}_b + \bar{G})^2$	$(a-1)(b-1)$
BS/A	$\sum^{a}\sum^{b}\sum^{i}(X_{abi} - \bar{P}_{i/a} - \bar{X}_{ab} + \bar{X}_a)^2$	$a(b-1)(n-1)$

Note in this breakdown that the AB interaction is treated as a Within-Subject effect because of the repeated measures on B. The application of these formulae are shown below:

BETWEEN SUBJECT VARIATION

$$SS_A = (5)(4)[(6.500 - 7.517)^2 + ... + (8.900 = 7.517)^2] \quad = 61.633$$

$$SS_{S/A} = 4[(5.25 - 6.500)^2 + ... + (8.50 - 8.900)^2] \quad = 36.600$$

$$DF_A = (3-1) = 2 \qquad MS_A = 61.63/2 \qquad = 30.817$$

$$DF_{S/A} = (3)(5-1) = 12 \qquad MS_{S/A} = 36.60/12 \qquad = 3.050$$

$$F_A = 30.817/3.050 = 10.104$$

If all assumptions (see below) were satisfied, this F-ratio could be evaluated for significance using the Table of the F-distribution (Table C, the Appendix), with 2 and 12 degrees of freedom. According to that table, the value of F required for significance at 2 and 12 degrees of freedom is 6.93 at the .01 level, thus we can conclude that this value is significant. This would be expressed as $F(2,12) = 10.104, p < .01)$.

WITHIN SUBJECT VARIATION

$$SS_B = (5)(3)[(5.667 - 7.517)^2 + ... + (8.200 - 7.517)^2 = 96.583$$

$$SS_{AB} = (5)[(4.60 - 6.500 - 5.667 + 7.517)^2 + ...$$
$$+ (11.60 - 8.900 - 9.067 + 7.517)^2] \qquad = 22.767$$

$$SS_{BS/A} = (3 - 5.25 - 4.60 + 6.50)^2 + ...$$
$$(10 - 8.50 - 11.60 + 8.90)^2 \qquad = 37.400$$

$$DF_B = (4-1) = 3 \qquad MS_B = 96.58/3 \qquad = 32.194$$

$$DF_{AB} = (4-1)(3-1) = 6 \qquad MS_{AB} = 22.77/6 \qquad = 3.794$$

$$DF_{BS/A} = (3)(4-1)(5-1) = 36 \qquad MS_{BS/A} = 37.40/36 \qquad = 1.039$$

$$F_B = 32.19/1.04 = 30.989 \qquad F_{AB} = 3.79/1.04 \qquad = 3.652$$

If all assumptions (see below) had been met, these two F-ratios could be evaluated for significance using the table of the F-distribution (Table C, the Appendix). The degrees of freedom for B

would be 3 and 36, and Table C indicates that a value of 4.51 would be significant at the .01 level. (using $df = 30$) The degrees of freedom for AB would be 6 and 36. Table C indicates that an F-ratio of 3.47 is required for significance at the .01 level for 6 and 30 (the next lowest value to 36 in the table) degrees of freedom. We could thus conclude that this F-ratio is also significant.

This information can be summarized in a table as follows:

Source	Sum of Squares	df	Mean Square	F-ratio
Between Ss				
A	61.633	2	30.817	10.104
S/A	36.600	12	3.050	
Within Ss				
B	96.583	3	32.194	30.989
AB	22.767	6	3.794	3.652
BS/A	37.400	36	1.039	
Total	254.983	59		

Assumptions from the Univariate Perspective

When considered from the univariate perspective, four sets of assumptions underly the split-plot factorial-design analysis of variance. In general, these are comparable to those already presented in earlier chapters, except that there is one extension because of the presence of the repeated measures factor. The assumptions are:

1. *Independent Random Sampling.* In this case, it is assumed that the subjects forming the various levels of the between groups factor are randomly assigned to the groups: or at least are samples from the populations of interest.

2. *Normality.* In this case, it is assumed that the distributions in the AB subpopulations are normally distributed. As we have already seen, the analysis of variance is robust with respect to violations of this assumption.

3. *Homogeneity of Variance.* There are actually three parts to this assumption as it applies to the split-plot factorial design. First, for the test of the effects of the between-groups factors, it is assumed that the variances of the various between groups are homogeneous in the population. In our example, therefore, it is assumed that there is homogeneity in the variances of the three groups of subjects means. Second, it is assumed that the various variance/covariance matrices for the between group factors are equivalent. In our example we have three levels of the between-group factor (A), and each one of these has a bXb variance/covariance matrix. It is assumed that these three matrices are equivalent. Third, it is assumed that the pooled variance/covariance matrix satisfies the assumption of circularity (see Chapter 5 for a discussion of this assumption).

4. *Null Hypotheses.* As we saw in the context of the completely randomized factorial design, there are two classes of null hypotheses, one referring to the main effects, and one referring to the interaction effects. The same is true for the split-plot factorial design. There is a distinction, however, in the test of these hypotheses in the split-plot design. For the case of the two-factor design, the error term for the between subjects effect is distinct from that for the within-subjects (or within blocks) effects, and the interaction of the between-subjects factor with the within-subjects (blocks) factor is considered a within-subjects effect. In our example, therefore, the effects due to A are considered between-subjects effects, and those for B, and AB are considered within-subjects effects.

Assumptions from the Multivariate Perspective

When viewed from the multivariate perspective, the assumptions are similar to those for the univariate model. The multivariate perspective applies only to the tests of within-subject effects, so that as far as the between-subjects effects are concerned the assumptions are as they were described above to refer to those effects. The biggest difference is that the assumption of circularity of the variance/covariance matrix is not necessary for the tests of within-subject effects. The assumption of random sampling is necessary, as is the case for all analysis of variance designs. Tests of the between-subjects effects rests on the assumption of within-groups homogeneity of variance of the subjects means, but providing sample sizes are equal, the analysis is robust to violations of this assumption (see Chapter 3). Tests of the within-subject effects (i.e., B and the AB interaction) require the assumption of Multivariate Normality, but again the tests are robust to violations of this assumption (see O'Brien and Kaiser, 1985).

ANALYZING THESE DATA USING SPSS WINDOWS

These data are analyzed using the **GLM-Repeated Measures** program. The following instructions assume that the data were typed into an ASCII file with the level of A, followed by the scores for each level of a repeated-measures factor on a line for each subject. In our example, there are four levels of the repeated-measures factor. It is assumed, further, that the file is on the A Drive in a file called **split.dat.**

The following steps are applicable to **SPSS 8.0** and **SPSS 9.0** except for the input of the ASCII or Text data file. In the example to follow, you are instructed at Step 3 to input your data following the procedures described in Chapter 1. The output for this example was obtained by using the freefield format in **SPSS 8.0**, and depending upon the input procedure you use, the output may be somewhat different. The answers are the same, however. Using the **WINDOWS** version of the program, you could simply type the Syntax file [the set of instructions required to run the procedure, including the relevant Data List and Execute statements (see page 30)], and then execute the job from inside the Syntax Editor (not discussed here), or use the program itself to create the syntax file. This latter procedure involves using the mouse to bring up a number of windows, and then selecting the appropriate options or typing in the required information (the **clope** procedure).

Steps in Using SPSS WINDOWS GLM-Repeated Measures

1. *Enter* **SPSS WIN**. This presents you with the SPSS Data Editor (see figure in Chapter 2, p. 46). At this point, you could begin to type in the data. However, we will assume here that you already have the data in a file on the A Drive, that this file is labelled **split.dat,** and that the data are in free or delimited format. For each participant there would be five values, the level of the between groups factor (labelled **a** in our example), and the four repeated measure scores.

2. *Click on* ***File*** *in the upper row of selections.* This will present you with a drop-down menu with a series of choices.

3. *Enter your ASCII (**SPSS 8.0**) or Text (**SPSS 9.0**) data file by following the steps on pages 17 to 20 for **SPSS 8.0**, or pages 20 to 28 for **SPSS 9.0***. For this example, the file will consist of five variables labelled **a, b1, b2, b3,** and **b4** respectively.

4. *Click on the **Statistics (SPSS 8.0)** or **Analyze (SPSS 9.0)** option on the menu bar.* This presents you with a drop-down menu. *Move your cursor to **General Linear Model**, and you are presented with another menu to the right with a choice of the following:*

SPSS 8.0	**SPSS 9.0**
GLM - General Factorial . . .	Univariate
GLM - Multivariate . . .	Multivariate
GLM - Repeated Measures . . .	Repeated Measures
Variance Components . . .	Variance Components

5. *Click on **GLM-Repeated Measures**.* This presents you with the Window, **GLM-Repeated Measures Define Factor(s).** This Window was presented in Chapter 5, but it is reproduced here to facilitate description of its use:

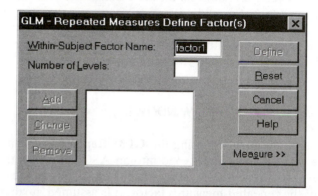

*There is a name (**factor1**) in the panel labelled **Within-Subject Factor Name.** If you wish to change it (as I did), you would click on the panel, delete factor1 and type in the name you wish (**b** in our example), then move the cursor to the pane for **Number of Levels,** and type in the number (**4** in our example). Otherwise the cursor would already be in this pane and you would simply type in the number of levels (**4**). Then click on **ADD.***

6. *Then click on **Define** (it will be darker and accessible at that point).* This produces another Window, **GLM-Repeated Measures.** We saw this Window in Chapter 5, but it is reproduced here because this version shows the presence of both Between- and Within-Subject factors:

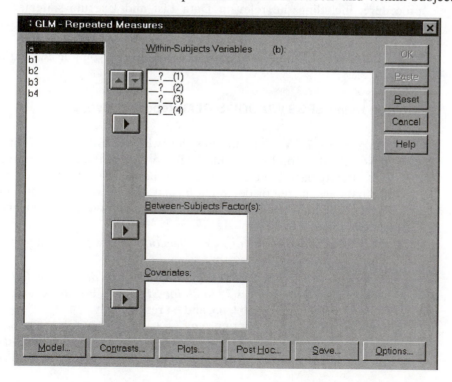

In this window, the first factor (i.e., **a**) is highlighted. *Click on the arrow for **Between Subjects Factor(s).** Then move your cursor to the repeated measures variables and add them to the **Within Subjects Variable(s)** by clicking on each one and clicking on the arrow for this pane.*

7. There are many choices available in this Window, but we will consider only one of them, **Options.** *Click on **Options.*** This produces another window. This window was also shown in Chapter 5, but is reproduced here to facilitate discussion of its use:

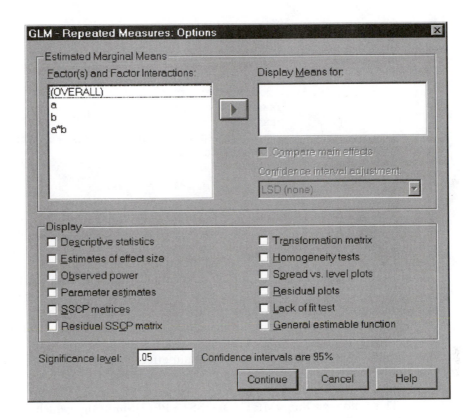

*Click on **Overall** in the white pane at the top left of the Window, and add to Display Means by clicking on the arrow to the left of the **Display Means for:** pane. Then click on **a**, and add to Display Means by clicking on the arrow; click on **b** and add to Display Means by clicking on the arrow; and click on **a*b** and click on the arrow.* This will result in four sets of tables for, (1) the grand mean, (2) the A means, (3) the B means, and (4) the AB means.

8. Select the following options by clicking on the small white pane preceding each:
   Descriptive Statistics
   Estimates of Effect Size
   Observed Power
   Homogeneity Tests
   *Then click on **Continue.***

9. This takes you back to the Window, **GLM-Repeated Measures.** *Click on **OK** to run the analysis of variance.*

10. This runs the analysis of variance program, and the answers are returned to the **SPSS Output Viewer,** as well as to your monitor. At this point, you can print your answers, save them in a file, or transfer them to some other editor.

11. To exit **SPSS,** *click on **File** (upper row of operations), and click on **Exit**.* Before you can exit, however, the program will ask if you wish to save the contents of the **SPSS Output Viewer,** as well as those of the Data Editor. If you have already saved them you will not have to do so again.

The Syntax File

If you were to follow the instructions given above, you would produce the following Syntax File (omitting the Data List and Execute lines):

```
GLM
b1 b2 b3 b4 BY a
/WSFACTOR = b 4 Polynomial
/METHOD = SSTYPE(3)
/EMMEANS = TABLES(OVERALL)
/EMMEANS = TABLES(a)
/EMMEANS = TABLES(b)
/EMMEANS = TABLES(a*b)
/PRINT = DESCRIPTIVE ETASQ OPOWER HOMOGENEITY
/CRITERIA = ALPHA(.05)
/WSDESIGN = b
/DESIGN = a .
```

The first line of the syntax file calls up the program **GLM,** which is a very general program. It can perform both multivariate analysis of variance procedures and univariate ones. As written it indicates that the four variables b1, b2, b3, and b4 are dependent variables, and the variable **a** is an independent variable. At this point, then the computer is ready to perform a single factor multivariate analysis of variance (see Chapter 11), and actually does perform the basic computations. The next line, /WSFACTOR ..., however, instructs the computer to consider the four dependent measures as observations in a repeated measures (or within subjects) factor, and thus to perform a split-plot factorial design analysis of variance instead, treating **a** as the between-subjects factor and **b** as the within-subjects factor with four levels. It also instructs the computer to perform trend analyses on the within subjects factor for both the main effect means and the interaction means (though in all probability you will not be interested in these analyses).

The following line, /METHOD=SSTYPE(3), indicates which method is used in making the calculations. (The program does not use the formulae that were presented earlier.) In this program, use is made of one of four methods for calculating the analysis of variance results. These are referred to as SSTYPE(1), SSTYPE(2), SSTYPE(3), or SSTYPE(4). If sample sizes are equal, all four methods give the same answers (and identical to those shown in our example), so which is chosen is irrelevant. If sample sizes are unequal, however, the various methods give different results that have different implications for interpretation. Many authors [see, for example, Kirk (1995)] recommend SSTYPE(3), but if you do have unequal sample sizes in your analysis you should consult a textbook like Kirk (1995) to ensure that you are using the correct method for your purposes. Note too, that in split-plot designs, you must have complete data for each individual across the repeated measure factor. Thus, when we speak of unequal sample sizes with respect to this analysis, we are referring to different numbers of respondents in the various **A** groups.

The statements defined by the keyword EMMEANS identifies the four tables of means we requested, viz., the grand mean (Overall), the main effect means for factor *A,* the main effect means for the repeated measures factor, *B,* and the *AB* means. The statement, /PRINT = DESCRIPTIVES ETASQ OPOWER HOMOGENEITY, results because of the four choices made in the OPTIONS window (see Step 8 above). It results in the computer providing information about the cell means as well as the main effect means, the estimates of effect size and power, and the test of homogeneity of variance. Each of these are discussed in the sections to follow when the corresponding results are presented.

The output for this program contains a number of different parts. Some are applicable to the *Univariate Approach* to the data analysis, and some are applicable to the *Multivariate Approach,* and some are applicable to both. The univariate and multivariate approaches are discussed here in separate sections. Most of the output that is appropriate to both approaches is presented immediately below. This information includes some identifying information and descriptive statistics, as well as the univariate test of the significance of the between-subject effects. This latter is appropriate to both the univariate and multivariate approaches to split-plot designs simply because there is not a multivariate test of these between-subject effects. If you opted, therefore, to use the multivariate approach to present the within-subjects results, you would still need the information concerning the between-subjects effects.

Identifying Information

The following table defines the constituents of the variable for the between-subjects analysis:

Within-Subjects Factors

Measure: MEASURE_1

B	Dependent Variable
1	$B1$
2	$B2$
3	$B3$
4	$B4$

This is followed by an indication of the number of levels of the between-subjects factor, and the number of subjects in each level:

Between-Subjects Factors

		N
A	1.00	5
	2.00	5
	3.00	5

Descriptive Statistics

The following table presents the summary statistics of the data. It is presented because the option Descriptive Statistics was selected in Step 8, page 135. Much of the information contained in this table is redundant with that obtained if you also select the Display Means options in Step 7, page 135. Ordinarily one of them would probably be omitted but both are shown here for completeness. It will be noted that this table presents the AB means and the B means, but not the A means. Using the Display options in Step 7 permits the researcher to output all means if desired. It will also be noted that the following table presents the standard deviations associated with the means. This is a bit different from the information provided by selecting the Display Means option.

Descriptive Statistics

	A	Mean	Std. Deviation	N
$B1$	1.00	4.6000	1.1402	5
	2.00	6.2000	1.6432	5
	3.00	6.2000	.8367	5
	Total	5.6667	1.3973	15
$B2$	1.00	6.4000	1.1402	5
	2.00	7.0000	1.8708	5
	3.00	8.0000	.7071	5
	Total	7.1333	1.4075	15
$B3$	1.00	7.6000	.8944	5
	2.00	7.2000	1.7889	5
	3.00	9.8000	.8367	5
	Total	8.2000	1.6562	15
$B4$	1.00	7.4000	1.1402	5
	2.00	8.2000	.8367	5
	3.00	11.6000	1.3416	5
	Total	9.0667	2.1536	15

TESTS OF BETWEEN-SUBJECTS EFFECTS

The analysis of variance summary table for the between-subjects factor in our example is as follows:

Tests of Between-Subjects Effects

Measure: MEASURE_1
Transformed Variable: Average

Source	Type III Sum of Squares	df	Mean Square	F	Sig.	Eta-Squared	Noncent. Parameter	Observed Power[a]
Intercept	3390.017	1	3390.017	1111.481	.000	.989	1111.481	1.000
A	61.633	2	30.817	10.104	.003	.627	20.208	.950
Error	36.600	12	3.050					

[a]Computed using alpha = .05

The term MEASURE_1 in the heading of this table refers to the transformed variable which is the mean of the four levels of B. In this analysis, the test of the Intercept is simply a test that the mean of all the observations differs significantly from 0. Where all the observations are positive numbers, this will generally be significant. If some of the numbers were negative and some positive, it may be of some interest to know that the mean departs significantly from 0 in one direction or the other, but generally researchers do not have an hypothesis bearing on this. The test of A is a test of whether or not the means for A (summing across B) vary more than can reasonably be expected on the basis of chance. The A means for this example are 6.50, 7.15, and 8.90 (see Table 2.A, page 147). The F-ratio is computed as:

$$\frac{MS_A}{MS_{S/A}} \quad \frac{30.817}{3.050} = 10.104$$

Note, in this equation, that $MS_{S/A}$ is used to refer to the term that **SPSS WINDOWS GLM** refers to as the Mean Square for Error. The degrees of freedom for this ratio are 2 for the numerator and 12 for the denominator. Since this F-ratio is significant, we can conclude that the 3 *means* *vary more than* could be reasonably attributed to chance. That is, we reject the null hypothesis that the variation in the A means is due to chance. We must investigate the means themselves to determine whether the hypothesis (see a, page 130) that the researcher had is actually supported, but we will consider this in a later section.

The F-ratios in this table have eta-squared and observed power estimates associated with them. As noted in Chapters 4 and 5, these eta-squared values are partial eta-squares. That is, they are the ratio of the sum of squares for the effect of interest over the sum of the sum of squares of the effect of interest plus that for the corresponding error term. Thus, the eta-squared for **A** is:

$$\eta^2 = \frac{SS_A}{SS_A + SS_{S/A}} = \frac{61.633}{61.633 + 36.600} = .627$$

Or alternatively:

$$\eta^2 = \frac{df_1 F}{df_1 F + df_2} = \frac{2(10.104)}{2(10.104) + 12} = .627$$

The power associated with this value is .950. This means that we would expect our results to be replicated 95% of the time at the .05 level. Thus, if we were reporting the results for the test of the main effects of **A**, we might note that significant effects were obtained for **A** ($F(2,12) = 10.104$, p < .003), that the proportion of variance accounted for by this effect was .627, and the probability of obtaining significance at the .05 level if the null hypothesis was false was .950.

TESTS OF WITHIN-SUBJECTS EFFECTS

The within-subjects effects can be analyzed using either a Univariate Approach or a Multivariate Approach. These are discussed in the following sections.

The Univariate Approach

The output for the univariate analysis of within-subjects effects is:

Tests of Within-Subjects Effects

Measure: MEASURE_1

Source		Type III Sum of Squares	df	Mean Square	F	Sig.	Eta-Squared	Noncent. Parameter	Observed Power[a]
B	Sphericity Assumed	96.583	3	32.194	30.989	.000	.721	92.968	1.000
	Greenhouse-Geisser	96.583	2.404	40.181	30.989	.000	.721	74.489	1.000
	Huynh-Feldt	96.583	3.000	32.194	30.989	.000	.721	92.968	1.000
	Lower-bound	96.583	1.000	96.583	30.989	.000	.721	30.989	.999
B*A	Sphericity Assumed	22.767	6	3.794	3.652	.006	.378	21.914	.918
	Greenhouse-Geisser	22.767	4.807	4.736	3.652	.012	.378	17.559	.861
	Huynh-Feldt	22.767	6.000	3.794	3.652	.006	.378	21.914	.918
	Lower-bound	22.767	2.000	11.383	3.652	.058	.378	7.305	.558
Error(B)	Sphericity Assumed	37.400	36	1.039					
	Greenhouse-Geisser	37.400	28.844	1.297					
	Huynh-Feldt	37.400	36.000	1.039					
	Lower-bound	37.400	12.000	3.117					

[a]Computed using alpha = .05

This analysis provides two sets of F-ratios, one for the B effect and one for the AB interaction. There are four rows of answers in each set. Note that for some statistics (Type III Sum Of Squares, F, and Eta-Squared) the values are identical within the set; for others (df, Mean Square, Sig., Non-central Parameter, and Observed Power) they can vary. This will be discussed in more detail below. For now, we will focus attention on the first row in each set, since these statistics are based on the definitional formulae presented earlier.

The F-ratio, with Sphericity Assumed (see table above), for B is computed as:

$$\frac{MS_B}{MS_{BS/A}} \quad \frac{31.194}{1.039} = 30.989$$

with 3 degrees of freedom for the numerator and 36 for the denominator. It will be noted in the table that the Mean Square for the denominator of this F-ratio is referred to as Error(B). I prefer to use the label $MS_{BS/A}$, because this labelling indicates that the variation is due to the interaction of the treatment B and Subjects computed within each group. We will use this label from now on. At any rate, this F-ratio is significant indicating that the four B means vary more than you could reasonably attribute to chance. In this case, the four means are 5.667, 7.133, 8.200 and 9.067 (see Table 3.B, page 147. This would appear to support the researcher's hypothesis (see b, page 130), but again post-hoc tests of means might be performed to determine which of the means differ significantly from each other.

The eta-squared associated with this effect is reported in the table as .721, which is the ratio of 96.583 to (96.583 + 37.40). This value of eta-squared can also be calculated using the formula involving the F-ratio and the associated degrees of freedom, as demonstrated previously. The power associated with this value of eta-squared is 1.00.

The F-ratio for the AB interaction, with Sphericity Assumed, is computed as:

$$\frac{MS_{AB}}{MS_{BS/A}} \quad \frac{3.794}{1.039} = 3.652$$

with 6 degrees of freedom for the numerator and 36 for the denominator. This F-ratio is significant indicating that there is a significant AB interaction. To understand the interaction, it is necessary to plot the means and to perform some further tests on them. This will be discussed in a later section. Again, note that the eta squared is 22.767/(22.767 + 37.40) = .378 (this value too can be computed using the F-ratio and associated degrees of freedom), and the associated power is .918.

Mauchly's Test of Sphericity and the Epsilon Multipliers

As noted in Chapter 5, one problem with F-ratios for within-subject effects is that they tend to have a positive bias if the assumption of circularity is violated. That is, violation of the assumption influences the magnitude of the Mean Squares in such a way that the F-ratios will tend to be inflated, increasing the chance to committing a Type I error. The assumption of circularity is simply that the variance of the differences among the repeated measures is equal in the population for all pairs of differences. In this case, there are 4 repeated measures, and therefore there are (4)(3)/2 or 6 such differences that could be computed (ie., $B_1 - B_2, \ldots B_3 - B_4$). Mauchly's (1940) test of sphericity, computed by **SPSS WINDOWS GLM** provides a test of the assumption of circularity of the pooled variance/covariance matrix. The arithmetic underlying this test is a bit complex. Suffice it to say that the test makes use of a statistic, W, that has associated with it an approximate chi-square test of significance. The **SPSS WINDOWS GLM** output for this example is as follows:

Mauchly's Test of Sphericity[b]

Measure: MEASURE_1

Within Subjects Effect	Mauchly's W	Approx. Chi-Square	df	Sig.	Epsilon[a]		
					Greenhouse-Geisser	Huynh-Feldt	Lower-bound
B	.667	4.347	5	.502	.801	1.000	.333

Tests the null hypothesis that the error covariance matrix of the orthonormalized transformed dependent variables is proportional to an identity matrix.

[a]May be used to adjust the degrees of freedom for the averaged tests of significance. Corrected tests are displayed in the layers (by default) of the Tests of Within Subjects Effects table.

[b]Design: Intercept+A
Within Subjects Design: B

As applied to these data, the lack of significance of the test ($\chi^2(5)$ = 4.347, ns) suggests that there is little reason to assume that the assumption of circularity has been violated. Thus, the F-ratios could well be evaluated at the degrees of freedom stated. Many statisticians (e.g., Kirk, 1995; Myers & Well, 1991), however, do not recommend this statistic and instead recommend another procedure that routinely adjusts the degrees of freedom of both numerator and denominator of all tests of within-subject effects. This adjustment derives from research by Box (1954), who demonstrated that an F-ratio based on within-subject effects follows the F-distribution with the degrees of freedom reduced to reflect the degree of violation of circularity. This procedure reduces the degrees of freedom for both the numerator and denominator for any within-subject F-ratio by multiplying them by a correction factor. Three such correction factors have been suggested, and **SPSS WINDOWS GLM** provides each of these *epsilon* multipliers in the preceding table.

SPSS WINDOWS GLM also gives adjustments to the Mean Squares by dividing the Sums of Squares by the adjusted degrees of freedom [see the table for tests of within-subjects effects (page 139)]. These adjustments also result in changes to Sig., Noncentral Parameter, and Observed Power. Various textbooks (see, for example, Kirk, 1995) suggest a three-step procedure for making adjustments to the degrees of freedom for the within-subject effects. This derives from the days when the epsilon multipliers had to be calculated by hand, and this procedure was rather laborious for all but the lower-bound epsilon.

In *Step 1,* you first determine whether or not the F-ratio is significant without any modification of the degrees of freedom (i.e., the first line in each step, identified as Sphericity Assumed, in the table of tests of within-subjects effects on page 139). If it is not, there is no need to use the epsilon multipliers. If it is, however, you could use the epsilon multipliers to adjust the degrees of freedom and conduct more conservative tests. The multipliers vary in terms of their conservativeness.

Step 2 uses the most conservative estimate, the *lower-bound epsilon.* This value is simply the reciprocal of the degrees of freedom for the repeated measures factor. If the F-ratio is significant using this value, then one could conclude that it was significant, even taking into account maximum violation of the assumption of circularity. This test is conservative, however, so if the F-ratio is not significant, it is recommended that you repeat the procedure using an epsilon multiplier based on the degree of non-circularity present in the sample data.

For *Step 3,* two estimates are available, one described in detail by Collier, Baker, Mandeville, and Hayes (1967) (and recommended by Greenhouse and Geisser, 1959) and one proposed by Huynh & Feldt (1976). The Greenhouse-Geisser estimate is the more conservative of the two.

Which you use is a matter of preference. Kirk (1995) recommends using the Greenhouse-Geisser estimate, while Myers and Well (1991) opt for the Huynh-Feldt one. Some researchers would do the computations with the next most conservative epsilon multiplier (i.e., the Greenhouse-Geisser), and if this was not significant, proceed with the least conservative (the Huynh-Feldt epsilon). Since **SPSS WINDOWS GLM** presents all three epsilon values (see table, p. 141) as well as the results of the actual calculations (see table, p. 139), researchers can choose the one they prefer so the three-step procedure is not necessary. Note in our example that the Huynh-Feldt value is 1.00, though this is not always the case. It can vary from 0 to values in excess of 1.0, but if it exceeds 1.0, **SPSS WINDOWS GLM** outputs the value of 1.00. We will illustrate the use of the *Greenhouse-Geisser epsilon.*

Evaluation of the *B* Effects.   Multiply the degrees of freedom for both the numerator and denominator of the *F*-ratio for *B* by the Greenhouse-Geisser epsilon as follows: (Note the Greenhouse-Geisser epsilon is given as .801 in the table on page 141, but it is actually .80123. This value is used in the following calculations, so that the answers agree with those given in the table on page 139.)

$$\text{Numerator} = (.80123)(3) = 2.404$$

$$\text{Denominator} = (.80123)(36) = 28.844$$

Generally, when reporting degrees of freedom in a manuscript, values are given in whole numbers. It is thus customary to round these values. I recommend always rounding up. Thus, the adjusted degrees of freedom in this example would be 3 for the numerator and 29 for the denominator. The alpha level presented in the table on page 139, however, evaluates significance for the actual degrees of freedom calculated above. If it were necessary for you to evaluate significance using the table of the *F*-distribution (Table C, Appendix), you would use 3 and 29 degrees of freedom, which could result in slightly different values. In any event, the *F*-ratio is significant in this case so you could proceed to conduct tests of significance between the *B* means, if such tests were meaningful.

Evaluation of the *AB* Effects.   Adjust the degrees of freedom for the numerator and denominator of the *F*-ratio for the *AB* interaction by multiplying by the Greenhouse-Geisser epsilon as follows:

$$\text{Numerator} = (.80123)(6) = 4.807$$

$$\text{Denominator} = (.80123)(36) = 28.844$$

You could evaluate $F = 3.652$ at 5 and 29 degrees of freedom by making use of a table of the *F*-distribution (Table C, Appendix). However, since GLM gives the alpha level in the table, it is not necessary to use Table C. This value is significant at the .05 level, thus you would report the result as follows [$F(5,29) = 3.652, p<.05$], indicating, in the body of the text or by footnote, that the degrees of freedom had been adjusted with the Greenhouse-Geisser epsilon.

Tests of Within-Subjects Contrasts.   **SPSS WINDOWS GLM** Repeated Measures routinely outputs a table of within-subjects contrasts. This table could be placed under either Univariate or Multivariate approaches to the analysis of the repeated components in the split-plot design. I chose to place it here because the statistics are univariate in form. This table (presented below) is comprised of a set of contrasts of each of the main effects of *B* and the *AB* interaction. The nature of the contrast can be specified when constructing the Syntax File (we didn't discuss it), but the default (identified as none in the contrast window) involves the use of orthogonal polynomials (polynomial is also one option available). In this form, the first test of *B* refers to a linear trend, the second, a quadratic trend, and so on. The corresponding tests for *B * A* refer to Treatment/Contrast interactions (see Kirk, 1995).

Personally, I recommend that you ignore this table unless you are interested in the particular contrast presented. In any event, the results should not be interpreted if the corresponding F-ratios from the tests of within-subjects effects (see page 139) are not significant. For the orthogonal contrasts in this example, you will note that the sum of the Sums of Squares of the contrasts add up to the corresponding Sum of Squares for that Effect. Thus, as we saw in the table of within-subject effects, the Sum of Squares for B equalled 96.583, which is 95.203 + 1.350 + .030 (the three values presented in the table of within-subjects contrasts for B). Similarly, the Sum of Squares for AB was 22.767, which is equal to 18.447 + 3.700 +.620, while that for Error(B) was 37.400, which equals 20.000 + 11.200 + 6.200.

Tests of Within-Subjects Contrasts

Measure: MEASURE_1

Source	B	Type III Sum of Squares	df	Mean Square	F	Sig.	Eta-Squared	Noncent. Parameter	Observed Power[a]
B	Linear	95.203	1	95.203	57.122	.000	.826	57.122	1.000
	Quadratic	1.350	1	1.350	1.446	.252	.108	1.446	.198
	Cubic	3.000E-02	1	3.000E-02	.058	.814	.005	.058	.056
$B * A$	Linear	18.447	2	9.223	5.534	.020	.480	11.068	.747
	Quadratic	3.700	2	1.850	1.982	.180	.248	3.964	.330
	Cubic	.620	2	.310	.600	.564	.091	1.200	.127
Error(B)	Linear	20.000	12	1.667					
	Quadratic	11.200	12	.933					
	Cubic	6.200	12	.517					

[a.] Computed using alpha = .05

The Multivariate Approach

As indicated earlier, the multivariate approach applies only to the within-subject effects. (Even if you had adopted this approach, you would report the univariate results for the between-subjects effects.) The within-subjects effects include tests of the main effects of B, and the AB interaction. **SPSS GLM** outputs the results of a multivariate analysis of variance for each of these effects. This consists of one table which presents four tests for each of the B and AB effects.

Multivariate Tests[d]

Effect		Value	F	Hypothesis df	Error df	Sig.	Eta-Squared	Noncent. Parameter	Observed Power[a]
B	Pillai's Trace	.838	17.236[b]	3.000	10.000	.000	.838	51.709	.999
	Wilk's Lambda	.162	17.236[b]	3.000	10.000	.000	.838	51.709	.999
	Hotelling's Trace	5.171	17.236[b]	3.000	10.000	.000	.838	51.709	.999
	Roy's Largest Root	5.171	17.236[b]	3.000	10.000	.000	.838	51.709	.999
$B * A$	Pillai's Trace	.778	2.336	6.000	22.000	.068	.389	14.014	.678
	Wilk's Lambda	.358	2.237[b]	6.000	20.000	.082	.402	13.422	.643
	Hotelling's Trace	1.412	2.118	6.000	18.000	.102	.414	12.706	.599
	Roy's Largest Root	1.049	3.845[c]	3.000	11.000	.042	.512	11.534	.660

[a]Computed using alpha = .05

[b]Exact statistic

[c]The statistic is an upper bound on F that yields a lower bound on the significance level.

[d]Design: Intercept+A
  Within Subjects Design: B

Evaluation of the *B* Effects.   The tests for the significance of B make use of the four multivariate tests of significance (Pillai's Trace, Wilks' Lambda, Hotelling's Trace, and Roy's Largest Root), but they all result in the same F-ratio. These tests are directly comparable with those reported in Chapter 5 for the main effects of the repeated measures factor. That is, they are single sample Hotelling's T^2 tests. The only difference between this test and the one reported in Chapter 5 is that there is a between-subjects factor in the present analysis, so that this test makes use of a pooled variance/covariance matrix (i.e., one could compute a variance/covariance matrix for each of the three A groups, and then average the values in each cell to obtain one-pooled matrix). The only major implication of this is that the degrees of freedom for the estimate of error in this design are different. They can be shown to be equal to $(N - (a - 1) - (b - 1))$ which is equivalent to $(N - a - b + 2)$. The observant student will notice that this is conceptually equivalent to the degrees of freedom for error identified in the previous chapter, except this estimate recognizes the existence of the A factor. The degrees of freedom for the numerator are defined as in the previous chapter. That is, they are $(b - 1)$.

When reporting these results, you would state that the multivariate test of the main effects of B was significant using notation such as $[F(3,10) = 17.236, p<.001]$ or Hotelling's $T^2(3,10) = 17.236$, $p<.001$). You could then report that the B means of 5.67, 7.33, 8.20, and 9.07 were more variable than you could reasonably attribute to chance. In order to determine differences between pairs of means, you would make use of the relevant test of means described under Tests of Means, Main Effects for B.

Evaluation of the *AB* Effects.   The multivariate test of the interaction of AB yields different values for the different tests (Pillai's Trace, Wilks' Lambda, Hotelling's Trace, and Roy's Largest Root), and different F-ratios as well. This is because the various tests evaluate the assumption of the interaction slightly differently. Different authors favor different tests, but monte carlo investigations generally find that Pillai's trace is the more robust with respect to violations of assumptions (Olson, 1976). We shall, therefore, focus on this test in this example.

We will not discuss this test in any detail here since it is identical in form to the Multivariate Analysis of Variance described in Chapter 11. In Chapter 11, we describe all the tests (i.e., Pillai's Trace, Wilks' Lambda, Hotelling's Trace, and Roy's Largest Root) in more detail, and even give the defining formulae for the more curious student. About the only difference between the data in this chapter and that in Chapter 11 is here the various dependent measures are the same test administered under different conditions, while in Chapter 11, they are different tests. All of the formulae, including those for the degrees of freedom are common to the two sets of tests. Thus, the results presented here refer to a test of whether or not the pattern of dependent measures is the same under the different levels of A. In Chapter 11, this has one implication (to be discussed there), here it has another. If the pattern of the dependent measures (i.e., the different B means) is different under the different levels of A, then this suggests that there is an interaction between A and B,

When reporting the results of this analysis, you would again indicate that you had adopted the multivariate approach, this time to test the interaction between A and B. You would report your statistics as [Pillai's Trace = .778, Approximate $F(6, 22) = 2.336$, ns]. Note that this result is different from that obtained with the univariate approach, even after adjusting the degrees of freedom using the Greenhouse-Geisser ϵ, and also different from the results suggested by Roy's Largest Root. It is therefore, necessary to decide beforehand which approach (the univariate or multivariate) that you are going to adopt, and the particular multivariate statistic you are going to use. It is not acceptable to go fishing and choose the statistic that best suits your taste. If you do, you simply compromise the meaning of Type I error.

If the multivariate test of the interaction had been significant, it would have indicated that the pattern of means of the various levels of B varied more than you could reasonably attribute to chance across the various levels of A. This is equivalent to saying that there is an interaction between A and B. If this were the case, it is likely that the researcher would wish to conduct some tests of the cell means. This would likely involve tests of the simple main effects. These are discussed below in the section on Tests of Simple Main Effects, pages 149–153.

Tests of Assumptions

One assumption underlying the F-ratio for the between subjects effects is the homogeneity of variance assumption underlying the different A groups. As we saw in the chapters on the single factor and completely randomized factorial design, the analysis of variance is robust to violations of this assumption provided sample sizes are equal. Although **SPSS WINDOWS GLM** performs Levene's tests of homogeneity of variance, as shown in the following table, these tests are not directly applicable to the assumption concerning the F-ratio for the main effects of A.

Levene's Test of Equality of Error Variances[a]

	F	$df1$	$df2$	Sig.
$B1$	2.220	2	12	.151
$B2$	1.043	2	12	.382
$B3$	3.072	2	12	.084
$B4$	1.149	2	12	.350

Tests that null hypothesis that the error variance of the dependent variable is equal across groups.

[a]Design: Intercept+A

Within Subjects Design: B

These tests are performed with respect to each level of the repeated measures factor for our split-plot analysis. They are relevant if you wish to conduct F-ratios of the effects at each level of B and were concerned that the assumption of homogeneity was satisfied in each case. If you wanted to perform the relevant test of homogeneity of variance for the main effects of A, however, it would be necessary for you to compute mean scores for each individual collapsing over the repeated measures factor, and conduct the analysis using **SPSS WINDOWS ONEWAY.** As stated, however, this is probably unnecessary if sample sizes are equal, or unless the variances are extremely disparate.

As we saw above, an assumption underlying the F-ratios for the within subjects effects is that of circularity of the pooled variance/covariance matrix. This is tested using Mauchly's test of Sphericity, and in any event adjustments to the degrees of freedom could be made using the *epsilon* multipliers. All of this assumes, however, that the variance/covariance matrices associated with each level of the between groups factor are themselves equivalent. Since we have three levels of A in our study, we have three bXb variance/covariance matrices, and before we pool them, we should determine whether or not they are equivalent. One test that has been proposed for this is the Box (1950) M test, and this is produced by **SPSS WINDOWS GLM** if you request the homogeneity tests (see Step 8, page 135). This output is as follows:

Box's Test of Equality of Covariance Matrices[a]

Box's M	38.709
F	.
$df1$	10
$df2$	42
Sig.	.

Tests the null hypothesis that the observed covariance matrices of the dependent variables are equal across groups.

[a]Design: Intercept+A

Within Subjects Design: B

The test itself requires solving for the determinant of each of the three variance/covariance matrices, and if this cannot be done (there are a few reasons why this might occur, which we will not discuss), the computer will report Box's M, but will not present values for the F-ratio or associated significance value for this statistic. In our example, the determinant could not be computed for one of our matrices, but the computer computed the Box M statistic, based on the remaining two matrices (it reduced the degrees of freedom accordingly). Note, however, that it did not output a corresponding F-ratio.[1]

TESTS OF MEANS

As discussed in earlier chapters, tests of means following an analysis of variance can involve either *planned* or *a posteriori* comparisons. As already seen, the arithmetic for planned comparisons is essentially the same as that for *a posteriori* comparisons, except they define Type I error in terms of the number of comparisons planned, not the number possible. This presentation here, then, will focus only on *a posteriori* tests.

Generally, when a significant F-ratio is obtained, a researcher is interested in making comparisons of means. In a two factor analysis of variance, such comparisons can involve either main effect or interaction means. Comparisons of means make use of one of three basic statistics, referred to here as q, t, and F, and a number of sampling distributions based on one of these statistics. Tests such as the Tukey Honestly Significant Difference, the Newman-Keuls test, and Duncan's New Multiple Range test make use of a statistic that takes the form of q (see below). Tests such as the Least-Significant Difference, the Dunn Bonferroni t, and Dunnett's comparison with a control condition are based on the t-statistic, while Scheffé's S statistic makes use of an F-ratio.

When conducting tests of means, it should be recognized that in the presence of a significant interaction, any interpretation of the associated main effects is questionable. This is because the significant interaction indicates that the means in the interaction cells act in ways that are not consistent with the main effects. Thus, where the interaction is significant, tests of significant main effects are generally not performed. Of course, if the interaction is not significant, then one would proceed to conduct tests of the contrasts involving significant main effects.

SPSS WINDOWS GLM Repeated Measures outputs tables of means and standard errors as requested in Step 7, page 135. The table output by the request for **OVERALL** is for the grand mean and is as follows:

1. Grand Mean

Measure:MEASURE_1

		95% Confidence Interval	
Mean	Std. Error	Lower Bound	Upper Bound
7.517	.225	7.025	8.008

[1]The concerned student might wonder how to proceed if we conclude that we had not satisfied the assumption of equivalence of the variance/covariance matrices, or as in this case, we cannot even evaluate the assumption. There isn't an easy answer to this question. One approach is to report the analysis, indicating the failure to satisfy (or test) the assumption, use the *epsilon* multiplier when reporting the F-ratios, and perform any tests of means using t-tests applied only to the data under examination (i.e., do not use Mean Squares, or df from the analysis of variance).

The F-ratio for the Intercept shown in the table of tests of between-subjects effects on page 138 is a test that this mean (7.517) is significantly greater than 0.

A second table that is output is the table of the means for the main effect of A. The F-ratio for A in the table of tests of between-subjects effects on page 138 is a test that these three means are more variable than would be expected on the basis of chance.

2. A

Measure:MEASURE_1

			95% Confidence Interval	
A	**Mean**	**Std. Error**	**Lower Bound**	**Upper Bound**
1.00	6.500	.391	5.649	7.351
2.00	7.150	.391	6.299	8.001
3.00	8.900	.391	8.049	9.751

The third table is for the means of B. The F-ratio for B presented in the table of tests of within-subjects effects on page 139 (or that presented in the multivariate tests for B on page 143) is a test of whether or not these means are more variable than one would expect on the basis of chance.

3. B

Measure:MEASURE_1

			95% Confidence Interval	
B	**Mean**	**Std. Error**	**Lower Bound**	**Upper Bound**
1	5.667	.323	4.963	6.371
2	7.133	.343	6.386	7.881
3	8.200	.323	7.496	8.904
4	9.067	.291	8.434	9.700

Tests of Main Effects

If the interaction is not significant, but a main effect is, it is meaningful to make comparisons of the main effect means. The form of the main effects of A and B are comparable but in the split-plot design the error terms for the corresponding F-ratios differ, and the test statistics reflect this difference by using the appropriate error term.

Main Effects for A

Assuming that factor A is based on between-subject comparisons, the form for the tests of A means are as follows:

$$q = \frac{\overline{X}_{a1} - \overline{X}_{a2}}{\sqrt{\dfrac{MS_{S/A}}{bn}}}$$

$$t = \frac{\overline{X}_{a1} - \overline{X}_{a2}}{\sqrt{\dfrac{2MS_{S/A}}{bn}}}$$

$$F = \frac{(\overline{X}_{a1} - \overline{X}_a)^2}{\dfrac{2MS_{S/A}}{bn}}$$

Depending on the test of interest, the results of these computations will be compared with values in the appropriate table corresponding to a particular sampling distribution. The following example will make use of the q- statistic as applied to the Tukey Honestly Significant Test (HSD), and compares the first and third means for the main effects of A.

$$q = \frac{6.500 - 8.900}{\sqrt{\dfrac{3.050}{(5)(4)}}} = \frac{-2.40}{.39} = -6.15$$

For the Tukey HSD test, we would compare the value of 6.15 against the value in the table of the Studentized Range for 3 steps (the number of A means), and degrees of freedom for the error term of 12 (see Table D, Appendix). This value is 3.77 ($p<.05$), and 5.05 ($p<.01$), thus we would conclude that this difference is significant at the .01 level. Of course, it is generally the case that a researcher would be interested in testing all possible pairs of means, and this can be done by hand using the formulae presented here.

It is possible to perform such posthoc tests using **SPSS WINDOWS GLM Repeated Measures** for the main effects of A by employing the **posthoc** option, which permits 18 possible tests, or the **EMMEANS** option which permits the three applications of the t-test (see Steps 6 and 7 respectively, pages 134–135). As stated in earlier chapters, these procedures do not present test statistics, but rather indicate only whether or not a difference is significant. This seems of limited value and, as a consequence, these options were not discussed in this chapter. Furthermore the standard error reported in the table (not shown here) is the standard error for t not q. Thus, it would be necessary to divide that value by $\sqrt{2}$ to calculate q by hand as shown in Chapter 3 (page 74).

Main Effects for B

Similar tests can be used for comparing the means for the main effect of factor B. When these means are based on within-subject comparisons, the form of the tests are slightly different. In the following, only the test for q is discussed, since we are directing attention to Tukey's HSD, though the generalizations to t and F are obvious:

$$q = \frac{\overline{X}_{b1} - \overline{X}_{b2}}{\sqrt{\dfrac{MS_{BS/A}}{an}}}$$

Tukey's HSD test comparing the first two B means is as follows:

$$q = \frac{5.67 - 7.13}{\sqrt{\dfrac{1.039}{(3)(5)}}} = \frac{-1.47}{.26} = -5.65$$

For the Tukey HSD test, we would compare the value of 5.65 against the tabled values of the Studentized Range for 4 steps and 36 degrees of freedom (see Table D, Appendix). These values are 3.85 ($p < .05$) and 4.80 ($p < .01$) for 4 and 30 degrees of freedom, the closest values in the table. Thus, we would conclude that the difference is significant at the .01 level. Again, it is likely that you would want to test all possible pairwise comparisons, which would involve hand calculations if you were to use the formulae presented in this chapter. It is true that **SPSS WINDOWS GLM Repeated Measures** does perform some tests of means. For a repeated measures factor, only the **EMMEANS** option (with the three applications of the t-test) is available, and this option does not use the formulae presented in this chapter. Instead, the Standard errors are based only on the data for the pair of interest in any comparison. As a consequence, the degrees of freedom would be equal to the number of pairs of subjects minus 1, rather than the degrees of freedom associated with the error term for B. This application is not discussed in this chapter.

Tests of Simple Main Effects

Tests of simple main effects are concerned with evaluating differences among cell means. These means are output by **SPSS WINDOWS GLM** Repeated Measures as part of the **EMMEANS** procedure, and are as follows:

4. A * B

Measure: MEASURE_1

A	B	Mean	Std. Error	95% Confidence Interval	
				Lower Bound	Upper Bound
1.00	1	4.600	.560	3.380	5.820
	2	6.400	.594	5.105	7.695
	3	7.600	.560	6.380	8.820
	4	7.400	.503	6.303	8.497
2.00	1	6.200	.560	4.980	7.420
	2	7.000	.594	5.705	8.295
	3	7.200	.560	5.980	8.420
	4	8.200	.503	7.103	9.297
3.00	1	6.200	.560	4.980	7.420
	2	8.000	.594	6.705	9.295
	3	9.800	.560	8.580	11.020
	4	11.600	.503	10.503	12.697

There are many ways of analyzing and interpreting interactions. One of the most common is to draw a graph (see Figure 1) of the means, and although this figure is often described as a graph of the interaction, it should be obvious that it also reflects any of the main effect differences that are in the data. Researchers then sometimes simply provide a verbal description of the graph. The problem with this approach is that often implications are made that some means differ significantly from others, when in fact no such test has been made. It is always a good idea to draw the graph, but it is recommended that this be augmented with the tests of significance that are appropriate. As was also the case for the factorial design analysis of variance, one such approach is a test of simple main effects.

Simple main effects involve contrasting means for one factor while holding the other factor constant. In a two-factor AB design, there are two possible sets of simple main effects, (a) the simple main effects of B holding A constant, and (b) the simple main effects of A holding B constant. In a split-plot factorial design, these two tests have different error terms and these must be accommodated in the tests of significance. Although both tests will be discussed here, it is recommended that in any analysis of variance only one should be conducted and discussed. Which is performed is often due to the researcher's major interest or preference, but often too, the plot (see Figure 1) will help a researcher decide which is the most appropriate.

Looking at Figure 1, a researcher may feel that it is most meaningful to hold Anxiety constant and determine how No. of Letters per Word influences learning. This would be an instance where one would perform simple main effects of B (No. of Letters per Word) holding A (Anxiety) constant. Thus, for example, the researcher might consider the High-Anxiety condition, and note that there is a linear increase in the Number of Trials needed to learn the material as the Number of Letters per Word increases. By comparing each mean with every other mean for the High-Anxiety condition, he/she can identify the pattern of significant differences. Similar analyses could be done for the Medium- and Low-Anxiety conditions, and the different patterns can be noted, described, and explained. One might anticipate that since each of these contrasts involves a within-subjects comparison, the differences needed for significance might be smaller since the error terms for such contrasts are often relatively smaller than those for between-subject contrasts.

Simple Main Effects of B Holding A Constant. The form of the q-test for the simple main effects of B is presented below. The forms for t and F are not given, but their generalization is obvious.

$$q = \frac{\overline{X}_{a1b1} - \overline{X}_{a1b2}}{\sqrt{\dfrac{MS_{BS/A}}{n}}}$$

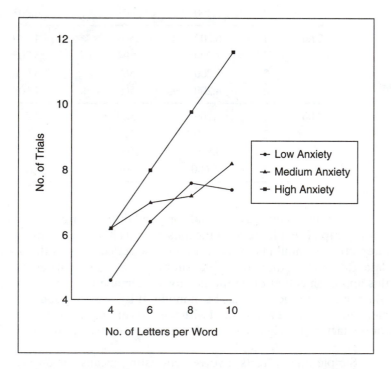

Figure 1. No. of Trials as a Function of Task Difficulty and Anxiety

Note, for this test, that the appropriate error term is the error term for both the main effect of B and the AB interaction. Applying this test to the means for A_1B_1 and A_1B_2 to compute Tukey's HSD yields the following:

$$q = \frac{4.60 - 6.40}{\sqrt{\frac{1.039}{5}}} = \frac{-1.80}{.46} = -3.91$$

This would be evaluated at 4 steps and 36 degrees of freedom using the table for the Studentized Range statistic (Table D, Appendix), and would be found to be significant at the .05 level. As indicated above, such calculations would have to be done by hand if the intention were to use the formulae presented here, and the associated degrees of freedom. Also, as indicated before, **SPSS WINDOWS GLM Repeated Measures** can perform the three t-tests which are part of the **EMMEANS** procedure. To do this, however, it is necessary to modify the **EMMEANS** statement for Tables (a * b) in the Syntax Editor as described in Chapter 4, page 98. In this case, however, the compare statement would refer to B the repeated measure factor, not A, the between-subjects factor. Also, as mentioned in Chapter 6, the standard error is based only on the pair being compared, and not on the error term from the full analysis as in the formulae presented here, and thus the degrees of freedom could be much smaller.

Simple Main Effects of *A* Holding *B* Constant. Some researchers might prefer not to make comparisons across the Number of Letters per Word at each level of Anxiety, but rather hold No. of Letters per Word constant, and make contrasts across the three levels of Anxiety. This would involve conducting tests of means for A holding B constant (i.e., tests of the simple main effect of A at B). When making such tests in a split-plot factorial design like the one under discussion, it is necessary to compute a pooled-error term and estimate of the degrees of freedom associated with this error term. This pooled-error term takes the form:

$$MS_{pooled} = \frac{SS_{S/A} + SS_{BS/A}}{df_{S/A} + df_{BS/A}}$$

and the degrees of freedom have the form (Satterthwaite, 1946):

$$df_{pooled} = \frac{(SS_{S/A} + SS_{BS/A})^2}{\frac{SS_{S/A}^2}{df_{S/A}} + \frac{SS_{BS/A}^2}{df_{BS/A}}}$$

The formula for the q-statistic would then have the following form, and the generalization to the t and F statistics would be as before:

$$q = \frac{\overline{X}_{a1b1} - \overline{X}_{a2b1}}{\sqrt{\frac{MS_{pooled}}{n}}}$$

Applying these formulae to the sample data yields the following:

$$MS_{pooled} = \frac{36.60 + 37.40}{12 + 36} = 1.54$$

$$df_{pooled} = \frac{(36.60 + 37.40)^2}{\dfrac{36.60^2}{12} + \dfrac{37.40^2}{36}} = 36.39$$

$$q = \frac{4.60 - 6.20}{\sqrt{\dfrac{1.54}{5}}} = -2.91$$

When using Tukey's HSD, you would evaluate the value of 2.91 at 3 steps (since there are 3 levels of A) and 37 (36.39 rounded up) degrees of freedom. The nearest tabled values are for 3 and 30, and since this value does not exceed the values given in Table D of the appendix, we would conclude that this difference is not significant.

Another approach to evaluating the significance of a test statistic based on a pooled error term was recommended by Cochran and Cox (1957). Kirk (1995, pp. 531-535) recommends the use of this procedure and provides an example. It can be used with the t, q, or F statistic. The following formula uses notation that was used above, and although it is slightly different in form from that given by Kirk (1995, p. 533) yields the same result.

$$h* = \frac{(h_1)(SS_{S/A}) + (h_2)(SS_{BS/A})}{SS_{S/A} + SS_{BS/A}}$$

where: $h*$ = Test statistic (t, q, or F) required for significance

h_1 = Test statistic (t, q, or F) required for significance for $df = df_{S/A}$

h_2 = Test statistic (t, q, or F) required for significance for $df = df_{BS/A}$

In our example, the degrees of freedom for S/A are 12, so that $h_1 = q(3,12) = 3.77$, while those for BS/A are 36, the nearest value of which in the table is 30 so that $h_2 = q(3,30) = 3.49$, thus:

$$h* = \frac{(3.77)(36.60) + (3.49)(37.40)}{36.60 + 37.40} = 3.63$$

Thus, any q value exceeding this value would be significant at the .05 level.

Again, it should be noted that ordinarily a researcher would probably make comparisons of all possible means in any given set, (i.e., for each level of B, evaluate the differences between all possible pairs of the three A means), and such computations would have to be done by hand.[2]

Generally, the pooled-error term is larger than that used for the within-subject contrasts and thus that the differences required for significance will tend to be larger than for those involving within-subject comparisons. It is nonetheless the case that a researcher may prefer this strategy, and if so these are the contrasts that should be made. Some researchers often perform both sets of contrasts (i.e., the simple main effects of B at A, and the simple main effects of A at B). I recommend against this strategy because it is in essence analyzing the same data twice and often little new information is obtained in both sets that cannot be gleaned from one.

---

[2] The interactive program, **POSTHOC**, I use asks if you wish to compute a pooled-error term, and if so, it asks for the relevant information and computes both the appropriate mean-square error, and the Satterthwaite estimate of the degrees of freedom, as well as the t, q, or F statistic.

Finally, it should be noted that **SPSS WINDOWS GLM Repeated Measures** does not perform tests of the simple main effects of A (the between-subjects factor) at B (the within-subjects factor). If it is desired to do this using **SPSS WINDOWS 8.0** or **9.0,** the most obvious approach is to perform a number of **ONEWAY** analyses of variance (see Chapter 3), one for each level of B (the repeated measures factor), and select the post hoc test of your choice. As before, however, it should be noted that no test statistics are given, and obviously, the estimates of error will be based only on the data in the particular analysis, and not those discussed in this chapter.

Rules for Determining Appropriate Error Terms

Why are there two different error terms depending upon which factor is being varied when conducting tests of simple main effects? The reason has to do with what sources of error actually contribute to the difference. A simple set of rules helps a researcher to determine whether or not it is necessary to construct a pooled-error term. They involve asking two basic questions:

1. What is the error term for the interaction means you are investigating?
2. What is the error term for the factor you are varying?

If the answers are the same for both questions, there is no need to construct a pooled-error term. This is the case, when one is investigating the AB interaction, and varying the Within Subjects B factor (in the present example). If the answers to the two questions are different, then it is necessary to compute a pooled-error term by summing the sums of squares for the two error terms and dividing this by the sum of the degrees of freedom for these error terms. This is the case when you are investigating the AB interaction, and varying the between-subjects A factor (in this example).

Chapter 7
Chi-Square Analysis of Frequency Data

There are times when researchers are interested in determining differences in the frequency of events. For example, given a sample of men and women, one might identify those who smoke and those who do not smoke, and then determine whether the number of smokers and non-smokers varies as a function of gender. Or, one may have a sample of students from the faculties of arts, social science, and science who have indicated their socioeconomic status as low, lower-middle, upper-middle, or high. The research question may be in determining whether or not there is an association between socioeconomic status and faculty of study. In each case, the intent is in determining if there is an *association* (*contingency* or *correlation*) between the two factors of interest.

There is another situation where one might be interested in drawing conclusions about frequency data. For example, assume that you had a frequency distribution of individuals on some variable, and that theory or previous research led you to believe that this distribution should have a particular shape. If this prior information permitted you to determine what the expected frequency would be for each of the obtained frequencies, you might wish to compare your obtained frequencies with the expected ones. In this case, you would be interested in determining the *goodness of fit* of your data to the model.

The above are two different contexts dealing with questions involving frequency data but each makes use of the χ^2 (chi-square) statistic. The general formula for the χ^2 statistic is:

$$\chi^2 = \Sigma \frac{(O - E)^2}{E}$$

where: O = the obtained frequency
E = the expected frequency

This statistic has a sampling distribution that is approximated by the density function for χ^2 with degrees of freedom equal to the number of obtained frequencies that are free to vary given whatever restrictions imposed (see below) provided that the null hypothesis is true. In this case, the null hypothesis is that in the population the observed frequencies equal the expected frequencies. Under such conditions, one would expect a given amount of variability based on sampling, but if this variability is greater than what would be expected on the basis of chance, then one would conclude that the null hypothesis is not true. One evaluates this in much the same way as one evaluates violation of the null hypothesis when using the t-distribution or the F-distribution.

The density function for the χ^2 distribution is given by the equation:

$$y = C(e^{-\frac{\chi^2}{2}} \chi^{2\frac{df-2}{2}})$$

This equation describes the shape of the χ^2 distribution. The value of C refers to an arbitrary constant used to determine the general height of the curve, e is the value of the base of the natural logarithm (2.7182818), and df refers to the degrees of freedom. As one might expect, the function differs for different degrees of freedom. The following figure shows the χ^2 distribution for three different degrees of freedom, 1, 5, and 10. In the figure, the horizontal axis refers to the various values of χ^2, while the vertical axis refers to the value of y. (For the special case in which $df = 1$, the value of y is infinite for $\chi^2 = 0$). Although y doesn't refer to a frequency in this equation, you can consider the curves depicted in the figure as describing frequency distributions for the various χ^2 distributions. As can be seen, the distribution changes quite a bit for different degrees of freedom.

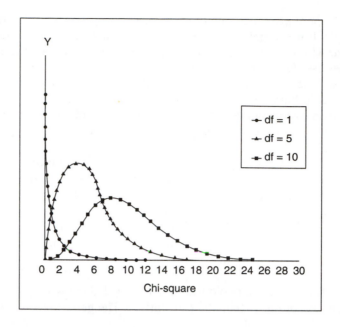

With 1 degree of freedom, the distribution is exponential. As the degrees of freedom increase to 5, it shows as an asymmetrical distribution with a long tail running to the right (note that it asymptotes on the X axis at 18). As degrees of freedom increase to 10, the distribution is somewhat less skewed, but nonetheless asymmetrical, asymptoting with the X axis behyond 24. It will be noted too, that the mean of the chi-square distribution increases (i.e., the centre of the distribution moves to the right) as the degrees of freedom increase. Since we know the function, we can determine that value for χ^2 such that 5% of the area of the curve is beyond it, or that value such that 1% of the area is beyond it, etc. In this way, we can identify values of χ^2 required for significance for any level of significance we desire. As might be expected given the sampling distributions shown in the figure, as df increases, the value required for significance also increases.

Tables of the χ^2 distribution give values required for significance at various alpha levels for different degrees of freedom. Table E, of the Appendix, presents this table of the χ^2 distribution. It will be noted that the degrees of freedom are presented on the left hand side of the table varying in steps of 1 from 1 to 30, and various probability levels varying from .99 to .001 are presented across the top. Values of χ^2 are presented in the table. Thus, as can be seen, for 1 degree of freedom, a value of 3.84 is required for significance at the .05 level, and a value of 6.84 is required at the .01 level.

A BIT OF HISTORY

The χ^2 distribution is often used in conjunction with frequency data, but it should be emphasized that it is a parametric distribution. In fact, the χ^2 statistic is actually the ratio of the sum of squared deviations of N observations from their sample mean divided by the population variance. This is written as:

$$\chi^2 = \frac{\Sigma\,(X - \overline{X})^2}{\sigma^2}$$

When equal-sized samples are drawn at random from a normal population, and this statistic is computed on each sample, this statistic has a sampling distribution with degrees of freedom equal to $(N - 1)$ that is described by the density function given previously.

A brief overview of the history of the chi-square distribution is presented by Cowles (1989), who indicates (p. 101, footnote 2) that the mathematics of the chi-square distribution can be traced back to the 1850's. Pearson (1900), however, was the first to introduce χ^2 as we know it today. This initial presentation was in the context of goodness of fit tests; later Pearson (1904, 1911) applied it to tests of association (contingency).

There are a number of issues that are commonly discussed when using χ^2 as a test statistic. Yates (1934) proposed that a correction be applied in the calculation of χ^2 when small expected frequencies exist and degrees of freedom = 1. Yates's correction for continuity is discussed below in the section on Tests of Association. Its effect is to reduce the magnitude of χ^2 slightly. In other circumstances, Cochran (1952) proposed that χ^2 not be applied if more than 20% of the cells have expected values less than 5.0, or if any are less than 1.0 (cf. Delucchi, 1993). These were singled out here because they are often applied in current-day computer packages, or at least alarms are raised. There are, however, a number of other issues that have been raised in the literature. Lewis and Burke (1949) discuss many of these issues and list nine errors that, at that time, were commonly made in the application of χ^2, but with the widespread use of computer packages to perform many of these calculations, some of their errors are less relevant today than they were in the past.

Delucchi (1993) published a followup article and extension of the Lewis and Burke paper and discusses many of the points raised by them. Two, in particular, are of interest. First, he reviews a number of articles dealing with the Yates correction for continuity, presenting both supporters and non-supporters for its use. He argues that using the correction results in a more conservative test, and generally recommends against it unless the marginal totals of one of the variables were purposely controlled to be certain values. He concedes, however, that there is still some debate over the use of the Yates correction.

Delucchi (1993) also discusses application of Cochran's (1952) rule and refers to a number of researchers who have debated its utility. Cochran's rule is that all expected values should be greater than 1, and no more than 20% should be less than 5 to make the chi-square analysis meaningful. Deluchi (1993) concludes that this is a reasonable and practical solution. This is fine as long as one satisfies Cochran's rule but is disconcerting when one does not. When faced with such a situation, researchers often collapse cells or increase sample sizes to overcome the problem. There are, however, other solutions many of which are discussed by Delucchi (1993).

ASSUMPTIONS UNDERLYING χ^2

There are two major assumptions underlying the χ^2 distribution and its use for evaluating hypotheses based on frequency data (cf. McNemar, 1969). To begin, it is necessary to emphasize that the χ^2 distribution is a continuous distribution, and as indicated at the beginning of the A Bit of History section, it actually refers to the sampling distribution of the ratio of a sample sum of squares to the population variance for samples drawn from a normal population. When applied to frequency data, therefore, an underlying assumption is that the sampling distribution of the deviations of the observed frequencies from the expected frequencies is normal. It's not really possible to test the validity of this assumption, though it is reasonable to assume that if the expected values are not too extreme, the assumption would be satisfied. If an expected value were particularly small, however, it is reasonable to assume that the assumption might be violated. If the expected value were 2, for example, the obtained frequencies less than this could only take values of 0 or 1, while there are many frequencies that could be greater. Under such conditions, the distribution of such differences would not be normal. This is one reason for being concerned about particularly low expected frequencies. Moreover, with small expected frequencies, even if the distribution of residuals were symmetrical, if not normal, the distribution of residuals would not be smooth, but instead would display a step function (a series of discrete changes). This is particularly true when $df = 1$, and thus the Yates correction for continuity was developed in order to make the distribution more continuous.

Another assumption is that the various replications must be independent of one another. This means that any individual can contribute only once to the frequency count. The total N in the table of frequencies must refer to the number of different subjects (i.e., individuals) in the investigation. It is not meaningful to include more than one observation from each subject in an analysis because these observations cannot be considered independent.

TESTS OF ASSOCIATION

The most common application of the χ^2 statistic is its use as a test of the association between two categorical variables. The simplest form of this test is with two dichotomous variables. Thus, consider a situation where a researcher wanted to determine if there is an association between smoking and gender. Assume that this researcher randomly sampled a large number of men and women and determined whether or not they smoked. The following table presents a summary of some fictitious results.

		Gender		
		Male	**Female**	**Total**
Do You Smoke?	No	44	32	76
	Yes	26	46	72
	Total	70	78	148

Inspection of this table reveals that a total of 148 individuals were investigated, and of these 70 were male and 78 female, while 76 reported that they did not smoke and 72 revealed that they did. These are termed the marginal restrictions in this table. Note, in this table that there was no attempt to sample the same number of males and females or smokers and non-smokers. That is, the marginal totals are not fixed at some given value. In some instances, it is possible that sampling would be done to equate the numbers in one of the marginal restrictions. Thus, for example, one might argue that it may have been better to sample an equal number of males and females, on the assumption that these numbers are equal in the population. This was not done in this example. In any event, the analysis of the data would proceed in exactly the same way, though the nature of the sampling may have other consequences in terms of interpretation. We will return to this point later in the section on Application of Chi-square to Tests of Goodness of Fit.

Examination of the frequencies within the table will demonstrate that there are more males who do not smoke in comparison with females who do not smoke, and more females who smoke relative to males who smoke. That is, there tends to be an association (or a contingency or correlation) between gender on the one hand and smoking behavior on the other. Note, that this does not imply any cause between one variable and the other, only an association. The question we might ask, therefore, is whether or not this association is significant.

In order to analyze these data by hand, it is necessary to determine the expected frequencies. This is done by assuming that if there was not an association between smoking and gender, one would expect that the number of non-smokers among the males would be proportional to the total number of males in the same way as the number of non-smokers would be proportional to the total number of individuals investigated. Referring to the value for the expected number of non-smoking males as E_{11} to signify that it is the value expected for the first row and the first column, this expression would be as follows:

$$\frac{E_{11}}{Col_1} = \frac{Row_1}{Total}$$

which is equal to:

$$\frac{E_{11}}{70} = \frac{76}{148} \quad \therefore \quad E_{11} = \frac{(70)(76)}{148} = 35.946$$

The expected values for the other cells could be determined using a similar rationale, but since this is a 2 X 2 table, the other values could be calculated more easily by way of subtraction. Thus, since the marginal restrictions indicated that there are a total of 70 men, if 35.946 of them are expected to not smoke, then obviously $70 - 35.946 = 34.054$ are expected to smoke. Similarly, since there are 76 individuals who do not smoke, and 35.946 of these are expected to be men, it follows that $76 - 35.946 = 40.054$ of them are expected to be women. Finally, there are $78 - 40.054 = 37.946$ (or $72 - 34.054 = 37.946$) women who are expected to not smoke.

Thus, the value of χ^2 would be:

$$\chi^2 = \Sigma \frac{(O - E)^2}{E}$$

$$\chi^2 = \frac{(44 - 35.946)^2}{35.946} + \frac{(32 - 40.054)^2}{40.054} + \frac{(26 - 34.054)^2}{34.054} + \frac{(46 - 37.946)^2}{37.946}$$

$$= 7.038.$$

The df for a χ^2 test of association are equal to the (number of rows -1) times the (number of columns -1), or $(r-1)(c-1)$. In this example, this equals $(2-1)(2-1) = 1$. To determine whether our obtained χ^2 is significant, therefore we would evaluate whether it is larger than the value of χ^2 required for significance at some given alpha level as indicated in a table for χ^2 (i.e., Table E, Appendix). As indicated in the table, the value of χ^2 required for significance at the .01 level for 1 df is 6.64 and, since our obtained value is larger than this, we would conclude that our value is significant at the .01 level. This would suggest that there is in fact a significant association between gender and smoking behavior.

In our Bit of History, we indicated that Yates (1934) suggested an adjustment should be made for 2 X 2 tables, to correct for discontinuity if some of the expected cell frequencies are low. Our smallest expected value was 34.054 so even with his concerns such an adjustment would not be necessary. However, to show you how the adjustment would be made, we will indicate it with respect to this table. The Yates correction for continuity involves reducing the absolute magnitude of the difference between the obtained and expected values by .5. Thus, the difference $44 - 35.946 = 8.054$ would be reduced to 7.554, that of $32 - 40.054 = -8.054$ to -7.554, etc. In this case, the χ^2, corrected for continuity using the Yates correction would be:

$$\chi^2 = \frac{7.554^2}{35.946} + \frac{-7.554^2}{40.054} + \frac{-7.554^2}{34.054} + \frac{7.554^2}{37.946}$$

$$= 6.192$$

According to Table E (Appendix) this value is significant at the .02 level (where a value of $\chi^2 = 5.41$ is required), but as can be seen it is conservative. Given Delucchi's (1993) cautions that this test is conservative, one might question whether it should be applied. In any event, it is not necessary in the present example because the expected values are all quite large. It is shown here, however, because it is routinely calculated by the **SPSS WINDOWS CROSSTABS** program, when $df = 1$.

Analyzing These Data Using SPSS WINDOWS CROSSTABS

There are two ways to analyze these data using **CROSSTABS,** depending upon whether the data are read in by subject, or the summary table is input.

Using Individual Data as Input. If the data were input by individual, it would be necessary to create a data file listing the data for each individual. In our example, there are 148 individuals, thus there would be 148 lines of data with two scores for each individual, the non-smoking/smoking score and the gender score. Since these two variables are both dichotomous, any values can be used for each. Thus, if one were to code the smoking variable as 1 = no smoking, 2 = smoking, and the gender variable as 1 = Male, 2 = Female, the data file would comprise 148 lines of data consisting of 1's and 2's. You could, however, use any dichotomous code you wish.

These data are analyzed using the **CROSSTABS** program. The following instructions assume that the data were typed into an ASCII (text) file with the scores for the two variables, smoking and gender on a line for each subject. It is assumed, further, that the file is on the A Drive in a file called **CHISQ.DAT.**

Steps in Using SPSS WINDOWS CROSSTABS

The following steps are applicable to **SPSS 8.0** and **SPSS 9.0** except for the input of the ASCII or Text data file. In the example to follow you are instructed at Step 3 to input your data following the procedures described in Chapter 1. The output for this example was obtained by using the freefield format in **SPSS 8.0,** and depending upon the input procedure you use, the output may be somewhat different. The answers are the same, however. Using the **WINDOWS** version of the program, you could simply type the Syntax file [the set of instructions required to run the procedure, including the relevant Data List and Execute statements (see page 30)], and then execute the job from inside the Syntax Editor (not discussed here), or use the program itself to create the syntax file. This latter procedure involves using the mouse to bring up a number of windows (the **clope** procedure), and then selecting the appropriate options or typing in the required information.

1. *Enter **SPSS WIN.*** This presents you with the **SPSS** Data Editor (see figure in Chapter 2, p. 46). At this point, you could begin to type in the data. However, we will assume here that you already have the data in a file on the A Drive, that this file is labelled chisq.dat, and that the data are in freefield (**SPSS 8.0**) or Delimited format (**SPSS 9.0**). For each participant there would be two values, the score for the "**smoke**" variable, and the one for the "**gen**" variable.

2. *Click on **File** in the upper row of selections.* This will present you with a drop-down menu with a series of choices.

3. *Enter your ASCII (**SPSS 8.0**) or Text (**SPSS 9.0**) data file by following the steps on pages 17 to 20 for **SPSS 8.0**, or pages 20 to 28 for **SPSS 9.0**.* For this example, the file will consist of two variables labelled **smoke** and **gen** respectively.

4. *Click on the **Statistics** (**SPSS 8.0**) or **Analyze** (**SPSS 9.0**) option on the menu bar.* This presents you with a drop-down menu. *Move your cursor to **Summarize** in SPSS 8.0 or **Descriptive Statistics** in SPSS 9.0,* and you are presented with another menu to the right with a choice of the following:

SPSS 8.0	**SPSS 9.0**
Frequencies . . .	Frequencies . . .
Descriptives . . .	Descriptives . . .
Explore . . .	Explore . . .
Crosstabs . . .	Crosstabs . . .
Layered Reports	

Case Summaries . . .
Report Summaries in Rows . . .
Report Summaries in Columns . . .

5. *Click on **CROSSTABS**.* This presents you with the Window, **CROSSTABS** (see figure below).

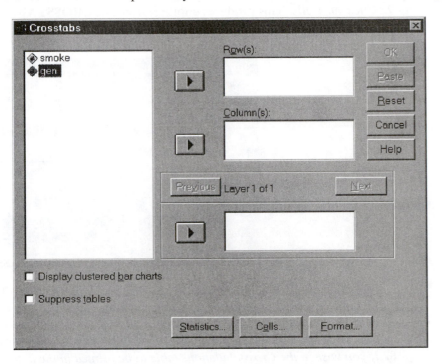

The two variables, **smoke** and **gen** appear in the white pane, *click on **smoke** and define it as the Rows variable by clicking on the arrow to the left of the Row(s) pane. Then click on **gen,** and define it as the Column(s) variable by clicking on the arrow to the left of the Column(s) pane.*

6. *Then click on **Statistics** at the bottom of the Window.* This produces another Window, **CROSSTABS: STATISTICS** (see figure below).

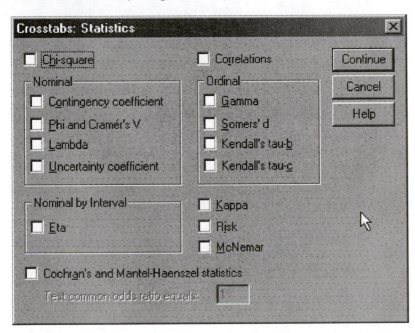

This Window presents a listing of all possible statistics that this program will produce (they may not all be meaningful or appropriate for your problem, however). *Click on the white square to the left of chi-square. Then click on* **Continue.** This returns you to the **CROSSTABS** Window.

7. *Click on* **Cells.** This produces another Window, **CROSSTABS: CELL DISPLAY** (see figure below).

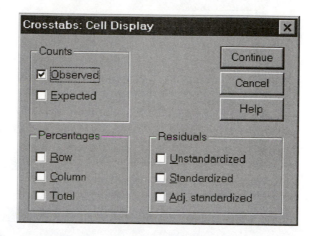

Note that there is a check-mark in the white square preceding **Observed** Counts. This is the Default Option. *I recommend that you also select* **Expected** *Counts and* **Unstandardized** *Residuals by clicking on the white squares preceding these two options. Once you have done this, click on* **Continue.** *This returns you to the* **CROSSTABS** *Window.*

8. *If you wished the Crosstabulations table to be printed in the default mode, you could ignore this step and continue directly to Step 9. If you wanted to change the format, Click on* **Format.** *This* presents the next Window, **CROSSTABS: TABLE FORMAT** (see following figure).

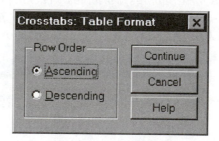

This Window allows you to control the format of the output. In our example, we are going to make use of the Ascending Row order, so no changes are necessary. *Click on* **Continue.**

9. This takes you back to the Window, **CROSSTABS.** *Click on* **OK** *to run the Chi-Square analysis.*

10. This runs the **CROSSTABS** program, and the answers are returned to the **SPSS Output Viewer,** as well as to your monitor. At this point, you can print your answers, save them in a file, or transfer them to some other editor.

11. To exit **SPSS,** *click on* **File** *(upper row of operations), and click on* **Exit.** *Before you can exit, however, the program will ask if you wish to save the contents of the* **SPSS** *Viewer as well as those of the Data Editor.* If you have already saved them you will not have to do so again.

The Syntax File.   If you were to follow the instructions given above, you would produce the following Syntax File:

```
CROSSTABS
    /TABLES= SMOKE BY GEN
    /FORMAT= AVALUE TABLES
    /STATISTIC=CHISQ
    /CELLS= COUNT EXPECTED RESID .
```

This syntax file indicates that the chi-square analysis is done because of the CROSSTABS statement, which consists of four parts. The first, /TABLES, indicates that the analysis is concerned with the association of SMOKE with GEN. The second, /FORMAT, indicates the format in which the Contingency Table will be organized. The third, /STATISTIC, indicates that we have requested only the basic χ^2 statistics (but other options are also available). The fourth component, identified by /CELLS =, indicates that we desire information concerning the count, the expected frequencies, and the residual. In many of these parts, however, you could obtain other information by requesting it.

Running this syntax file presents the following set of output. The first table presented gives general information about the number of valid and missing cases. This table should be examined to make sure that it corresponds to your knowledge of the data.

Case Processing Summary

			Cases			
	Valid		Missing		Total	
	N	Percent	*N*	Percent	*N*	Percent
SMOKE*GEN	148	100.0%	0	.0%	148	100.0%

The second table presents a summary of the information concerning the cells. It is as follows:

SMOKE*GEN Crosstabulation

			GEN		
			1.00	2.00	Total
SMOKE	1.00	Count	44	32	76
		Expected Count	35.9	40.1	76.0
		Residual	8.1	−8.1	
	2.00	Count	26	46	72
		Expected Count	34.1	37.9	72.0
		Residual	−8.1	8.1	
Total		Count	70	78	148
		Expected Count	70.0	78.0	148.0

Value Labels are not presented in this table, but they could be, if desired. Recall, however, that a value of **smoke** equal to 1 means a non-smoker, while 2 refers to a smoker. Similarly, a value of **gen** equal to 1 means male, while 2 means female. We have also seen many of the other values presented in the table in the example we worked out previously. The obtained cell frequencies are 44, 32, 26, and 46, respectively. The expected frequencies are shown as 35.9, 40.1, 34.1, and 37.9 rounded to one decimal place. (We carried ours to three places in our calculations to avoid large differences from the χ^2 calculations done by the computer that would be due to rounding. Of course, when doing the computations, the computer carries a number of decimal places.) The values of 8.1, −8.1, etc., are the (unstandardized) residuals rounded to one decimal place. (We carried three decimal places, thus the values we used in our calculations were 8.054, etc.). The row totals, 76 and 72, and the column totals, 70 and 78 are also indicated, as is the total number of participants, 148.

The third table presents four chi-square statistics (χ^2) computed on these data.

Chi-Square Tests

	Value	df	Asymp. Sig. (2-sided)	Exact Sig. (2-sided)	Exact Sig. (1-sided)
Pearson Chi-Square	7.038[b]	1	.008		
Continuity Correction[a]	6.192	1	.013		
Likelihood Ratio	7.099	1	.008		
Fisher's Exact Test				.009	.006
Linear-by-Linear Association	6.991	1	.008		
N of Valid Cases	148				

[a]Computed only for a 2x2 table

[b]0 cells (.0%) have expected count less than 5. The minimum expected count is 34.05

The first line of output, labelled Pearson Chi-Square, (i.e., 7.038) is the typical value of χ^2 used in research, and the one we calculated in our example. The significant χ^2 value simply indicates that the association is significant. That is, given these data, it is reasonable to conclude that in the population there is an association between Gender and Smoking such that smoking is associated with women and non-smoking is associated with men. If we were presenting this information in a document, we would indicate it as $[\chi^2(1) = 7.04, p < .01]$.

The other summary statistics can be interpreted similarly. The one labelled Continuity Correction applies the Yates correction for continuity as described previously. If presenting this in a document, it would be written as $[\chi^2(1) = 6.192, p < .05]$, and a statement made that the Yates correction for continuity had been applied.

The other statistics labelled Likelihood Ratio, Fisher's Exact Test, and Linear-by-Linear Association will not be discussed here. Finally, the Minimum Expected Frequency (34.05) reported as a note to the table is simply a statement of the smallest expected frequency obtained in this analysis. It refers to the value for the Males-Yes category which was rounded to 34.1 in the previous table.

Using a Summary Table as Input. In some circumstances, a researcher already has the summary table of the frequencies, and wishes to calculate the values of χ^2 without having to input the data by subject. This can be done easily using a slight modification of the steps described on pages 160–162 for running the **CROSSTABS** program. Thus, assume your **chisq2.dat** file was comprised of four lines of data, where the first number on each line indicates the value of the smoking variable, the second, the value of the gen variable, and the third, the frequency of cases in that cell. The data file would then look as follows:

```
1 1 44
1 2 32
2 1 26
2 2 46
```

To run the data in this form would involve an additional step preceding step 4 on page 160. To perform this step, you must be in the Data Editor. If you are not, *click on the data file in the task bar at the bottom of the screen* (generally labelled Untitled . . .). *Then, click on **DATA** on the Menu Bar* (at the top of the screen). This produces a drop-down menu. *Click on the **Weight Cases** option* (at the bottom of the menu). This presents the following Window:

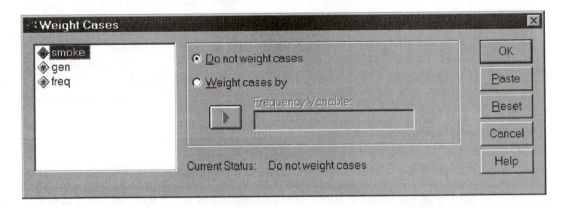

*Click on Weight cases by. Click on **freq**, then click on the arrow, and then on **OK.*** At this point, you continue on with step 4 on page 160 (but note that the **Window, Crosstabs,** appears a bit different).

This modification results in a syntax file that differs slightly from the one presented previously. The output would appear as in the previous example, but the syntax would be as follows:

```
WEIGHT BY FREQ.
CROSSTABS
        /TABLES= SMOKE BY GEN
        /FORMAT= AVALUE TABLES
        /STATISTIC=CHISQ
        /CELLS= COUNT EXPECTED RESID .
```

Relation of χ^2 to Tests of Proportions in 2 X 2 Tables

The observant student would have noticed that really all we are doing here is comparing the proportions of males (coded **1**) and females (**2**) who smoke(**2**) or don't smoke(**1**), or alternatively the proportion of smokers and non-smokers who are male (or female). Considering, the first example, we would say that the proportion (p_1) of males who smoke is 26/70 = .3714, while the proportion (p_2) of females who smoke is 46/78 = .5897. McNemar (1969) gives as a test of proportions, the equation:

$$Z = \frac{p_1 - p_2}{\sqrt{pq\left(\frac{1}{N_1} + \frac{1}{N_2}\right)}}$$

where:

$$p = \frac{26 + 46}{70 + 78} = .4865 \quad q = 1.0 - .4865 = .5135$$

Thus:

$$Z = \frac{.3714 - .5897}{\sqrt{((.4865)(.5135)(.0142857 + .0128205)}} = -2.653$$

The absolute value of this Z statistic is greater than 2.56, the value required for significance at the .01 level, thus, we can conclude that the proportion of males who smoke is significantly smaller than the proportion of females who smoke. More to the point for this discussion, we would observe that if our obtained value of $Z = -2.653$ were squared, it would equal 7.038, which is the value of χ^2 obtained in our analysis. That is, the tests are equivalent in that they both test the same hypothesis. Thus, *for 2 X 2 tables,* a significant association indicates a significant difference in the proportions. Of course, as indicated earlier, we could have tested the difference in the proportions of non-smokers for males vs. females instead, or the difference in the proportions of smokers vs. non-smokers for males, etc., The absolute value of the Z statistic would be the same in all instances. The interested student might want to perform these calculations to demonstrate that this is the case.

Analyzing *r* X *c* Tables

Sometimes the type of χ^2 analysis we want to perform involves a table larger than a 2 X 2. For example, consider the case in which we want to determine whether there is an association between faculty of registration at university (classified as arts, social science and science) and socioeconomic status (classified as Lower, Lower-Middle, Upper-Middle and Upper). Since there are three categories of faculty of registration and four categories of socioeconomic status, this is a 3 X 4 chi-square. A table may appear as follows:

	Socioeconomic Status				
	Low 1	Lower-Middle 2	Upper-Middle 3	Upper 4	Row Total
Arts (1)	10	11	37	52	110
Social Sc. (2)	21	72	105	37	235
Science (3)	16	28	65	43	152
Column Total	47	111	207	132	497

As before, these computations could be done by hand. The expected value for the Arts, Low SES cell (E_{11}) would be computed as $E_{11} = (47)(110)/497 = 10.402$, $E_{12} = (111)(110)/497 = 24.567$, $E_{13} = (207)(110)/497 = 45.815$, and $E_{14} = 110 - 10.402 - 24.567 - 45.815 = 29.216$. The values for the second row could be calculated similarly, while those for the third row could be obtained by subtraction. Then, by summing the squared residuals divided by their expected values, one could compute the χ^2 statistic.

If we were to perform the analysis using **SPSS WINDOWS CROSSTABS,** we could read in the data by subject, or as a summary table of frequencies. If we used the summary table of frequencies, the data file, **chisq3.dat,** would be as follows:

```
1 1 10
2 1 21
3 1 16
1 2 11
2 2 72
3 2 28
1 3 37
2 3 105
3 3 65
1 4 52
2 4 37
3 4 43
```

We could run these data following the steps described on pages 160 to 162, with the additions prior to step 4 described on pages 164–165. If we did, we would obtain the following syntax file:

```
WEIGHT BY FREQ.
CROSSTABS
     /TABLES= FACULTY BY SES
     /FORMAT= AVALUE TABLES
     /STATISTICS = CHISQ
     /CELLS=COUNT EXPECTED RESID.
```

I have requested the same information as before in the Cells and Statistics statements. This syntax file yields the following output:

Case Processing Summary

	Cases					
	Valid		Missing		Total	
	N	Percent	N	Percent	N	Percent
FACULTY*SES	497	100.0%	0	.0%	497	100.0%

FACULTY*SES Crosstabulation

			SES				
			1.00	2.00	3.00	4.00	Total
FACULTY	1.00	Count	10	11	37	52	110
		Expected Count	10.4	24.6	45.8	29.2	110.0
		Residual	−.4	−13.6	−8.8	22.8	
	2.00	Count	21	72	105	37	235
		Expected Count	22.2	52.5	97.9	62.4	235.0
		Residual	−1.2	19.5	7.1	−25.4	
	3.00	Count	16	28	65	43	152
		Expected Count	14.4	33.9	63.3	40.4	152.0
		Residual	1.6	−5.9	1.7	2.6	
Total		Count	47	111	207	132	497
		Expected Count	47.0	111.0	207.0	132.0	497.0

Chi-Square Tests

	Value	df	Asymp. Sig. (2-sided)
Pearson Chi-Square	46.607[a]	6	.000
Likelihood Ratio	46.385	6	.000
Linear-by-Linear Association	4.627	1	.031
N of Valid Cases	497		

[a]0 cells (.0%) have expected count less than 5.
The minimum expected count is 10.40

Note in this example that the χ^2 statistic (46.607) has 6 degrees of freedom and that it is significant. It has 6 degrees of freedom because the number of degrees of freedom, as we saw, is equal to the (number of rows − 1) times the (number of columns − 1) (i.e., $(3 - 1)(4 - 1) = 6$). Since the value of χ^2 is significant, it indicates that in the population, there is an association between faculty of registration and SES. Note, however, the value of the χ^2 statistic tells you nothing about the nature of this association, only that there is an association. If one wished to determine the nature of the association, it would be necessary to examine the table further (i.e., provide a post hoc interpretation).

Post Hoc Interpretation. Unfortunately, if you investigate a number of statistics textbooks, few of them give you much guidance as to how to proceed at this point. We will consider three different ways to proceed, but it should be emphasized that any or all of them may not be applicable to all situations. The reason for this is that the χ^2 test of association evaluates the null hypothesis with respect to the whole table, and any post hoc test involves an hypothesis based on only some parts of the table, or on some restructuring of the table.

Method I: Examining the Cells. One way to proceed is simply to examine the table. That is, it will be noted that two cells have relatively large positive residuals [Arts(coded **1**)/Upper SES(**4**), +22.8; Social Science(**2**) /Lower Middle SES (**2**), +19.5], and two have relatively high negative residuals [Social Science(**2**)/Upper SES(**4**), −25.4; Arts(**1**)/Lower Middle SES(**2**), −13.6]. Thus, from visual inspection, one might interpret the significant χ^2 as indicating mostly that relatively more arts students come from Upper SES families (+22.8), with fewer from Lower-Middle SES families (−13.6), while relatively more social science students come from Lower-Middle SES (+19.5) with fewer from Upper SES families (−25.4). If we wish, we could even quantify how much of the χ^2 each of these four values contribute to the overall χ^2. Recalling that the χ^2 statistic of 46.61 is computed by summing the squared residuals divided by the expected values, we could determine the contribution for each cell. Thus, the contribution from the Arts/Upper SES cell would be:

$$\frac{22.8^2}{29.2} = 17.80$$

This cell, then, accounts for 17.80/46.61 = 38.2% of the total χ^2. In like manner, the Social Science/Lower-Middle SES cell accounts for 7.24/46.61 = 15.5% of the χ^2, the Social Science/Upper SES cell accounts for 10.34/46.61 = 22.2%, and the Arts/Lower-Middle SES cell accounts for 7.52/46.61 = 16.1%. In total, therefore, these cells account for 92% of the χ^2 value. You might, therefore, wish to restrict your interpretation to this type of visual inspection with or without calculating the percentage contributions. Sometimes, of course, it happens that although the χ^2 is significant, none of the cells make a contribution that is that much larger than any other cell. This does not mean that you cannot make a verbal description, but it does make it more complex.

Another way to consider the cell data is to assess the extent to which the deviation of an obtained frequency from the expected frequency in a cell is significant. There are at least two ways to perform this type of analysis, both of which derive from research by Haberman (1973). One uses the standardized residuals (see also, Beasley & Schumacker, 1995), and the other uses adjusted standardized residuals (see also, Agresti, 1996). Although neither of these statistics have a standard normal distribution (see MacDonald & Gardner, in press), they can be treated as standardized normal deviates. In a Monte Carlo investigation of a 3 X 4 table, MacDonald and Gardner (in press) have demonstrated that if a standardized residual is greater than 1.96 (the value of Z required for significance at the .05 level), the deviation can be considered as significant at the .05 level, and this controls the experimentwise Type I error rate close to .05. Similarly, if a Bonferroni adjustment is made to control for the number of such tests that can be made, the adjusted standardized residuals similarly can be treated as standardized normal deviates. The Bonferroni adjustment involves dividing the desired alpha level (i.e., .05) by the number of cells (r X c), and requiring the adjusted standardized residual to be greater than the Z required for this adjusted alpha level. In our example, there are $3 \times 4 = 12$ cells. Thus, the alpha level would be .05/12 = .004. Inspection of Table A (see Appendix) indicates that a $Z = 2.85$ is required for significance at the .004 level, two-tailed. Any adjusted standardized residual that exceeds this value would then be considered significant. Mac Donald and Gardner (in press) demonstrate that this approach controls the Type I error rate experimentwise at .05, at least for a 3 X 4 table.

Standardized and adjusted standardized residuals are produced in **SPSS** by selecting these options in step 7 (page 162). MacDonald and Gardner (in press) recommend using the adjusted standardized residual with the Bonferroni adjustment. Often **SPSS** outputs these residuals to only one decimal place. If more decimal places are desired, this is easily done. *Simply move your cursor to the table of interest in your output, and double-click on the left mouse button to set the table in the edit mode. Then double-click on the right mouse button.* This brings up a Menu. *Click on **Select Table**. Then double-click on the right mouse button again, and select **Cell Attributes**.* This produces another Menu, and you *select the option #.#, and then indicate in the window below the number of decimal places desired (2 should be sufficient), then click on **OK**.* The table will now show all values in that table with the number of decimal places you desire. Note this procedure can be used with all tables in **SPSS** output.

Method II: Examining Specific Contrasts. A second strategy would be to investigate specific contrasts derived from the table. This can take one of two basic forms.

One commonly used procedure involves extracting a 2 X 2 table of interest from the r X c table. Thus, we could focus attention on a table that considers the distinction between Arts (coded **1**) and Social Science (**2**) and between Lower-Middle (**2**) and Upper SES (**4**). Such an analysis would produce the following results:

	Lower Middle	**Upper**	**Row Total**
Arts	11	52	63
Social Science	72	37	109
Column Total	83	89	172

This analysis produces a χ^2 of 37.76. If this is treated as a 2 X 2 analysis (without recognizing that it is actually a part of a larger table), this value might be considered significant ($p < .01$) because it exceeds the value of 6.64 which is required for significance at the .01 level for 1 df. If this conclusion is drawn, it must be realized that it does not relate directly to the original r X c analysis. It is a post hoc analysis resulting from selecting extreme cells from the larger table, and as such can capitalize on Type I error. To counter this, it is wise to adopt a conservative Type I error rate by performing a Bonferroni adjustment as detailed in the next paragraph.

The number of 2 X 2 tables that can be formed from an r X c table is given by the value of k in the following equation:

$$k = \frac{r!}{2!(r-2)!} \frac{c!}{2!(c-2)!}$$

where the expression ! (factorial) refers to a series multiplication. That is, $r! = r(r-1)(r-2)(r-3) \ldots (1)$, 2! refers to 2(1), and $(r-2)!$ refers to $(r-2)(r-3) \ldots (1)$, etc. In our example, this would be:

$$k = \frac{3!}{2!(3-2)} \frac{4!}{2!(4-2)!} = \frac{(3)(2)(1)}{((2)(1))(1)} \frac{(4)(3)(2)(1)}{((2)(1))((2)(1))} = 18$$

A Bonferroni adjustment involves dividing .05 by k (i.e., .05/18 = .0027), and requiring the obtained value of χ^2 to exceed the tabled value with this alpha level at 1 df. Since most tables of χ^2 give values for alpha only as low as .001 (e.g., $\chi^2(1) = 10.83$), any finer adjustments would require access to a computer program that calculates probability values for χ^2. Of course, since χ^2 at 1 df is equal to Z^2, one could use tables of the Normal distribution (see Table A, Appendix) to get at some finer gradations of alpha levels.

Regardless of how you define alpha, it will be recalled that this test is equivalent to testing hypotheses concerning proportions. Thus, this analysis could be interpreted as indicating that the proportion of arts students who are from Upper SES (52/63) is larger than the proportion of social science students who are from Upper SES (37/109), or, alternatively, that the proportion of Lower-Middle SES students in arts (11/83) is significantly lower than the proportion of Upper SES students in arts (52/89), etc., but this conclusion is based only on information from respondents who are either Lower-Middle or Upper SES from these two faculties. As we saw, there are a number of ways of extracting 2 X 2 tables from a larger table (18 in our example), but each one reflects a specific hypothesis. If you adopt this strategy, you should extract very few such tables. The important thing to remember is that hypotheses of this type are not derived directly from the value of χ^2 calculated on the entire table.

The second procedure is sometimes considered when there is no particular 2 X 2 table of interest in the r X c table, and it seems meaningful to collapse categories to form one 2 X 2 table involving all the data. If the two variables were ordinal, this could be done by collapsing each of them into a dichotomy. Thus, in our example, SES is an ordered variable, so that we might collapse Low and Lower-Middle SES into one category called Lower, and Upper-Middle and Upper into another, which we might label Higher. This would give us a total sample of 158 in the lower category and 339 in the upper. Or we might wish to have one group defined as Upper ($N_1 = 132$), and the aggregate of the other three as Lower ($N_2 = 365$). Regardless of how the cells are collapsed, the new classification should make substantive sense. It is also a good idea to attempt to make the two groups as near to equal in size as possible, and to avoid particularly small frequencies if at all practicable.

It is more difficult to collapse faculty of registration into two categories, since they represent three distinct and unordered categories. One might, however, argue that one could form a dichotomy of arts on the one hand and social science and science on the other, arguing that the one faculty refers to non-scientists, and the other two to scientists. Or, one might group arts and social science together and contrast them with science, arguing that the latter is more of an objective set of disciplines, etc. Or, one might even form one group of social scientists, and the other of arts and sciences, using an historical argument (i.e., the arts and sciences were academic disciplines that originated before the social sciences). As you can see, collapsing groups based on a nominal classification is even more difficult to justify than one based on ordinal categories, but in any event, the procedure might be used to form a 2 X 2 table, which as we have already seen is easier to interpret. The important point to realize, however, is when such reclassification is done, it changes the nature of the data, and thus the question asked.

Note, as an example, however, that if we had collapsed SES categories 1 and 2 to make a Lower classification, and 3 and 4 to make a Higher one, and had collapsed arts and social science together to contrast it with science, the 2 X 2 table would appear as follows:

	Lower	Higher	Row Total
Arts & Social Sc.	114	231	345
Science	44	108	152
Column Total	158	339	497

The χ^2 value for this analysis is .816 with 1 df, thus with the reclassification of faculty and SES, there is now no evidence of an association between faculty of registration and socioeconomic status. A close examination of the original table indicates that this is what should have occurred because of the pattern of large residuals revealed there. By reclassifying the variables the way we did, we covered up the association which largely involved distinctions between arts and social science at two levels of SES. One must be careful, therefore, when reclassifying the variables.

One must also be careful as to how one defines Type I error. There doesn't appear to be any clear way to determine how many ways it is possible to collapse the table, and thus to come up with a meaningful Bonferonni adjustment. I suspect that most researchers would simply evaluate this as a χ^2 with 1 df. Obviously, however there are a great many ways of collapsing the table, so this must be considered a very liberal solution. If one does use this approach, it would seem that at a minimum, one should adopt a Type I error rate of .01. Also, any such grouping should be based on decisions before the data are inspected. If the grouping is done after the pattern of results have been observed, and is designed to show the best association evident, the concept of Type I error is seriously compromised, and would have very little meaning.

Method III: Simple Effects. A third strategy is discussed by Delucchi (1993). In our example, consider that the variable, Faculty of Registration, is defined as a, and a can take values from 1 to 3, while the variable SES is defined as b and can take values from 1 to 4. We could then calculate three proportions for each of the four levels of SES as shown below [or alternatively, four proportions for each of the three levels of faculty of registration (not shown)]. In this approach, one considers the original chi-square analysis as an omnibus test, much like the F-ratio in an analysis of variance. In the present instance, the overall χ^2 evaluates the hypothesis:

$$\begin{vmatrix} p(a_1|b_1) \\ p(a_2|b_1) \\ p(a_3|b_{1)} \end{vmatrix} = \begin{vmatrix} p(a_1|b_2) \\ p(a_2|b_2) \\ p(a_3|b_2) \end{vmatrix} = \begin{vmatrix} p(a_1|b_3) \\ p(a_2|b_3) \\ p(a_3|b_3) \end{vmatrix} = \begin{vmatrix} p(a_1|b_4) \\ p(a_2|b_4) \\ p(a_3|b_4) \end{vmatrix}$$

$$\begin{vmatrix} \dfrac{10}{47} \\ \dfrac{21}{47} \\ \dfrac{16}{47} \end{vmatrix} = \begin{vmatrix} \dfrac{11}{111} \\ \dfrac{72}{111} \\ \dfrac{28}{111} \end{vmatrix} = \begin{vmatrix} \dfrac{37}{207} \\ \dfrac{105}{207} \\ \dfrac{65}{207} \end{vmatrix} = \begin{vmatrix} \dfrac{52}{132} \\ \dfrac{37}{132} \\ \dfrac{43}{132} \end{vmatrix}$$

That is, the null hypothesis is that the vector (set) of proportions at b_1 equals the vector at b_2, and so on to b_4 (or the hypothesis could be rewritten to refer to the three vectors with four proportions in each expressed as proportions of b at a). A significant χ^2 statistic suggests that the hypothesis is false, and that the vectors (sets) of proportions are not all equal. To investigate this further, it would be necessary to perform specific post hoc tests. That is, one would evaluate whether or not specific proportions differ significantly from each other. In his presentation, Delucchi (1993) does not recommend tests of significance, but instead focuses on the calculation of confidence intervals for various proportions. Since our focus here is on tests of significance, I will continue with that strategy, but will use the general rationale he proposes.

In this approach, we would be interested in evaluating the differences between specific proportions. As was the case with the factorial design analysis of variance, we could hold one factor constant and vary another. Thus, we might ask whether or not the proportion of arts students from Lower-Middle SES differs significantly from the proportion of arts students from Upper SES. In terms of the previous equation, we have thus extracted two of the proportions of interest, and expressed a post hoc hypothesis as follows:

$$Ho: \quad p_{a1|b2} = p_{a1|b4} \quad ; \quad \frac{11}{111} = \frac{52}{132}$$

Since this involves the difference between two proportions, it could be evaluated by calculating the χ^2 for the following 2 X 2 table:

	Lower Middle	Upper	Row Total
Arts	11	52	63
Other	100	80	180
Column Total	111	132	243

If we were to analyze this table using the **CROSSTAB** program from **SPSS WINDOWS,** we would obtain a χ^2 value of 27.294 with 1 degree of freedom. However, since this is a post hoc test from the original χ^2 analysis, we would evaluate our value not at 1 *df*, but at $(r-1)(c-1)$ *df*, based on the original table. That is, we would determine whether our obtained value of 27.29 is significant at 6 *df*. In this case it is (you need a value of $\chi^2 = 12.59$ for significance at the .05 level for 6 *df* according to Table E, the Appendix), so we would conclude that the proportion of arts students from Lower-Middle SES was significantly lower than that from the Upper SES. One problem that Delucchi (1993) points out with this procedure is that it has low power (i.e., probability of rejecting the null hypothesis when it is false), and this would be particularly true when there are a large number of rows and/or columns. Delucchi (1993) proposes a variant on this procedure to compensate for this loss in power to some extent, but since it is in the context of confidence intervals, we will not discuss it here.

An alternative way of defining Type I error could make use of the Bonferroni logic discussed earlier. In this case, the number of possible tests of simple effects that could be performed (k) is equal to:

$$k = r\frac{c!}{2!(c-2)!} + c\frac{r!}{2!(r-2)!}$$
$$= 3\frac{[(4)(3)(2)]}{(2)(2)} + 4\frac{[(3)(2)]}{(2)(1)} = 30$$

Thus, alpha would be defined as .05/30 = .0017. Research in our laboratory has demonstrated that by using alpha defined in this way, and evaluating χ^2 at 1 *df*, the error rate is reasonably well controlled, though still a bit conservatively.

TESTS OF GOODNESS OF FIT

As was noted in the section A Bit of History, Pearson's first application of χ^2 was to the problem of goodness of fit; analysis of contingency tables came later. The goodness of fit application is concerned with determining how closely a set of obtained frequencies compares with frequencies that would be expected from theory. In early days, astronomers were concerned with determining whether or not errors in observations were normally distributed, while biologists investigated the distribution of various attributes, and the goodness of fit of a series of obtained frequencies to theoretical expectation was based largely on visual inspection. Pearson (1900) developed the χ^2 statistic to provide a more objective means of determining whether obtained frequencies differed from theoretical expectations. We have already seen the formula for the χ^2 statistic, but we will repeat it here. It is as follows:

$$\chi^2 = \Sigma \frac{(O - E)^2}{E}$$

where: O = the obtained frequency
E = the expected frequency

There are many situations in which tests of goodness of fit can be used. For example, if you had a set of frequency data and some expectation of how they should be distributed, you could employ the χ^2 statistic to determine whether your obtained frequencies conformed to these expectations. Consider, for example, that an instructor had a class of 200 students, and that he/she was expected to have 10% of the class obtain A grades, 30% obtain B grades, 30% C grades, 25% D grades, and 5% failing grades. The following table shows a sample set of frequencies that might have been obtained, the values expected based on the above breakdown, and the computations needed to compute the value of χ^2:

Grade	O	E	$(O - E)^2$	$(O - E)^2/E$
A	15	20	25	1.25
B	70	60	100	1.667
C	70	60	100	1.667
D	39	50	121	2.42
F	6	10	16	1.6
	200	200		$\chi^2 = 8.604$

This analysis of goodness of fit leads to a value of χ^2 equal to 8.604. The number of degrees of freedom for this analysis is the number of categories minus one, or $(5 - 1) = 4$. To determine whether this value is significant, therefore, it would be necessary to determine how large a value of χ^2 would be required for significance at 4 df. Looking at Table E of the Appendix would indicate that this value is 9.49 ($p < .05$). Thus, we would conclude that our value of χ^2 is not significant. If we wished to present this value and the associated information in a written document, we would write it as ($\chi^2(4) = 8.61$, ns).

Obviously then, regardless of its name in the literature, this is a test of the badness of fit not goodness of fit, in that the larger the value of χ^2 the poorer the fit. If the value were significant, this would indicate that the obtained frequencies do not fit the expected values very well. Because we really do not want to obtain significance when conducting tests of goodness of fit, we should perhaps err on the side of making a Type I error, and rather than adopt a Type I error rate of 5%, it might be more meaningful to adopt an error rate of 10 or 20%. If we did adopt a Type I error rate of 20%, we would find by investigating the Table for χ^2 at 4 df that we would require a value of 5.99 for significance. Since our value exceeds this value we would conclude that the frequencies of grades obtained did differ significantly from the expected values, and we would report this using the notation $(\chi^2(4) = 8.61, p < .10)$ since this is the nearest value in the table. As you can see, this is one problem with the χ^2 test of goodness of fit. There is some leeway involved in determining what constitutes significance or departure from a good fit. As a rule of thumb, there is much to be said for simply setting the Type I error at .20.

It will be noted in this analysis that one of the expected cell frequencies was fairly low (i.e., 10). If we were to eliminate this, by grouping the D and F categories together, this would give an obtained frequency for this new cell of 45, and the expected value would be 60. We could, if we wish, recompute the value of χ^2 for this modified set of cells. If we did we would obtain a χ^2 value of 1.25 + 1.67 + 1.67 + (45 − 60)^2/60 = 8.34, with 3 df (since we now only have four categories). A value of χ^2 of 4.64 is required for significance at the .20 level with 3 df, and 7.82 at the .05 level, thus in this case we would conclude that our obtained frequencies differ significantly from the expected values. We would report the result as $[\chi^2(3) = 8.34, p < .05]$, since this is the closest value in the table.

If we wished to perform the analysis using the five categories in the original example, and using **SPSS WINDOWS,** we would make use of the NPAR program. As before, we could read the data in by subject or by weighted category. If we were to read it in by subject, the DATA LIST would refer only to the one variable, GRADE, and the data would consist of as many lines of data as there are students (in this case, 200) with each student's grade indicated by category (i.e., 1, 2, 3, 4, or 5 in this case). If we were to read in the data in summary table form, the data file would consist of five lines of data, each line consisting of the grade and the corresponding frequency, as follows:

```
1  15
2  70
3  70
4  39
5  6
```

Analyzing These Data Using SPSS WINDOWS NPAR

We will direct attention here to running the analysis with the data in summary table form in a file called **fit.dat** on the A Drive.

Steps in Using SPSS WINDOWS NPAR. The following steps are applicable to **SPSS 8.0** and **SPSS 9.0** except for the input of the ASCII or Text data file. In the example to follow you are instructed at Step 3 to input your data following the procedures described in Chapter 1. The output for this example was obtained by using the freefield format in **SPSS 8.0,** and depending upon the input procedure you use, the output may be somewhat different. The answers are the same, however. Using the **WINDOWS** version of the program, you could simply type the Syntax file [the set of instructions required to run the procedure, including the relevant Data List and Execute statements (see page 30)], and then execute the job from inside the **Syntax Editor** (not discussed here), or use the program itself to create the syntax file. This latter procedure involves using the mouse to bring up a number of windows, and then selecting the appropriate options or typing in the required information (the **clope** procedure).

1. *Enter SPSS WIN.* This presents you with the **SPSS Data Editor** (see figure in Chapter 2, p. 46). At this point, you could begin to type in the data. However, we will assume here that you already have the data in a file on the A Drive, that this file is labelled fit.dat, and that the

data are in freefield (**SPSS 8.0**) or Delimited format (**SPSS 9.0**). In our example, there would be five lines of data, with each line containing the grade (i.e., 1, 2, or 3 etc.), and the other the number of individuals obtaining that grade.

2. *Click on **File** in the upper row of selections.* This will present you with a drop-down menu with a series of choices.

3. Enter your ASCII (**SPSS 8.0**) or Text (**SPSS 9.0**) data file by following the steps on pages 17 to 20 for **SPSS 8.0,** or pages 20 to 28 for **SPSS 9.0.** For this example, the file will consist of two variables labelled **grade** and **freq** respectively.

4. *Click on **DATA** on the Menu Bar.* This produces a drop-down menu. *Click on the **Weight cases** option (at the bottom of the menu).* This presents the **Weight Cases** Window (see figure, page 165) except that this one will include only grade and frequency in the white pane. *Then click on **Weight by cases**. Click on **freq**, then click on the arrow, and then on **OK**.*

5. *Click on the **Statistics (SPSS 8.0)** or **Analyze (SPSS 9.0)** option on the menu bar.* This presents you with a drop-down menu. *Move your cursor to **Non-Parametric Tests** and you are presented with another menu to the right with a choice of the following in both* **SPSS 8.0** *and* **SPSS 9.0:**

    Chi-Square...
    Binomial...
    Runs
        1-Sample KS
        2 Independent samples
        K Independent samples
        2 Related samples
        K Related samples

6. *Click on **Chi-Square**.* This presents you with the Window, **Chi-Square Test** (see figure below).

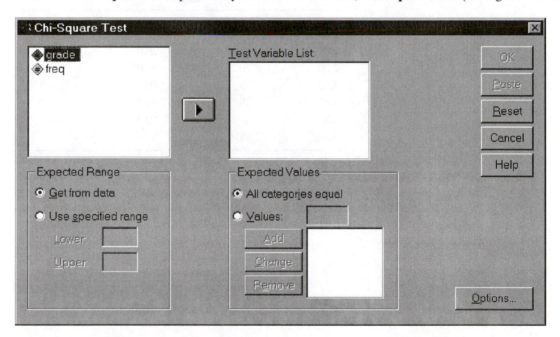

The two variables, **grade** and **freq** appear in the white pane, with **grade** highlighted. *Click on **grade** and add it to the **Test Variable List** by clicking on the arrow. Then click on the white circle preceding **Values**.* This puts a dot in the circle and moves the cursor to the white pane to the right. *Type in the first expected frequency (i.e., 20), then click on **ADD**. Type in each of the other expected frequencies (60, 60, 50, 10), clicking on **ADD** after each one.*

7. *Click on **OK** to run the **Chi-Square** analysis.*

8. This runs the chi-square program, and the answers are returned to the **SPSS Output Viewer,** as well as to your monitor. At this point, you can print your answers, save them in a file, or transfer them to some other editor.

9. To exit **SPSS,** *click on **File** (upper row of operations), and click on **Exit.** Before you can exit, however, the program will ask if you wish to save the contents of the SPSS Output Viewer as well as those of the Data Editor.* If you have already saved them you will not have to do so again.

The Syntax File.   If you were to follow the instructions given above, you would produce the following Syntax File:

```
WEIGHT BY FREQ.
    NPAR TESTS CHISQUARE = GRADE (1,5)
    / EXPECTED = 20 60 60 50 10.
```

Many of the commands in this file are comparable to others presented in this chapter. The data are analyzed, however, using the program **NPAR** rather than **CROSSTABS** from **SPSS WINDOWS.** In this job, we have requested the **CHISQUARE** option as the **TEST** on the **NPAR** line, and have indicated that the classifications are based on the variable **GRADE.** We indicated that the expected frequencies for the five categories are as indicated, but we could have read in the expected proportions instead of the frequencies. The format is the same, and the answers are identical, provided the expected frequencies add to the same total as the observed frequencies.

The results for this syntax file are presented below:

Grade

	Observed *N*	Expected *N*	Residual
1.00	15	20.0	−5.0
2.00	70	60.0	10.0
3.00	70	60.0	10.0
4.00	39	50.0	−11.0
5.00	6	10.0	−4.0
Total	200		

Test Statistics

	GRADE
Chi-Square[a]	8.603
df	4
Asymp. Sig.	.072

[a]0 cells (.0%) have expected frequencies less than 5
The minimum expected cell frequency is 10.0

As can be seen, the χ^2 value is the same as that obtained by our hand calculations (8.604), allowing for rounding error. If we were to adopt a Type I error rate of .20, we would thus conclude that the distribution of grades differed significantly from the expected values $[\chi^2(4) = 8.603, p < .10]$ since this is the closest value in Table E of the Appendix. As with the example with the test of Association with more than 1 *df,* the interpretation is not any more detailed than this.

We might also use tests of goodness of fit if we wished to evaluate whether or not our samples are representative of our expectations. Thus, in our analysis of the relationship of Gender to Smoking, we claimed that we randomly sampled individuals to obtain the given results. Since we did not fix the numbers of males and females, or the number of smokers and non-smokers at any given values, we could evaluate whether or not it is reasonable to assume that the numbers of smokers and non-smokers, or males and females followed expected values. For example, we could assume that the numbers of males and females in the population are equal, and test whether our marginal totals for gender (70 and 78) fit our expectations of equal proportions (or any other proportion we thought was appropriate). Or, if we had reason to believe that there were 55% non-smokers and 45% smokers in the population (or any other proportions), we could evaluate whether this expectation is reasonable given our marginal totals of 76 and 72. If we obtained results suggesting our marginal totals did not meet our expectations, we could conclude either that our expectations were incorrect, or there was something wrong with our sampling procedures.

Also, in our analysis of the relationship of faculty of registration and socioeconomic status, we could evaluate our marginal statistics to determine whether or not they conformed to expectations. Let us assume, for example, that the university records indicated that 25% of students were in arts, 40% were in social science, and 35% were in science. We could determine whether or not the students we sampled conformed to these values by performing a χ^2 analysis using the **NPAR** program from **SPSS WINDOWS** as we did in the previous example. If this χ^2 was significant, we could conclude either that the university figures were incorrect or that there was something wrong with our sampling procedures. Assuming that there is no reason to question the university figures, we might wish to re-examine our sampling procedures. We might find, for example, that proportionately more of our sampling was done near cafeterias that were frequented more by students from one faculty than another. This would lead to the conclusion that our sampling was not truly representative of the larger population.

There are many other uses of the chi-square distribution that we have not discussed in this chapter, and other procedures that can be used to evaluate hypotheses concerning frequency data. Hopefully, however, this chapter gives you some insight into one of the oldest procedures used for data analysis.

Chapter 8
Bivariate Regression and Correlation

This chapter is concerned with procedures that assess the relationship between two variables. That is, the focus of attention is on the differences between individual respondents, but more than that, it is on how differences on one attribute (or variable) relate to differences on another attribute or variable. Because attention is directed to differences between individuals as opposed to differences between groups or treatments, the investigation of such relationships is often referred to as the study of individual differences. Until now, most of the procedures that we have discussed (i.e., Chapters 2 to 6) involved comparisons between means. That is, we were interested in determining whether the mean of one group or condition differed significantly from another, or whether there were differences among sets of means, etc., and we were not interested in the nature of the differences between the individuals. If anything, such differences were treated as "error," and helped define the estimates of error in our tests of significance (i.e., the t-tests and F-ratios).

In this chapter, we change our focus. Now, the basic data of interest consist of pairs of observations on a series of individuals. We often refer to these pairs of observations as X and Y, and they represent observations on two different variables such as height and weight, or anxiety and performance, or IQ and grades in school, etc. We are not interested in comparing the means of X and Y (it wouldn't make sense to ask if the average height was more than the average weight), but instead we want to know if there is a relationship between X and Y, and, if so, the nature of that relationship. The statistics of interest are concerned with the relationship between the two variables.

BASIC NOTIONS

When investigating the linear relationship between two sets of variables, we can distinguish between two aspects. One is the nature of this relationship, and the other is its strength. This chapter will consider linear relationships; non-linear relationships are discussed toward the end of the next chapter (see Chapter 9, the section on "Investigating Curvilinear Relations Between Two Variables").

The nature of the relationship between two variables is investigated in *bivariate regression* and is defined by an equation that describes how one variable changes as a result of changes in the other variable. In defining this relationship, one variable (e.g., X) is considered the independent variable, and the other (e.g., Y) is considered the dependent variable. That is, Y is considered to vary as a function of X. The nature of the relationship is defined by an equation that takes the general form:

$$Y' = a + bX$$

where $Y' =$ the value of Y predicted given the value of X.

If we were to plot a graph of the relationship of Y on X, this would consist of a vertical axis to represent the Y values and a horizontal axis to represent the X values. This type of graph is referred to as a scatterplot. The data for each individual is represented as a point in space. The values of Y', as calculated using the above equation, would describe a straight line passing through these points. Consider, for example, a situation where you wished to make a scatterplot of height (Y) on weight (X). For each individual, you would locate the value on the X axis that corresponded to her/his weight, and the value on the Y axis that corresponded to her/his height, and then plot a point where these two values intersect in space. If you had data for 20 individuals, this would result in 20 points being plotted. The figures below present examples for scatterplots for relationships that are positive, negative, or zero.

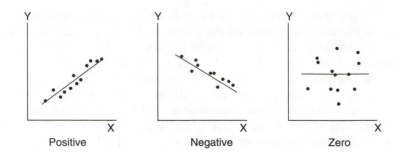

As you can see for the scatterplot representing a *positive* relationship, there is a tendency for the points to be higher on Y as the values on X increase. That is, high values on the horizontal axis (X) tend to be associated with high values on the vertical axis (Y) and low values on the horizontal axis tend to be associated with low values on the vertical axis. A straight line drawn to represent this relationship shows this positive trend. A different pattern is present for a *negative* relationship. In this case, high values of X tend to be associated with low values of Y, while low values of X tend to be associated with high values of Y. The straight line describing this pattern shows this negative trend. Finally, for a *zero* relationship, there is no clear trend in the data. Whether values are low or high on the horizontal axis (X) has no obvious relationship with values on the vertical axis (Y). The straight line describing this relationship is a line that is parallel to the horizontal axis. In fact, this line would be drawn at the value of the mean for Y.

The strength or degree of the relationship is defined in terms of the *correlation* between the two variables, and it reflects how closely the points fall near a straight line with either a positive or negative slope. If the points are all very close to the line, we would describe the relationship as a strong one; if the points tend to be far away from the line, we would describe the relationship as weak. As you can see, the relationship would be considered weak in the case where the relationship is zero, which makes sense because there is no relationship between the two variables (i.e., Y doesn't change systematically with changes in X). A measure of the strength of the relationship is provided by the correlation coefficient (r). The value of r can vary from -1 to $+1$ (depending on the general slope of the line), and the absolute value of r is the measure of the strength of the relationship. If the absolute value is close to 1, the relationship is considered strong; if it is close to 0 it is considered weak. Absolute values varying between 0 and 1 are sometimes referred to as slight, moderate, etc., depending on how close the number is to 1, but the definition of weak, slight, moderate, and strong, etc., is often arbitrary, depending in part on the variables being studied, the sample size, and the expectations of the researcher.

A BIT OF HISTORY

The study of bivariate regression and correlation can be traced back to a series of publications in the late 1800s and early 1900s, and many of these publications involve individuals who contributed in other ways to the field of data analysis and statistics. Cowles (1989, Chapter 10, pp. 121–147) presents a brief and interesting account of this history, and some of the philosophical and controversial issues that surround it.

For all practical purposes, indices of bivariate regression and correlation as we know them today began with a publication on laws of heredity by Galton (1877). In that article, he discussed the inheritance of weight and size of pea seeds, and introduced a measure of *reversion* that he referred to as r. He noted that there was a relation between the size of (parent) pea seeds and the size of pea seeds grown from them (the offspring), as well as the weight of the parents and the weight of their offspring. Large parents tended to produce large offspring, and small parents tended to produce small offspring. He noted too, however, that although large parents often produced offspring that were even larger than their parents (while small pea seeds often produced offspring that were even smaller than their parents), on average offspring of the larger seeds tended not to be as large as their parents, and the offspring of the smaller peas seeds were not as small as their parents. This is sometimes referred to as regression toward the mean.

In 1884, Galton opened a laboratory at the International Health Exhibition where he charged an entrance fee to people, measured a number of their attributes (e.g., height, strength, sensory acuities, etc.), and gave them a record of their results. Following the exhibition, he opened another laboratory at the South Kensington Museum, and continued obtaining information on a number of attributes of individuals for eight more years. One study that grew out of this (Galton, 1885) investigated the relation between parents' and children's heights, obtaining results that were comparable to those obtained with the pea seeds. In this article, he referred to this phenomenon as *regression* instead of reversion. In time, the term *regression* came to be associated with the slope of the best fitting line, and the value of this slope became known as the regression coefficient.

Galton also introduced a measure of *co-relation,* but the *correlation coefficient,* as we know it today, was introduced by Pearson (1896), who also presented much of the theory underlying correlation as well as its mathematical foundation. Later researchers provided information that permitted tests of significance associated with correlation. For example, Gosset (Student, 1908b) investigated the empirical sampling distribution of r when samples are obtained from a population in which the correlation is 0, while Fisher (1915) developed the mathematics underlying the sampling distribution of $r,$ and ultimately proposed the t-test of significance associated with regression and correlation that we use today.

BIVARIATE REGRESSION

Given two variables, it is possible to compute two regression equations. One involves the regression of Y on $X,$ where Y is considered the dependent variable and X is the independent variable. The other involves the regression of X on $Y,$ where X is the dependent variable and Y is the independent variable. Different equations result, as we shall see. Often, of course, it makes sense to consider only one of the variables as the dependent variable, so an equation treating this one as the independent variable would not make any interpretative sense, but arithmetically at least the equation can be determined. At other times, of course, it is not meaningful to consider either variable as dependent or independent. For example, if you were interested in the relationship between the personality variables of extraversion and sociability, it is hard to know which to consider as dependent and which as independent. When we come to discuss correlation, we will see that it doesn't really matter.

Regression of Y on X

In regression, one variable is considered to be dependent upon the other. In the discussion to follow, we will consider the variable Y to be the dependent variable, and X to be the independent variable, and we can investigate the regression of Y on $X,$ for example, the regression of weight (Y) on height (X). The regression equation for Y on X describes a linear relationship as follows:

$$Y' = a_{yx} + b_{yx}X$$

where the subscripts for a and b (i.e., yx) are used to formally indicate that the dependent variable is Y and the independent variable is X.

There are two unknown values in this equation, a_{yx}, and b_{yx}. The value of a_{yx} refers to the Y *intercept* or the *constant* (i.e., the value of Y' when X equals 0), and is determined as follows:

$$a_{yx} = \overline{Y} - b_{yx}\overline{X}$$

The value of b_{yx} is the *regression coefficient,* and is the slope of the straight line that best fits the data. The value of b_{yx} represents that increment in Y' associated with a unit increase in X. The value of b_{yx} is calculated as follows:

$$b_{yx} = \frac{\Sigma(X - \overline{X})(Y - \overline{Y})}{\Sigma(X - \overline{X})^2}$$

Following is a set of sample data for 10 subjects on two variables, X and Y. Note in the table that we also include the values of the mean and standard deviation for each variable, as well as the deviations of each observation from the mean for that variable.

X	Y	$X - \overline{X}$	$Y - \overline{Y}$
3	6	−4	−2.6
4	8	−3	−.6
5	9	−2	.4
5	7	−2	−1.6
6	9	−1	.4
7	10	0	1.4
8	8	1	−.6
9	10	2	1.4
11	10	4	1.4
12	9	5	.4
$\overline{X} = 7.00$	$\overline{Y} = 8.60$		
$S = 2.98$	$S = 1.35$		

We can use these data to calculate the values for a_{yx} and b_{yx}. Thus:

$$a_{yx} = 8.60 - .30(7.00) = 6.50 \qquad b_{yx} = \frac{24}{80} = .30$$

The regression equation for these data then would be:

$$Y' = 6.50 + .30X$$

With this equation, you could determine the predicted value for each individual. For example, if $X = 5$,

$$Y' = 6.50 + (.30)(5) = 8.0$$

You might calculate the predicted values of Y for each individual. The following table presents the values of X, Y, and Y' for this sample of data.

X	Y	Y'
3	6	7.4
4	8	7.7
5	9	8.0
5	7	8.0
6	9	8.3
7	10	8.6
8	8	8.9
9	10	9.2
11	10	9.8
12	9	10.1

If prediction were perfect, each Y score would equal each Y' score, and the sum of squared deviations of the Y score from the Y' score would be 0. Obviously, in this case, prediction is not perfect. We could, if we wished, examine this table more closely. For example, we could calculate the mean of the Y' values. If we did, we would discover that it was 8.60, the same as the mean for the Y values. Furthermore, we could compute the sum of the squared deviations of each Y value from the corresponding Y' value. That is:

$$(6 - 7.4)^2 + (8 - 7.7)^2 + \ldots + (9 - 10.1)^2 = 9.20$$

This value of 9.20 is a measure of the differences between the predicted and obtained values of Y. It is often referred to as the *Residual Sum of Squares*.

Similarly, we could compute the sum of the squared deviations of each Y' from their mean. That is:

$$(7.4 - 8.6)^2 + (7.7 - 8.6)^2 + \ldots + (10.1 - 8.6)^2 = 7.2$$

This value of 7.2 is a measure of the differences among the predicted values. It is often referred to as the *Regression Sum of Squares*.

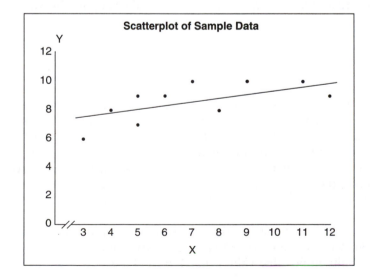

Scatterplot of Sample Data

The figure above presents a scatterplot of the regression of Y on X, with the regression line superimposed on it. As can be seen, there is a tendency for the values of Y to increase with increases in X. That is, there tends to be a positive relation between X and Y. Although there appears to be a slight bend in the actual scatter of points, this bend is not indicated by the straight line. In the next chapter, procedures will be described that permit an investigator to determine whether a non-linear function may better describe the relationship between two variables.

Standard Error of Estimate

One measure that is used to assess the amount of error in predicting Y is the standard error of estimate. There are at least three ways of calculating the value of the standard error of estimate that can be found in various textbooks, but they all involve the Residual Sum of Squares. One form of this is given in terms of the following equation [see, for example, Freund (1974)]:

$$SE = \sqrt{\frac{\Sigma(Y - Y')^2}{N - 2}}$$

$$= 1.072$$

The other forms of the equation involve dividing by N (see McNemar, 1969), or $(N - 1)$ (see Ferguson, 1966) instead of $(N - 2)$, and obviously yield somewhat different values. It is beyond the scope of this chapter to discuss the reasons for these different forms of this equation. Suffice it to say, we have adopted the form given in the preceding equation because it is consistent with the form used by **SPSS WINDOWS** that we will discuss later in this chapter (see Performing a Regression Analysis with **SPSS WINDOWS,** page 189).

The smaller the value of SE, the better the prediction, or stated another way, the smaller the errors of prediction. There is another way in which the standard error of estimate can be very useful. That is, we can use the standard error of estimate to establish confidence intervals for our estimated values. We saw, for example that with our equation, an individual with an X value of 5, would have a predicted Y value of 8.0. We might ask, however, what sort of range we might expect in this prediction. To determine this, we could compute confidence intervals for this prediction. We could, for example, determine the 95% confidence interval; that range of values that we would expect our value to take 95% of the time in the population. Assuming that the errors are normally distributed around the regression line, we could compute this value as follows:

$$Y' = (a_{yx} + b_{yx}X) \pm 1.96 SE$$

$$Y' = (6.50 + (.30)(5)) \pm (1.96)(1.072) = 8.0 \pm 2.10$$

That is, 95% of the time, we would expect that in a population for which this set of data can be considered a random sample, an individual obtaining an X value of 5, would be expected to obtain a Y value as low as $8.0 - 2.10 = 5.90$, and as high as $8.0 + 2.10 = 10.10$. In this example, therefore, although one would consider that $SE = 1.072$ is relatively small, we can see that there is still a fairly large error in our possible prediction, at least in this case. Given a fairly low score on X of 5, we would predict that an individual's score on Y could vary anywhere from approximately 6 to 10, which in our example is essentially the range of the Y values given.

In a similar fashion, the 95% confidence interval corresponding to an X value of 9 is 7.10 to 11.30. That is, the expected value can vary from roughly 7 to 11. This still represents considerable variability in possible values that Y could be expected to take. You could, of course, calculate the confidence intervals for each other predicted value in the above table. Note that the interval is simply the predicted value plus or minus 2.10 for these data.

Regression of X on Y

As discussed earlier, it is possible to calculate two regression equations with bivariate data. The regression of X on Y is comparable to that of the regression of Y on X, except that the equations now become:

$$X' = a_{xy} + b_{xy}Y$$

where:

$$a_{xy} = \overline{X} - b_{xy}\overline{Y}$$

and:

$$b_{xy} = \frac{\Sigma(X - \overline{X})(Y - \overline{Y})}{\Sigma(Y - \overline{Y})^2}$$

Using the data in the example:

$$a_{xy} = 7.00 - (1.46)(8.60) = -5.56 \qquad b_{xy} = \frac{24}{16.4} = 1.46$$

And, the regression equation is:

$$X' = -5.56 + 1.46Y$$

We could also, of course, calculate the Residual Sum of Squares, the Regression Sum of Squares, the standard error of estimate, and 95% confidence intervals for each predicted value of X. This is left as an exercise for you (though you might find it easier to do using **SPSS WINDOWS** instead of doing the hand calculations).

BIVARIATE CORRELATION

The nature and degree of the relationship between two variables X and Y is assessed by the Pearson product-moment correlation (r). As we saw above, the two regression equations are different, and although it may not be obvious, the reason for this is due to the fact that the means and standard deviations of X and Y are different. Before calculating the values of a and b, the data for X and Y could first be standardized so that they both had the same means and standard deviations. This can be done by making use of standard scores defined as follows:

$$Z_x = \frac{X - \overline{X}}{S_x} \qquad Z_y = \frac{Y - \overline{Y}}{S_y}$$

where S_x and S_y are unbiased estimates of their population standard deviations.

In this form, the means of Z_x and Z_y are both 0, the standard deviations are both 1.0, and the sum of the squared values of both Z_x and Z_y are equal to $(N-1)$ (i.e., $\Sigma Z_x^2 = \Sigma Z_y^2 = (N-1)$). If we were to calculate the regression coefficients a and b for these variables, we would find that regardless of whether or not we calculated the regression of Z_y on Z_x, or vice versa, the regression coefficients would be the same. Consider, for example, the regression of Z_y on Z_x. Using the equations presented earlier (p. 182) but using the data in standard score form instead of the original measures:

$$a = \bar{Z}_y - b\bar{Z}_x = 0$$

since the means of both Z_y and Z_x are 0, and

$$b = \frac{\Sigma Z_x Z_y}{\Sigma Z_x^2} = \frac{\Sigma Z_x Z_y}{(N-1)} = \frac{5.964}{9} = .663$$

The major point to be made here is that one would obtain this value regardless of which variable Z_x or Z_y were considered the dependent variable. In some contexts, this is referred to as the regression coefficient in standard score form, and called Beta. More commonly, it is called the Pearson product moment correlation coefficient, and designated by the symbol r.

It isn't necessary, of course, to first standardize the data if you wish only to compute the correlation between two variables, X and Y. With a bit of algebra, it can be shown that an equivalent expression is:

$$r = \frac{\Sigma(X - \bar{X})(Y - \bar{Y})}{\sqrt{\Sigma(X - \bar{X})^2 \, \Sigma(Y - \bar{Y})^2}}$$

$$r = \frac{24}{\sqrt{(80)(16.4)}} = .663$$

Even this equation can be a bit difficult when computing this value by hand, but a bit of algebra produces yet another equivalent expression, this one using the data directly without having to calculate the deviation scores. This expression is:

$$r = \frac{N\Sigma XY - \Sigma X \Sigma Y}{\sqrt{[N\Sigma X^2 - (\Sigma X)^2][N\Sigma Y^2 - (\Sigma Y)^2]}} = \frac{(10)(626) - (70)(86)}{\sqrt{[(10)(570) - 70^2][(10)(756) - 86^2]}}$$
$$= .663.$$

Proportion of Variance in Common

The value of r provides a description of the nature of the relationship between the two variables (i.e., positive or negative), as well as an index of the strength of the relationship (i.e., the magnitude of the absolute value of r). The square of r provides somewhat more information about the relationship in that it is an index of the proportion of the total sum of squares that is accounted for by the regression. That is:

$$r^2 = \frac{\Sigma(Y' - \bar{Y})^2}{\Sigma(Y - \bar{Y})^2} = \frac{7.2}{16.4} = .439$$

Thus, given a correlation of .663, we can state that $.663^2 = .439$ of the variance in Y is common to the variance in X, or alternatively that these two variables share 43.9% of the variance in common.

TESTS OF SIGNIFICANCE

We have seen how to compute the values for a, b, and r, but a question that follows once we have computed any of these values is the nature of any generalizations that we can make as a result. That is, we know that, in our sample, the correlation between X and Y is .663, but we might wonder what generalizations we might make of the population from which our sample was drawn. In correlation, tests of significance evaluate how likely it is to obtain the result you did, providing the value in the population (ρ, rho) is 0. That is, with respect to correlation, for example, the null hypothesis is:

Ho: $\rho = 0$.

For a two-tail test, the alternative hypothesis is:

Ha: $\rho \neq 0$

For a one-tail test, the alternative hypothesis is:

Ha: $\rho > 0$, or $\rho < 0$ depending upon the prediction.

Similar observations apply to a and b.

The Sampling Distribution of r

Assume there is a population comprising two variables with a given correlation. If we were to obtain a series of random samples from this population and compute the correlation for each one, we would not expect to obtain this actual population correlation in each sample. We would expect that sometimes we would obtain the same correlation as in the population, but that sometimes we would obtain correlations that are lower, and sometimes correlations that are higher. The following figure shows two distributions of correlations for 1000 samples of $N = 10$ each drawn from two populations, one where the correlation in the population (r) was equal to 0, and one where it was equal to .60. As you can see, there was considerable variability in the correlations obtained. For the population for which the correlation was 0, these correlations range from −.85 to .80. Note too that, for this population, the distribution of correlations was relatively normally distributed around 0. In fact, the mean of the 1000 correlations was equal to −.02. When I tested each of these correlations to determine whether or not they were significant, I found that only 45 of the 1000 were significant at the 5% level. That is, when the correlation in the population was 0, only 4.5% of the correlations were found to be significant at the .05 level. (In theory, you would expect 5% of them to be significant, so that if I were to repeat the study, I might obtain a value slightly greater than 5% next time.)

For the population in which the correlation was .60, the correlations range from −.45 to .90, and the distribution is obviously not normal, but is in fact skewed to the left. The mean of the 1000 correlations was .56, and tests of significance revealed that 447 of the 1000 were significant at the 5% level (note, this means that 553 were not significant). That is, the tests were correct only 44.7% of the time in concluding that the population correlation was not 0. If we increased the sample size to 20, we would find that more of the correlations would be significant, and if we continued to increase the sample size even more would be. This is because sample size has a big effect on the power of the test to correctly identify a non-zero correlation in the population. No amount of change in sample size would influence the number of significant correlations found in the previous case where the population correlation was 0.

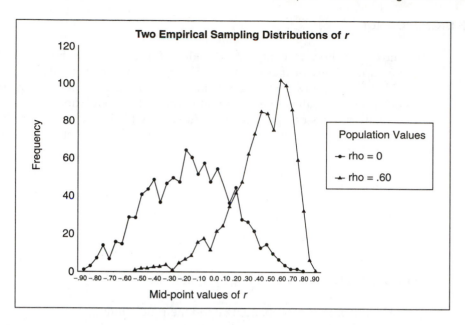

Significance of *r* and *b*

The equation for the test of significance of r is identical to that for the significance of b_{yx} and b_{xy}. It is:

$$F = \frac{r^2}{\dfrac{1 - r^2}{N - 2}} = \frac{r^2(N - 2)}{1 - r^2}$$

This F-ratio has 1 degree of freedom associated with the numerator and $(N - 2)$ degrees of freedom associated with the denominator. As applied to the sample data, it is:

$$F = \frac{.663^2(8)}{(1 - .663^2)} = 6.261$$

at 1 and 8 degrees of freedom. One could determine the significance of this statistic by comparing it with the table of the F-distribution (see Table C, the Appendix), and if this were done it would be found that it is significant at the .05 level. If it were desired to present this information in an article, it would be expressed as $(r = .663, F(1,8) = 6.26, p < .05)$.

An equivalent test is the t-test as follows:

$$t = \frac{r}{\sqrt{\dfrac{1 - r^2}{N - 2}}} = \frac{.663}{\sqrt{\dfrac{1 - .663^2}{8}}} = 2.502$$

This t-test would be evaluated at $(N - 2)$ degrees of freedom (8 in the example) and would be evaluated for significance by determining whether it exceeds the value of t for 8 degrees of freedom in the table of t (see Table B, the Appendix). In this case it is significant at the .05 level. To present this information, one would write ($r = .663$, $t(8) = 2.502$, $p < .05$). It will be noted, of course, that the t given above is simply the square root of the previous F-ratio (i.e., $2.502^2 = 6.261$).

These same two statistics (F and t) are also appropriate for evaluating the significance of the two regression coefficients. Thus to determine whether or not $b_{yx} = .30$ or $b_{xy} = 1.46$ is significant, one would perform the identical calculations. For the sample data, the F-ratio for each value of b would be 6.261 at 1 and 8 degrees of freedom, or the equivalent t-ratio of 2.502 at 8 degrees of freedom. Alternatively, the t-test for b can be written as:

$$t = \frac{b}{\sigma_b}$$

or b divided by the standard error of b. It is beyond the scope of this chapter to discuss the standard error of b except to say that it is a measure of the variability in b expected due to sampling fluctuations. The important point here is that this t-value would have the same value as the previous equation for t.

PERFORMING A REGRESSION ANALYSIS WITH SPSS WINDOWS

Analyzing the Data Using SPSS WINDOWS

The data presented in the previous example could be typed into a data file in which the X and Y scores for each participant are given on a line with blanks separating each score (that is, in free form in **SPSS 8.0,** or delimited in **SPSS 9.0**) Assume that this file was called **corrchp.dat** and that it was stored on the A Drive in ASCII (or Text) form.

Steps in Using SPSS WINDOWS REGRESSION. The following steps are applicable to **SPSS 8.0** and **SPSS 9.0** except for the input of the ASCII or Text data file. In the example to follow you are instructed at Step 3 to input your data following the procedures described in Chapter 1. The output for this example was obtained by using the freefield format in **SPSS 8.0,** and depending upon the input procedure you use, the output may be somewhat different. The answers are the same, however. Using the **WINDOWS** version of the program, you could simply type the Syntax file [the set of instructions required to run the procedure, including the relevant Data List and Execute statements (see page 30)], and then execute the job from inside the Syntax Editor (not discussed here), or use the program itself to create the syntax file. This latter procedure involves using the mouse to bring up a number of windows (the **clope** procedure), and then selecting the appropriate options or typing in the required information.

1. *Enter **SPSS WIN.*** This presents you with the **SPSS** Data Editor (see figure in Chapter 2, page 46). At this point, you could begin to type in the data. However, we will assume that you already have the data in a file on the A Drive, that the file is labelled **corrchp.dat,** and that the data are in freefield (**SPSS 8.0**) or Delimited (**SPSS 9.0**) format. For each participant, there would be two values, the score for **X,** and the score for **Y.** Of course, if you wished to calculate the correlations among a number of variables, you could have more than two in the list.

2. *Click on **File** in the menu bar.* This will present you with a drop-down menu with a series of choices.

3. Enter your ASCII (**SPSS 8.0**) or Text (**SPSS 9.0**) data file by following the steps on pages 17 to 20 for **SPSS 8.0,** or pages 20 to 28 for **SPSS 9.0.** For this example, the file will consist of two variables X and Y respectively.

4. *Click on the **Statistics** (SPSS 8.0) or **Analyze** (SPSS 9.0) option on the top row.* This presents you with a drop-down menu. *Move your cursor to Regression, and you are presented with another menu to the right with a choice of the following in **SPSS 8.0** or **SPSS 9.0:***

SPSS 8.0	**SPSS 9.0**
Linear . . .	Linear . . .
Curve Estimation . . .	Curve Estimation . . .
Logistic . . .	Binary Logistic . . .
Probit . . .	Multinomial Logistic
Nonlinear . . .	Probit . . .
Weight Estimation . . .	Nonlinear . . .
2-Stage Least Squares . . .	Weight Estimation . . .
Optimal Scaling	2-Stage Least Squares . . .
	Optimal Scaling

5. *Click on **Linear.*** This presents you with the Window, **Linear Regression** (see figure below).

   Note that the variable X is highlighted. *Add X to the Independent(s) pane by clicking on the appropriate arrow. You can then add the dependent variable to Dependent by clicking on Y, and then the appropriate arrow.*

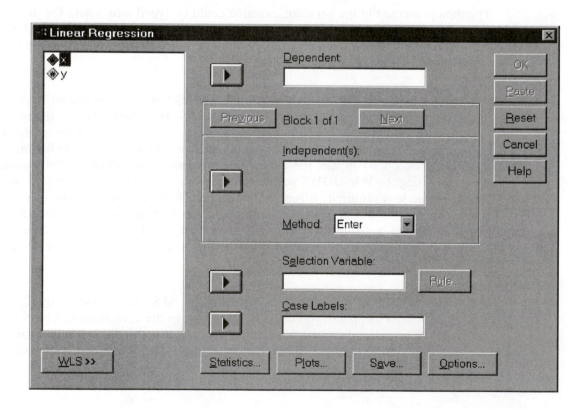

6. *Click on **Statistics** at the bottom of the Window.* This gives another Window, **Linear Regression Statistics** (see figure below).

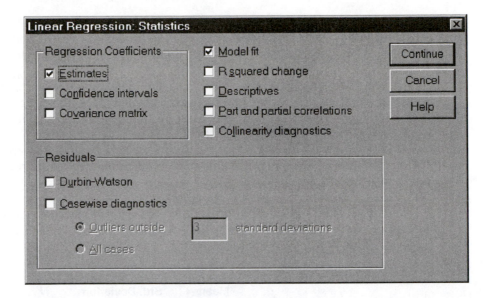

The choices, **Estimates** and **Model Fit,** are selected by default, but many other options are available. *Add **Descriptives** to obtain means, standard deviations, correlations, significance, and N's. Click on **Continue.*** This returns you to the **Linear Regression Window.**

7. *If you wished to add to the default options, you could click on **Options** and, if you did, this would give you another Window, **Linear Regression Options.*** We are not going to add any options, so we will omit that step. *Instead, click on **OK** to run Linear Regression.*

8. This runs the Regression program, and the answers are returned to the **SPSS Output Viewer** as well as to your monitor. At this point, you can print your answers, save them in a file, or transfer them to some other editor.

9. To exit **SPSS,** *click on **File** (upper row of operations), and click on **Exit.*** Before you can exit, however, the program will ask if you wish to save the contents of the Output Viewer as well as those of the Data Editor. If you have already saved them, you will not have to do so again.

The Syntax File.   If you followed the above instructions, you would construct the following syntax file:

```
REGRESSION
  /DESCRIPTIVES MEAN STDDEV CORR SIG N
  /MISSING LISTWISE
  /STATISTICS COEFF OUTS R ANOVA
  /CRITERIA=PIN(.05) POUT(.10)
  /NOORIGIN
  /DEPENDENT y
  /METHOD=ENTER x.
```

The regression procedure is invoked by the keyword REGRESSION, and all the variables are to be analyzed. The keyword DESCRIPTIVES instructs the computer to include in the output the means and standard deviations of all variables, as well as the number of cases, the correlations among these variables, and an indication of their significance level. The MISSING statement indicates that if a subject has missing data, he/she will be omitted from all calculations. The STATIS-TICS statement indicates that we desire the regression coefficients, the correlation between the variables, and the analysis of variance table evaluating the significance of the correlation. The CRI-TERIA and NOORIGIN statements are of little interest in the present case where there are only two variables, and will not be discussed at this point. More will be said about them in the next chapter dealing with multiple correlation. The statements, DEPENDENT and METHOD indicates that we want Y to be considered the dependent variable, and X the independent variable.

Before discussing the output concerning the regression analysis, I should point out that the Regression program that we are using is really designed for multiple regression analysis (see Chapter 9). Consequently some of the output is a bit unnecessary for bivariate regression. Specifically, aspects of the output refer to "Model 1." This is because the program could be used to compute more than one regression equation for the dependent variable if there were more than one independent variable and it was desired to add more predictors in the same run. Each different analysis would constitute a different model.

The descriptive statistics for the sample data are presented in the following table. You will note that the values in this table are the same as those computed in the example presented earlier.

Descriptive Statistics

	Mean	Std. Deviation	N
Y	8.6000	1.3499	10
X	7.0000	2.9814	10

The output for the correlation follows. It consists of the correlation matrix (in this case there are only the two variables X and Y), an indication of the significance of the correlation, and the number of observations for each variable.

Correlations

		Y	X
Pearson Correlation	Y	1.000	.663
	X	.663	1.000
Sig. (1–tailed)	Y	.	.018
	X	.018	.
N	Y	10	10
	X	10	10

The following table presents a summary of the variables entered into the regression equation. Since there is only one independent variable, this table indicates that X is the independent (predictor) variable, and Y is the dependent variable (see footnote b following the table).

Variables Entered/Removed[b]

Model	Variables Entered	Variables Removed	Method
1	X[a]	.	Enter

[a]All requested variables entered
[b]Dependent Variable: Y

The analysis of variance table is presented next. You will recall that the F-ratio is a test of the significance of the regression coefficient, as well as of the correlation coefficient. Note that the values in the table are identical to those used in our earlier discussion. The values of the Sum of Squares and the associated degrees of freedom (df) are as indicated earlier. The Mean Squares are obtained by dividing the Sums of Squares by their respective degrees of freedom, and the F-ratio presented following is the ratio of the Mean Square for the Regression divided by the Mean Square for the Residual. It will be noted that the value of the F-ratio in the table is the same as that obtained using the equation of F to test the significance of r or b given above (see page 188).

ANOVA[b]

Model		Sum of Squares	df	Mean Square	F	Sig.
1	Regression	7.200	1	7.200	6.261	.037[a]
	Residual	9.200	8	1.150		
	Total	16.400	9			

[a]Predictors: (Constant), X
[b]Dependent Variable: Y

The next table, labelled "Coefficients" presents information about the regression equation. Note, that it indicates that B (the regression coefficient that we referred to as b_{yx}) is .30, and that the constant (we called this a_{yx}) is 6.50. The output also gives the standard errors for these two statistics, the results of t-tests evaluating whether or not they differ significantly from 0, and the probability values associated with these two t-tests. Note that the value of t for the regression coefficient is 2.502, which is the value obtained for the t-test of the regression coefficient given above (page 188). Note, too, that this value is equal to the square root of the F-ratio discussed above. The other value given in the table is referred to as "Beta," and it will be noted that this is identical to the value of the correlation between X and Y given in the table of correlations on page 192 as well as that for "R" given in the table of the Model Summary presented later.

Coefficients[a]

Model		Unstandardized Coefficients		Standardized Coefficients		
		B	Std. Error	Beta	t	Sig.
1	(Constant)	6.500	.905		7.181	.000
	X	.300	.120	.663	2.502	.037

[a]Dependent Variable: Y

The last table presents a summary of the correlational analysis. We have not yet discussed all of the statistics listed in this output, but we can review those that we have discussed. The dependent variable is identified as Y, and X is the independent variable entered on Step 1. When we are dealing with bivariate regression, there will only be one step, but in multiple regression (see the next chapter), there may well be more independent variables, and thus more steps. The output then lists the following:

R Since there is only one predictor, this is in fact the bivariate correlation (r). It has a value of .663.

R Square	This is the squared value of r, and is an expression of the proportion of variance common to X and Y. That is, 43.9 % of the variation in Y is accounted for by X.
Adjusted R Square	This is a reduction of r^2 to take into account the number of participants and the number of predictors in the equation. It is sometimes referred to as the shrunken value of r, and in this instance it is equal to .369. This statistic is appropriate to multiple regression (see the next chapter), and is not used in the context of bivariate correlation (but see the paragraph below on the Relation of the Adjusted R square to the Standard Error).
Standard Error	This is the standard deviation of the errors of estimate Note that the value of 1.0724 agrees with the value of 1.072 we obtained in the earlier example.

Model Summary

Model	R	R Square	Adjusted R Square	Std Error of the Estimate
1	.663[a]	.439	.369	1.0724

[a]Predictors: (Constant), X

Interpreting the Results of this Analysis

Taken together, we could note that the correlation between X and Y is .663, and that it is significant ($p < .05$). The correlation is positive, so we know that high scores on X are associated with high scores on Y and low scores on X are associated with low scores on Y. If we wished to present the value of the correlation in an article, we would use the notation ($r(8) = .663, p < .05$). Similarly, we could make use of the standard error of estimate, and point out that it is 1.072, or use this value to calculate confidence intervals for any individual value we predicted using the regression equation. Finally, we could refer directly to the regression equation by stating the equation as:

$$Y' = 6.50 + .30X$$

If we felt it were desirable, we could also indicate the values of a_{yx} and b_{yx} using the notation [$a = 6.50, t(8) = 7.18, p < .0001$], and [$b = .30, t(8) = 2.50, p < .05$]. It wouldn't be necessary to indicate the subscripts for a and b, because it should be obvious from the presentation which is the dependent variable and which is the independent variable.

Relation of Adjusted R Square to Standard Error

In bivariate regression, there is a direct relation between the adjusted r-square and the standard error. Earlier, there was an equation given to calculate the standard error expressed as a function of the squared differences between the obtained Y values and the predicted Y values (see page 184). An equivalent expression is:

$$SE = S_y \sqrt{1 - r_{adj}^2}$$

Solving this equation for r^2, using the value of SE calculated from the earlier expression and the unbiased estimate of S_y, yields the adjusted r-square. That is:

$$r^2_{adj} = \frac{S_y^2 - (SE)^2}{S_y^2} = \frac{1.35^2 - 1.072^2}{1.35^2} = .369$$

PERFORMING A CORRELATIONAL ANALYSIS WITH SPSS WINDOWS

Analyzing the Data Using SPSS WINDOWS

The data for this example consists of four variables, X and Y from the previous example, and two new variables identified as A and B. The data file is not shown, but these data were typed into a data file in which the four scores for each participant are given on a line with blanks separating each score, that is in free format. Assume that this file was called **corfour.dat** and that it was stored on the A Drive in ASCII (Text) form.

Steps in Using SPSS WINDOWS BIVARIATE CORRELATIONS. The following steps are applicable to **SPSS 8.0** and **SPSS 9.0** except for the input of the ASCII or Text data file. In the example to follow you are instructed at Step 3 to input your data following the procedures described in Chapter 1. The output for this example was obtained by using the freefield format in **SPSS 8.0,** and depending upon the input procedure you use, the output may be somewhat different. The answers are the same, however. Using the **WINDOWS** version of the program, you could simply type the Syntax file [the set of instructions required to run the procedure, including the relevant Data List and Execute statements (see page 30)], and then execute the job from inside the Syntax Editor (not discussed here), or use the program itself to create the syntax file. This latter procedure involves using the mouse to bring up a number of windows, and then selecting the appropriate options or typing in the required information.

1. *Enter SPSS WIN.* This presents you with the **SPSS** Data Editor (see figure in Chapter 2, page 46). At this point, you could begin to type in the data. However, we will assume that you already have the data in a file on the **A Drive,** that the file is labelled **corfour.dat,** and that the data are in freefield (**SPSS 8.0**) or Delimited (**SPSS 9.0**) format. For each participant, there would be four values, the scores for **A, B, X,** and **Y.**

2. *Click on File in the menu bar.* This will present you with a drop-down menu with a series of choices.

3. Enter your ASCII (**SPSS 8.0**) or Text (**SPSS 9.0**) data file by following the steps on pages 17 to 20 for **SPSS 8.0,** or pages 20 to 28 for **SPSS 9.0.** For this example, the file will consist of two variables X and Y respectively.

4. *Click on the Statistics (SPSS 8.0) or Analyze (SPSS 9.0) option on the top row.* This presents you with a drop-down menu. *Move your cursor to Correlate, and you are presented with another menu to the right with a choice of the following:*
    Bivariate . . .
    Partial . . .
    Distances . . .

5. *Click on Bivariate.* This presents you with the Window, **Bivariate Correlations,** and the variable **a** is highlighted (see figure below).

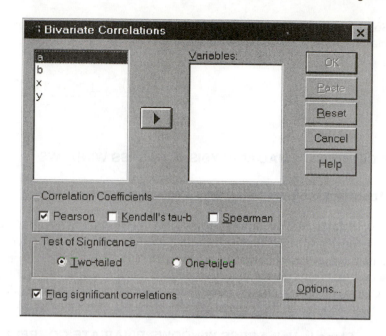

*Add all the variables **a** to **y** to the Variables pane. You can do this one at a time by clicking on each one and then clicking on the arrow. Alternatively, you can add all the variables at once by putting the cursor on **a**, holding down the left mouse button, and dragging the cursor down to **y**. This highlights **a** to **y**, and when you click on the arrow, all are added to the pane.*

6. You will note that **Pearson, Two-tailed,** and **Flag significant correlations** are selected by default. We do not want any of the other choices here, but we do want to select something from **Options.** *Therefore, click on **Options**.* This produces the next Window, **Bivariate Correlations: Options** (see below).

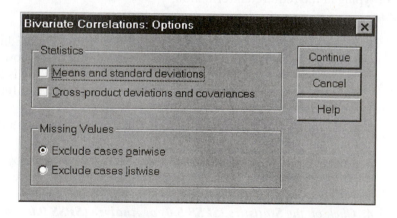

7. **Exclude cases pairwise** has been selected by default. *Click on **Means and standard deviations*** to provide these statistics. *Then click on **Continue**.* This returns you to the **Bivariate Correlations** Window.

8. *Click on **OK** to run **Correlations**.*

9. This runs the **Correlations** program, and the answers are returned to the **SPSS Output Viewer** as well as to your monitor. At this point, you can print your answers, save them in a file, or transfer them to some other editor.

10. To exit **SPSS,** *click on* **File** *(upper row of operations), and click on* **Exit.** Before you can exit, however, the program will ask if you wish to save the contents of the **Output Viewer** as well as those of the **Data Editor.** If you have already saved them, you will not have to do so again.

The Syntax File. If you followed the above instructions, you would construct the following syntax file:

```
CORRELATIONS
 /VARIABLES=a b x y
 /PRINT=TWOTAIL NOSIG
 /STATISTICS DESCRIPTIVES
 /MISSING=PAIRWISE.
```

This syntax file provides the following output. Listing the variables as indicated in the section VARIABLES results in the computer outputting the square matrix of correlations among all the variables. The statement PRINT instructs the computer to provide two-tailed tests of significance, and to flag the correlations that are significant. The keyword STATISTICS followed by Descriptives results in a listing of the variables, the number of cases in each, the mean and the standard deviation. It will be noted that these values agree with the earlier examples for the variables X and Y.

Following are the two tables of output:

Descriptive Statistics

	Mean	Std. Deviation	N
A	13.6000	2.9515	10
B	24.8000	3.7357	10
X	7.0000	2.9814	10
Y	8.6000	1.3499	10

Correlations

		A	B	X	Y
Pearson Correlation	A	1.000	−.411	.177	.067
	B	−.411	1.000	−.589	.071
	X	.177	−.589	1.000	.663*
	Y	.067	.071	.663*	1.000
Sig. (2-tailed)	A	.	.238	.625	.854
	B	.238	.	.073	.847
	X	.625	.073	.	.037
	Y	.854	.847	.037	.
N	A	10	10	10	10
	B	10	10	10	10
	X	10	10	10	10
	Y	10	10	10	10

*Correlation is significant at the 0.05 level (2-tailed)

The first section of the table above presents the correlation coefficients. It will be noticed that the table is symmetric, in that the values above the diagonal are the same as those below the diagonal. As can be seen, the variables are shown to have a correlation of 1.000 with themselves, but otherwise the correlation range from $-.589$ for the correlation between B and X to .663 for the correlation between X and Y. The asterisk (*) following this correlation indicates that this is the only correlation that is significant, with the Type I error defined as .05, two-tailed (see the footnote after the table). The second section of the table shows the actual probabilities associated with each correlation. Thus, the two-tailed probability associated with the correlation of $-.411$ was .238; that associated with the correlation of .663 was .037. Again, note that these are two-tailed probabilities. If a one-tailed probability were preferred (because the direction of the correlation was predicted) these probability levels would be divided by 2. Thus, the one-tailed probability associated with the correlation of $-.589$ would be $.073/2 = .0366$. The third section shows the sample size on which each correlation was based. In the present example, there were 10 observations for each correlation, but if there had been some missing data for some of the variables, and if the "exclude cases pairwise" option was selected in Step 7 (p. 196), these values would vary. If there were missing data for some of the variables, and the "exclude cases listwise" option were selected at Step 7, the sample sizes would be equal in this section of the table and would equal the number of subjects who have complete data on all the variables listed.

TESTS OF SIGNIFICANCE INVOLVING CORRELATION COEFFICIENTS

We have already seen on page 188 that the test of the significance of the correlation coefficient and the unstandardized regression coefficient are equivalent and that this test can be expressed as an F-ratio with 1 and $(N-2)$ degrees of freedom. We saw too that the square root of this ratio produces an equivalent test using the t-statistic. These two statistics test the null hypothesis that the population correlation (or the population regression coefficient) is 0. If the test is significant, we conclude that the value in the population is not 0, and that consequently we have found evidence that there is an association between the two variables (i.e., X and Y) in question. There are, however, other tests that can be applied to test this assumption, as well as other assumptions involving correlation coefficients. The following sections discuss some of the more common tests.

Each of these tests make use of the standard normal deviate, Z. The sampling distribution underlying this statistic is the standard normal distribution which has a mean of 0.0 and a standard deviation of 1.0. The table for the standard normal distribution is given in Table A of the Appendix. The proportion of area underlying sections of this distribution are well known, and three values in particular are often used when conducting tests of significance. One is the value of $Z = (\pm 1.65)$ which encompasses 90% of the area underlying the curve. That is, 90% of the standard normal distribution lies between ± 1.65, thus this value is spoken as the value of Z that is significant at the .10 level. This means that we would expect an absolute value of Z greater than 1.65 less than 10% of the time on the basis of chance. If a test of significance yields a Z value greater than this, we then say that it is significant at the .10 level. In much the same way, a value of Z greater than 1.96 is said to be significant at the .05 level, and one of 2.58 is characterized as significant at the .01 level. These values refer to two-tailed tests. If a one-tailed test is of interest, these various probability values would be divided by two, and the values would be described as being significant at the .05, .025, and .005 levels, respectively.

Other Tests of the Significance of r

The test discussed earlier that made use of the t or F statistic is the one most commonly used to test the significance of r, however, there is at least one other test in the literature. This test is an easy one to apply and is applicable when sample size is large. (The definition of large is often somewhat arbitrary, and a value of around 100 might be considered a reasonable cutoff.) In essence, however, the approximation to the standard normal deviate improves as sample size increases. In any event, the null hypothesis is **Ho:** $\rho = 0$, and the test statistic is:

$$Z = r \sqrt{N - 1}$$

where Z is a standard normal deviate.

Thus, assume that you had a correlation between height and weight of .27 in a sample of 100 individuals. Applying this test statistic would yield:

$$Z = .27\sqrt{99} = 2.69$$

which is significant at the .01 level (see Table A, the Appendix).

Comparing Two Correlations from Independent Samples

There are some circumstances in which it is desired to test the significance of the difference between two correlations based on the same variables but drawn from two different samples. In this case, the null hypothesis is that the correlations in the two corresponding populations are identical; that is, **Ho:** $\rho_1 = \rho_2$ for independent samples.

This test makes use of the Fisher z transformation, which involves a logarithmic transformation of the two sample correlations. The formula for the transformation applied to both sample values is:

$$z_r = \frac{1}{2} \log_e \frac{(1 + r)}{(1 - r)}$$

Each of these Fisher z values is itself normally distributed with a standard error of $1/(n - 3)$ where n is the sample size for the correlation in question, and a test of the difference of these two values is:

$$Z = \frac{z_{r1} - z_{r2}}{\sqrt{\dfrac{1}{N_1 - 3} + \dfrac{1}{N_2 - 3}}}$$

The resulting Z is a standard normal deviate and as indicated in the previous example values greater than 1.96 and 2.58 are indicative of significance (using a two-tailed test) at the .05 and .01 levels, respectively.

As an example of this statistic, assume that you had sampled 100 men and found a correlation of .27 between weight and height, while the corresponding correlation in a sample of 60 women was .43. The Fisher z transformation for these two values would be .277 and .460, respectively, and the value of Z would be $(.277 - .460)/.1667 = -1.10$. Since this value is not greater than 1.96 in an absolute sense, we can conclude that we have found no evidence to indicate that the correlation between weight and height is different in men and women.

Comparing Correlated Correlations with a Common Variable

There are situations in which it is sometimes of interest to determine whether one variable (Variable 1) correlates higher with Variable 2 than it does with Variable 3. Consider, for example, that you had conducted a study in which you had assessed students' grades in school, intelligence and scholastic motivation. You may wish to ask the question "Do grades in school correlate more highly with intelligence than with scholastic motivation?" Two tests are presently recommended to test this hypothesis.[1] In both cases, the null hypothesis can be expressed as **Ho:** $\rho_{12} = \rho_{13}$ for correlated correlations.

One test proposed by Dunn and Clark (1969) is:

$$Z = \frac{(r_{12} - r_{13})\sqrt{N}}{\sqrt{(1 - r_{12}^2)^2 + (1 - r_{13}^2)^2 - 2r_{23}^3 - (2r_{23} - r_{12}r_{13})(1 - r_{12}^2 - r_{13}^2 - r_{23}^2)}}$$

Defining grades in school as variable 1, intelligence as variable 2, and scholastic motivation as variable 3, and assuming that $r_{12} = .50$, $r_{13} = .40$, and $r_{23} = .30$, and that sample size was 200, the value of Z would be 1.404. Since this value does not exceed 1.96, we have no evidence to conclude that the correlation between Variables 1 and 2 in the population is different from the correlation between Variables 1 and 3 in the population.

An alternative test has been proposed by Meng, Rosenthal and Rubin (1992). This test is as follows:

$$Z = (z_{r12} - z_{r13})\sqrt{\frac{n - 3}{2(1 - r_{23})h}}$$

where the values z_{r12} and z_{r13} are Fisher z transformations as discussed above (p. 199). The values of h and f are as follows:

$$h = \frac{1 - f(r_{12}^2 + r_{13}^2)/2}{1 - (r_{12}^2 + r_{13}^2)/2}$$

and:

$$f = \frac{1 - r_{23}}{2(1 - (r_{12}^2 + r_{13}^2)/2)}$$

Applying this test yields a value of Z equal to 1.393. Since this value is not significant (i.e., it is less than 1.96), we can conclude that we have found no evidence to reject the null hypothesis that the correlation between grades in school and intelligence is equivalent to the correlation between grades in school and scholastic motivation in the population.

---

[1]There is a third test proposed by Hotelling (1940), but it is recognized to be somewhat limited as to its generalizability. See, for example, Meng, Rosenthal & Rubin (1992).

Comparing Correlated Correlations with Different Variables

There are other instances where there is interest in comparing two correlations based on data from the same sample, but involving different variables. One such situation is known as cross-lagged panel analysis (Kenny, 1979). This is a complex area, with a number of assumptions necessary to justify the statistic, which will not be discussed here. The necessary statistic is as follows:

$$Z = \frac{(r_{14} - r_{23})\sqrt{N}}{\sqrt{(1 - r_{14}^2)^2 + (1 - r_{23}^2)^2 - r_{14}r_{23}(r_{12}^2 + r_{13}^2 + r_{24}^2 + r_{34}^2) - 2(r_{12}r_{34} + r_{13}r_{24}) + C}}$$

where:

$$C = 2(r_{14}r_{12}r_{13} + r_{14}r_{24}r_{34} + r_{12}r_{24}r_{23} + r_{13}r_{34}r_{23})$$

This test is typically used in the analysis of cross-lagged panel analysis, and is used to infer the direction of causation between two variables measured on two occasions. Assume, for example, that you had a measure of scholastic motivation taken at two time periods separated by six months. Let us refer to the first assessment as Variable 1 and the second as Variable 3. Assume further that you also had two assessments of academic achievement taken at these same two time periods. Let us refer to them as Variable 2 and Variable 4 respectively. The question of interest may be "Does academic motivation (Variable 1) at time 1 'cause' academic achievement at time 2 (Variable 4), or does academic achievement at time 1 (Variable 2) 'cause' academic motivation at time 2 (Variable 3)?" We might conclude that the former is correct if r_{14} was significantly greater than r_{23}. If r_{14} was significantly less than r_{23}, we might conclude the latter. If the two correlations did not differ significantly we might conclude that we have no evidence for deciding one way or another. In the previous sentence, I continually made use of the term "might" to emphasize that this is just one possible set of interpretations that could be made. As indicated earlier, this use of the test is dependent upon a number of assumptions, and side restrictions, and some researchers would disagree with the logic in any case. The best that can be said is that the null hypothesis under investigation with this statistic is **Ho:** $\rho_{14} = \rho_{23}$ for correlated correlations.

As an example, consider the following data:

$$r_{12} = .50 \quad r_{13} = .70 \quad r_{14} = .40 \quad r_{23} = .35 \quad r_{24} = .80 \quad r_{34} = .60, \text{ sample size } (N) = 100.$$

As applied to these equations, this would yield a value of $Z = .577$. Since this value is not greater than 1.96, we have no evidence to suggest that either variable is more likely than the other to cause the other. If the value of Z were greater than 1.96, then we could conclude that the correlation of .40 was significantly greater than that of .35, and that consequently we have evidence to suggest that academic motivation "causes" academic achievement.

Testing the Significance of an Average Correlation

On some occasions, we have correlations between two variables from more than one sample, and we wish to determine whether the average of these correlations is significant. This test makes use of the Fisher z transformation for each correlation weighted by the sample size. The equation is as follows:

$$z_{AV} = \frac{(N_1 - 3)z_{r1} + (N_2 - 3)z_{r2} + \cdots + (N_k - 3)z_{rk}}{(N_1 - 3) + (N_2 - 3) + \cdots + (N_k - 3)}$$

and:

$$Z = z_{AV}\sqrt{((N_1 - 3) + (N_2 - 3) + \cdots (N_k - 3))}$$

If the value of Z is greater than 1.96, then we can conclude that the average correlation is significantly greater than 0.

Consider an example where there are three independent samples with data as follows:

$$r_1 = .50, N = 33 \quad r_2 = .70, N = 53 \quad r_3 = .40, N = 63$$

The z_r values are as follows:

$$z_1 = .549 \quad z_2 = .867 \quad z_3 = .424$$

Therefore, the value of z_{av} is .609, and the value of Z is 7.21. Since this value of Z is greater than 2.58, we would conclude that the average correlation is significant at the .01 level.

On occasion, a researcher may wish to report the correlation corresponding to the value of z_{av} that was computed. This can be determined by using the following formula:

$$r = \frac{e^{2z} - 1}{e^{2z} + 1}$$

$$r = \frac{e^{2(.609)} - 1}{e^{2(.609)} + 1} = \frac{e^{1.218} - 1}{e^{1.218} + 1} = \frac{2.3804}{4.3804} = .543$$

That is, after transforming the individual correlations to Fisher z scores, and computing a weighted average of them, the resulting average Fisher z can be transformed back to a correlation coefficient. Although it isn't obvious, the formula above is simply a variant of the one for the Fisher z given on page 199, except that it is expressed in terms of r rather than z.

Chapter 9
Multiple Regression and Multiple Correlation

203

Multiple regression and multiple correlation are concerned with the relationship of one variable on the one hand with a number of variables on the other. They are two aspects of the same analytic procedure. You will recall from the simple bivariate case that the concepts of regression and correlation, though different from one another, are close relatives. In the bivariate case, regression is concerned with determining the nature of the relationship between one variable, often referred to as a dependent or criterion variable, and another variable, often referred to as an independent or predictor variable. As we saw in the previous chapter, the important characteristic of bivariate regression is that the result is an equation that describes the nature of the linear relationship between a random dependent variable and a fixed independent variable.

Bivariate correlation, on the other hand, is concerned with determining the strength or the degree of linear relationship between two variables. In this context, there is no distinction between dependent and independent variable. Rather, interest is in the degree of covariation between two random variables. The result in bivariate correlation is a number that varies from -1.0 to $+1.0$, where the sign ($+$ or $-$) provides an index of the nature of the covariation. Negative correlations indicate that high scores on one variable tend to be associated with low scores on the other, while positive correlations indicate that high scores on one variable are associated with high scores on the other and low scores on one are associated with low scores on the other.

The magnitude of the bivariate correlation coefficient tells us how close the relationship between the two variables is to a straight line. The closer the absolute value is to 1.0, the closer the relationship is to a straight line. As the magnitude of the correlation nears 0.0, the nature of the relationship departs more and more from a straight line. Although it is not often characterized as such, another way of considering correlation is in terms of the degree of linear relation of one variable with the predicted value of that variable based on the regression equation. Viewed in this light, correlation (or more precisely, the correlation squared) is also a measure of the accuracy of prediction using a linear regression model (see Chapter 8).

BASIC NOTIONS

Similar distinctions can be made for multiple regression and multiple correlation. Multiple regression is concerned with the nature of the relationship between one dependent or criterion variable (Y) and a set of independent or predictor variables (Xs). The result of a multiple regression analysis is an equation of the form:

$$Y' = a + b_1X_1 + b_2X_2 + \cdots + b_kX_k$$

where　a = the constant. The value of Y' when all of the X values are 0.0.
　　　　b_1, b_2, etc are the unstandardized regression coefficients.
　　　　X_1, X_2, etc are the predictors.

If the variables are considered in standard score form, the regression equation is as follows:

$$Z'_Y = \beta_1Z_1 + \beta_2Z_2 + \cdots + \beta_kZ_k$$

where　Z'_Y = the predicted value of Z_Y.
　　　　β_1, β_2, etc are the standardized regression coefficients.
　　　　Z_1, Z_2, etc are the predictors in standard score form.

Multiple correlation is similar to bivariate correlation in that it describes the degree of linear relationship between two variables. In multiple correlation, however, one of the variables is the criterion (or dependent variable) and the other is the linear aggregate of the independent (predictor) variables. This linear aggregate is formed by computing weights (the regression coefficients) such that the correlation of this aggregate with the criterion is as large as possible. The multiple correlation can be calculated using the following formula:

$$R = \sqrt{\beta_1 r_{x_1} + \beta_2 r_{x_2} + \cdots + \beta_k r_{x_k}}$$

As can be seen, the multiple correlation is a function of the correlation of the predictors (Xs) with the criterion (Y) and the standardized regression coefficients. It can take values varying from 0.0 to 1.0. As with bivariate correlation, the closer the value is to 1.0, the closer the relationship is to a straight line. Since the multiple correlation is always positive, the nature of the relationship is not reflected in the sign of the multiple correlation. Rather, the nature of the relationships of the dependent variable to each of the predictors *in the context of the total regression equation* is shown in the sign of the regression coefficient for each predictor.

Multiple regression/correlation is an extremely general and flexible procedure, and it should come as no surprise that it has many uses. In this chapter, we will discuss the following four applications:

1. The establishment of a prediction equation. That is, given a number of predictor variables, we might wish to determine those weights for the variables that maximize prediction.
2. The selection of a subset of predictors. That is, rather than consider all possible predictors, a researcher may want only a certain number of predictors that gives almost as good prediction as the whole set.
3. The investigation of curvilinear relationships between two variables. If we wish to determine the nature of the function linking one variable (Y) with another variable (X), multiple regression can be used to investigate curve components (i.e., non-linear relationships).
4. The investigation of interactions among continuous predictors. This use permits us to determine whether one variable (Y) might moderate the relationship between one variable (X) and another (Z).

A BIT OF HISTORY

Like many correlational procedures, multiple regression and correlation can be traced back to the pioneer efforts of Galton and Pearson. Galton first introduced the notion of regression, and Pearson generalized this to the concept of correlation, however an article by Yule (1897) is seen as the initial publication dealing with partial and multiple correlation. Yule (1907) is credited with developing the notational system (e.g., $R_{1.234\ldots p}$) that is still commonly used today (and in this chapter).

An article by Guilford (1931) is seen as an important landmark in the use of multiple regression in psychology (cf. Lovie, 1979). It was concerned with the prediction of affective reactions to two colors based on ratings of the pleasantness of the two colors when viewed separately. Other developments came later. There were many attempts to develop systems to select the best set of variables in a prediction equation, but these were ultimately replaced by the various indirect procedures used today in **SPSS WINDOWS REGRESSION** (see below). In addition, a number of researchers were concerned with the issue that multiple correlations tend to be artificially high, because they capitalize on chance relations among the variables. These gave rise to the development of many different "shrinkage formulae" (e.g., Wherry, 1931; Herzberg, 1969). Finally, even early on, there was a recognition that multiple regression was related to other analytic procedures, but it was articles by Cohen that popularized some of them in psychology. Thus, Cohen (1968) demonstrated that the various forms of analysis of variance could be reduced to special cases of multiple regression, and Cohen (1978) demonstrated that multiple correlation could be used to investigate curvilinear relationships between variables, as well as interactions between continuous independent variables.

TESTS OF SIGNIFICANCE

There are basically two tests of significance associated with multiple regression and correlation, one having to do with the significance of the multiple correlation and one having to do with the significance of the change in multiple correlation as a result of adding one or more predictors. In the case where the change is the result of adding one predictor, this test is equivalent to the square of the t-test of the significance of the regression coefficient for that variable. That is, if adding one variable to the prediction equation significantly increases the magnitude of the multiple correlation then its regression coefficient will differ significantly from 0.

Testing the Significance of *R*

The formula for testing the significance of a multiple correlation is as follows:

$$F = \frac{R^2/p}{(1 - R^2)/(N - p - 1)}$$

where F = an F-ratio with p degrees of freedom in the numerator and $(N - p - 1)$ degrees of freedom in the denominator.
R^2 = the squared multiple correlation.
p = the number of predictors.
N = the Number of Subjects.

This provides a test of the difference of a multiple correlation from 0. As the number of predictors increases, it is possible that this test will be significant even though there is not really much of a relationship. This is because the expected value (i.e., the mean of the sampling distribution) of a multiple correlation is not 0, but is a function of the number of predictors and the number of subjects. According to McNemar (1969, p. 203) the expected value of the squared multiple correlation is dependent on the number of predictor and the number of subjects. The relation can be expressed as follows:

$$E(R^2) = \frac{p}{(N - 1)}$$

That is, if one had 5 predictors and 11 subjects, the expected value of R^2 given no prediction at all is .50 (and $R = .71$). Because of this biased nature of the multiple correlation, it is therefore possible for the F-ratio to be significant even though none of the predictors contribute significantly to prediction.

Sample Size and the Number of Predictors. The preceding discussion demonstrates that particularly when N is small and p is large, it is possible to obtain a multiple correlation that is significantly different from 0, even when there is not a true relationship in the population. This is one reason why it is often recommended that when computing a multiple correlation, attention be directed to the ratio of the number of subjects relative to the number of predictors. Many different values have been recommended. For example, Pedhazur (1982) comments that a ratio of 30 to 1 is often suggested. He also notes, however, that some researchers reject this and argue that you should have at least 400 subjects in any event. Stevens (1986), on the other hand, recommends a ratio of 15 to 1, and Tabachnick and Fidell (1989) claim that a bare minimum would be 5 to 1, though they also state that a ratio of 20 to 1 is to be preferred. In point of fact, one can compute a multiple correlation as long as $N > p + 2$, but the value of R would be very close to 1.0, and it, as well as the various regression coefficients, would be very unstable from a sampling point of view. As N relative to p increases, the results become more stable and it is the relative degree of stability that different researchers find acceptable that accounts for the different recommendations.

Testing the Difference Between Two Multiple Correlations

This test is appropriate to the situation where it is desirable to compare the magnitude of two multiple correlations based on the same data where one multiple correlation contains all of the predictors in the other as well as one or more additional ones. That is, we are concerned here with determining whether an additional set of predictors contributes to a significant increase in prediction. The formula for this test is:

$$F = \frac{(R^2_2 - R^2_1)/(p_2 - p_1)}{(1 - R^2_2)/(N - p_2 - 1)}$$

where: F = an F-ratio with $(p_2 - p_1)$ and $(N - p_2 - 1)$ degrees of freedom.
R^2_2 = the squared multiple correlation with the greater number of predictors.
R^2_1 = the squared multiple correlation with the fewer number of predictors.
p_2 = the greater number of predictors.
p_1 = the lesser number of predictors.
N = the sample size.

Where $(p_2 - p_1) = 1$, this formula is equivalent to the square of the t-test of significance of the regression coefficient for the variable that was added. That is, consider an equation that had four predictors, and thus the standardized regression coefficients $\beta_1, \beta_2, \beta_3, \beta_4$. The test of the significance of any one standardized regression coefficient is:

$$t_{\beta_2} = \sqrt{\frac{R^2_{Y.1234} - R^2_{Y.134}}{(1 - R^2_{Y.1234})/(N - 4 - 1)}}$$

In this formula, we are computing the value of t for β_2, in an equation that has four predictors, thus variable 2 is missing from the second R^2, and the degrees of freedom in the denominator are $(N - 4 - 1)$. Note too that if the standardized regression coefficient is significant, so to is the corresponding unstandardized regression coefficient (b_2 in this example). In fact, the t-value for b_2 will be identical to that for β_2. You might demonstrate this to yourself by calculating by hand the values for the stepwise analysis on pages 222 to 225.

PARTIAL AND PART CORRELATIONS

It is easier to understand the rationale underlying multiple regression/correlation if one understands the statistics of partial and part correlation. *Partial correlation* refers to the correlation between two variables (e.g., Y and X_1) when you have removed, from both variables, any variation you can attribute to another variable (e.g., X_2). That is, you actually subtract from both Y and X_1 that part of those two variables that can be accounted for by the third variable, X_2. You might well ask, how do you do this, and the answer is "nothing to it." To remove X_2 from X_1 you would simply calculate the regression of X_1 on X_2 as described in the previous chapter. This would yield predicted X_1 values as follows:

$$X'_1 = a + b X_2$$

If you then created a new variable $X_1 - X'_1$, you have created a new variable (i.e., $X_1 - X'_1$) that is orthogonal to X_2. Thus, when you remove variation from one variable that is related to the other, this is referred to as residualizing, or orthogonalizing that variable. That is, removing from X_1 whatever in X_1 can be attributed to X_2 results in a residualized variable, and this residualized variable will be independent of X_2 regardless of the original correlation of X_1 and X_2. The partial correlation is just like a bivariate correlation as described in the last chapter. It can vary from -1 to $+1$, and the sign and magnitude of the correlation is an indication of the strength of the relationship. The only difference is that what is being correlated is the residuals in Y with the residuals in X_1. When there are only three variables, as in the present example, the partial correlation is given as follows:

$$r_{YX_1 \cdot X_2} = \frac{r_{YX_1} - r_{YX_2} r_{X_1 X_2}}{\sqrt{(1 - r_{YX_2}^2)(1 - r_{X_1 X_2}^2)}}$$

The interpretation of a partial correlation then is very much like that for a bivariate correlation, except it now refers to the correlation between Y and X_1 controlling for any differences in X_2. Suppose, Y was grades in school, X_1 was intelligence, and X_2 was academic motivation. The partial correlation between grades and intelligence partialling out motivation is the correlation between grades and intelligence, if everyone were equal in motivation. Thus, if motivation was positively related to both grades and intelligence, part of the original correlation between grades and intelligence could be attributed to motivation. By computing the partial correlation, you can get an idea of how the two variables would relate to each other if you could control for differences in the other variable.

The *Part Correlation* is the correlation between two variables (e.g., Y and X_1) when you have removed, from one of the variables (e.g., X_1), any variation you can attribute to another variable (e.g., X_2). That is you take out of X_1 any of the score that you can attribute to X_2, but you don't take this variability out of Y. When there are only three variables, as in this example, the part correlation is given as follows:

$$r_{Y(X_1 \cdot X_2)} = \frac{r_{YX_1} - r_{YX_2} r_{X_1 X_2}}{\sqrt{(1 - r_{X_1 X_2}^2)}}$$

The interpretation of this correlation is comparable to that above except you remove the variation for one variable (e.g., X_2) from only one of the variables (e.g., X_1). However, it too is simply a bivariate correlation, but in this case only one of the variables is residualized. As such, the interpretation of the part correlation is a bit different from that of the partial correlation. In this case, you are saying that if you removed any variation in X_1 that was common to X_2, the resulting variable would correlate with Y a given amount. Obviously, inspection of the two formulae given above will show that the value of the partial correlation will always be larger than that for the part correlation, but that the signs will always agree. It is beyond the scope of this chapter to discuss this any further, but it should be pointed out that the tests of significance for the partial and part correlations are t-tests that yield identical answers, even though the formulae for these t-tests (not shown here) look different. It turns out furthermore that the t-tests of significance of the Beta coefficient and the unstandardized regression coefficient also give the same answers as those for the partial and part correlation. In short, if one has a significant Beta or b regression coefficient, this means that one also has a significant partial and part correlation. Finally, although the formulae for partial and part correlation coefficients become somewhat more complex than those shown above when more than one variable is partialled, all of the comments made above still apply.

In the sections to follow, it is argued that one should not interpret regression coefficients, either standardized or unstandardized, because their interpretation can be misunderstood or misrepresented. Part and partial correlations are however, relatively easy to interpret, and in a subsequent section, we will see how one can easily transform the test of significance of the regression coefficients into a part correlation. We will recommend at that point that if you want to interpret a regression coefficient, you restrain yourself and interpret the part correlation instead. I focus attention on the part correlation rather than the partial correlation, not because of any preference for the former, but rather because it is a bit more complicated to derive partial correlations from the output presently available in **SPSS. SPSS** has the option to output partial and part correlations, so that if this option is selected, either one could be interpreted, rather than attempting to interpret the standardized regression coefficients.

You will note that, in the two equations above, one difference rests in the expressions on the left, where the notation $YX_1 \cdot X_2$ is meant to show that X_2 is removed from both Y and X_1, whereas the notation $Y(X_1 \cdot X_2)$ indicates that X_2 is removed only from X_1. The other difference is in the denominators of the expressions on the right, where the expression $(1 - r^2_{YX2})$ is missing from the second equation.

ON THE INTERPRETATION OF REGRESSION COEFFICIENTS

It is generally recommended that one not attempt to interpret regression coefficients or attempt to assess the importance of predictors based on the results of a regression analysis (cf. Winne, 1983). As Winne (1983) demonstrates, it is possible that the residualized variable may not be the same as the original variable. That is, if you remove from your measure of Intelligence, any variability you can attribute to motivation, the residualized measure of intelligence may rank individuals much differently than the original measure of intelligence did. This would be the case if there were a high correlation between intelligence and motivation. When residualizing variables, one can always ask how different the residualized variable is from the original variable. If any interpretative focus is placed on the part correlation, the nature of the variability removed from the residualized variable is made explicit. One might well argue that therefore you could interpret the standardized regression coefficients (i.e., the Betas) as long as you explicitly indicate what has been residualized. The problem with this argument is that it assumes that the relative ordering of standardized regression coefficients is the same as that for the part correlations, and this is not always the case. This will be discussed later in the section, What Can I Do if I Want to Interpret the Individual Contributions? (page 212).

If the X variables precede the Y variable temporally, and there are relations between them, it can be said that the Xs are predictors of Y, and the regression equation can be viewed as a prediction equation. It is common for researchers to therefore want to interpret the resulting regression coefficients. I strongly recommend against attempting to make any psychological interpretation of either standardized or unstandardized regression coefficients. The reasons for this recommendation are discussed in the following two sections. In these sections we take a close look at both unstandardized and standardized regression coefficients in order to see precisely what they mean, and what they don't mean. This will be done in the context of two predictors though this generalizes completely to the case of more than two predictors.

Unstandardized Regression Coefficients

To understand the meaning of unstandardized regression coefficients, consider the special case of two predictors. In this case, the prediction equation takes the form:

$$Y' = a + b_1 X_1 + b_2 X_2$$

This equation describes a plane in three dimensional space. If we were to consider a graphical representation of the regression of Y on X_1 and X_2 with the plane superimposed, the value a would be the height of the ordinate when the two Xs equal 0, b_1 would be the slope of the plane in the Y vs. X_1 surface, and b_2 the slope in the Y vs. X_2 surface. In such a diagram X_1 and X_2 would be shown at right angles to each other because in the regression model the two Xs are independent of each other. Since it is often the case that the Xs are not independent, this means that the X-axes actually represent X-variables that are mutually orthogonalized—or residualized such that they refer respectively to the X-variable in question once any variation common to the other X-variable has been removed. That is, an unstandardized regression coefficient is the slope of the plane on the axes common to the dependent variable and the X-variable in question once that X-variable has been made orthogonal to the other X-variable. This generalizes to the case of more than two predictors. Moreover, if these other predictors are not independent of those in the equation (which is usually the case), this means that each time a predictor is added, the unstandardized regression coefficients of all other predictors can change—sometimes quite dramatically. That is, unstandardized regression coefficients represent the slope of the plane on a residualized predictor in a set of predictors; unstandardized regression coefficients are not measures of the predictive capacity of the X-variables, nor are they measures of correlation. As a consequence, they should not be interpreted as such.

Standardized Regression Coefficients

Standardized regression coefficients are the regression coefficients applied to the regression equation when the data are considered in standard score form rather than in raw score form. Although it is often the case that these coefficients take values that vary from −1.0 to +1.0, this is not a required limitation, and they can take values well beyond these limits (see the example for X**2 on page 229).

The regression equation in standardized form is:

$$Z'_Y = \beta_1 Z_1 + \beta_2 Z_2$$

Note that in this equation there is no constant. That is because the Z'_Y intercept is always 0. Note, too, that the Beta coefficients are weights applied to standard scores. Since standard scores are on comparable scales with means of 0 and variances of 1.0, this means that the relative magnitudes of the beta coefficients are indicative of the relative contributions of the standardized variables to the prediction equation. That is, if $\beta_1 = .50$ and $\beta_2 = .25$, then variable Z_1 is weighted twice as much in the equation as is the residualized variable Z_2.

It can also be shown that the sum of the squared Z'_Y values divided by N ($\Sigma Z'_Y{}^2/N$), which is the variance of the predicted values, is equal to the square of the multiple correlation and that this is equal to:

$$R^2 = \beta_1^2 + \beta_2^2 + 2 r_{12} \beta_1 \beta_2$$

That is, the square of the multiple correlation is equal to the sum of the squared standardized regression coefficients plus two times the product term (including the correlation). Thus, one cannot simply square the Beta coefficient to obtain some index of the proportion of variance accounted for by a predictor since this would ignore the product term involving each pair of predictors. This emphasizes once again that the magnitude of the regression coefficients is a function of all the predictors in the equation. This formula generalizes to the case of more than two predictors by including the squares of the additional regression coefficients plus two times each of the other product terms.

Relation of Unstandardized to Standardized Regression Coefficients

It should also come as no surprise that there is a direct relation between the standardized and unstandardized regression coefficients. With some algebra, it can be shown that the relation between, for example β_1 and b_1, is:

$$\beta_1 = b_1 \frac{S_1}{S_Y}$$

where b_1 = the unstandardized regression coefficient for X_1.
        S_1 = the standard deviation of predictor X_1.
        S_Y = the standard deviation of the criterion Y.

Thus, given the unstandardized regression coefficients, and the standard deviations of the predictor and the criterion, one can calculate the value for the standardized regression coefficients. These standardized regression coefficients are all based on the same scale of unitless measurement, thus if one wants to make comments about the relative sizes of the regression coefficients this can be done with the standardized, but not the unstandardized coefficients. It should also be noted that because of possible differences in the magnitudes of the standard deviations, the relative magnitudes of the standardized and unstandardized regression coefficients can be quite different. Thus, in the example on page 220, it can be seen that although the unstandardized regression coefficient for $X5$ is the largest in terms of absolute value of the five in the set, the corresponding standardized regression coefficient has the smallest absolute value in its set.

Structure Coefficients

Rather than discuss the importance of variables to the prediction equation in terms of their standardized regression coefficients, it has been recommended that one instead calculate the correlations of each variable in the regression equation with the values of Y' calculated from the regression equation. These are often referred to as structure coefficients (Pedhazur, 1982), and since they represent the correlations of variables with a dimension (i.e., the Y') are interpreted much like factor loadings. The nature of the predicted value then is described in much the same way as a factor. There are, however, problems with these structure coefficients. Although they are simply the correlation of a predictor with the predicted value, they can also be calculated using the following formula:

$$s_i = \frac{r_{yi}}{R}$$

where s_i = the structure coefficient for the ith predictor.
        r_{yi} = the correlation of the criterion with the ith predictor.
        R = the multiple correlation of the set of predictors with the criterion.

Examination of this formula will indicate that to some extent the magnitude of the structure coefficient will be a function of the magnitude of the multiple correlation. That is, with a small value of the multiple correlation, even variables with relatively low values of the correlation with the criterion would have relatively large structure coefficients.

Assessing the Importance of Predictors

These considerations with respect to the meaning of the unstandardized regression coefficients, standardized regression coefficients and structure coefficients demonstrate the difficulties involved in interpreting the nature of any prediction equation and the importance of any given predictor. [For further discussion of the difficulties associated with attempting to interpret regression coefficients, see Winne (1983)]. The unstandardized regression coefficients are influenced by the scale of measurement of any given predictor and the nature of any other predictors in the equation. The standardized regression coefficients are all on the same unitless scale, thus their relative magnitudes do reflect their contribution to the regression equation in standard form, but they too are influenced by the other predictors in the equation. In point of fact, it is possible to obtain Beta coefficients that are not significant that are larger than other Beta coefficients in the same equation that are significant, thus making it difficult to place too much reliance on their relative magnitudes. [The reason for this anomaly has to do with the fact that the standard errors of the b (and the Beta) coefficients are influenced by the correlation of a predictor with all other predictors.]

The structure coefficients indicate how well any given predictor correlates with the weighted aggregate and thus indicates its contribution to the aggregate, but it can be inflated when the multiple correlation is low. Because of these considerations, it is recommended that if one wants to make any comment concerning the importance of a predictor this should be based simply on its correlation with the criterion. After all, when you're talking about a predictor, as opposed to one predictor in a set of predictors, the best indication of its relation to the criterion is its correlation with the criterion.

What Can I Do if I Want to Interpret the Individual Contributions?

As indicated above, interpretation of regression coefficients, in either standardized or unstandardized form, is fraught with difficulties. You might well ask yourself, therefore, how should I proceed if I have performed a multiple regression analysis, and I want to say something about each variable in the regression equation? As suggested above, you should focus your interpretation on either the partial or part correlations. Which you choose is not important, except that the partial correlations will always be greater in magnitude. If you have had **SPSS** output these values, you can choose the one you want, and interpret it accordingly. The interpretation in any event will be the same. I recommend the part correlation, only because it is easy to calculate this value if one has the t-value for the regression coefficient, the squared multiple correlation, and the degrees of freedom associated with the residual term in the multiple regression. The formula is as follows:

$$Part\ Correlation = \sqrt{\frac{t^2(1 - R^2)}{df}}$$

This formula will always yield a positive value thus, if the Beta coefficient is negative, the part correlation is negative so the sign must be changed. In any event, the resulting values will be part correlations and can be interpreted like any part correlation.

THE ESTABLISHMENT OF A PREDICTION EQUATION

The basic application of multiple regression is to establish an equation that maximizes the prediction of a variable (Y) by obtaining the best weighted aggregate of a series of predictors (Xs). This is very useful in situations where you want to use scores on a series of variables to predict scores on some other variable. For example, this technique has been used to form equations to predict the probable degree of success of students in graduate or professional programs. If prediction is demonstrated to be good, the equation can be used in selecting promising new students.

This procedure is implemented in **SPSS WINDOWS** by using the program **REGRESSION.** Consider the following sample data.

Y	X_1	X_2	X_3	X_4	X_5
97	89	78	5	42	1
92	86	74	2	31	1
90	91	77	5	29	1
85	76	67	3	36	1
84	87	81	4	32	1
82	87	63	5	29	2
81	73	76	4	31	1
80	75	74	1	41	2
77	70	68	5	26	1
75	67	69	3	35	1
75	74	73	4	33	1
74	75	54	5	28	2
73	73	75	2	36	1
73	72	64	5	30	2
71	73	53	4	20	2
70	70	74	7	30	1
70	73	66	8	35	2
70	69	62	5	26	2
70	72	57	6	40	1
67	73	68	4	30	2
66	71	60	7	27	1
66	68	64	8	25	2
63	70	61	3	28	2
61	73	65	6	11	1
61	72	56	5	24	2
60	68	55	7	30	2
59	69	54	6	22	1
57	66	60	9	10	2
54	67	56	6	16	2
50	69	56	6	15	2

These fictitious data involve scores for 30 students on 6 variables. The variables are as follows:

Y Grades in Computer Analysis in Psychology
X_1 Grades in Introductory Statistics
X_2 Grades in Introductory Psychology
X_3 Anxiety
X_4 Computer Aptitude
X_5 Faculty of Major (Coded: 1 = Social Science 2 = Other)

Analyzing the Data Using SPSS WINDOWS

The data presented in the previous example could be typed into a data file in which the six scores for each participant are given on a line with blanks separating each score (that is, in freefield form in **SPSS 8.0,** or delimited in **SPSS 9.0**) Assume that this file was called **mulreg.dat** and that it was stored on the A Drive in ASCII (or Text) form.

Steps in Using SPSS WINDOWS REGRESSION.   The following steps are applicable to **SPSS 8.0** and **SPSS 9.0** except for the input of the ASCII or Text data file. In the example to follow you are instructed at Step 3 to input your data following the procedures described in Chapter 1. The output for this example was obtained by using the freefield format in **SPSS 8.0**, and depending upon the input procedure you use, the output may be somewhat different. The answers are the same, however. Using the **WINDOWS** version of the program, you could simply type the Syntax file [the set of instructions required to run the procedure, including the relevant Data List and Execute statements (see page 30)], and then execute the job from inside the Syntax Editor (not discussed here), or use the program itself to create the syntax file. This latter procedure involves using the mouse to bring up a number of windows, and then selecting the appropriate options or typing in the required information.

1. *Enter SPSS WIN.* This presents you with the **SPSS Data Editor** (see figure in Chapter 2, page 46). At this point, you could begin to type in the data. However, we will assume that you already have the data in a file on the A Drive, that the file is labelled **mulreg.dat,** and that the data are in freefield (**SPSS 8.0**) or Delimited (**SPSS 9.0**) format. For each participant, there would be six values, $Y, X_1, X_2, X_3, X_4,$ and X_5.

2. *Click on **File** in the menu bar.* This will present you with a drop-down menu with a series of choices.

3. Enter your ASCII (**SPSS 8.0**) or Text (**SPSS 9.0**) data file by following the steps on pages 17 to 20 for **SPSS 8.0**, or pages 20 to 28 for **SPSS 9.0.** For this example, the file will consist of the six variables.

4. *Click on the **Statistics (SPSS 8.0)** or **Analyze (SPSS 9.0)** option on the top row.* This presents you with a drop-down menu. *Move your cursor to **Regression,** and you are presented with another menu to the right with a choice of the following in **SPSS 8.0** or **SPSS 9.0**:*

SPSS 8.0	**SPSS 9.0**
Linear . . .	Linear . . .
Curve Estimation . . .	Curve Estimation . . .
Logistic . . .	Binary Logistic . . .
Probit . . .	Multinomial Logistic
Nonlinear . . .	Probit . . .
Weight Estimation . . .	Nonlinear . . .
2-Stage Least Squares...	Weight Estimation . . .
Optimal Scaling	2-Stage Least Squares . . .
	Optimal Scaling

5. *Click on **Linear.** This presents you with the Window, **Linear Regression,** and the variable Y is highlighted (see figure below).*

   *The dependent variable **Y** is highlighted. Add it to **Dependent** by clicking on **Y,** and then the appropriate arrow. Then add all the predictors, X1 to X5, to the **Independent**(s) pane. You can do this one at a time by clicking on each one and then clicking on the appropriate arrow. Alternatively, you can add all the predictors at once by putting the cursor on the first one, holding down the left mouse button, and dragging the cursor down to **X5.** This highlights **X1** to **X5,** and when you click on the arrow, all are added to the pane.*

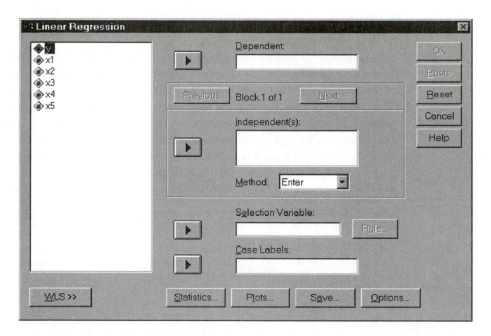

6. This window permits you to choose among a number of alternative methods for performing the multiple regression analysis. The default method is **Enter.** The various options are **Enter, Stepwise, Remove, Backward,** and **Forward,** which can be found by *clicking on the small arrow to the right of the white pane containing the option **Enter.*** Since we are using **Enter** in this example, no changes are necessary. We will discuss the other options later in the section on The Selection of a Subset of Predictors (p. 222).

7. *Click on **Statistics** at the bottom of the Window.* This gives another Window, **Linear Regression Statistics** (see figure, below).

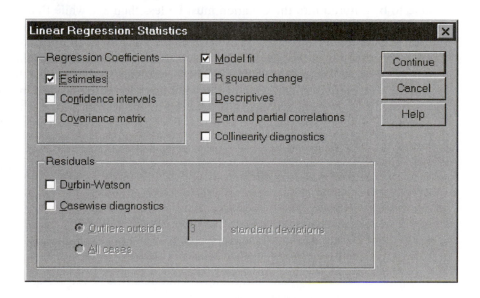

The choices, **Estimates** and **Model Fit,** are selected by default, but many other options are available. *Click on **Descriptives** to obtain **means, standard deviations, correlations, significance,** and **N's.*** It is also desirable to click on **Part** and **partial correlations** *if you wish to*

interpret these values. That was not done in this example. *Click on* **Continue.** *This returns you to the* **Linear Regression Window.**

8. *If you wished to add to the default options, you could click on* **Options.** *If you did, this would give you another Window,* **Linear Regression Options.** We are not going to add any options, so we will omit that step. *Instead, click on* **OK** *to run* **Linear Regression.**

9. This runs the **REGRESSION** program, and the answers are returned to the **SPSS Output Viewer** as well as to your monitor. At this point, you can print your answers, save them in a file, or transfer them to some other editor.

10. To exit **SPSS,** *click on* **File** *(upper row of operations) and click on* **Exit.** Before you can exit, however, the program will ask if you wish to save the contents of the **Output Viewer** as well as those of the **Data Editor.** If you have already saved them, you will not have to do so again.

The Syntax File. If you followed the above instructions, you would construct the following syntax file:

```
REGRESSION
        /DESCRIPTIVES MEAN STDEV CORR SIG N
        /MISSING LISTWISE
        /STATISTICS COEFF OUTS R ANOVA
        /CRITERIA=PIN(.05) POUT(.10)
        /NOORIGIN
        /DEPENDENT Y
        /METHOD=ENTER X1 X2 X3 X4 X5.
```

The REGRESSION statement has a number of components. The DESCRIPTIVES statement instructs the computer to output the descriptive statistics indicated. If part and partial correlations had also been included (it was not in this example), this would show as ZPP on this line. The /MISSING statement indicates that only those participants with complete data are to be analyzed. This is the default condition, and I strongly recommend that you always use it. The /STATISTICS line indicates the statistics to be output. The /CRITERIA statement indicates that the probability for a variable to be entered into the equation must be less than .05, while that needed to exclude a variable that has already been added is less than .10. These are the default values, but in fact they are not used in the forced Entry method used here. They are more appropriate for the Indirect methods to be described later in this chapter. The /NOORIGIN statement is similarly a default option and will not be discussed here. The /DEPENDENT statement indicates that the dependent variable is Y, and the statement /METHOD indicates what method should be used in computing the multiple correlation. In the present instance, it is followed by the word ENTER which means that the computer is to force all the variables listed after the ENTER statement into the equation. This is sometimes referred to as the *Method of Forced Entry,* or the *Direct* approach.

The Output. This syntax file produces the following summary of the analysis that was performed:

Variables Entered/Removed[b]

Model	Variables Entered	Variables Removed	Method
1	$X5, X3, X1, X4, X2^a$	.	Enter

[a] All requested variables entered.
[b] Dependent Variable: Y

This table indicates that the dependent variable is Y (see footnote b) and the Independent variables entered into the equation were $X1$ to $X5$. Their order of listing in the table (i.e., $X5, X3,$

etc.) does not appear to be related to any of the statistics associated with this analysis (i.e, the magnitudes of either the standardized or unstandardized regression coefficients, etc.). Finally, the table indicates that the "Enter" (i.e., the Direct Entry) method was used.

The output also yields the following table of information about the means and standard deviations for each variable:

Descriptive Statistics

	Mean	Std. Deviation	N
Y	71.7667	11.3523	30
$X1$	73.9333	6.9129	30
$X2$	65.3333	8.3184	30
$X3$	5.0000	1.8754	30
$X4$	28.2667	8.0298	30
$X5$	1.5000	.5085	30

The means and standard deviations tell you a lot about your data, and should be considered carefully when interpreting a multiple regression analysis. If the means are extreme in terms of the possible values your measures can take, this could indicate a floor or ceiling effect, and possibly a badly skewed distribution. This could place limits on the magnitude of the bivariate correlations you could obtain, and thus influence the results of the multiple regression analysis. Similarly, if the standard deviations are very low, this could also influence the magnitude of the bivariate correlations and thus the results of the multiple regression analysis. As we already noted in Chapter 1, it really isn't easy to characterize a standard deviation as high or low. It depends on the nature of the measurement. That is, in this example, the standard deviation of $X5$ is very small relative to that of $X2$, but $X5$ is a dichotomous measure and thus we wouldn't expect it to have a large standard deviation. Thus, when we speak of a high or low standard deviation, this has to be considered in terms of the types of values that would be expected (i.e., the types of values in the population).

SPSS WINDOWS REGRESSION also provides the following information about the correlations among the measures:

Correlations

		Y	X1	X2	X3	X4	X5
Pearson Correlation	Y	1.000	.807	.730	−.513	.681	−.469
	$X1$	.807	1.000	.572	−.340	.395	−.314
	$X2$	.730	.572	1.000	−.424	.531	−.554
	$X3$	−.513	−.340	−.424	1.000	−.483	.217
	$X4$	.681	.395	.531	−.483	1.000	−.312
	$X5$	−.469	−.314	−.554	.217	−.312	1.000
Sig. (1-tailed)	Y	.	.000	.000	.002	.000	.004
	$X1$	.000	.	.000	.033	.015	.046
	$X2$	.000	.000	.	.010	.001	.001
	$X3$	.002	.033	.010	.	.003	.125
	$X4$	.000	.015	.001	.003	.	.046
	$X5$	.004	.046	.001	.125	.046	.
N	Y	30	30	30	30	30	30
	$X1$	30	30	30	30	30	30
	$X2$	30	30	30	30	30	30
	$X3$	30	30	30	30	30	30
	$X4$	30	30	30	30	30	30
	$X5$	30	30	30	30	30	30

As we saw in the previous chapter, the table of Correlations consists of three matrices. The first one is the matrix of correlations, and as can be seen, there are some reasonably high values (they range from $-.554$ to $.807$). The second matrix presents the significance levels (in terms of one-tailed tests) for each one of the correlations (if you wish to determine the two-tailed significance, simply double the values reported in the table). As can be seen, all five predictors correlate significantly ($p<.01$, one-tailed) with the dependent variable, and most correlate substantially with each other. Only one of the correlations is not significant at the .05 level (one-tailed), and four at the .05 level (two-tailed). The third matrix presents the sample sizes for each correlation. Note in this case that the N for each correlation is 30. As indicated earlier, I strongly urge you to ensure that all your Ns are equal even though the program does permit you to base your correlations on varying sample sizes.

Statistics Relevant to the Multiple Correlation Analysis

The output for the multiple correlation analysis provides two sets of data, one concerning the multiple correlation, and one concerning the multiple regression. For this example, the results pertaining to the multiple correlation are as follows:

Model Summary

Model	R	R Square	Adjusted R Square	Std. Error of the Estimate
1	$.922^a$	.851	.820	4.8186

^{a}Predictors: (Constant), $X5$, $X3$, $X1$, $X4$, $X2$

These results indicate that the multiple correlation of Y with the weighted aggregate of the five predictors is .922 and the square of this value is .851. As discussed earlier, the order of the predictors indicated in footnote **a** has no interpretative significance.

Adjusted Squared Multiple Correlation. The adjusted R square is one of many possible adjustments that have been suggested to shrink the obtained multiple correlation to take into account the fact that the procedure capitalizes on every degree of association in the sample when calculating the multiple correlation. This particular shrinkage formula was proposed by Wherry (1931) to overcome the overestimation of the relationship resulting from any chance covariation. It is computed using the following formula:

$$AdjR^2 = 1 - (1 - R^2)\frac{(N-1)}{(N-p-1)}$$

As can be seen, the degree of reduction is based largely on the relationship of the number of predictors to the number of subjects. The utility of this adjustment has been questioned (see, for example Stevens, 1986; Tabachnick & Fidell, 1989). Stevens (1986) recommends other formulae proposed by Herzberg (1969) which have a much greater effect on the result, and Tabachnick and Fidell (1989) refer to one proposed by Browne (1975). The point is that there are many ways of estimating a "shrunken" multiple correlation depending upon how one characterizes the purpose of such an estimate. **SPSS WINDOWS REGRESSION** has opted for the Wherry (1931) adjustment.

Standard Error. The standard error of estimate in the table refers to the standard error of the residuals. It is defined as:

$$SE = \sqrt{\frac{\Sigma(Y - Y')^2}{N - p - 1}}$$

Note that this is simply the square root of the Residual Mean Square (see next table), and it gives some idea of the accuracy of prediction. The smaller this value, the less the errors of prediction. It can also be shown to be a function of the squared multiple correlation and the total sum of squares. It is given by the formula:

$$SE = \sqrt{\frac{(1 - R^2)SS_{Total}}{(N - p - 1)}}$$

where $SS_{Total} = SS_{Regression} + SS_{Residual}$.

$$= \sqrt{\frac{(1. - .851)(3737.367)}{24}} = 4.82$$

Analysis of Variance Summary Table. The analysis of variance summary table is presented below:

| | ANOVA^b | | | | | |
Model		Sum of Squares	df	Mean Square	F	Sig.
1	Regression	3180.106	5	636.021	27.392	.000^a
	Residual	557.261	24	23.219		
	Total	3737.367	29			

^{a}Predictors: (Constant), $X5$, $X3$, $X1$, $X4$, $X2$
^{b}Dependent Variable: Y

There are three sources of variation described in this table, Regression, Residual, and Total. The Regression Sum of Squares is an index of how well the predictors predict the dependent variable. It has $(p - 1) = 5$ degrees of freedom associated with it, where p = the number of predictors. The Residual Sum of Squares is a measure of the error in predicting the dependent variable. It has $(N - p - 1) = 24$ degrees of freedom associated with it. The Total Sum of Squares is the sum of the Regression and Residual Sums of Squares. It has $(N - 1) = 29$ degrees of freedom associated with it. Note that the Mean Squares are the Sums of Squares divided by their respective degrees of freedom. Note, too, that the ratio of the Regression Sum of Squares to the Total Sum of Squares is equal to the squared multiple correlation from the preceding table. That is:

$$R^2 = \frac{3180.106}{3737.367} = .851$$

The F-ratio can be computed by dividing the Regression Mean Square by the Residual Mean Square, or by using the formula given earlier (p. 206). If the F-ratio is significant, it suggests that it is unreasonable to assume, based on the results obtained, that the multiple correlation in the population is 0. In other words, we can conclude that a relationship exists. A word of caution is in order, however. This F-ratio tests whether or not it is reasonable to expect the population correlation to be 0, but as indicated earlier the expected value of a multiple correlation is not 0. In fact, using the formula on page 206, it can be shown in the present case to be equal to:

$$\sqrt{\frac{5}{29}} = .42$$

Regression Statistics

The **SPSS WINDOWS** program **REGRESSION** outputs the following data with respect to the multiple regression when all variables are entered into the equation:

Coefficients[a]

Model		Unstandardized Coefficients		Standardized Coefficients		
		B	Std. Error	Beta	t	Sig.
1	(Constant)	−14.261	14.422		−.989	.333
	X1	.860	.160	.524	5.382	.000
	X2	.244	.162	.179	1.506	.145
	X3	−.554	.562	−.092	−.985	.334
	X4	.434	.140	.307	3.093	.005
	X5	−2.002	2.116	−.090	−.946	.354

[a]Dependent Variable: Y

This table contains the unstandardized regression coefficients (B), the standard error of the unstandardized regression coefficients (Std. Error), the standardized regression coefficients (Beta), the t-ratio evaluating the significance of the difference of the b (and the Beta) coefficients from 0, and the alpha level (Sig.). Consideration of the t-ratios will reveal that they are simply the ratio of the unstandardized regression coefficients to their standard error. However, as indicated above in the section on significance testing it was shown that the square of this t can also be computed by comparing two multiple correlations, one including all the variables, and the other omitting the variable in question. In any event, the t-tests indicate whether the regression coefficients (and the constant) differ significantly from 0.

In this table, it will be noted that only the regression coefficients for $X1$ and $X4$ are significant. This suggests that, although a significant multiple correlation was obtained considering all five predictors, only predictors $X1$ and $X4$ contribute significantly to the regression equation when all five predictors are considered. Note too that an investigation of the table of correlations on page 217 will reveal that although $X1$ had the highest correlation with the criterion, $X4$ was the third, not the second, highest correlate and that all predictors correlated significantly with the criterion even though three of them do not enter into this equation significantly. This should be an indication to you that the interpretation of the regression coefficients is not as straightforward as one might think.

As indicated earlier, some individuals use multiple correlation to determine the "best" predictors of a criterion, and then use this information to characterize predictors as good or poor. Thus, with information like that obtained here, they would state that $X1$ (Grades in Statistics) and $X4$ (Computer Aptitude) are good predictors of Y (Grades in Computer Analysis in Psychology), while $X2$ (Grades in Introductory Psychology), $X3$ (Anxiety), and $X5$ (Faculty of Major) are poor predictors. As we have seen, however, this is nonsense. All variables correlated significantly with Y, and in fact $X2$ correlated more highly with Y than did $X4$. A good predictor (or a bad predictor, for that matter), as defined by regression coefficients, is a function of what else is in the regression equation.

The major thing that can be said is that considering all five predictors, the regression equation in unstandardized form takes the form:

$$Y' = -14.261 + .860X_1 + .244X_2 - .554X_3 + .434X_4 - 2.002X_5$$

If you were to use this equation to compute the predicted values of Y and then correlate this new variable with the obtained values of Y, you would obtain a correlation of .92, the value of the multiple correlation. Similarly, the regression equation in standardized form takes the form:

$$Z'_Y = -.524Z_{X1} + .179Z_{X2} - .092Z_{X3} + .307Z_{X4} - .090Z_{X5}$$

And if you were to correlate these Z'_Y values with Z_Y, the correlation would be .92, the value of the multiple correlation.

Interpreting Contributions of Predictors, Revisited

The preceding has argued against attempts to interpret regression coefficients. Earlier, it was suggested that if some interpretation is desired, one could direct attention to the part or partial correlations. A formula was also given to show how part correlations could be computed from information often available in regression output. We shall apply that here to the regression coefficient for the variable X_4, Computer Aptitude. In the table above, the Beta is given as .307, the t-value as 3.093, the degrees of freedom for the residual as 24, and the R^2 as .851. Therefore the part correlation is:

$$part\ correlation = \sqrt{\frac{(3.093^2)(1 - .851)}{24}} = .244$$

To interpret this, we could say that there is a significant correlation between Y (Grades in Computer Analysis) and Computer Aptitude ($X4$) once you have partialed out of Computer Aptitude any variability in common with the combined effects of Grades in Introductory Statistics, Grades in Introductory Psychology, Anxiety, and College Major. You will note that this part correlation is somewhat lower than the original correlation of Computer Aptitude and Grades in Computer Analysis which was .681, but in some applications, the part correlation may be larger than the original one. In much the same way, we could compute and interpret the part correlations for each of the other variables in the regression equation. If we did, the values would be as follows:

Variable	Initial Correlation	Variables removed	Beta	Part Correlation
$X1$ Introductory Statistics	.807	$X2, X3, X4, X5$	.524	.424
$X2$ Introductory Psychology	.730	$X1, X3, X4, X5$	.179	.119
$X3$ Anxiety	−.513	$X1, X2, X4, X5$	−.092	−.078
$X4$ Computer Aptitude	.681	$X1, X2, X3, X5$	.307	.244
$X5$ College Major (SS vs. Other)	−.469	$X1, X2, X3, X4$	−.090	−.075

It will be noted in this example that some of the part correlations are considerably lower than the initial correlations, indicating that when you remove variability associated with the collection of the other variables, the relationship can change drastically. This occurs presumably because the initial correlation is due to this common variation, however, it also could be due to some random variability in the particular set of data, that may not be present in another sample. Thus, even interpreting the part correlations can be hazardous, but in any event their interpretation will be much better understood by others than will an attempt to interpret the regression coefficients as somehow reflecting relationships between the criterion and the predictor variables.

THE SELECTION OF A SUBSET OF PREDICTORS

As indicated above, not all of the variables contributed significantly to prediction when considered as a set. One might ask therefore what the multiple correlation would be if we were to select a subset of the predictors. One thing we might do since we have already computed the multiple correlation using all of the predictors, is to rerun the analysis in the direct mode but enter only Variables $X1$ and $X4$ since they were the only two that contributed significantly to prediction. (You might wish to do this for yourself!) If we did, we would obtain a multiple correlation of .90 and a regression equation that takes the form:

$$Y' = -22.733 + 1.046X_1 + .607X_4$$

Alternatively, we might use a strategy that searches through the variables and their interrelations and generates the best possible regression equation with the least number of variables. There are a number of different ways of approaching this task, not all of which give the same answer. These approaches depend on the data to determine which variables are added, and as such their use is questioned by many researchers (see, for example Tabachnick & Fidell, 1989). The procedures used in **SPSS WINDOWS REGRESSION** include Stepwise Inclusion, Forward Selection, and Backward Elimination.

Stepwise Inclusion

In this procedure, predictor variables are entered into the equation one at a time in a series of steps. The **SPSS WINDOWS REGRESSION** program computes the multiple correlation, performs the analysis of variance, and calculates regression coefficients and tests of significance for the variables entered into the equation at that point as well as potential beta coefficients and partial correlations for those not yet entered. In the stepwise method, if a variable no longer contributes significantly to prediction it is eliminated from the equation. This procedure is repeated until a regression equation is obtained in which all the variables contribute significantly to prediction.

This type of analysis is run using the steps described on pages 214 to 216, with the exception that the method **Stepwise** is chosen on Step 6, page 215. The **SPSS WINDOWS REGRESSION** syntax file for this approach with the sample data is as follows:

```
REGRESSION
      /DESCRIPTIVES MEAN STDDEV CORR SIG N
      /MISSING LISTWISE
      /STATISTICS COEFF OUTS R ANOVA
      /CRITERIA=PIN(.05) POUT(.10)
      /NOORIGIN
      /DEPENDENT y
      /METHOD=STEPWISE x1 x2 x3 x4 x5.
```

The procedure begins by entering first the variable that correlates highest with the criterion (assuming this correlation is significant) and calculating the regression equation. It then computes the partial correlation of each variable with the criterion, partialling out any variation in common with the variable already entered, and determines whether any of these partial correlations are significant. If any one is significant, it then enters the variable with the highest partial correlation, calculates the regression equation, tests the significance of each regression coefficient, and eliminates any variable for which the regression coefficient is not significant. It then computes new partial correlations for the variables not in the equation removing variation that can be attributed to variables in the equation, and repeats the process. It continues this until none of the partial correlations are significant. The output from this syntax file produces the following four tables of output. The sequence followed in this analysis is shown in the first table as follows:

Model Summary

Model	R	R Square	Adjusted R Square	Std. Error of the Estimate
1	.807[a]	.650	.638	6.8303
2	.898[b]	.806	.792	5.1807
3	.916[c]	.840	.821	4.8004

[a]Predictors: (Constant), $X1$
[b]Predictors: (Constant), $X1$, $X4$
[c]Predictors: (Constant), $X1$, $X4$, $X2$

At each step (referred to as Model in the table), the computer calculates the multiple correlation, and performs the analysis of variance to test the significance of the multiple correlation. The table above presents information concerning the variable added at each step, the multiple correlation, and related statistics. Thus Model 3 refers to a model in which variables $X1$, $X4$, and $X2$ have been added to the equation. These results of the analyses of variance for each model are summarized in the next table:

ANOVA[d]

Model		Sum of Squares	df	Mean Square	F	Sig.
1	Regression	2431.102	1	2431.102	52.111	.000[a]
	Residual	1306.265	28	46.652		
	Total	3737.367	29			
2	Regression	3012.696	2	1506.348	56.124	.000[b]
	Residual	724.670	27	26.840		
	Total	3737.367	29			
3	Regression	3138.231	3	1046.077	45.395	.000
	Residual	599.136	26	23.044		
	Total	3737.367	29			

[a]Predictors: (Constant), $X1$
[b]Predictors: (Constant), $X1$, $X4$
[c]Predictors: (Constant), $X1$, $X4$, $X2$
[d]Dependent Variable: Y

The computer computes the unstandardized and standardized regression coefficients for each step, and tests to determine whether they are all significant. The following table summarizes this output:

Coefficients[a]

Model		Unstandardized Coefficients		Standardized Coefficients		
		B	Std. Error	Beta	t	Sig.
1	(Constant)	−26.156	13.622		−1.920	.065
	$X1$	1.324	.183	.807	7.219	.000
2	(Constant)	−22.733	10.358		−2.195	.037
	$X1$	1.046	.151	.637	6.906	.000
	$X4$	.607	.130	.429	4.655	.000
3	(Constant)	−28.258	9.886		−2.858	.008
	$X1$	.874	.159	.532	5.512	.000
	$X4$	.482	.132	.341	3.649	.001
	$X2$	.333	.143	.244	2.334	.028

[a]Dependent Variable: Y

Note that each model corresponds to a different step. Thus, Model 1 refers to the first step in which the variable $X1$ was entered into the regression equation. It consists of the constant (−26.156) and related statistics, and the regression coefficients and related statistics for the first predictor ($X1$). You will note from the table of correlations given on page 203 that this variable has the highest correlation with the criterion (.807). Model 2 refers to the second step, wherein $X4$ was added to the equation, and so on. Note that at Model 3 all the regression coefficients are significant indicating that all three variables, $X1$, $X4$, and $X2$, contribute significantly to prediction. Note too, that the regression coefficients (both unstandardized and standardized) for variables in the equation at earlier steps change in later steps as new variables are added. Thus, the b coefficient for Variable $X4$ was 1.324 in step 1, 1.046 in step 2, and .482 in step 3. That is, the regression coefficients will change from step to step if there are any correlations among the predictors because as discussed earlier the regression coefficients refer to the residualized variables.

The next table presents information for the variables not added to the equation at each step (Model). This information includes the value of the Beta coefficient if the variable were added to the equation, a t-test of significance of this value, and the partial correlation of the criterion with that variable once the variation of the other variables in the equation had been removed. It should be noted that the t-test of *Beta In* is equivalent to the t-test for the partial correlation, hence the latter is not repeated in the table. Finally, the table presents *Collinearity Statistics* in the form of a measure of Tolerance. We shall not discuss this statistic in this chapter. The table is as follows:

Excluded Variables[d]

Model		Beta In	t	Sig.	Partial Correlation	Collinearity Y Statistics Tolerance
1	$X2$	.399[a]	3.454	.002	.554	.673
	$X3$	−.270[a]	−2.472	.020	−.430	.884
	$X4$	.429[a]	4.655	.000	.667	.844
	$X5$	−.239[a]	−2.163	.040	−.384	.901
2	$X2$	.244[b]	2.334	.028	.416	.563
	$X3$	−.120[b]	−1.234	.228	−.235	.740
	$X5$	−.157[b]	−1.784	.086	−.330	.859
3	$X3$	−.088[c]	−.955	.349	−.188	.721
	$X5$	−.086[c]	−.913	.370	−.180	.692

[a]Predictors in the Model: (Constant), $X1$
[b]Predictors in the Model: (Constant), $X1$, $X4$
[c]Predictors in the Model: (Constant), $X1$, $X4$, $X2$
[d]Dependent Variable: Y

Examination of the last section of this table indicates that neither variable $X3$ nor $X5$ will add significantly to prediction. Thus, the process is terminated because the PIN (probability to enter) is reached.

Forward Selection

This procedure is similar to Stepwise inclusion in that it starts with the best single predictor, adds as the next predictor the one that has the highest partial correlation, and so on. Like the stepwise approach, it too tests the multiple correlation and the regression coefficients for significance, and continues on until none of the remaining variables will add significantly to prediction. It differs from stepwise inclusion in that it does not eliminate any predictors from the equation that no longer contribute significantly to prediction once a new variable has been added. In this way, it is possible to end up with a set of predictors that gives maximum prediction *for this sample,* but for which some of the variables in the set no longer contribute significantly to prediction. You would run this type of analysis by selecting **Forward** at Step 6 in the instructions for running **SPSS WINDOWS REGRESSION** (see page 215).

Backward Elimination

This procedure is the opposite of Forward Selection. It starts by entering all variables into the regression equation and then eliminating one by one those variables that contribute least to prediction in the given equation. The procedure is complete when only those variables that contribute significantly to prediction are left in the equation. You run this type of analysis by selecting **Backward** at Step 6 in the instructions for running **SPSS WINDOWS REGRESSION** (see page 215).

Use of any of these three procedures is not generally recommended. Their results are quite dependent on the nature of the data in the sample, and may not be stable from a sampling point of view. They have their uses to be sure. They can serve a purpose in initially selecting a good set of predictors, but if so, the results should be followed up with a cross validation study. Moreover, Cohen and Cohen (1975) recommend that if these indirect procedures are used, corrections for shrinkage should use the total number of independent variables in the initial pool, not the number selected, in the computations. This is not done by **SPSS WINDOWS REGRESSION,** and thus even the Wherry (1931) shrinkage estimate would have to be calculated by hand.

INVESTIGATING CURVILINEAR RELATIONS BETWEEN TWO VARIABLES

Multiple regression can be used to investigate the nature of the functional relationship between two variables, the dependent variable Y, and the independent variable X. By making use of powers of the independent variable, it is possible to determine whether the nature of the function is linear, quadratic, cubic, etc., or combinations of these components. One approach to this problem was first introduced into psychology by Cohen (1978). It is based on the notion of adding powers of X (i.e., X, X^2, X^3, etc.) to the regression equation one at a time and noticing whether or not that power adds significantly to prediction. If it does, this will be indicated by a significant t-ratio for the regression coefficient for that power. The following table presents data that might be subjected to this type of analysis.

X	Y
2	15
2	16
4	16
5	15
6	16
7	15
8	15
8	17
10	16
10	17
11	17
12	18
13	18
14	19
14	20
15	20
15	21
16	21
16	22
17	22
18	23
19	24
20	24
21	26
22	27
22	28
23	30
23	31
23	32
24	33

These data are plotted in Figure 1. The Y values are shown on the vertical axis and the values of X are shown on the horizontal axis. It will be noted that the plot is somewhat curvilinear with a tendency for the Y values to increase with increases in X.

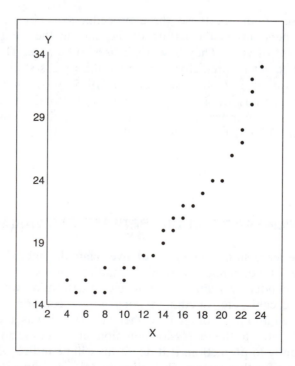

Figure 1.   Scatter plot of Y on X (Curvilinear Function)

Analyzing the Data Using SPSS WINDOWS

The steps for analyzing the data are comparable to those presented earlier (pages 214 to 216). In this example, we will assume that the data are in an ASCII or Text file on the A drive and that the file is labelled **curve.dat.** This file consists of the two values X and Y for each participant. Thus, in Step 3 (page 214) we will enter only these two variables, X and Y. Then at Step 4, you select **Curve Estimation** (which presents the following window):

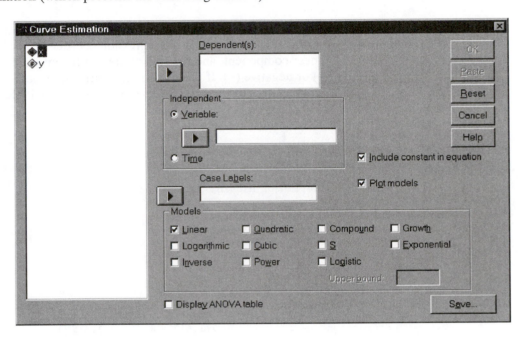

Note in the above Window, that **X** is highlighted. *Add **X** to the Independent pane by clicking on the appropriate arrow. Then click on **Y** and add it to the **Dependent(s) Window** by clicking on the appropriate arrow.*

You can then select the model of your choice. This chapter deals only with the use of curve functions based on partialled powers. Using this technique, **SPSS WINDOWS Curve Estimation** allows only the **linear, quadratic,** and **cubic** components in the Window selection. In most instances, however, the linear, quadratic and cubic components are sufficient, so we shall restrict ourselves to these components only. You will note that **Linear** has already been selected by default. *Select quadratic and cubic by clicking on the white panes preceding these alternatives. Then click on the **Display ANOVA table** to obtain the analysis of variance results.* This is very important, because otherwise the output can be very misleading. *Then click on **OK** to run the analysis.*

It should be noted that there are a number of other curve functions such as logarithmic, exponential, growth, etc., that can be investigated with this program. I strongly recommend that you do not use these functions until you have read a textbook that deals with the procedure in question. As indicated above, this chapter deals only with the use of partialled powers.

If you were to follow the instructions given above, you would obtain the following syntax file:

```
CURVEFIT /VARIABLES=y WITH x
 /CONSTANT
 /MODEL=LINEAR QUADRATIC CUBIC
 /PRINT ANOVA
 /PLOT FIT.
```

The CURVEFIT statement instructs the computer to perform a curve-fitting analysis of the relationship between y treated as the dependent variable and x as the independent variable. This curve fitting analysis is simply a multiple regression analysis in which the predictors are X, X^2 and X^3, and they are added in successive steps. This involves computing an equation that includes a CONSTANT and a series of curve components. The MODEL statement indicates that three curve components will be considered: the linear, the quadratic, and the cubic. Each of these are tested in a series of discrete steps as follows:

Step 1: To determine whether there is a linear relation between Y and X, **SPSS** WINDOWS CURVEFIT enters X as the lone predictor. If the regression coefficient for X is significant, this indicates that there is a linear component, and the sign of the coefficient will indicate whether the relationship is positive (+) or negative (−). If the regression coefficient is not significant, this indicates that there is no linear component. In the present case, this yields a multiple correlation of .92948, (note, this is simply the correlation between X and Y) and the following information about the regression equation:

```
Dependent variable.. Y Method.. LINEAR

Listwise Deletion of Missing Data

Multiple R            .92948
R Square              .86393
Adjusted R Square     .85907
Standard Error        2.08608

Analysis of Variance:

                 DF      Sum of Squares      Mean Square
Regression        1          773.61778        773.61778
Residuals        28          121.84889          4.35175

F =    177.77182           Signif F = .0000

------------------- Variables in the Equation --------------------

Variable           B          SE B        Beta        T      Sig T

X              .766717      .057505     .929477    13.333    .0000
(Constant)   10.399291      .890612                11.677    .0000
```

The regression coefficient is significant, therefore, we can conclude that there is a linear relationship between the dependent variable (Y) and the independent variable (X), and moreover that the relationship is positive. This is also very evident from an examination of the figure on page 226.

Step 2: To determine whether there is a quadratic component, the computer enters X and X^2 (X**2) into the equation. If the regression coefficient for X^2 is significant, this indicates that there is a quadratic component. If the regression coefficient is not significant, this indicates that there is no quadratic component.

In the present example, we obtain the information reported below. You will note that the multiple correlation is .98886, that it is significant, and more importantly that the regression coefficient for X^2 is also significant. The test of the significance of the regression coefficient for X is not considered at this point. In fact, it can be shown that it too is a test of a quadratic component at this stage. If the function contained both a linear and a quadratic component, the former would be indicated at Step 1.

```
Dependent variable.. Y                       Method.. QUADRATI

Listwise Deletion of Missing Data

Multiple R               .98886
R Square                 .97785
Adjusted R Square        .97621
Standard Error           .85708

            Analysis of Variance:

            DF    Sum of Squares      Mean Square

Regression   2         875.63265        437.81632
Residuals   27          19.83402           .73459

F =     595.99818      Signif F =    .0000

------------------- Variables in the Equation -------------------

Variable            B        SE B       Beta         T     Sig T
X            -.435452    .104714    -.527890    -4.159    .0003
X**2          .044924    .003812    1.495942    11.784    .0000
(Constant)  16.453815    .630759                26.086    .0000
```

Step 3: To determine whether there is a cubic component, the computer enters X, X^2, and X^3 (X**3). The test of significance of the regression coefficient for X^3 is a test of the cubic component. This run yields the following output:

```
Dependent variable.. Y                       Method.. CUBIC

Listwise Deletion of Missing Data

Multiple R               .98960
R Square                 .97930
Adjusted R Square        .97692
Standard Error           .84428

            Analysis of Variance:

DF              Sum of Squares       Mean        Square

Regression       3          876.93358      292.31119
Residuals       26           18.53309         .71281

F =     410.08223      Signif F = .0000

------------------- Variables in the Equation -------------------

Variable            B        SE B       Beta         T     Sig T
X            -.042770    .308430    -.051849     -.139    .8908
X**2          .008998    .026857     .299628      .335    .7403
X**3          .000918    .000679     .741360     1.351    .1884
(Constant)  15.414946    .988638                15.592    .0000
```

Note that, in this case, the multiple correlation is significant but none of the regression coefficients are. This latter occurs because all three predictors (X, X^2, and X^3) refer to cubic components at this stage and there is not a cubic component in this relationship. The actual test of whether or not there is a cubic component, however, is the test of significance of the regression coefficient for X^3. The tests for X and X^2 in this step are of no interest. The tests of the linear component was performed in Step 1, while that for the quadratic component was performed in Step 2.

Given these results, we would draw the function for this curve by using the values obtained at Step 2. Thus, the equation for this function is:

$$Y' = 16.453815 - .435452X + .044924X**2$$

In order to know exactly what the function looks like, it is necessary to plot it for various values of X spanning the entire range of X. In order to do this, you could compute values of Y' for each value of X and plot the results. As can be seen in Figure 1 on page 226, the function has both a positive linear component (it moves upward from left to right), and a quadratic component (it shows one bend).

SPSS WINDOWS Curve Estimation prints a graph of the functions if you leave the default option Plot Models as indicated in the window shown on page 227. The graph is as follows:

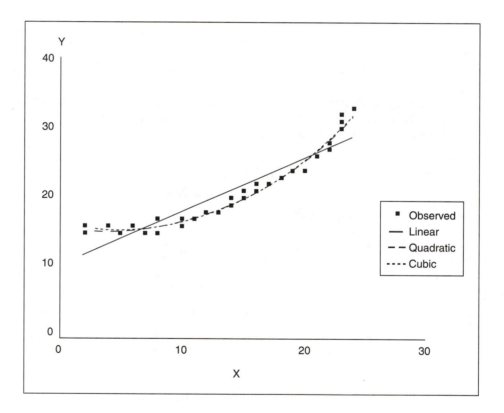

The graph consists of the observed values (shown by the small squares) as well as plots for (a) the linear function, (b) the quadratic function, and (c) the cubic function (the legend for each line is shown at the right of the figure). The lines for each function are based on the equations formed by the unstandardized regression coefficients (labelled B in the output) for the function in question (i.e., the linear, the quadratic, and the cubic). The equation for the quadratic function was given above (see page 230).

This procedure can be used to evaluate the nature of any type of relation between a dependent variable Y and an independent variable X. **SPSS WINDOWS Curve Estimation,** as used in this example, assesses only linear, quadratic and/or cubic functions through the window selection, but this generally should be sufficient. More complex functions would generally be difficult to interpret.

INVESTIGATING INTERACTIONS BETWEEN CONTINUOUS VARIABLES

Multiple regression can also be used to assess interactions between continuous variables. Like the procedure for investigating curvilinear relations, this too was introduced into psychology by Cohen (1978). The following table presents sample data.

Z	X	Y
31	5	10
28	5	2
34	6	9
33	7	8
36	7	9
27	8	3
24	8	4
24	8	3
23	9	3
24	10	5
21	10	4
35	10	8
36	10	8
19	11	4
38	12	5
37	12	7
19	13	5
20	13	5
18	14	2
37	15	9
19	16	3
36	17	9
18	17	2
37	18	9
20	19	4

The following procedures can be used to assess whether or not there is an interaction between X and Y in their relation to Z. If there is a significant interaction, this indicates that X moderates the relation between Y and Z, as well as that Y moderates the relation between X and Z.

Analyzing the Data Using SPSS WINDOWS

The steps for analysing the data are comparable to those presented earlier (pages 214 to 216). In this example, we will assume that the data are in an ASCII or Text file on the A drive and that the file is labelled **xydat.dat.** This file consists of the three values **Z, X,** and **Y** for each participant. Thus, in Step 3 (page 214) we will define these three variables, **Z, X** and **Y.** To proceed, you must be in the **Data Editor.** If the **Output Viewer** is predominant, switch to the **Data Editor.** Before progressing to Step 4, *click on Transform in the upper menu.* This produces a drop-down menu with a number of options. *Click on Compute,* and this yields the following Window.

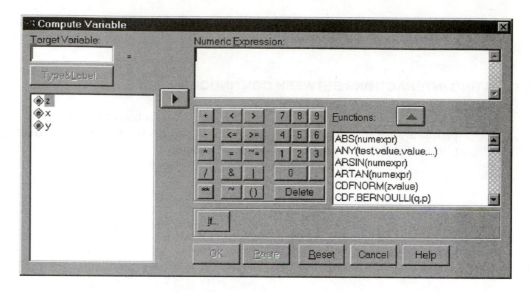

Click on the white pane under **Target Variable,** *and type in the variable name* **xy.** Then in the **Numeric Expression** window, *type in the expression* **x*y.** This produces the statement **Compute xy = x * y** in the Syntax file. Once you have done this *click on* **OK.** This should return you to the **Data Editor,** now with the new variable, *XY,* defined. At this point, continue to Step 4 (page 214), *click on* **Statistics (SPSS 8.0)** *or* **Analyze (SPSS 9.0)** from the menu bar, and *proceed with the subsequent instructions.* This means, *you would choose* **Linear** *at Step 5, and follow the subsequent instructions, realizing that the dependent variable is* **Z,** *and that the predictors are* **X, Y,** *and* **XY.**

If you were to follow the instructions given above, you would obtain the following syntax file:

```
COMPUTE xy = x*y .
EXECUTE .
REGRESSION
 /DESCRIPTIVES MEAN STDDEV CORR SIG N
 /MISSING LISTWISE
 /STATISTICS COEFF OUTS R ANOVA
 /CRITERIA=PIN(.05) POUT(.10)
 /NOORIGIN
 /DEPENDENT z
 /METHOD=ENTER x y xy .
```

This syntax file would yield the following output:

Descriptive Statistics

	Mean	Std. Deviation	N
Z	27.7600	7.4904	25
X	11.2000	4.1231	25
Y	5.6000	2.6926	25
XY	61.7600	38.7344	25

Correlations

		Z	X	Y	XY
Pearson Correlation	Z	1.000	−.179	.790	.583
	X	−.179	1.000	−.090	.567
	Y	.790	−.090	1.000	.701
	XY	.583	.567	.701	1.000
Sig. (1-tailed)	Z	.	.196	.000	.001
	X	.196	.	.334	.002
	Y	.000	.334	.	.000
	XY	.001	.002	.000	.
N	Z	25	25	25	25
	X	25	25	25	25
	Y	25	25	25	25
	XY	25	25	25	25

Variables Entered/Removed[b]

Model	Variables Entered	Variables Removed	Method
1	XY, X, Y[a]	.	Enter

[a]All requested variables entered.
[b]Dependent Variable: Z

Model Summary

Model	R	R Square	Adjusted R Square	Std. Error of the Estimate
1	.851[a]	.724	.684	4.2080

[a]Predictors (Constant), XY, X, Y

ANOVA[b]

Model		Sum of Squares	df	Mean Square	F	Sig.
1	Regression	974.711	3	324.904	18.349	.000[a]
	Residual	371.849	21	17.707		
	Total	1346.560	24			

[a]Predictors: (Constant), XY, X, Y
[b]Dependent Variable: Z

Coefficients[a]

Model		Unstandardized Coefficients		Standardized Coefficients	t	Sig.
		B	Std. Error	Beta		
1	(Constant)	29.263	5.469		5.351	.000
	X	−1.231	.452	−.678	−2.722	.013
	Y	.284	.799	.102	.355	.726
	XY	.173	.067	.895	2.577	.018

[a]Dependent Variable: Z

As can be seen in the correlation matrix, there is a substantial correlation between variables Z and Y but not Z and X, and also fairly high correlations between XY and both X and Y. When all three variables, X, Y, and XY are entered into the equation, this results in a multiple correlation of .851, a significant F-ratio (18.349) for the Regression, and significant unstandardized coefficients for the Constant, X, and XY. Since we performed this analysis to determine if there was an interaction between X and Y in the prediction of Z, we are interested only in the regression coefficient for XY. If the regression coefficient for this product term is significant, it indicates that there is an interaction between X and Y and their relation to Z. That is, X is said to moderate the relation between Y and Z, and Y is said to moderate the relation between X and Z. If the regression coefficient for the XY term was not significant, it would indicate that X and Y do not interact in their relation with Z (i.e., neither variable moderates the other in its relation with Z).

The important point for our purpose is that the regression coefficient for XY is significant, indicating that there is a significant interaction between X and Y. The tests of significance of the regression coefficients for X and Y are of no interest. The significance for X simply indicates that X adds significantly to prediction after Y and XY have been considered. It does not mean that X is a significant predictor. Similarly, the lack of a significant regression coefficient for Y does not mean that Y is not a significant predictor; it means simply that Y does not add significantly to prediction when X and XY are in the equation. In fact, as we saw in the correlation matrix, Y is a very good predictor. A more complete discussion of this and the distinction between moderators and mediators is presented by Baron and Kenny (1986).

The information contained in the table of coefficients can be used to write the regression equation as:

$$Z' = 29.263 - 1.231X + .284Y + .173XY$$

In order to fully understand the results of this analysis, it is recommended that you construct a scatterplot of Z as a function of X (or Y) and then superimpose on this the function identified by the

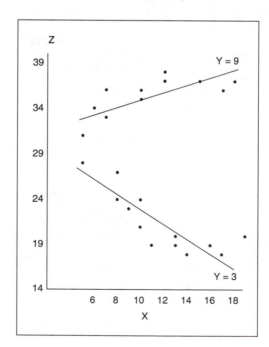

Figure 2.   Plot of Z against X with XY interaction imposed

regression analysis. Figure 2 presents the scatter plot of Z and X, with the interaction between X and Y superimposed.

The interaction was determined by solving for the value of Z' for various combinations of X and Y. In order to obtain the values to plot the interaction shown in Figure 2, the four combinations of low values of X and Y (7 and 3, respectively, in this example) and high values of X and Y (17 and 9, respectively) were used. The results of these four calculations were then used to draw the two lines, one corresponding to the function for low values of Y, and the other for the high values of Y. Other values of X and Y could have been used, of course, but the lines that would have resulted would be represented in the arc described by the two shown. Interpretation of the interaction would indicate, therefore, that for low values of Y increases in X are associated with decreasing values of Z, while for high values of Y increases in X are associated with increases in Z. It is recommended that the interaction always be plotted because this is the only way to ensure that the interaction is correctly understood.

Chapter 10
Factor Analysis

Research on individual differences is concerned with how scores on one measure (variable) relate to scores on another measure or measures. This differs from research that is interested in how some treatment influences behavior. In this latter type of research the focus of attention is largely on the mean of the scores, and the statistical procedures employed include the t-test, analysis of variance and the like. Individual differences are often considered as error in estimating the effects of the treatment. For example, in a completely randomized single factor analysis of variance, the Mean Square Within is nothing more than the (weighted) mean of the variances within each treatment group. Research concerned with individual differences, on the other hand, treats the differences between individuals as the material of interest, and concerns itself with asking questions of the type, "How do differences in this measure relate to differences in that measure?" Where only two measures are concerned, this is often answered by using the Pearson product-moment correlation coefficient. Thus, if one is interested in whether or not tall people are more sociable than short people, the typical procedure would be to correlate scores on a measure of Sociability with individuals' heights. Where more than two measures are involved, researchers are often concerned with the pattern of relationships among the measures.

Factor analysis is a generic term used to describe a family of techniques that have as their purpose the investigation of the relationships among a set of individual difference variables. The basic idea underlying the procedures is that any given measure of an individual difference variable can be thought of as being made up of a number of components, and by studying the relationships among a set of measures it is possible to identify these various components. It is generally assumed that there are fewer components responsible for the relationships than there are variables. These components can be thought of as latent variables while the measures themselves can be thought of as indicator variables. For example, a test of knowledge of statistics would be an indicator variable (or measure), but could be thought of as being made up a number of latent variables (components) such as knowledge of statistics, intelligence, math anxiety, etc.

Factor analysis is unlike many other "statistical procedures" in that it is not concerned with how some treatment variable influences behavior. Rather, it is concerned with how variables relate to one another. In many, but not all, factor analytic procedures there isn't even any assessment of statistical significance. In the procedures to be discussed in this chapter, statistical significance is not used in assessing the nature of the factors identified. Instead of stating that this factor is significant or that this variable is significantly related to that factor, etc., comments are made such that this factor accounts for a given percentage of the total variance or that this variable is highly or moderately related to that factor, etc. Some students find this lack of reliance on statistical significance discomforting, but it should be remembered that even the judgment that something is "significant" is based on an arbitrary decision as to what constitutes significance, $p < .05$, $p < .01$, $p < .001$, etc.

A BIT OF HISTORY

The basic principle underlying factor analysis can be traced back to Galton (1889), who conceived of the concept of a latent variable or trait to explain the relationships among measured variables. Or it could be attributed to Pearson, who extended Galton's concept of regression to develop the measure of correlation (frequently the basis for factor analysis), and who subsequently (1901) outlined the principles underlying principal-axis factor analysis, one of the techniques still in use today. Most researchers, however, credit Spearman (1904) for developing the first common factor model (cf. Mulaik, 1972) and with subsequently introducing the term "factor" (Spearman, 1927). He made use of the concept of tetrad difference to support his contention that measures of talent were composed of two factors, a general ability common to all the measures (referred to as "g"), and a set of abilities specific to each measure. Other researchers (see, for example, Thomson, 1956) disagreed with this conceptualization, arguing instead that there were only groups of common factors. Still other researchers proposed instead that there was a hierarchy of abilities starting with a general ability factor and extending to less general abilities (see, for example, Vernon, 1961). Much of this development and discussion was focused in Great Britain.

In the United States, Thurstone (1947) argued against the concept of a common factor and for that of multiple factors, which he called the primary mental abilities. He introduced the notion of simple structure and proposed that any given factor should be defined primarily by a largely non-overlapping subset of variables. He proposed that factors should be rotated to uncover this simple structure. Subsequently, other researchers (see, for example, Carroll, 1953, 1957; Kaiser, 1958) proposed analytic procedures that could identify simple structure by means of computer application. The stage was set for the development of the major computer packages **SPSS, SAS,** and **BMDP** to provide easy-to-use programs to perform the factor analysis and the subsequent rotation.

All of the preceding procedures are concerned with the use of exploratory methods. That is, one starts with a matrix of associations (e.g., correlations) and seeks to identify the factors that underlie these associations. Another approach begins with a theory about what factors are responsible for the associations, and seeks to test the adequacy of this theory. This is the technique of confirmatory factor analysis. Some of Thurstone's research was concerned with this type of approach. Today, a proponent of this type of analysis is Jöreskog (1969).

GENERAL RATIONALE

As indicated above, the basic idea underlying factor analysis is that the measure of any variable is potentially composed of a series of latent variables. The objective of factor analysis then is to uncover these underlying latent variables (also referred to as dimensions or factors). This is done by investigating the relationships among a series of variables by studying how they relate to a series of dimensions. If two or more variables are shown to relate highly to the same dimension, it can be said that they share this dimension in common. By determining what variables relate to a given dimension and considering what is common to them, and noting how they differ from variables that don't relate to this dimension, one can derive an understanding of this dimension. This dimension then is the latent variable. Note the two-stage related process in this logic:

1. Determine what variables relate "highly" to a dimension.
2. Identify the dimension in terms of what is common to the variables that relate highly to the dimension, and different from those variables that do not relate highly to the dimension.

Types of Factor Analysis

There are basically two different approaches to factor analysis, and within these two approaches a number of different analytical procedures to satisfy the stated objectives. The two basic approaches are *exploratory factor analysis* and *confirmatory factor analysis*. Exploratory factor analysis begins with the relationships among the indicator variables and strives to uncover the dimensions underlying them. Confirmatory factor analysis begins with a model or theory of the nature of the dimensions underlying a set of indicator variables and seeks to determine to what extent the dimensions explain the relationships among the variables. This chapter is concerned with the first of these two approaches, exploratory factor analysis.

There are a number of exploratory factor analytic procedures. **SPSS WINDOWS** performs seven (there are more) of these in its program, **Factor.** In **Factor,** these are referred to as Extraction Methods. They are:

a. *PC*—Principal Components Analysis

b. *PAF*—Principal Axis Factor Analysis

c. *ML*—Maximum Likelihood Factor Analysis

d. *ALPHA*—Alpha Factor Analysis

e. *IMAGE*—Image Analysis

f. *ULS*—Unweighted Least Squares Analysis

g. *GLS*—Generalized Least Squares Analysis

Although this chapter will focus attention on Principal Components Analysis, it should be emphasized that the different procedures share many features in common with this method. They differ in the nature of the mathematics used, but many of the concepts to be introduced in this chapter are common to all the methods. Moreover, the different methods tend to provide very similar answers concerning the dimensionality underlying any given set of variables (see MacIntyre (1990) for a clear presentation and example of the similarities among some of these methods).

Stages in Factor Analysis

There are three stages in a Principal Components Analysis, and these stages are common to many different types of factor analysis. Stage 1 is concerned with the computation of the relationships among the variables. This is generally expressed in the form of a *Correlation Matrix*. Stage 2 involves extraction of the factors. These factors are the mathematically-based dimensions that describe the principal components of variance in the correlation matrix, and the matrix of correlations of the variables with these dimensions forms the *Initial Factor Matrix*. Stage 3 is concerned with identifying factors that more parsimoniously (i.e., more simply) describe the relations among the variables. This is achieved by rotating the factors described in the initial factor matrix to produce a more interpretable structure. The resultant matrix of associations of the variables with the rotated factors is the *Rotated Factor Matrix*.

Stage 1. The Correlation Matrix. The most common approach to Principal Components Analysis is to make use of the matrix of correlations among all the variables to assess their interrelationships, although other measures of association could be used. **SPSS WINDOWS FACTOR** permits the use of correlation or variance/covariance matrices, but we will focus attention on the use of the correlation matrix. The correlation matrix presents the relationships among the variables two at a time, and careful inspection of this matrix can help the researcher to see how all the variables relate to one another. However, if there are a large number of variables, it is often difficult to keep track of the various relationships and patterns of relationships. If, for example, there were 10 variables, there would be $(10)(9)/2 = 45$ correlations to consider; if there were 20 variables, there would be 190 correlations. Obviously, it is not easy to perform a careful inspection.

Principal Components Analysis "extracts" the dimensions from this matrix. In this context, the Fundamental theorem in Factor analysis is that the correlation between any two variables can be expressed as the sum across all dimensions of the cross products of the correlations of these two variables with the dimensions. The Fundamental Theorem is stated as follows:

$$r_{XY} = a_{X,I}A_{Y,I} + a_{X,II}a_{Y,II} + \cdots + a_{X,K}a_{Y,K}$$

where: $a_{X,I}$ is the correlation of variable X with Factor I (the first dimension)

$a_{Y,I}$ is the correlation of variable Y with Factor I, etc.

Stage 2. The Initial Factor Matrix.   The dimensions themselves are simply weighted aggregates of the variables expressed in standard score form. Thus, each dimension or factor can be viewed as a sort of *super-variable* (cf. Tabachnick & Fidell, 1989) that is made up by aggregating scores on all the variables in the analysis. That is, an individual's score in standard score form on a Factor is equal to:

$$F_i = w_1 Z_{1,i} + w_2 Z_{2,i} + \cdots + w_m Z_{m,i}$$

where: F_i is an individual's score on the Factor
w_1, w_2, etc. are weights applied to each variable
$Z_{1,i}$, $Z_{2,i}$, etc. are an individual's standard score on the variables

The different methods of factor extraction differ in terms of the operations used to determine these weights. Principal Components uses matrix algebra to select weights for each factor so that the variance of the scores on the Factor is as large as possible. Given m variables, it is possible to extract m factors. In Principal Components Analysis, the first factor will be extracted using weights such that the variance of the scores for Factor I will be as large as possible. These weights are scaled such that the sum of their squared values equals 1.0. One could compute the correlations of each variable with this Factor. Having done this, one could then partial out the correlation of each variable with the Factor from the correlations among the variables. What is left is a matrix of residual correlations (i.e., partial correlations) where any variation common to the first factor has been removed. Factor II will be extracted from this residual matrix, and thus will be independent of the first factor. It will have weights such that the variance of scores on that factor will be the next largest, and so on.

In Principal Components Analysis, the set of weights (ws) for any one factor is often referred to as an *eigenvector*. A matrix of these weights would consist of as many columns as there are factors, and as many rows as there are variables. This matrix is often referred to as the *Pattern Matrix*. In Principal Components Analysis, each of the factors is independent of one another because of this partialling out process. This could be demonstrated by computing a score for each factor for each individual and correlating these scores. The resulting correlations among the Factors would all be 0. One might also compute the variance of each Factor. The variances of these Factors are referred to as *eigenvalues*.

As indicated above, once the factors have been extracted, it is possible to determine how the variables relate to them by correlating the scores on the variables with the scores on the factors. These correlations of the variables with the Factors are referred to as *factor loadings*, and the matrix of these factor loadings is often referred to as the *Structure Matrix*. The factor loadings are the a's in the equation for the Fundamental Theorem presented on page 239. A high positive correlation between a variable and a factor indicates that the variable tends to measure something in common with the factor. A high negative correlation indicates that the variable tends to measure the opposite of what the factor describes. A very low correlation indicates that there is nothing in common between the variable and the factor.

If you were to square the factor loadings for each variable and sum the resulting values for each factor, you would obtain the eigenvalue. These eigenvalues are, as we have seen, the variance for each factor, and can be calculated using the following equation:

$$\lambda = a^2_1 + a^2_2 + \cdots + a^2_m$$

where: λ = the eigenvalue for a Factor
a^2_1 = the squared factor loading for variable 1 on the Factor, a^2_2 the squared factor loading for variable 2, and so on for all (m) variables

If you were to sum the squared factor loadings across the factors for each variable, the resulting values are the *communalities* for each variable. The communality, designated by h^2, for a variable is a measure of how much variance the variable has in common with all the other variables in the matrix, at least as reflected in the factors that have been extracted. The formula for this computation is:

$$h^2 = a_1^2 + a_2^2 + \cdots + a_p^2$$

where: h^2 = the communality for a variable

a_1^2 = the squared factor loading for the variable 1 on the first factor, 1, a_2^2 the squared factor loading for the variable on the second factor, and so on for all p factors.

Stage 3. The Rotated Factor Matrix.   One problem with Principal Components Analysis is that the factors are extracted in order of the amount of variance they account for, rather than in terms of how well they actually describe the relationships among the variables. For example, if you were to consider the factors two at a time and plot a graph depicting the factor loadings and their relation to the two factors, you would find that in general the variables are not particularly close to either of the two factors. Many researcher recommend, therefore, that the axes be rotated so that they tend to come closer to the points representing the variables. This is referred to as *rotation* in factor analysis. The purpose of rotation is to provide a more parsimonious or simpler description of the relationships among the variables.

There are many types of rotation procedures that can be employed. Rotational procedures can be distinguished in terms of the nature of the solution they produce. These solutions can be either *orthogonal* or *oblique*. Orthogonal solutions are those in which the rotated factors retain the independence of the factors that characterizes the original Principal Components Analysis. The factors are kept independent of one another, thus the interpretation of any one factor does not affect the interpretation of any other. This is done by keeping the factors at right angles to each other when performing the rotations. Oblique solutions, on the other hand, are those in which the factors themselves are allowed to be correlated with one another. This means that the interpretations of the factors can overlap to some extent, depending on the degree of correlation between any two factors. This correlation is allowed in the rotational procedure by letting the factors be at less (or more) than right angles with one another. The interpretation of oblique factors is a bit more complex than that for orthogonal factors and will not be discussed any further. This is not that problematic because generally orthogonal solutions provide very meaningful descriptions of the data, and non-orthogonality can be accounted for in the interpretation. However, it is usually a good idea to plot the rotated factors just to ensure they provide a meaningful fit to the data. This can be done directly in **SPSS WINDOWS FACTOR** (but this use of the command is not discussed here).

The rotational procedures provided by **SPSS WINDOWS FACTOR** are as follows:

Orthogonal Solutions
a. **VARIMAX**
b. **EQUAMAX**
c. **QUARTIMAX**

Oblique Solutions
d. **DIRECT OBLIMIN**
e. **PROMAX**

The Varimax solution (Kaiser, 1958) is the most commonly used procedure and will be the only one discussed in this chapter. Generally, however, the three orthogonal procedures yield similar solutions. If the factor structure is orthogonal, even the oblique solutions will provide comparable results. That is, oblimin will not force an oblique solution if the underlying structure is orthogonal. MacIntyre (1990) provides a very clear discussion with examples of the comparability of the different rotational procedures for a given set of data.

MAJOR ISSUES IN FACTOR ANALYSIS

Like all other multivariate procedures, there are a number of issues associated with factor analysis that should be considered. Some of these have already been alluded to above. In this section, we will consider five issues in a bit more detail.

Principal Components vs. Principal Axis Factor Analysis

We have already seen that there are numerous forms of data reduction referred to as factor analysis. The Principal Components Method was described above as one in which the factors are isolated in terms of the amount of variance they extract. Within this general approach, however, you will sometimes see a distinction between Principal Components and Principal Axis or Primary Factor Analysis. The mathematical solution underlying these two approaches is very similar, but the theoretical underpinnings are quite different. Principal Components Analysis is concerned with analyzing all the variance associated with the variables, whereas Principal Axis Factor Analysis is concerned with analyzing only the variance that is common to the variables. Much could be said about this distinction, but suffice it to say that the practical implications of the distinction lies in the definition of the important variance for a variable. If it is the total variance that is of interest, then in standard score form the variance associated with a variable is 1.0. If it is the common variance that is of interest, then it is the common variance (i.e., the communality) that is of interest. This is reflected in the analysis in terms of the value put into the diagonal of the correlation matrix. In Principal Components Analysis, the diagonal values are 1.0, and the number of factors extracted will equal the number of variables. In Principal Axis Factor Analysis, we attempt to estimate the common variance associated with each variable. There are a number of approaches to this problem, but a common one is to use the squared multiple correlation of a variable with all the other variables in the matrix as the estimate of common variance for that variable. If you recall from the previous chapter, this was the definition of R^2. Thus, to perform a Principal Axis Factor Analysis, **SPSS WINDOWS FACTOR** uses R^2 to estimate the communality for each variable. However, because all the variance for the variables is no longer represented in the matrix, the number of factors the solution will produce is something less than the number of variables. A decision must therefore be made as to the number of factors to extract. These decisions are based on the Principal Components Analysis. The net result of this is that if you were to perform a Principal Axis Factor Analysis on **SPSS WINDOWS FACTOR,** some of the initial statistics would be identical to those for the Principal Components Analysis.

It is beyond the scope of this chapter to go into the distinction between these two forms of analysis any further. The preceding observations were made simply to point out the difference. Although there is not much made of the distinction between the two in this chapter, there are different opinions in the literature. Pedhazur and Schmelkin (1991) argue, for example, that Principal Components Analysis and Principal Axis Factor Analysis refer to very different models, that under certain conditions they can give very different answers, and moreover that it is not meaningful to rotate principal components. This view can be contrasted with that of Stevens (1996) who focuses attention on Principal Components Analysis as a factor analytic procedure, because he argues it is psychometrically sound and mathematically simpler than Principal Axis Factor Analysis. Moreover, he recommends that principal components can be rotated to improve interpretability. As you can see, there are very different interpretations, and you can find many examples in the literature of preference for one over the other. As I indicated above, however, we are directing attention in this chapter to the use of principal components.

Sample Size

Since factor analysis is a multivariate procedure, there are, as you might expect, concerns about the issue of sample size. Traditionally, it has been argued that sample size should be at least as large as 100 to 300 (cf. Cattell, 1978; Comrey, 1973). But you will find many factor analytic studies with samples smaller than this. Some researchers have proposed that the number of subjects should bear some relation to the number of variables. For example, Nunnally (1978) proposed a 10 to 1 subjects to variable ratio, but Guadagnoli and Velicer (1988) cite a series of references recommending ratios that vary from 2 to 1 to 20 to 1 (note the similarity with multiple regression). Finally, some researchers recommend that a researcher should consider the ratio of the number of subjects to the number of factors expected. There is some merit in all of these recommendations. Clearly, the larger the sample size, the more stable the results. Correlation coefficients are relatively stable from a sampling point of view with large sample sizes. Furthermore, the stability of the factor is greater when there are a number of defining variables. Thus, logically, it makes sense that sample size should be large in general, and that with more variables or more factors, one needs more subjects.

A Monte Carlo study of rotated principal components by Guadagnoli and Velicer (1988) appears to question some of this logic, however. They found that by far the most important feature that influences the stability of the results is the saturation of the factor. If the factors are well defined [i.e., the factor loadings are large (in the order of .8 in the population)], sample sizes as low as 50 are relatively stable. And this is true for many variables as well as relatively few variables. That is, if the factors are well defined in the population, they will be relatively stable from a sampling point of view. Guadagnoli and Velicer (1988) point out, moreover, that their study used artificial data where any one variable contributed to only one factor in the population, which is rather unusual in applied situations. In any event, they still recommend that in applied contexts sample sizes be in the range of 100 to 200. They point out too, that if one is concerned primarily with the general pattern of results, rather than the sampling distribution of specific factor loadings, and if a factor is defined by at least four variables with relatively large loadings (greater than $\pm$ .60), interpretation is meaningful even with smaller samples. Attempting to summarize this, one might conclude that even with sample sizes in the neighborhood of 100, if one is cautious in one's interpretation, and verifies it by considering the pattern of correlations in the correlation matrix, general conclusions based on the factor analysis may well be justified. Of course, the proof of the pudding is in replication, and if factor analyses of other samples support the conclusions drawn, then the issue of sample size loses some of its urgency.

Number of Factors

A primary objective of factor analysis is to reduce the number of dimensions necessary to describe the relationships among the variables. Thus, although m factors can be extracted to account for the relationships among m variables, generally attention is directed only to those dimensions that account for most of the relationships. In adopting this strategy, it is assumed that to the extent that there are common themes (i.e., patterns or clusters) underlying the relationships, fewer dimensions will be needed to account for them. It is assumed too, that the correlations themselves reflect sampling variations so that it is meaningful to extract only as many dimensions needed to account for the major degree of relationship. Some non-zero correlations will be left over once the contributions of the major dimensions are removed, but these are considered to reflect random error.

There are a number of ways of determining the "right" number of factors. One commonly used method, and the one used as the default in **SPSS WINDOWS FACTOR,** is Kaiser's (1960) eigenvalue-one criterion. This approach assumes that all factors with eigenvalues greater than 1.0 are meaningful and should be retained in the final solution. The rationale underlying this method is that the variance for a variable is 1.0 in standard score form and that, if a factor doesn't account for any more variance than a single variable, then it, as a weighted aggregate of all the variables, isn't reducing the complexity of the final solution. As such, the factor should not be considered as a dimension accounting for any of the relationships among the variables.

A second approach to the number of factors problem is to perform what is referred to as the Scree Test (Cattell, 1966). This procedure involves drawing a graph in which the eigenvalues are plotted against the factors arranged in order from 1 to m. Since factors are extracted in terms of the magnitude of their eigenvalues, this results in a graph in which the values decrease as the factor number increases. This plot has been likened to a side view of a mountain, and the problem is to determine when the mountain ends and the plane at the base of the mountain begins. Using the mountain analogy, one could argue that the plane will never be perfectly flat because of the rubble (i.e., the scree) that falls from the mountain. In the scree plot, the rubble corresponds to a general levelling off of the eigenvalues. Application of the Scree Test, then, involves determining when there is a major bend in the elbow indicating a break between the "mountain" and the "rubble." This involves a judgment on the part of the researcher based on a visual inspection of the graph. Sometimes there is evidence of two screes. That is, the eigenvalues tend to level off after the initial drop, and then show another drop with levelling off again (sometimes more than once) further along. Cattell (1966) recommends in such cases that one base decisions on the first scree; that is retain all factors before the first elbow.

Both of the above procedures are concerned with determining when essentially all of the association among the variables has been accounted for, and deciding that any remaining association basically reflects sampling fluctuations. This can be determined directly by considering the residual matrix once the given number of factors has been extracted. Presumably this residual matrix will consist of correlations that vary within sampling fluctuations around 0. Although this might sound like the only real way of determining whether all meaningful factors have been extracted, a bit of reflection will reveal that this involves deciding how many factors to extract before calculating the residual matrix, and then making a decision about whether each of the residual correlations are essentially 0 allowing, of course, for some Type I errors. Thus, if this procedure were to be followed, one would find herself/himself deciding whether one residual matrix was more like a matrix of zeroes than another. This itself would be a difficult decision to make, and a difficult one to describe, because of the large number of correlations involved. In any event all three procedures generally lead to similar (though not necessarily identical) conclusions, thus either the eigenvalue-one or the Scree test is preferred by most researchers. Under some circumstances, particularly where there is a large number of variables, the eigenvalue-one criterion can lead to a decision to retain one or a few more factors than the other methods, so many researchers consider both the Scree test and the eigenvalue-one criteria in combination.

The Rotation Issue

There is a long historical debate about whether or not factors should be rotated, and if so by what method. When the method of analysis is principal components, the components themselves have meaning, and one can mount an argument for not performing rotations (see, for example, Pedhazur & Schmelkin, 1991). The factors are linear aggregates of the variables, and are extracted in terms of the magnitude of the variances of the factors. On the other hand, there are also good reasons for rotating principal components (see, Stevens, 1996). When the form of analysis is Principal Axis Factor Analysis or most other forms of analysis, then rotation is commonly performed.

As indicated above the purpose of rotation is to provide a more parsimonious (simple) description of the relationships. The notion of rotation was suggested by Thurstone (1947) to achieve what he termed *simple structure*. Simple structure is demonstrated in a factor matrix when the Factor Loadings are such that each variable contributes to a minimum number of factors, and each factor is defined by a number of variables. The table below illustrates a pure case of simple structure.

Variables	I	II	III
1	X	0	0
2	X	0	0
3	X	0	0
4	0	X	0
5	0	X	0
6	0	X	0
7	0	0	X
8	0	0	X
9	0	0	X

This table presents information about 9 variables and three factors. The Xs represent high loadings (either positive or negative) and the 0s represent low (or near zero) loadings. As can be seen in this table, each variable contributes to only one factor, and each factor has a predominance of low (near zero) loadings. In this example, each factor is defined by the same number of variables (each has three high loadings), but this is not necessary. The important thing is that each factor has a number of high loadings, and a number of low loadings. Moreover, when you consider the factors two at a time, you will note that each display is a completely different pattern of high and low loadings from the other. That is, the factors are very different. Once you have satisfied these conditions, it will be the case that the factors provide a very simple interpretation of the data.

The example above characterizes each variable as contributing to only one factor. This would be true if each of the measures were relatively pure measures of the factor in question. Many measures, however, are comprised of more than one dimension. That is, they would contribute to more than one factor. Consider Variable 6, for example. If it had high loadings on both Factor II and III (i.e., Xs in both columns), this would indicate that it contributes to both dimensions. This would occur if it correlates highly with Variables 4 and 5, as well as with Variables 7, 8, and 9. This pattern would still be an instance of simple structure, except in this case this one variable is shown to be more complex than the rest. That is, simple structure does not require that all variables have only one high loading. If variables are complex, they will tend to load on more than one factor, but generally speaking each variable should show one or more high loadings and a number of near-zero loadings across the factors. Moreover, each factor should show a number of high loadings (generally, you need at least three to define a factor) and a number of near-zero loadings.

Factor Scores

Once a principal components analysis has been performed, it is sometimes desirable to compute scores to represent the factors in question. These scores could be formed from the original Principal Components matrix or from the rotated matrix. It is beyond the scope of this chapter to discuss how factor scores are computed. Suffice it to say that these scores can be computed, and then these scores can be used in other analyses. **SPSS WINDOWS FACTOR** calculates three different types of factor scores. The important characteristic of these scores is that they correlate with each other in the same way as the corresponding factors correlate. Thus, if you have performed an orthogonal rotation, and then compute factor scores from the rotated matrix, the correlations among these factor scores will be 0. To the extent that you have interpreted the factor scores, you can then use these scores as representing the factors in other analyses. Thus, for example, if you wished to use these scores as predictors in a multiple regression analysis, this would mean that these predictors are mutually independent. As we saw in the last chapter, there are advantages in using independent predictors in multiple regression.

PERFORMING A PRINCIPAL COMPONENTS ANALYSIS WITH SPSS WINDOWS

You can perform a factor analysis using the Principal Components procedure, and obtain a rotated solution by making use of the **SPSS WINDOWS** program **FACTOR.** There are a number of options that can be invoked when using this program, but attention here will be focussed only on some of them. Consider the data presented in the following table. They are fictitious data representing scores of 20 elementary school students on 7 variables (note, the sample size is too small, and there are relatively few variables). In the table, we assume that variables 1 to 4 are measures of mathematical skills, assessing proficiency in *Addition, Subtraction, Multiplication,* and *Division,* respectively, with possible ranges of scores from 0 to 25 on each measure. Assume further that variables 5 to 7 are measures of English Skills. Variable 5 could be a short measure concerned with a student's appreciation of the functions performed by *nouns* in English sentences, with a possible range of scores varying from 5 to 20, while variables 6 and 7 could be longer measures with possible ranges from 0 to 60. Variable 6 could be a measure of the number of *adverbs* correctly identified as to grammatical function while variable 7 could be the number of *adjectives* correctly identified.

Add	Subt	Mult	Div	Noun	Adv	Adj
9	12	5	10	7	45	52
10	14	8	10	6	42	51
13	13	9	12	10	43	54
18	16	12	15	18	46	56
16	17	15	16	11	39	54
15	16	16	13	14	43	56
19	21	18	15	11	44	53
19	24	19	16	7	40	51
16	19	14	16	10	40	52
11	17	10	17	18	46	54
9	11	8	11	10	45	51
10	12	11	8	16	42	54
12	13	12	10	9	39	49
15	12	11	10	11	45	51
11	14	10	9	12	47	54
16	15	14	10	18	48	55
10	13	14	12	17	48	54
12	13	16	11	19	49	53
11	17	18	12	17	49	54
19	18	20	16	18	50	57

Steps in Using SPSS WINDOWS FACTOR

The following steps are applicable to **SPSS 8.0** and **SPSS 9.0** except for the input of the ASCII or Text data file. In the example to follow you are instructed at Step 3 to input your data following the procedures described in Chapter 1. The output for this example was obtained by using the freefield format in **SPSS 8.0,** and depending upon the input procedure you use, the output may be somewhat different. The answers are the same, however. You could, if you prefer, transfer into the **Syntax Editor** and simply type the Syntax file [the set of instructions required to run the procedure, including the relevant **Data List** and **Execute** statements (see page 30)], and then execute the job from inside the **Syntax Editor** (not discussed here). We will use the **clope** method instead and create the syntax file by employing the mouse to bring up a number of windows, and then selecting the appropriate options or typing in the required information.

1. *Enter **SPSS WIN**.* This presents you with the **SPSS Data Editor** (see figure in Chapter 2, p. 46). At this point, you could begin to type in the data. However, we will assume here that you already have the data in a file on the A Drive, that this file is labelled **fac1.dat,** and that the data are in freefield (**SPSS 8.0**) or Delimited format (**SPSS 9.0**).

2. *Click on **File** in the upper row of selections.* This will present you with a drop-down menu with a series of choices.

3. *Enter your ASCII (**SPSS 8.0**) or Text (**SPSS 9.0**) data file by following the steps on pages 17 to 20 for **SPSS 8.0**, or pages 20 to 28 for **SPSS 9.0**.* For this example, the file will consist of the seven variables labelled **V1** to **V7.**

4. *Click on the **Statistics (SPSS 8.0)** or **Analyze (SPSS 9.0)** option on the menu bar.* This presents you with a drop-down menu. *Move your cursor to **Data Reduction**, and you are presented with another menu to the right with a choice of the following:*
   Factor
   Correspondence Analysis
   Optimal Scaling

5. *Click on **Factor**.* This presents you with the Window, **Factor Analysis,** and the variable V1 is highlighted (see figure below).

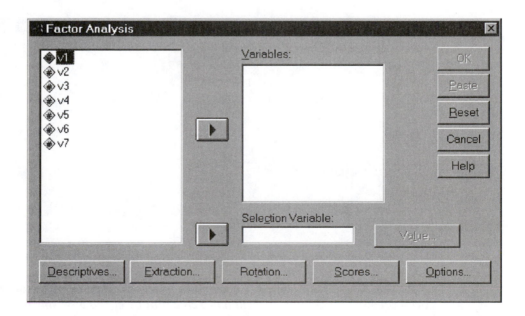

*Add all the variables, **V1** to **V7**, to the **Variables pane**. You can do this one at a time by clicking on each one and then clicking on the appropriate arrow. Alternatively, you can add all the variables at once by putting the cursor on the first one, holding down the left mouse button, and dragging the cursor down to **V7**. This highlights **V1** to **V7**, and when you click on the arrow, all are added to the pane.*

6. This Window also allows you to make a number of additional choices. We shall discuss only **Descriptives, Extraction,** and **Rotation.** *Click on Descriptives.* This presents the Window, **Factor Analysis Descriptives** (see below).

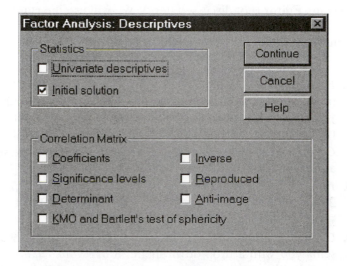

Note that **Initial solution** is already selected as the default option. We will add **Univariate descriptives,** as well as **Coefficients** and **Reproduced** (under Correlation Matrix) by *clicking these choices. Then click on **Continue**.* This will return you to the Window, **Factor Analysis.**

7. *Click on **Extraction**. This produces the Window, **Factor Analysis Extraction** (see figure below).*

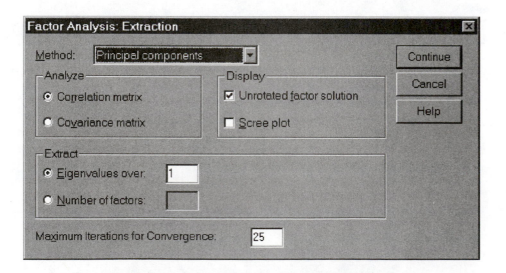

Note that **Correlation matrix, Eigenvalues over,** and **Unrotated factor solution** have already been selected by default. *We will add **Scree plot** by clicking on this option as well. Then click on **Continue**.* This returns you to the Window, **Factor Analysis.**

8. *Click on **Rotation** at the bottom of the Window.* This gives another Window, **Factor Analysis Rotation** (see figure below).

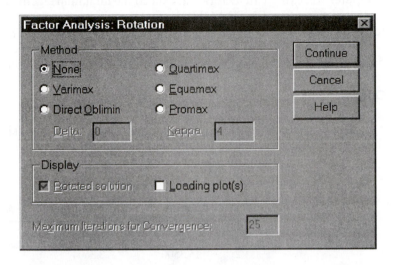

Note that the option **None** has been chosen as the method by default. *We will change this by clicking **Varimax**.* Then click on **Continue.** This returns you to the Window, **Factor Analysis.** *Since we don't want to use any of the other selections, click on **OK** to run **Factor Analysis.***

9. This runs the **Factor Analysis** program, and the answers are returned to the **SPSS Viewer** as well as to your monitor. At this point, you can print your answers, save them in a file, or transfer them to some other editor.

10. To exit **SPSS**, *click on **File** (upper row of operations), and click on **Exit.*** Before you can exit, however, the program will ask if you wish to save the contents of the **Viewer** as well as those of the **Data Editor.** If you have already saved them, you will not have to do so again.

The Syntax File. If you followed the above instructions, you would construct the following syntax file:

```
FACTOR
 /VARIABLES v1 v2 v3 v4 v5 v6 v7 /MISSING LISTWISE
 /ANALYSIS v1 v2 v3 v4 v5 v6 v7
 /PRINT UNIVARIATE INITIAL CORRELATION REPR EXTRACTION ROTATION
 /PLOT EIGEN
 /CRITERIA MINEIGEN(1) ITERATE(25)
 /EXTRACTION PC
 /CRITERIA ITERATE(25)
 /ROTATION VARIMAX
 /METHOD=CORRELATION
```

The program, **FACTOR,** is executed with the VARIABLES statement defining the variables to be included in the analysis. The MISSING statement indicates that subjects with missing data will be deleted listwise (i.e., they will be ignored in the analysis). The ANALYSIS statement indicates that the analysis will make use of all the variables, V1 to V7. Multiple analysis statements can be run, thus allowing researchers to use different numbers of variables in other runs without having to change the earlier Variables statement. The PRINT statement indicates what results are to be listed in the output file. In the present case, the computer has been instructed to output the univariate statistics, the initial statistics, the correlation matrix, the matrix of reproduced and residual correlations based on the final factor solution, the extraction statistics and the results of the varimax rotation. The PLOT EIGEN statement directs the computer to provide plots of results. In this case, the computer is instructed to output the Scree plot, but other options are available. The CRITERIA statement indicates that the computer will extract all factors that exceed the minimum eigenvalue of 1.0, and that it will limit itself to 25 iterations. The EXTRACTION statement indicates which type of initial extraction is to be performed, in this case it is PC, the Principal Components analysis. The ROTATION statement indicates which form of rotation to perform; in this case the Varimax procedure. The METHOD statement indicates that the correlation matrix will be the matrix to be analyzed.

Output

Descriptive Statistics.   This section of the output consists of the means, standard deviations, and sample size for the variables included in this analysis.

Descriptive Statistics

	Mean	Std. Deviation	Analysis N
$V1$	13.5500	3.5165	20
$V2$	15.3500	3.3604	20
$V3$	13.0000	4.0911	20
$V4$	12.4500	2.8186	20
$V5$	12.9500	4.3222	20
$V6$	44.5000	3.4412	20
$V7$	53.2500	2.0229	20

It is useful to study this information to understand the nature of the variables included in the analysis. These results refer to the raw score data. Thus, in this example, Variable 1 has a mean of 13.55 and a standard deviation of 3.52. The mean tells us that the average score on Variable 1 is between 13 and 14. If Variable 1 had a possible range of scores from 0 to 25, this would indicate that average scores are around the centre of possible scores. If, on the other hand, the possible range of scores were from 0 to 100, this would indicate that the average scores were generally quite low on this measure in this sample. Similarly, the standard deviation tells us the extent to which individuals differ on this score. A small standard deviation indicates relatively little variability while a large one indicates considerable variation. More information about the nature of the individual variables could be provided by a frequency distribution, and it is often recommended that researchers get to know their data better by examining these distributions (cf. Norusis, 1991), but at a minimum much can be gained by considering the means and standard deviations.

The above table also indicates that the number of individuals in this sample is 20. If some individuals had missing observations and the researcher had used the default option, the value indicated in this section of output would refer to the number of individuals who had complete data since the correlations would be computed only on the sample of complete data. There is an option in which the researcher can request that the correlations be computed with pairwise deletion, so that all available data for any given correlation is used. This option is not recommended, but if a researcher were to use it, the output would show the maximum number of observations for each variable. Note, too, that if the data did contain some missing observations and these were indicated by blanks in the data file, the freefield format could not be used in **SPSS 8.0** but Delimited could be used in **SPSS 9.0.**

Correlation Matrix.   The correlation matrix describes the bivariate relations involving all the variables. In the output to **SPSS FACTOR,** the matrix is shown as a square matrix, with the diagonal values (i.e., the correlation of each variable with itself) shown as 1,000, and the correlations between each pair of variables shown both above and below the diagonal. Thus, the correlation of $V1$ and $V2$ is .744, and it appears in both the first row and second column, and the second row and first column. The correlation matrix is the matrix on which the factor analysis is based, and thus it is a good idea to study it also to appreciate the nature of the relationships among the variables taken two at a time. Often, it is advisable to inspect this matrix carefully once the final solution has been interpreted to ensure that the interpretation of the factors is consistent with the bivariate relationships described here. The correlation matrix is as follows:

Correlation Matrix

		$V1$	$V2$	$V3$	$V4$	$V5$	$V6$	$V7$
Correlation	$V1$	1.000	.744	.684	.643	.082	−.115	.313
	$V2$	.744	1.000	.708	.777	−.049	−.198	.149
	$V3$	.684	.708	1.000	.516	.378	.150	.350
	$V4$	.643	.777	.516	1.000	.119	−.122	.293
	$V5$	.082	−.049	.378	.119	1.000	.702	.718
	$V6$	−.115	−.198	.150	−.122	.702	1.000	.525
	$V7$	.313	.149	.350	.293	.718	.525	1.000

In the correlation matrix, you will note that Variables 1 and 2 correlate quite highly with one another, but that Variable 1 correlates more highly with Variable 7 than does Variable 2. Similarly, Variables 1 and 3 are highly intercorrelated, but both correlate similarly with Variable 7. That is, considering the variables two or three at a time, we can detect some patterns in the relationships. Note, too, that Variables 1 to 4 correlate highly among themselves and that Variables 5 to 7 correlate highly among themselves, but that the correlations between the two sets of variables are generally quite low. This is another pattern reflected in this matrix. As can be seen, there are only 21 correlations in this matrix, but it is still not an easy matter to see all the possible patterns that might arise.

Communalities. Initially, the communalities for each variable are 1.00, the variance for the variable in standard score form. Once the number of factors has been accounted for, however, the communalities are lower, and reflect for each variable the proportion of the variance for that variable accounted for by the factors. The following table presents these communalities.

Communalities

	Initial	Extraction
$V1$	1.000	.785
$V2$	1.000	.889
$V3$	1.000	.732
$V4$	1.000	.722
$V5$	1.000	.871
$V6$	1.000	.782
$V7$	1.000	.745

Extraction Method: Principal Component Analysis.

In the above table, it will be observed that the communality for variable $V1$ is .785. That is, the factor analysis has accounted for 78.5% of its variance. Variable $V2$ has the largest communality (.889), and variable $V4$, the lowest (.722). A researcher should consider these communalities. If the communality for a variable is particularly low (e.g., <.50), this means that the factor analysis does not account for much of the variance associated with that variable. That is, the variable doesn't have much in common with the other variables in the analysis. This could be due to one of three reasons. One, the variable is simply very different from the other variables in that it really is a measure of something distinct. Two, the measurement of the variable is very unreliable, and thus the observations on that variable represent largely chance variation. Three, an insufficient number of factors were extracted. An investigator can assess the relevance of the latter reason by considering closely the decision rule used to determine the number of factors. An examination of the residual matrix would indicate whether there still exist some high residual correlations involving the variable in question. If so, this would argue for extracting at least one more factor. It is not possible to distinguish between the first two reasons from the factor analysis alone, but if one knew that the reliability of the measure was high, then she/he might well conclude that the first reason is most likely. In any event, it is important to consider the communality estimates when interpreting a factor analysis.

Eigenvalues and Variance Explained.   The following table presents the eigenvalues for the analysis, as well as estimates of the variance accounted for by the final solution.

Total Variance Explained

Component	Initial Eigenvalues			Extraction Sums of Squared Loadings			Rotation Sums of Squared Loadings		
	Total	% of Variance	Cumulative %	Total	% of Variance	Cumulative %	Total	% of Variance	Cumulative %
1.000	3.281	46.873	46.873	3.281	46.873	46.873	3.132	44.746	44.746
2.000	2.245	32.076	78.949	2.245	32.076	78.949	2.394	34.203	78.949
3.000	.520	7.430	86.379						
4.000	.381	5.447	91.826						
5.000	.287	4.100	95.926						
6.000	.194	2.772	98.699						
7.000	.091	1.301	100.00						

Extraction Method: Principal Component Analysis.

There are actually two sets of results output in this table. The section entitled "Initial Eigenvalues" presents the eigenvalues, percent of variance, and cumulative percent of variance for each factor arranged in order of the magnitude of the eigenvalues. In this case, the first eigenvalue is 3.281, and this accounts for 46.873% (i.e. [(3.281/ 7.00)*100]) of the variance. Note that each of the eigenvalues is greater than 0 and that their sum is 7.00 (i.e., 3.281 + 2.245 + ... + .091 = 7.00). If an eigenvalue is ever equal to 0, this indicates that the matrix of correlations is "ill-conditioned" and that a factor analysis should not be performed. (It is beyond the scope of this chapter to discuss the reasons for this.) The section entitled "Extraction Sum of Squared Loadings" reproduces this information for the number of factors extracted in the analysis (in this case two). Note, that the sums of the squared loadings are identical to the eigenvalues. Two factors were extracted in this example, because at Step 7 of the set-up (see page 248), we chose the default option of extracting all factors for which the eigenvalues were greater than 1. The section labelled "Rotation Sums of Squared Loadings" presents the same information for the rotated factors. Note that the sums of the squared factor loadings are different from those reported in the section on "Extraction Sum of Squared Loadings," but that their sum (3.132 + 2.394) is equal to the sum of the eigenvalues (3.281 + 2.245). Note too, that before and after rotation the two factors together account for 78.9% of the variance, even though individually, the percentage of variance accounted for by each factor differs before and after rotation.

Scree Plot. This section presents a plot of the eigenvalues against the factors. This plot permits the researcher to determine the number of factors that he/she feels best represents all the meaningful variance described by the correlation matrix.

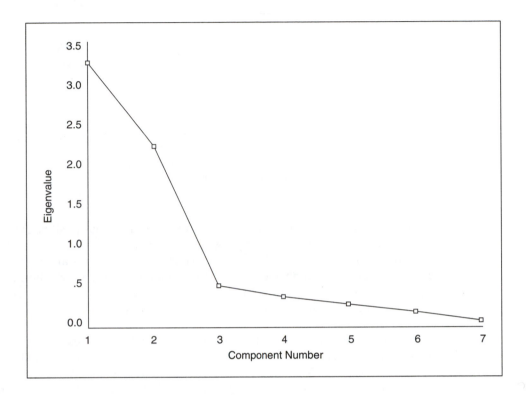

Inspection of this plot would suggest that two factors account for the major meaningful variance in the matrix of correlations. This conclusion is based on a decision of where the elbow appears in the plot. In this case, it is at Factor 3, which suggests that the amount of variance accounted for by Factors 3 and following are all low and more or less equivalent. This would in turn suggest that the variances for each of these factors essentially reflect sampling fluctuations. In essence, then, the researcher is looking here to distinguish the mountain (i.e., principal components based on true covariation) from the "scree" (i.e., principal components based on random error).

Initial Factor Matrix. The initial factor matrix in this analysis is the Principal Components factor matrix. It is a Structure Matrix because it consists of the correlations of each variable with each Principal Component. **SPSS WINDOWS FACTOR** does not output the Pattern Matrix for the Principal Component solution because this is an orthogonal solution, and the Pattern Matrix is comparable to the Structure Matrix in this case.

The Structure Matrix (**SPSS WINDOWS FACTOR** labels it the Component Matrix) is shown below, and in this example it can be seen to consist of two factors. This decision concerning the number of factors is based on the eigenvalue-one rule, not on the results of the Scree plot presented above, although both decisions agree in this case. That is, only two factors had eigenvalues greater than 1.0, and this is the default decision in **SPSS WINDOWS FACTOR.** Fewer or more factors could be extracted by using options available in the **Factor Analysis Extraction** Window (see Step 7, page 248). For example, you could lower the value for the minimum eigenvalue from that chosen as the default, or you could select the Number of Factors option, and type in the number desired.

Component Matrix[a]

	Component	
	1.000	**2.000**
$V1$	.836	−.295
$V2$	.824	−.458
$V3$	.856	−.007
$V4$	.797	−.295
$V5$	.426	.831
$V6$	.163	.869
$V7$	.573	.645

Extraction Method: Principal Component Analysis.
[a]2 components extracted.

Inspection of this matrix will reveal that the first factor has positive (and generally reasonably substantial) loadings from all variables, while the second factor has a combination of positive and negative loadings. This pattern is typical of Principal Components analyses (and others too) unless there are a substantial number of negative correlations in the correlation matrix. In all Principal Components analyses, all factors after the first will have a combination of positive and negative loadings in the initial factor matrix.

If you were to square the factor loadings and sum the squares of these loadings over the number of variables for each factor, you would find that the resulting sum equals the eigenvalue for that factor. That is, $.836^2 + .824^2 + ... + .573^2 = 3.281$. In short, the eigenvalue is the sum of the squares of the factor loadings for each Principal Components factor. Moreover, if you were to square each factor loading and sum it over the factors for each variable, you would find that this results in the communality for that variable. That is $.836^2 + (−.295)^2 = .785$. In short, the communality for a variable is the sum of the squares of the factor loadings for that variable.

Reproduced Correlation and Residual Correlation Matrix.   This section presents the reproduced correlation matrix and the residual correlation matrix. A researcher often would not output this information. It was done here for explanatory purposes. The diagonal values in the top matrix are the communalities, and these are identical to those presented in the preceding table. Note that the diagonal values are marked by a superscript b. Such marking is not necessary in the small matrix presented here, but for large matrices this notation makes it easier to identify the diagonal. Also, note that footnote b indicates that these diagonal values are the communalities.

Reproduced Correlations

		$V1$	$V2$	$V3$	$V4$	$V5$	$V6$	$V7$
Reproduced Correlation	$V1$	.785[b]	.824	.717	.753	.111	−.120	.289
	$V2$	.824	.889[b]	.708	.792	−.030	−.264	.177
	$V3$	.717	.708	.732[b]	.684	.358	.133	.486
	$V4$	.753	.792	.684	.722[b]	.094	−.127	.266
	$V5$	.111	−.030	.358	.094	.871[b]	.791	.780
	$V6$	−.120	−.264	.133	−.127	.791	.782[b]	.654
	$V7$	.289	.177	.486	.266	.780	.654	.745[b]

Reproduced Correlations (*continued*)

		V1	V2	V3	V4	V5	V6	V7
Residual[a]	V1		−.079	−.033	−.110	−.030	.005	.023
	V2	−.079		.000	−.015	−.020	.066	−.028
	V3	−.033	.000		−.168	.020	.016	−.136
	V4	−.110	−.015	−.168		.025	.005	.027
	V5	−.030	−.020	.020	.025		−.089	−.062
	V6	.005	.066	.016	.005	−.089		−.129
	V7	.023	−.028	−.136	.027	−.062	−.129	

Extraction Method: Principal Component Analysis.

[a]Residuals are computed between observed and reproduced correlations. There are 8 (38.0%) nonredundant residuals with absolute values > 0.05.

[b]Reproduced communalities

The reproduced correlation matrix is obtained by applying the equation for the Fundamental Theorem (see p. 239) to the factor loadings presented in the initial factor matrix. That is, the reproduced correlation between Variables 1 and 2 is (.836)(.824) + (−.295)(−.458) = .824; that between Variables 5 and 7 is (.426)(.573) + (.831)(.645) = .780. This matrix of correlations is that accounted for by the factor analysis. To determine how well the original correlation matrix is accounted for by the factor analysis, we could compute the residual correlation matrix by subtracting each value in the reproduced correlation matrix from the corresponding value in the original (observed) correlation matrix. This produces the residual correlation matrix, presented in the bottom matrix. Thus, the residual value for the correlation between Variables 1 and 2 is .744 − .824 = −.079. (This is not an arithmetic error. It is true that .744 − .824 = −.080, but the computer carries all values to a large number of decimal places, thus the difference between −.079 and −.080 is due to rounding.) If the solution describes most of the relationships in the original matrix, these residual values should be close to 0. To provide a rough index of the adequacy of the fit, **SPSS WINDOWS FACTOR** counts the number of residuals that have an absolute value greater than .05. In footnote *a* to the table example, it states that 8 of the 21 correlations (38.0%) exceed .05.

A note also should be made about possible differences between the table you might produce if you were to run this example and the table as shown here. The default output makes use of floating point arithmetic for very small (and large numbers). In the original output for this table the residual correlation between variable 1 and 2 was shown as −7.9 E−.02, which is read as $−7.9 \times 10^{-2} = −.079$. *You can change the floating point arithmetic in* **SPSS** *by double-clicking the mouse while the cursor is in the table containing these numbers.* This puts the table in the edit mode (indicated by a fuzzy border around the whole table). *Then by moving your cursor so that it is in a numeric field in the table, click the right mouse.* This brings up a menu. *Left click on* **Select Table.** This will result in the table turning black. *Again, with your mouse in a numeric field, click on the right mouse.* This brings up another table. *Left click on* **Cell properties.** *This will produce a Window. Left click on #.#, and this will open a window asking for the number of decimal values. Type in the number (three was used in this example), and left click the mouse.* All values in the table will now appear with the number of decimal values indicated, and there will be no floating point values. *Click on the table to exit the* **Edit** *mode, and click outside the table to unselect the table.* This procedure can be used for all tables if desired.

Rotated Factor Matrix.   This section presents the results obtained after the initial factor matrix is rotated to produce a more parsimonious (easier to interpret) solution. In this example, the Varimax solution was used. The resulting factor matrix (structure matrix) is sometime referred to as the Varimax matrix, or as in the **SPSS WINDOWS FACTOR** output, as the Rotated Component Matrix. The output also indicates how many iterations were required to obtain the maximum fit (the maximum permitted by default in **SPSS WINDOWS FACTOR** is 25).

Rotated Component Matrix[a]

	Component	
	1.000	**2.000**
$V1$	.885	.044
$V2$	.936	−.112
$V3$	.795	.318
$V4$	.849	.029
$V5$	.079	.930
$V6$	−.179	.866
$V7$	.286	.814

Extraction Method: Principal Component Analysis.
Rotation Method: Varimax with Kaiser Normalization.
[a]Rotation converged in 3 iterations.

The Component Transformation Matrix is that matrix which, when multiplied with the initial factor matrix, produces the rotated matrix. This Factor Transformation Matrix has no interpretative value. All the interpretation is based on the Rotated Factor Matrix.

Component Transformation Matrix

Component	1	2
1	.925	.379
2	−.379	.925

Extraction Method: Principal Component Analysis.
Rotation Method: Varimax with Kaiser Normalization.

The rotated factor matrix is obtained by rotating the initial factor matrix. The figure below shows a plot of the variables in terms of both the initial factor matrix (using the axes I and II), and the rotated factor matrix (using the axes I′ and II′).

This figure is obtained by plotting a point to represent each variable on the two factors. The plot is actually done using axes I and II, and the rotation is done subsequently. The values plotted are the factor loadings from the initial factor matrix. Thus, the coordinates for Variable 1 are .836 and −.295, while those for Variable 7 are .573 and .645. One thing that stands out from an examination of Figure 1 is that the axes corresponding to Factors I and II do not fall very close to the points. The purpose of rotation is to bring the axes closer to the points. When an orthogonal rotation is performed, the restriction is imposed that the rotated axes must be kept at right angles to each other.

The rationale underlying the Varimax criterion is that the rotation will be continued until the sum of the variances of the squared factor loadings for each factor is as large as possible. For each factor, the variance would be large when, given the restrictions imposed by the location of points, some of the squared factor loadings are large while others are small (thus producing a structure like that described earlier as simple structure). Under these conditions, the rotated axes will be as close as possible to some of the points.

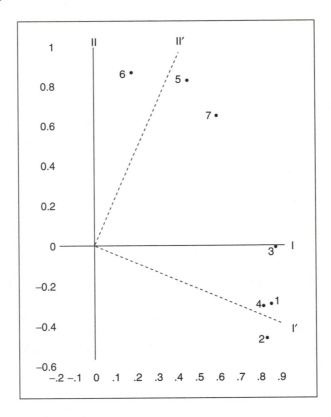

The figure shows the factors produced by the Varimax procedure. The rotated factors are indicated by the broken lines and are labelled I' and II' respectively. The rotated loadings are obtained by reading off the values of the coordinates from these new axes. Thus, the rotated factor loadings for Variable 1 are .885 and .044 for Factors I' and II', respectively; those for Variable 7 are .286 and .814. Viewed from the perspective of the rotated factors, it can be seen that Variables V1, V2, V4, and to some extent V3 are quite close to Factor I', while Variables V5, V6, and V7 are closest to Factor II'. That is, these axes are closer to clusters of points than are the unrotated axes (I, and II). Both sets of axes, I and II on the one hand, and I' and II' on the other, can be used to locate the points in space. And the location of the points in space is fixed. All that differs is the frame of reference used to describe the location of the points in space. Generally, since the points are closer to the rotated axes, many feel that this is the more parsimonious (i.e., simplest) way of describing the data. Depending on one's purposes, however, one might favor the unrotated axes. The important point is that they are simply two different ways of describing the same data.

By drawing both the rotated and unrotated axes in this figure, we can see the relation of the varimax solution to the principal components solution for these data. Ordinarily, the rotated factors would not be superimposed on the figure depicting the principal components solution. It is more the case that a separate figure would be drawn showing the rotated solution.

Interpretation of Rotated Factor Loadings

The Varimax matrix is interpreted by considering each factor and determining what is common to all the variables that load highly on a factor and not common to all the variables obtaining low loadings. To begin answering this question, one must first determine what constitutes a high loading. Many researchers use .30 as a cut-off. Others temper this as a function of the sample size. Thus, if the sample size were 100 or more, they might consider .30; if it were less, they might choose a higher number such as .40 or .50.

If we were to choose .50 because of the very small sample size (20) in this example, we might make the following observations. Factor I obtains high loadings (i.e., greater than ± .50) from four variables, *viz.,* Variables 1 to 4. Since each of these variables involve a measure of arithmetic skills, we might feel that Factor I is best characterized as representing *Quantitative Skill.* That is, we propose that since Variables 1 to 4 are tests of Addition, Subtraction, Multiplication and Division respectively, high levels of proficiency in all of these measures indicate high levels of quantitative skill. If Variables 5 to 7 also involved measures of arithmetical operations, this characterization might not seem that reasonable since Variables 5 to 7 do not also contribute very much to this factor. However, as we saw, Variables 5 to 7 measure skill in the proper use of Nouns, Adverbs, and Adjectives, and it is reasonable to expect that they would not also contain high levels of quantitative skill. Considering the nature of the variables, and the loadings on Factor I, its identification as a *Quantitative Skill* dimension seems quite reasonable.

Factor II obtains high loadings from Variables 5 to 7. Since each of these measure proficiency in English grammar, it seems meaningful to define Factor II as a *Verbal Skill* dimension. The reasoning for the definition of this factor follows the same logic as that used for Factor I. One might quibble as to the name, preferring instead *Grammatical Sensitivity,* or *English Proficiency,* etc., but the fact remains that these three measures correlate highly with Factor II while the others do not. Hence, Factor II is interpreted in terms of what is believed to be common to these three measures and different from Variables 1 to 4.

Since this is a Varimax rotation, we would further conclude that these two factors, *Quantitative Skill* and *Verbal Skill* are independent of one another. Note, however, if we had adopted a cutoff value of .30, we might conclude that there is some small component of *Verbal Skill* in Variable 3 (the Multiplication test), or we might wish to redefine Factor II to characterize it in terms of that which would be common to measures of Noun, Adverb and Adjective use as well as Multiplication skill. In any event, Variable 3's contribution to Factor II is relatively slight. We might also wish to make similar observations about the contribution of Variable 7 (Adjective Use) to Factor I. The point is the cut-off values are arbitrary to some extent, and factor interpretation is more of an art than a science (whatever that might mean). With this particular data set, it is unlikely that many researchers would make these extended interpretations, however, if the sample size were 300, such speculations might be of interest. If nothing else, they might cause the researcher to look more closely at the measures of Variables 3 and 7, or perhaps to examine the possible connections between measures of multiplication and Verbal Skills, and between measures of Quantitative Skills and adjective use.

The figure on the facing page shows a graphical depiction of the components of Variable 3 as demonstrated in our analysis.

The Varimax rotated factor loadings were .795 and .318 for Factors I and II respectively. The squares of these values are .631 and .101, thus a factor analyst would conclude that for Variable 3 (Multiplication), 63.1% of it is composed of Quantitative Skill, 10.1% of Verbal Skill, and the remaining 26.8% of other factors not identified in this study or to error. This is shown in the Pie Diagram. *Quantitative Skill* is shown to account for .631 of the pie, while *Verbal Skill* accounts for .101, and Other and Error accounts for .268 of it. It is conceivable that the bulk of the "Other and Error" could be due simply to errors of measurement and random errors operating during testing. On the other hand, it might be due to a factor that we have not included in our investigation. With the data we have presented here, it is not possible to determine which alternative is correct. There are, however, ways of doing so, though their discussion is beyond the scope of this Chapter.

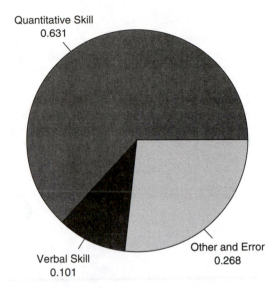

Quantitative Skill
0.631

Verbal Skill
0.101

Other and Error
0.268

Schematic Representation of the Components of Variable 3 (Multiplication)

Another point that should be emphasized is that the factor structure obtained in any investigation is only an estimate of the structure in the population. And the stability of this estimate is heavily influenced by the size of the sample. If we were to perform another investigation, even using only the same measures as in this example, we would not obtain identical results because of differences due to sampling fluctuations. Obviously, if our sample size was 300, the results would be much more stable than they are for the sample of 20 students that we used in this example. Moreover, if we were to add some other variables, the factor structure could change, particularly if these additional variables represented another factor.

Chapter 11
Multivariate Analysis of Variance

Multivariate Analysis of Variance refers to a class of analysis of variance procedures where the effects of one or more factors on a number of dependent variables are assessed. It is similar to the univariate analysis of variance with which you are already familiar, though there are, of course, differences. The major difference is that in a univariate analysis of variance there is only one dependent variable while there can be many dependent variables in a multivariate analysis of variance. Another difference is that multivariate analysis of variance appears much more esoteric. It has many rather mystical concepts associated with it, with names such as **eigenvalue, discriminant function**, **canonical variate** and the like, Greek letters like λ (lower case lambda), Λ (upper case lambda) and Π (upper case pi, a symbol indicating a multiplicative function), and the matrix algebra underlying the technique is more complex than the simple arithmetic for univariate analysis of variance. Yet another difference is that there are a number of apparently different tests of significance of the same effect rather than the single F-ratio for each effect in univariate analysis of variance. And finally, to add to the complexity, **SPSS WINDOWS** currently has two programs, **GLM** and **MANOVA,** that perform multivariate analyses of variance providing some elements of different output in each analysis that might be of interest to researchers. Currently, one of these programs, **GLM,** is accessible through Windows (with their associated clicking and hoping), while the other, **MANOVA** is run directly from the Syntax Window. The net result is that multivariate analysis of variance can appear very mysterious. In this chapter, however, we plan to show that the basic concepts are, in fact, rather straightforward and that the technique can be used quite easily. You will also recall that we discussed special applications of multivariate analysis of variance in our discussions of Single-Factor Repeated Measures Designs (Chapter 5), and Split-Plot Analysis of Variance (Chapter 6).

AN ILLUSTRATIVE EXAMPLE OF THE DIFFERENCE

In order to understand the basic difference between univariate and multivariate analysis of variance, consider an example of an experiment involving a completely randomized single-factor analysis of variance. Such an experiment might involve four levels of a treatment factor, such as four different strategies used to learn a list of words. Subjects would be randomly assigned to one of four conditions using either (a) rote learning, (b) visual imagery, (c) verbal learning strategies or (d) a control (no specific method) condition, and would be instructed in the use of the strategy to which they had been assigned. In this case then, the independent variable (or treatment factor) would be Type of Learning Strategy and the dependent variable might be the number of trials necessary to learn the words so that they could be recited without error. These data would be analyzed using the **SPSS WINDOWS** program **ONEWAY.** As you will recall from Chapter 3, this program presents a basic output consisting of an analysis of variance summary table which includes an F-ratio for the Treatment Factor. If this F-ratio is significant, researchers generally make use of some post hoc test of means to identify which treatment means, if any, differ significantly from one another.

Suppose, however, that the researcher was interested in studying the effects of these four different treatment conditions on not only the number of trials necessary to learn the words, but also the mean number of errors made while learning, and the total amount of time spent on learning the words. One possibility would be to do three separate single-factor analyses of variance using ONEWAY. Another is to recognize that since there are three dependent variables, the problem is no longer a univariate one; it is now a multivariate one. In this event, one would analyze these data as a multivariate analysis of variance and use either the **SPSS** program **GLM** or **MANOVA.** The output for these programs includes both multivariate and univariate tests of significance of both the constant and the Treatment Factor. Moreover, for the tests of multivariate effects, both programs provide not one, but four F-ratios for the Multivariate effects. On the output, these statistics are referred to as **Pillai's Trace, Hotelling's Trace, Wilks' Lambda,** and **Roy's Largest Root.** Examination of the output for the univariate effects, however, will reveal that they are the same as those obtained if each dependent variable had been analyzed separately using **SPSS WINDOWS ONEWAY.**

A BIT OF HISTORY

The history of multivariate analysis of variance parallels that of univariate analysis of variance and is not that much more recent. We saw in earlier chapters that, although the rationale underlying the t-test was developed in 1908, it wasn't used until 1925. And it was in 1925 that Fisher introduced the fundamentals of analysis of variance. We saw too that the t-test is a special case of the single factor analysis of variance, and that Hotelling (1931) developed the multivariate generalization of the t-test (which has come to be known as Hotelling's T^2) to compare two groups on a number of dependent variables simultaneously. A year later, Wilks (1932) published the multivariate extension of analysis of variance. Thus, there are parallels, and the history of the multivariate analogues is almost as long as that of their univariate counterparts. There is a difference of less than 10 years in the ages of the univariate and multivariate versions of this class of statistics.

Despite their similarities in age, multivariate analysis of variance is not as well known to researchers as is univariate analysis of variance. The growth of multivariate analysis of variance was hampered much more by the complexity of the underlying mathematics than were the univariate analogues. It is generally recognized (cf. Cowles, 1989) that the popularity of analysis of variance procedures was delayed somewhat by the nature of Fisher's writing. A textbook by Snedecor (1937) is generally regarded as a much more readable source. Cowles retells the story of a European researcher who told an American colleague, "When you see Snedecor again, tell him that over here we say, 'Thank God for Snedecor; now we can understand Fisher.'"

The same criticisms might well be levelled at earlier presentations of multivariate analysis of variance, and it is difficult to determine just who the "Snedecor" of the multivariate procedures was. In the preface to his influential book, Morrison (1967) claims that his book could be used at an undergraduate or graduate level in the "sciences," claiming that the "mathematical and statistical prerequisites are minimal" (p. vii). This is certainly true enough, but many students in the social sciences would still find it rough going. In the last 10 years or so, there has been an increase in the number of textbooks that help the student and researcher to work through the intricacies of multivariate analysis of variance (see for example, Stevens, 1986; Tabachnick & Fidell, 1989).

More to the point, the availability of computer packages such as **SPSS, SAS,** and **BMDP** brought multivariate analysis of variance into greater use. Another publication that has served to increase the use of multivariate analysis of variance is that by Hummel and Sligo (1971). They demonstrated that if a researcher had a number of dependent variables and employed univariate analysis of variance data analytic procedures, the Type I error associated with the experiment as a whole (i.e., the experimentwise error rate) could be controlled if the univariate analyses of variance were preceded by a significant multivariate effect. Subsequent to this publication, many journal editors requested multivariate analyses in such situations simply to control Type I error and, although this is a limited use of multivariate analysis of variance, it has served to introduce researchers to the technique. It remains to be seen whether researchers will interpret the multivariate results now that some computer programs provide the information to permit such interpretation.

BASIC RATIONALE

The purpose of a multivariate analysis of variance is to analyse a set of dependent variables in an analysis of variance design as a set, as opposed to each dependent variable separately. Basically, as we will see in more detail later, multivariate analysis of variance asks the question as to whether or not there is at least one way of combining the dependent variables to see whether the combination differs as a function of the different levels of the treatment factor. This combination is called a *discriminant function* (or a *canonical variate* or *super variable*) and is simply a weighted aggregate (sum) of the scores of the form:

$$V = w_1 X_1 + w_2 X_2 + w_3 X_3$$

where: V is the score for an individual on the weighted aggregate of the dependent variables, w_1, w_2, etc . . . , are weights assigned to each dependent variable and are determined in such a way as to make the means of V as different as possible for the treatment groups, X_1, X_2, etc . . . , are the individuals' scores on each dependent variable.

Viewed in this way, V could be viewed as a type of super variable (cf. Tabachnick & Fidell, 1989). In psychology, we often calculate totals of items, etc., to form a variable. We are doing the same thing here, except that the elements may not be items, and the elements are weighted to maximize the differences between the groups on the total score.

Although the example described above refers to a single factor analysis of variance, multivariate analysis of variance can be used with any type of design when there is more than one dependent variable. That is, it is appropriate to a completely randomized single factor analysis of variance, a factorial design, a split plot analysis of variance, a repeated measures design, or a randomized blocks factorial design, etc. In each case, it is comparable to the corresponding univariate design except that it has more than one dependent variable. We saw too that multivariate analysis of variance can be used instead of the univariate analysis where there are repeated measures, as in the single factor repeated measures analysis of variance design (Chapter 5) or the split plot design (Chapter 6).

Why Perform a Multivariate Analysis of Variance?

There are two reasons for performing a multivariate analysis of variance. The most frequently used one in psychology is to control for Type I error. That is, the general rationale underlying any test statistic is that if the null hypothesis is true, one would expect that statistic to exceed some specified value less than a given percentage of the time on the basis of chance. Thus, assuming an alpha level of .05, whenever one does a single factor analysis of variance, there is a 5% chance of rejecting the null hypothesis when it's true. If you did two independent analyses of variance, however, your chance of obtaining significant results on at least one of the analyses would be roughly .05 + .05 or $(2)(.05) = .10$. That is, although the Type I error for the analysis is only 5%, the experimentwise Type I error is approximately 10%. With three independent analyses of variance, the experimentwise Type I error is about 15% and so on. That is, the chances of finding at least one significant effect increases as the number of independent analyses of variance increases (though not, strictly speaking, multiplicatively as suggested by the example). Of course, when you have to perform a number of univariate analyses of variance on different dependent measures, these analyses are not independent of one another so the above example doesn't apply exactly (for more detail, see Hummel & Sligo, 1971). But it is the case that the experimentwise error rate will be greater than 5% nevertheless.

There is a way of controlling the experimentwise error rate when you have a number of dependent variables. Hummel and Sligo (1971) conducted a Monte Carlo investigation and found that, if one first performed a multivariate analysis of variance and considered the univariate tests only if the multivariate test was significant ($p < .05$), then the experimentwise Type I error rate was kept at 5%. This is true, of course, because multivariate analysis of variance performs only one analysis for each effect on the set of dependent variables, thus setting the experimentwise Type I error rate for each effect at .05. If one adopts this strategy, then, once it has been demonstrated that there is a significant multivariate effect, a researcher can proceed to perform the univariate analyses of variance and evaluate each one with alpha = .05.

The second (but less frequently used in psychology) reason for conducting a multivariate analysis of variance is to capitalize on the power associated with considering the set of dependent variables as a unit. The basic rationale underlying the multivariate test is one in which a weighted aggregate of the dependent variables is formed where the weights assigned to each variable are chosen so as to make the various groups (in our example above, there were four groups) as different as possible on the aggregate. In short, if there is a possible difference to be found in the set of dependent variables, the multivariate analysis of variance should find it, while at the same time controlling the Type I error rate for the collection of variables if no effect exists. A significant multivariate effect indicates that there is at least one way of combining the dependent variables into a weighted aggregate that differentiates among the groups. With single factor designs, at least, it is possible that by studying the nature of the weighted aggregates [referred to as *discriminant functions* or *canonical variates* (or *super variables* by Tabachnick & Fidell, 1989)], you can sometimes gain an insight into the effects of the treatment on this composite variable. In this chapter, the terms discriminant function and canonical variate are used interchangeably, but you can think of it simply as a super variable!

These two approaches to multivariate analysis of variance have somewhat different purposes, and in **SPSS WINDOWS** are best conducted using different programs, as follows:

1. If the primary intent of performing the analysis is to control for Type I error because of the use of more than one dependent variable, one wishes to present the multivariate results and follow them with the univariate results. If that is all that is intended, **SPSS WINDOWS GLM** provides all the information that is required. In this approach, the researcher would first present the test of significance for the multivariate effects. If the multivariate test was significant, the researcher can proceed to discuss the univariate effects. If the multivariate test were not significant, however, it would not be meaningful to consider any of the univariate F-ratios that had significance values less than .05 as being significant. These apparently significant F-ratios would be interpreted as reflecting Type I error (cf. Hummel & Sligo, 1971). Thus, with this purpose, the information that is needed includes the test of significance for the multivariate effect, the tests of significance for each of the univariate effects, and possibly post hoc tests of the means for the univariate effects. **SPSS WINDOWS GLM Multivariate** provides all of this (though the production of the post hoc tests is not discussed in this chapter), as well as information about the power and proportion of variance accounted for by the multivariate and univariate effects.

2. If one is performing the multivariate analysis of variance to obtain information concerning the canonical variates (the second reason discussed above), further considerations are required. This would involve a presentation of the significant multivariate effect (as above), but this would then be followed by an assessment of the significance of the canonical variates, and interpretation of any that were significant. The relevant information for this is not output by **SPSS WINDOWS GLM Multivariate** but can be obtained using **SPSS WINDOWS MANOVA.** Researchers may also want to follow up any discussion of the canonical variates by a presentation of the univariate effects as discussed in the preceding paragraph, and **SPSS WINDOWS MANOVA** also presents the information to permit this.

An Example

We will focus our attention on a Single Factor Multivariate Analysis of Variance though, as indicated above, the procedure can be used for any type of design. For any given analysis, if there are *a* treatment levels and *p* dependent variables, there are a number of possible canonical variates (i.e., weighted aggregates) that can potentially differentiate the groups. Moreover, the canonical variates will be independent of each other. The number of such aggregates will be the lesser of $(a - 1)$ or p. Thus, if there were $a = 3$ treatment levels and $p = 3$ dependent variables, there are $(a - 1) = 2$ possible canonical variates.

Consider an example where there are four treatment conditions and four dependent variables. The data could appear as follows:

Treatment 1				Treatment 2				Treatment 3				Treatment 4			
$X1$	$X2$	$X3$	$X4$	$X1$	$X2$	$X3$	$X4$	$X1$	$X2$	$X3$	$X4$	$X1$	$X2$	$X3$	$X4$
3	11	15	15	9	11	14	13	10	17	14	13	4	12	11	16
4	16	14	12	4	8	13	16	3	10	12	15	4	12	12	13
6	17	16	12	3	7	12	15	11	16	12	14	5	14	12	14
4	14	17	14	2	6	16	11	2	13	15	16	6	15	13	12
1	6	15	15	8	13	13	12	9	14	12	14	7	14	14	12

Assume that the four treatments were four different ways of motivating individuals to learn (No Incentive, Ridicule for Errors, Praise for Success, and Monetary Reward) and that the dependent measures were $(X1)$ Evaluation of the Task, $(X2)$ Evaluation of the Experimenter, $(X3)$ Number of Errors, and $(X4)$ Self-rated Depression. Thus, in this study, the researcher may hypothesize that these different motivational techniques might influence not only how difficult it is for individuals to learn the material but also their feelings of Depression and evaluation of the task and the experimenter.

USING SPSS WINDOWS GLM MULTIVARIATE

As indicated earlier, there are two programs that can be used in **SPSS WINDOWS** to analyze this type of data. If a researcher is interested only in determining whether there are significant multivariate effects, and then identifying the significant univariate effects, the program **GLM** provides all the necessary information. This section will focus on the use of this program. The following instructions assume that the data were typed into an ASCII (Text) file with the level of a, and the four dependent scores on each line, and that the file was on the A Drive in a file called **mandat.dat.**

Steps in Using SPSS WINDOWS GLM Multivariate

These data are analyzed using the **GLM Multivariate** program. The following steps are applicable to **SPSS 8.0** and **SPSS 9.0** except for the input of the ASCII or Text data file. In the example to follow you are instructed at Step 3 to input your data following the procedures described in Chapter 1. The output for this example was obtained by using the freefield format in **SPSS 8.0,** and depending upon the input procedure you use, the output may be somewhat different. The answers are the same, however. Using the **Syntax Editor,** you could simply type the Syntax file [the set of instructions required to run the procedure, including the relevant Data List and Execute statements (see page 30)], and then execute the job from inside the **Syntax Editor** (not discussed here). Instead, we will use the program itself to create the syntax file. This latter procedure involves using the **clope** procedure, whereby you make use of the mouse to bring up a number of windows, and then select the appropriate options or type in the required information.

1. *Enter SPSS WIN.* This presents you with the SPSS **Data Editor** (see figure in Chapter 2, p. 46). At this point, you could begin to type in the data. However, we will assume here that

you already have the data in a file on the A Drive, that this file is labelled **mandat.dat,** and that the data are in freefield or delimited format. For each participant there would be five values, the level of the between groups factor (labelled **a** in our example), and the scores on the four dependent measures.

2. *Click on **File** in the upper row of selections.* This will present you with a drop-down menu with a series of choices.

3. *Enter your ASCII (**SPSS 8.0**) or Text (**SPSS 9.0**) data file by following the steps on pages 17 to 20 for **SPSS 8.0**, or pages 20 to 28 for **SPSS 9.0**.* For this example, the file will consist of five variables labelled **a, X1, X2, X3,** and **X4,** respectively.

4. *Click on the **Statistics** (**SPSS 8.0**) or **Analyze** (**SPSS 9.0**) option on the menu bar.* This presents you with a drop-down menu. *Move your cursor to **General Linear Model,** and you are presented with another menu to the right with a choice of the following:*

   SPSS 8.0   **SPSS 9.0**
   GLM-General Factorial . . .   Univariate
   GLM-Multivariate . . .   Multivariate
   GLM-Repeated Measures . . .   Repeated Measures
   Variance Components . . .   Variance Components

5. *Click on **GLM-Multivariate.*** This presents you with the Window, **GLM Multivariate,** and the variable **a** (or whatever you named the first variable) is highlighted (see figure below).

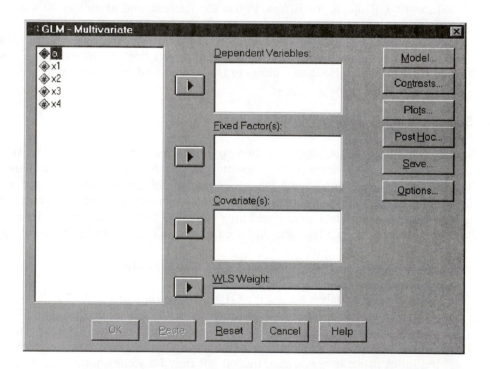

*Add this (i.e., **a**) to the **Fixed Factors** by clicking on the appropriate arrow. Then move your cursor to **x1**, hold down the left button of the mouse and drag the cursor down until all of **x1, x2, x3,** and **x4** are highlighted then click on the arrow for dependent variables.*

6. At this point, you have a number of choices, **MODEL, CONTRASTS, PLOTS, POST HOC, SAVE** and **OPTIONS.** If you click on **MODEL,** this provides a Window which allows you to choose between different models. Where sample sizes are equal, this will have no effect on the analysis. Hence, we will not discuss it here. The default model is **SSTYPE3,** which corresponds to the Unique Sums of Squares Model (Overall & Spiegel, 1969, Model I), which is often

considered the most appropriate when you have unequal sample sizes (but see the discussion of the different models in Chapter 4).

7. The only choice we will use here is **Options.** *Click on **Options.*** This presents the **GLM-Multivariate: Options** Window (see figure below).

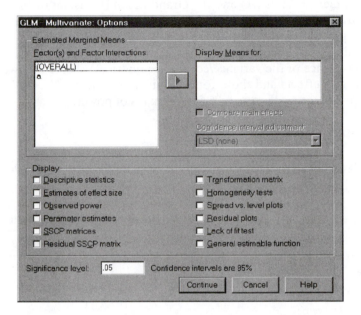

8. *Select the following options by clicking on the small white pane preceding each of:*
   Descriptive Statistics
   Estimates of Effect Size
   Observed Power
   Homogeneity Tests
   *Then click on **Continue.***

9. This takes you back to the Window, **GLM Multivariate.** *Click on **OK** to run the analysis of variance.*

10. This runs the **GLM** program, and the answers are returned to the **SPSS Output Viewer,** as well as to your monitor. At this point, you can print your answers, save them in a file, or transfer them to some other editor.

11. To exit **SPSS,** *click on **File** (upper row of operations), and click on **Exit.** Before you can exit, however, the program will ask if you wish to save the contents of the **Output Viewer** as well as those of the **Data Editor.** If you have already saved them you will not have to do so again.*

The Syntax File

If you follow the previous instructions, you will create the following Syntax file:

```
GLM
 x1 x2 x3 x4 BY a
 /METHOD = SSTYPE(3)
 /INTERCEPT = INCLUDE
 /PRINT = DESCRIPTIVE ETASQ OPOWER HOMOGENEITY
 /CRITERIA = ALPHA(.05)
 /DESIGN = a .
```

The **GLM** statement indicates that the computer is to use the **GLM** program in **SPSS WINDOWS**, and that there are four dependent variables, $x1$, $x2$, $x3$, and $x4$, and one independent variable (a). The METHOD statement indicates that if there are unequal sample sizes, the computer will employ the SSTYPE(3) method to estimate the sums of squares. The GLM program will generate basic information about the multivariate analysis of variance, and will produce output for the Treatment Effects (A) and the Grand Mean (Constant or Intercept). Because of the PRINT statement, the computer will also output a table of **descriptive** statistics, information about eta squared and power in both the univariate and multivariate analysis of variance tables, and two tables concerning tests of homogeneity of variance (one involving Levene's test, and the other Box's test of equivalence of the variance/covariance matrices). There are two levels of output, those for the multivariate effects and those for the univariate effects. The CRITERIA statement indicates that the Type I error rate is set at .05 for estimates of power.

Output

This syntax file yields the following basic output. The first table defines the levels of the Treatment factor, and the number of observations in each level.

Between-Subjects Factors

		N
A	1.00	5
	2.00	5
	3.00	5
	4.00	5

The next table presents the means, standard deviations and sample sizes for the four dependent variables, $X1$, $X2$, $X3$ and $X4$ for each of the four treatment levels of A. It also presents the grand mean, standard deviation and sample size (labelled "Total") for each dependent variable. It is informative to review all of this information to look for any irregularities such as large variation in sample sizes or standard deviations that, as we have already seen in earlier chapters, can influence the validity of the univariate results. (They can also influence the validity of the multivariate results.) In addition, the information about the means will be needed in some calculations necessary to interpret the univariate effects (see below).

Descriptive Statistics

	A	Mean	Std. Deviation	N
$X1$	1.00	3.6000	1.8166	5
	2.00	5.2000	3.1145	5
	3.00	7.0000	4.1833	5
	4.00	5.2000	1.3038	5
	Total	5.2500	2.8814	20
$X2$	1.00	12.8000	4.4385	5
	2.00	9.0000	2.9155	5
	3.00	14.0000	2.7386	5
	4.00	13.4000	1.3416	5
	Total	12.3000	3.4504	20

Descriptive Statistics

	A	Mean	Std. Deviation	N
$X3$	1.00	15.4000	1.1402	5
	2.00	13.6000	1.5166	5
	3.00	13.0000	1.4142	5
	4.00	12.4000	1.1402	5
	Total	13.6000	1.6670	20
$X4$	1.00	13.6000	1.5166	5
	2.00	13.4000	2.0736	5
	3.00	14.4000	1.1402	5
	4.00	13.4000	1.6733	5
	Total	13.7000	1.5594	20

Tests of Multivariate Effects. There are four multivariate tests of significance given by **SPSS GLM.** They are Pillai's Trace, Wilks' Lambda, Hotelling's Trace, and Roy's Largest Root, and these tests are made for both the Intercept and the Treatment. The tests of significance for the Intercept simply assesses whether one can compute a canonical variate (V) such that the grand mean deviates significantly from 0. This test is of little if any interest to most researchers in most contexts, and will not be discussed any further. Those for the Treatment Effect (A) are of interest. The computations underlying the four tests of the Treatment Effect differ (see Tables 1 and 2 at the end of this chapter for the defining formulae and sample calculations), but in essence they all have the same meaning. If they are significant, it means the collection of dependent variables differ among the treatment conditions. Following is the table for these tests:

Multivariate Tests[d]

Effect		Value	F	Hypothesis df	Error df	Sig.	Eta-Squared	Noncent. Parameter	Observed Power[a]
Intercept	Pillai's Trace	.998	1902.588[b]	4.000	13.000	.000	.998	7610.353	1.000
	Wilks' Lambda	.002	1902.588[b]	4.000	13.000	.000	.998	7610.353	1.000
	Hotelling's Trace	585.412	1902.588[b]	4.000	13.000	.000	.998	7610.353	1.000
	Roy's Largest Root	585.412	1902.588[b]	4.000	13.000	.000	.998	7610.353	1.000
A	Pillai's Trace	1.396	3.266	12.000	45.000	.002	.465	39.187	.982
	Wilks' Lambda	.141	3.170	12.000	34.686	.004	.479	31.949	.932
	Hotelling's Trace	2.911	2.830	12.000	35.000	.008	.492	33.962	.949
	Roy's Largest Root	1.472	5.522[c]	4.000	15.000	.006	.596	22.087	.913

[a]Computed using alpha = .05

[b]Exact Statistic

[c]The statistic is an upper bound on F that yields a lower bound on the significance level.

[d]Design: Intercept+A

Although the values of the various test statistics for A differ, generally all four tests give comparable results. That is, if one is significant, they all tend to be significant but not necessarily, and not necessarily at the same alpha level. The general consensus, however, is that Pillai's Trace is the most robust in that it is not that affected by violations of assumptions (see Olson, 1976); thus it is recommended here that you use it routinely as the test statistic.

This table also presents values of eta squared, the noncentrality parameter, and observed power for the tests of the Intercept and the Treatment Effects (A). These values are computed for the multivariate effects, but are comparable in meaning to those for univariate effects discussed earlier in Chapters 4, 5, and 6. Moreover, the estimates of eta squared can be computed directly from the F-ratio and the degrees of freedom using the same formula as presented in the earlier chapters (see, particularly, Chapters 5 and 6). The eta squared values indicate the percentage of variance accounted for by the Effects, and differ slightly for the different test statistics for A. Thus, if using Pillai's Trace, the proportion of variance accounted for at the multivariate level is:

$$\eta^2 = \frac{df_1 F}{df_1 F + df_2} = \frac{12(3.266)}{12(3.266) + 45} = .465$$

That is, 46.5% of the variance in the collection of the four dependent variables is accounted for by the different strategies when investigated using Pillai's Trace statistic. The power of detecting a true difference, using this test statistic with Type I error set at .05 is .982. That is, with effects in the population as large as those indicated by this study, the chances are that 98.2% of the time, you would obtain a Pillai's Trace statistic significant at the .05 level.[1]

Tests of Univariate Effects. If the multivariate test is significant, a researcher can go on to consider the univariate F-ratios. These are presented for tests of both the Intercept and the Treatment factor. The univariate tests for the Intercept assesses whether the grand mean for each dependent variable differs significantly from 0, and this is seldom of interest to researchers in psychology. The univariate tests of the Treatment factor are of interest, however. Both sets of tests are presented as follows in the **SPSS GLM** output:

Tests of Between-Subjects Effects

Source	Dependent Variable	Type III Sum of Squares	df	Mean Square	F	Sig.	Eta-Squared	Noncent. Parameter	Observed Power[a]
Corrected Model	$X1$	28.950[b]	3	9.650	1.199	.342	.184	3.596	.261
	$X2$	76.200[c]	3	25.400	2.709	.080	.337	8.128	.546
	$X3$	25.200[d]	3	8.400	4.870	.014	.477	14.609	.819
	$X4$	3.400[e]	3	1.133	.424	.739	.074	1.271	.116
Intercept	$X1$	551.250	1	551.250	68.478	.000	.811	68.478	1.000
	$X2$	3025.800	1	3025.800	322.752	.000	.953	322.752	1.000
	$X3$	3699.200	1	3699.200	2144.464	.000	.993	2144.464	1.000
	$X4$	3753.800	1	3753.800	1403.290	.000	.989	1403.290	1.000
A	$X1$	28.950	3	9.650	1.199	.342	.184	3.596	.261
	$X2$	76.200	3	25.400	2.709	.080	.337	8.128	.546
	$X3$	25.200	3	8.400	4.870	.014	.477	14.609	.819
	$X4$	3.400	3	1.133	.424	.739	.074	1.271	.116

(*Table continued on next page*)

---

[1]It is curious that the formula presented above does not appear to apply to η^2 for Wilks' Lambda (Λ) in this case. Applying the formula yields a value of .523, not .479 as it appears in the table. Moreover, partial η^2 can be defined for Wilks' Lambda as $1 - \Lambda^{1/b}$ where b is as defined in Table 1, page 285. This also yields $\eta^2 = .523$. Finally, applying the formula presented above to the Wilks' Lambdas for multivariate effects reported in Chapter 5, page 123 and Chapter 6, page 143 yields the values reported there. I have no explanation for the discrepancy.

Tests of Between-Subjects Effects

Source	Dependent Variable	Type III Sum of Squares	df	Mean Square	F	Sig.	Eta-Squared	Noncent. Parameter	Observed Power[a]
Error	$X1$	128.800	16	8.050					
	$X2$	150.000	16	9.375					
	$X3$	27.600	16	1.725					
	$X4$	42.800	16	2.675					
Total	$X1$	709.000	20						
	$X2$	3252.000	20						
	$X3$	3752.000	20						
	$X4$	3800.000	20						
Corrected Total	$X1$	157.750	19						
	$X2$	226.200	19						
	$X3$	52.800	19						
	$X4$	46.200	19						

[a]Computed using alpha = .05
[b]R Squared = .184 (Adjusted R Squared = .030)
[c]R Squared = .337 (Adjusted R Squared = .213)
[d]R Squared = .477 (Adjusted R Squared = .379)
[e]R Squared = .074 (Adjusted R Squared = –.100)

This table appears complex (more so because it spans two pages), but it contains some redundant information and in fact is simply a set of four completely randomized single factor analyses of variance. The first section labelled Corrected Model is identical in this example to the third one labelled A, and is simply the information concerning the Treatment Effects for each of the dependent variables. Note that the Sum of Squares for $X1$ is 28.950. This is the sum of squares that you would obtain if you were to conduct an analysis of variance for $X1$ using the **SPSS WINDOWS** program **ONEWAY.** The section labelled Error presents the Within Cells statistics. The Sum of Squares for X1 is 128.800, and is the Sum of Squares for the Within Cells that you would obtain if you were to conduct a completely randomized single factor analysis of variance for the variable X1 as discussed in Chapter 3. The section labelled Corrected Total is the sum of the sums of squares for A and Error for each variable. That is, for $X1$, 157.750 = 28.950 + 128.800. The section labelled "Total" includes the variation from the Intercept, and is generally not referred to in most analysis of variance summary tables. Considering the output for each of the dependent variables, these results demonstrate that, although the multivariate tests indicated that there was a significant effect for A, there was only one significant univariate effect (and that was for Variable $X3$).

This table also presents information about eta squared, the noncentrality parameter, and observed power for the Intercept and the Treatment Effect for each dependent variable. As can be seen, the proportion of variance accounted for by the treatments for $X3$ is .477 (the highest of the values for the dependent variables), and the probability of rejecting the null hypothesis (assuming the Type I error rate was set at .05) was .819 (also the highest of the dependent variables).

Tests of Assumptions. We requested tests of two assumptions concerning homogeneity when we created the syntax file (see step 8, page 267). The first concerns the data at the multivariate level and refers to the null hypothesis that the variance/covariance matrices involving the four dependent measures are the same for the four different treatment groups. This is tested by Box's test of Equality of Covariance Matrices, and the results are presented below.

Box's Test of Equality of Covariance Matrices[a]

Box's M	83.177
F	1.413
$df1$	30
$df2$	704
Sig.	.072

Tests the null hypothesis that the observed covariance matrices of the dependent variables are equal across groups.

[a]Design Intercept+A

This test indicates that Box's M is equal to 83.177, and is not significant [$F(30,704)$ = 1.413, ns]. This suggests that we have no evidence to conclude that the four different variance/covariance matrices are not drawn from populations with identical variance/covariance matrices. This means that we do not have to be too concerned that our test of the multivariate effects (i.e., Pillai's Trace) is biased. One problem with Box's M statistic, however, is that it is sensitive to violations of multivariate normality, and thus even if it is significant, one cannot be sure that the variance/covariance matrices are not equivalent. Also, if sample sizes are equal, violation of the assumption of equivalence of the variance/covariance matrices has little effect, particularly on Pillai's Trace. For all of these reasons, it is generally recommended that this test be used with caution, and primarily only if sample sizes are very disparate (e.g., ratios of 20:1). Under these conditions, it would be necessary to investigate the variance/covariance matrices for each treatment condition to determine whether the sample sizes are positively or negatively related to the discrepancies. A positive relationship would indicate that the Type I error for the multivariate test would be underestimated, while a negative relationship (i.e., small variances/covariances associated with large sample sizes) would inflate the probability of rejecting a true null hypothesis at the multivariate level. With equal sample sizes the test can be ignored. It was introduced here simply because it is produced by **SPSS WINDOWS GLM.**

The second test of homogeneity output by **SPSS WINDOWS GLM** concerns the data at the univariate level and refers to the assumption of homogeneity of variance for each of the dependent variables considered one at a time. This assumption is assessed by Levene's test which was discussed in Chapters 2, 3, and 4. The results for these data are presented below:

Levene's Test of Equality of Error Variances[a]

	F	$df1$	$df2$	Sig.
$X1$	7.427	3	16	.002
$X2$	2.071	3	16	.144
$X3$	.341	3	16	.796
$X4$	1.012	3	16	.413

Tests the null hypothesis that the error variance of the dependent variable is equal across groups.

[a]Design Intercept+A

As can be seen in the table, significant departure from homogeneity of variance was obtained only for the first dependent variable, $X1$, [$F(3,16)$ = 7.427, $p < .002$]. As we saw in earlier chapters, however, if sample sizes are equal as they are in this example, violations of this assumption have little effect on the corresponding univariate F-test for treatment differences. We would thus not be concerned with this violation in this case. Also, as we saw when we considered the univariate tests of significance, only the F-ratio for $X3$ was significant, and there is no indication that homogeneity of variance for this variable was compromised in this example.

USING SPSS WINDOWS MANOVA

SPSS WINDOWS MANOVA cannot be run using the Windows click and hope method. Instead, it is run directly from the Syntax Window. One way to do this is to prepare the syntax file as an ASCII file or text file before entering **SPSS.** We will use that approach here. Assume that we had prepared the following file in ASCII (text) format and it was stored on the A Drive in a file called **manova.sps.** In **SPSS 8.0,** the file would appear as follows:

```
Data list file 'a:mandat.dat' free/a x1 x2 x3 x4.
Manova x1 x2 x3 x4 by a(1,4)
  /discrim=stan raw corr
  /print=signif(multiv, univ, eigen, dimenr)
  /design.
```

In **SPSS 9.0**, the MANOVA lines are the same as in the above example. The data input lines are as follows:

```
Data List file 'a:mandat.dat' free records = 1/a x1 x2 x3 x4.
Execute.
```

We would then *enter **SPSS,** and click on **File** in the Menu Bar. We would then select **Open,** indicate that the file is on the A Drive, and select **manova.sps.** This would appear on the monitor in the **Syntax** window. *We could then click on **Run,** select **all,** and run the analysis. The output would appear in the following order. **SPSS WINDOWS** does not output this information in graphics, but rather in a courier font as a series of lines of information. I have retained that font here so that the output can be distinguished from the explanations that I have interspersed throughout it.

The first section of output reproduces the syntax file, presents a message about the notation to follow, and yields basic information about the data file. The following output was obtained in **SPSS 8.0,** so there may be a few minor differences in **SPSS 9.0.**

```
Data list file 'a:mandat.dat' free/a x1 x2 x3 x4.
Manova x1 x2 x3 x4 by a(1,4)
  /discrim=stan raw corr
  /print=signif(multiv, univ, eigen, dimenr)
  /design.
```

```
The default error term in MANOVA has been changed from WITHIN CELLS to
WITHIN+RESIDUAL. Note that these are the same for all full factorial
designs.

* * * * * * A n a l y s i s   o f   V a r i a n c e * * * * * *

    20 cases accepted.
     0 cases rejected because of out-of-range factor values.
     0 cases rejected because of missing data.
     4 non-empty cells.

     1 design will be processed.
- - - - - - - - - - - - - - - - - - - - - - - - - - - - - - - - - - - - - - -
```

This is followed by the output for the multivariate effects. You will note that this output is comparable (though not presented in as fancy a fashion) to that produced by **GLM** except for the number of decimal places. You will note too that the output provides a set of parameters defined as S, M, and N in the line labelled Multivariate Tests of Significance. These parameters are used in formulae to calculate the F-ratios and associated degrees of freedom (see Tables 1 and 2 at the end of this chapter). The presentation of the values for S, M, and N is followed by the statistics for each of the four tests and the approximate F-ratios, hypothesis (numerator) degrees of freedom, error (denominator) degrees of freedom and alpha levels (labelled Sig. of F) for the first three tests listed. Note that the value of Roy's Largest Root is different from that presented in the output from **GLM,** but that is due to a slight change in the definition of this statistic in the two programs. In **GLM,** Roy's Largest Root is simply the first eigenvalue, while in **MANOVA** it is the equivalent of the eta-squared presented for Roy's Largest Root in **SPSS WINDOWS GLM** (see page 269).

The formulae used to calculate the various statistics are presented in Table 1, and their application to this example is described in Table 2. As Table 1 indicates, the values associated with the statistics differ because they involve different summaries of eigenvalues computed on the data and different formulae for computing the F-ratios and degrees of freedom. These formulae will not be discussed here. The important point is to choose beforehand which test statistic is the one of interest to you, and to use it in making decisions concerning the results obtained. Different researchers choose different test statistics. As indicated earlier, I recommend that you routinely choose Pillai's statistic unless you have good reason to choose one of the others. (A good reason isn't that one of the others is significant, while Pillai's is not).

```
* * * * * * A n a l y s i s   o f   V a r i a n c e - design 1 * * * * * *

EFFECT .. A
Multivariate Tests of Significance (S = 3, M = 0, N = 5 1/2)

Test Name        Value  Approx. F Hypoth. DF   Error DF  Sig. of F

Pillais        1.39644   3.26562     12.00       45.00     .002
Hotellings     2.91099   2.83013     12.00       35.00     .008
Wilks           .14104   3.16971     12.00       34.69     .004
Roys            .59554

- - - - - - - - - - - - - - - - - - - - - - - - - - - - - - - - - - -
```

To now, all we know about the multivariate effects is that they are significant. If a significant multivariate effect is obtained in a single factor design, however, it is sometimes of interest to attempt to interpret the canonical variates. One bit of information necessary in this regard concerns the values of the eigenvalue associated with each canonical variate. As indicated above, a multivariate analysis of variance will produce the lesser of $[(a-1), p]$ independent discriminant functions, and each discriminant function has an eigenvalue associated with it. The eigenvalue is simply a measure of how much the groups differ on the discriminant function in question. If canonical variate scores were obtained for a function on each individual and an analysis of variance was obtained on these scores, the eigenvalue (λ) is:

$$\lambda = \frac{SS_{Treatments}}{SS_{Within}}$$

With the instructions given in the syntax file, **SPSS WINDOWS MANOVA** yields the following output concerning the eigenvalues:

```
Eigenvalues and Canonical Correlations

Root No.    Eigenvalue      Pct.    Cum. Pct.    Canon Cor.

    1          1.472        50.582      50.582        .772
    2          1.016        34.918      85.500        .710
    3           .422        14.500     100.000        .545
```

As can be seen, the first function has an eigenvalue of 1.472, and this function accounts for 50.582% of the relative variation discriminating between the treatment groups [i.e., (1.472/(1.472 + 1.016 + .422))*100 = 50.582]. The eigenvalue for the next discriminant function is 1.016 and it accounts for 34.918% of the variance, while the last eigenvalue accounts for 14.50%. Together, the three discriminant functions account for 100% of the variation in the *sample* data. Note, eigenvalues are always output in decreasing order of magnitude.

The output also provides values for the canonical correlation (labelled Canon. Cor.) for each function. The canonical correlation is another measure of the relation between the treatment factor and the discriminant function, and it always varies from 0 to 1.0. Squaring the canonical correlation provides a value analogous to eta-squared in analysis of variance. In this case, it is a measure of the proportion of variance in the *population* (for the discriminant function) accounted for by the treatment factor. Thus the treatment factor accounts for $.772^2 = .596$ (or 59.6%) of the variance in the first discriminant function, while it accounts for $.710^2 = .504$ (or 50.4%) of the variance in the second discriminant function, and $.545^2 = .297$ (or 29.7%) in the third. Note that whereas the set of percentages of variance referred to in the previous paragraph adds to 100, this set does not. Nor should it! The two are very different conceptually. The first set indicates the relative importance of the discriminant functions for differentiating among the groups. The second set indicates how strongly the treatment conditions differentiate the subjects on the discriminant function in question.

Information for Assessing Multivariate Effects

The statement DISCRIM = STAN RAW CORR presented in the syntax file produces information that is needed to understand the nature of the multivariate effects that were obtained in the study. The addition of DIMENR in the PRINT statement produces the *Dimension Reduction Analysis* which yields a test of whether or not the eigenvalues are significant. This is given in the following output.

```
Dimension Reduction Analysis

Roots         Wilks L.      F       Hypoth. DF   Error DF   Sig. of F

1 TO 3         .14104    3.16971      12.00       34.69       .004
2 TO 3         .34872    3.23586       6.00       28.00       .015
3 TO 3         .70319    3.16573       2.00       15.00       .071
```

The nature of the computations is somewhat complex and will not be discussed in any detail. Suffice it to say that the first line is concerned with testing the significance of the first eigenvalue. In point of fact, the test makes use of all the eigenvalues (in this case, there are three). For this test, the F-ratio is 3.16971 at 12 and 34.69 degrees of freedom. This F-ratio is significant ($p < .004$) indicating that when considering all three canonical variates, there is a significant effect due to the Treatments. The second line of the output presents a test of the significance of the effects of the Treatments on the remaining canonical variates, once the first is removed. This F-ratio is 3.23586 at 6 and 28 degrees of freedom, and it too is significant ($p < .015$). The third line is a test of the significance of the third canonical variate, and it is not significant. In this example, therefore, there were three canonical variates, and the test of significance considering all of them was significant, as was the test of the last two, while the test of the last one was not significant. These three tests, considered together, indicate that the treatments had an effect on the first and second canonical variates but not on the last one.

The next section of output presents a summary of the univariate tests of significance. Note that they are comparable to those presented by **SPSS WINDOWS GLM,** except for differences in the number of decimal points in the output.

```
- - - - - - - - - - - - - - - - - - - - - - - - - - - - - - - - - - - - - - - -
EFFECT .. A (Cont.)
Univariate F-tests with (3,16) D. F.

Variable   Hypoth. SS   Error SS   Hypoth. MS   Error MS       F    Sig. of F

X1          28.95000   128.80000     9.65000    8.05000   1.19876     .342
X2          76.20000   150.00000    25.40000    9.37500   2.70933     .080
X3          25.20000    27.60000     8.40000    1.72500   4.86957     .014
X4           3.40000    42.80000     1.13333    2.67500    .42368     .739
- - - - - - - - - - - - - - - - - - - - - - - - - - - - - - - - - - - - - - - -
```

Computing Centroids on the Canonical Variates

Having determined that the first two eigenvalues were significant, we might wish to determine the nature of each canonical variate. Earlier, it was stated that the canonical variate was a weighted aggregate. For the present example, this would take the form:

$$V = w_1 X_1 + w_2 X_2 + w_3 X_3 + w_4 X_4$$

Expressed this way, the weights are referred to as raw (or unstandardized) discriminant function coefficients. The output yields the following information:

```
EFFECT .. A (Cont.)
Raw discriminant function coefficients
                      Function No.

Variable         1          2          3

X1             .382      -.089      -.421
X2            -.520       .157       .043
X3            -.162      -.793      -.316
X4            -.292      -.132      -.663
```

Thus, the first discriminant function has the form:

$$V = (.382)X_1 + (-.520)X_2 + (-.162)X_3 + (-.292)X_4$$

We will investigate these scores a little later. We will find then that, if we were to compute these scores for each individual in each group and then compute the means of these scores we would have means for the groups on this canonical variate. Rather than do this, however, we can compute the means directly by applying the raw discriminant function coefficients directly to the means of the variables. Thus, these means can be computed by multiplying the means for $X1$, $X2$,

$X3$, and $X4$ for each treatment group by the appropriate weight and adding them together. The means for the four treatment groups on the first canonical variate are:

Treatment 1. $(.382)(3.6) - (.520)(12.8) - (.162)(15.4) - (.292)(13.6) = -11.75$

Treatment 2. $(.382)(5.2) - (.520)(9.0) - (.162)(13.6) - (.292)(13.4) = -8.81$

Treatment 3. $(.382)(7.0) - (.520)(14.0) - (.162)(13.0) - (.292)(14.4) = -10.92$

Treatment 4. $(.382)(5.2) - (.520)(13.4) - (.162)(12.4) - (.292)(13.4) = -10.90$

These means (called centroids) are often adjusted in discriminant function analysis to have a mean of 0, but **SPSS WINDOWS MANOVA** doesn't make this adjustment. This is of little consequence, however, since it doesn't affect the relative differences between the means. Note, the weights generated by **SPSS WINDOWS MANOVA** for this example created negative values for the means. Note too that Treatment 1 (the No Incentive condition) has the lowest mean (-11.75) , while Treatment 2 (Ridicule) has the highest mean (-8.81), and Treatments 3 (Praise) and 4 (Monetary Reward) have intermediate means (-10.92 and -10.90, respectively). Thus, if we could agree on an appropriate label for the canonical variate, we could make a concluding statement about this multivariate effect. To do this, it is necessary to interpret the discriminant function. This is discussed in a later section (see Interpreting Discriminant Functions).

Since the second eigenvalue is significant, we could also calculate the means of the second canonical variate for the four Treatment conditions. In this case, we would use the Raw discriminant function coefficients for the second function. These means are:

Treatment 1. -12.32
Treatment 2. -11.60
Treatment 3. -10.63
Treatment 4. -9.96

Again, note that in this example all of the means for the second canonical variate are negative. Note too that the pattern of means is somewhat different from that obtained with the first canonical variate. In this case, Treatment 1 has the lowest mean and Treatment 4 has the highest mean, with Treatments 2 and 3 intermediate. Clearly, the results are different in this case, which they should be, given that this function is independent of the first.

At this point, it would be nice if we could provide a simple *a posteriori* test of the differences between the group centroids for each canonical variate. One such test exists, the Roy-Bose procedure (see, for example, Marascuilo & Levin, 1983, pp. 324–329), which is typically used to calculate confidence intervals for the centroids to determine whether or not they can be considered representative of the same population centroid. This procedure is beyond the scope of this chapter, however, and in any event it is not used that frequently in psychology. Often, if researchers do wish to compare the centroids between the two groups, they restrict their contrast to verbal description. Thus, assuming that a researcher had identified the nature of the canonical variates (and applied names to them), she/he might discuss the results by simply referring to the values of the centroids. With respect to the first canonical variate, a researcher might say simply that Treatment 2 has the highest centroid which is clearly different from Treatment 1, while Treatment conditions 3 and 4 are intermediate. For the second canonical variate, he/she would state that Treatment 4 has the highest centroid, Treatment 1 has the lowest, and Treatments 2 and 3 are intermediate. Further discussion would rest on the labels applied to the canonical variates and the meaning associated with them.

Computing Individual Scores on the Canonical Variates

As we saw earlier, we could use the raw discriminant function coefficients to create a new variable—a canonical variate, or a super variable for each eigenvalue that is significant. For each individual, we could compute a score on the first canonical variate using the formula:

$$V_{ij1} = (.382)X_1 + (-.520)X_2 + (-.162)X_3 + (-.292)X_4$$

This would produce the following scores for the individuals.

Treatment 1	Treatment 2	Treatment 3	Treatment 4
−11.38	−8.35	−11.08	−11.17
−12.56	−9.41	−10.38	−10.45
−12.64	−8.82	−10.15	−11.40
−12.59	−8.16	−13.10	−11.12
−9.55	−9.31	−9.87	−10.38

If we were to conduct a single factor analysis of variance on these values (using **SPSS WINDOWS ONEWAY,** for example), we would obtain the following results:

Analysis of Variance

Source	df	Sum of Squares	Mean Squares	F Ratio	F Prob.
Between Groups	3	23.5642	7.8547	7.8530	.0019
Within Groups	16	16.0035	1.0002		
Total	19	39.5677			

Note in this output that, as indicated on page xxx, the eigenvalue is nothing more than:

$$\lambda = \frac{SS_{Treatments}}{SS_{Within}} = \frac{23.5642}{16.0035} = 1.472$$

Note too, that the Mean Square Within is 1.00 (with rounding). Moreover, the means of these data correspond to the centroids referred to above. It is tempting to use this information to perform *a posteriori* tests of the centroids as we did with the means following a univariate analysis of variance; however, this would be inappropriate because the centroids are multivariate statistics, and the sampling distributions used with standard *a posteriori* tests are applicable to univariate statistics. Problems associated with the use of univariate sampling distributions with multivariate statistics have been discussed by Neufeld and Gardner (1990).

You might demonstrate these calculations to yourself by performing an analysis of variance on the data for the second function. If you do, you will confirm that the ratio of $SS_{between}$ to SS_{within} is the same as the eigenvalue for the second canonical variate (1.016), and the F-ratio is 5.4211 with 3 and 16 degrees of freedom.

It should be noted that these univariate analyses of variance of the canonical variates are performed here only to give you some idea of the meaning of the eigenvalue. It is not meaningful to perform such analyses because this is a univariate analysis and the canonical variate is a multivariate statistic. Because the sampling distributions of univariate and multivariate statistics are not comparable, it is quite possible to obtain "significant" results with this univariate form of analysis even though the eigenvalue is not significant.

Interpreting Discriminant Functions

There are two sets of information that are typically used when attempting to interpret canonical variates. I say "when attempting to interpret canonical variates" because it must be recalled that each canonical variate is a weighted aggregate that maximally separates the groups. Canonical variates are thus mathematical functions, and not necessarily meaningful measures. As you might imagine, there is some disagreement about the usefulness and meaningfulness of canonical variates, as well as in the way in which they can be interpreted. If one wants to interpret the canonical variates, however, it is generally agreed that attention be directed to either the standardized discriminant function coefficients or the correlations of the variables with the discriminant functions, or both.

Earlier, when we discussed the calculation of the canonical variates you will recall that we weighted the variables by the raw discriminant function coefficients. Thus, it has been recommended that the interpretation of these canonical variates can be ascertained in terms of the magnitude and sign of these coefficients, since these coefficients represent the unique contribution of each variable to the canonical variate. This is generally not recommended any more, however.

The reason for not using the raw discriminant function coefficients to determine the unique contributions of each variable to the aggregate is that the raw coefficients are influenced by the standard deviation of the variables themselves. Some researchers (see, for example, Stevens, 1986) suggest that one can gain information about the redundancy of the variables making up the canonical variate by considering the standardized discriminant function coefficients. That is, variables with relatively large standardized discriminant function coefficients provide non-redundant information to the canonical variate. **SPSS WINDOWS MANOVA** provides the standardized discriminant function coefficients when the syntax file is constructed as shown earlier. It is recommended, therefore, that rather than use the raw discriminant function coefficients for interpretation, one use the standardized discriminant function coefficients instead. These coefficients are simply the raw discriminant function coefficients multiplied by the square root of the Mean Square Within for the respective variables. That is, for $X2$,

$$Standardized\ coefficient = -.520 * \sqrt{9.375} = -1.592$$

By standardizing the coefficients, it puts the coefficients for all of the variables on the same scale, making direct comparisons more meaningful. The standardized discriminant function coefficients for this example are as follows:

```
Standardized discriminant function coefficients
          Function No.
Variable          1          2          3
X1             1.083      -.252     -1.195
X2            -1.592       .482       .130
X3             -.212     -1.042      -.416
X4             -.478      -.216     -1.084
- - - - - - - - - - - - - - - - - - - - - - - - - - - - - - - - - - - - -
```

Thus, for Function I, it can be seen that both $X1$ and $X2$ contribute highly to the definition of the canonical variate, $X1$ positively, and $X2$ negatively. Variables $X3$ and $X4$ make much smaller (and negative) unique contributions. Note, that whether or not we consider the raw discriminant function coefficients or the standardized discriminant function coefficients, the first function is basically a complex difference score in which weighted elements of variables $X2$, $X3$, and $X4$ are subtracted from $X1$. The standardized discriminant function coefficients simply take into account variations due to the standard deviations of the measures. These standardized weights represent the unique contributions of the variables to the canonical variate; thus, one way to interpret the meaning of the canonical variate is to label it based on the variables that make the largest unique contributions to it. That is, to compute this canonical variate, you subtract elements of evaluation of the experimenter, self-ratings of Depression, and the number of errors made on the task from evaluation of the task (see page 265 for identification of the variables). If this type of score has psychological meaning, you could consider the canonical variate as a score almost like any other score you might compute.

Given this, and focussing on the standardized weights, it appears that the first canonical variate is made up largely of Evaluation of the Task ($X1$) minus Evaluation of the Experimenter ($X2$). One might thus interpret the first canonical variate as a measure of *Resultant Positive Affect Toward the Experiment*. Individuals who obtain high scores on this canonical variate have a positive evaluation of the experiment (controlling for Evaluation of the Experimenter). Individuals with low scores have a relatively low impression of the experiment (controlling for Evaluation of the Experimenter). This interpretation ignores the relatively small contributions from Number of Errors ($X3$) and self-rated Depression ($X4$), though the interpretation could be extended to include them.

We could use a similar logic to interpret Function II. Thus, it is defined primarily by low scores on Variable $X3$ (Errors), but with a slight contribution from Evaluation of the Experimenter ($X2$). Individuals with high scores on this canonical variate make relatively few errors and tend to have a positive evaluation of the experimenter. Individuals with low scores would have made many errors and been somewhat critical of the experimenter. We might therefore identify this function as *Rewarded Learning*. Again, this interpretation tends to ignore the small contributions from $X1$ and $X4$ because they add so little to the aggregate, but the interpretation might be extended.

To this point, we have attempted to interpret the canonical variates in terms of the unique contributions of the variables to their definition. Since these refer to unique contributions, however, it is possible that by the nature of the residualization (recall this concept from Multiple Regression, see Chapter 8) the variables may be somewhat different from their original state. Rather than interpreting a canonical variate score solely in terms of how the scores are aggregated, it is generally recommended that this interpretation be substantiated by also examining how the canonical variates correlate with the variables themselves. This requires examination of the within cells correlations between each dependent variable ($X1$, $X2$, $X3$, and $X4$ in this case) and the canonical variates (see, for example, Marascuilo & Levin, 1983; Stevens, 1986; Tabachnick & Fidell, 1989). These correlations, often called structure coefficients, are much like factor loadings in factor analysis and are interpreted in much the same way. Loadings greater in magnitude than .30 are considered in defining the canonical variate (though, obviously, this might be tempered by sample size).

The structure coefficients for this example are given on the **SPSS WINDOWS MANOVA** output as follows:

```
Correlations between DEPENDENT and canonical variables
                   Canonical Variable
Variable           1          2          3
X1               .094       .303      -.530
X2              -.510       .311      -.252
X3              -.244      -.899       .096
X4              -.072       .048      -.406

- - - - - - - - - - - - - - - - - - - - - - - - - - - - - - - - - -
```

The correlations for the first discriminant function are not particularly large, but the suggestion is that the canonical variate correlates negatively with Evaluation of the Experimenter. We defined the first canonical variate as a measure of Resultant Positive Affect Toward the Experiment, and as such we would have expected it to correlate positively with Evaluation of the Task, $X1$ (which it does, but slightly), and negatively with Evaluation of the Experimenter, $X2$. That it correlates primarily negatively with Evaluation of the Experimenter suggests that this Affect is complexly influenced by participants' reactions to the experimenter. We might conclude, therefore, that participants with Resultant Positive Affect Toward the Experiment were those who were relatively dissatisfied with the experimenter. They also tend to make fewer errors ($X3$).

The correlations for the second discriminant function tend to confirm our original definition of the second canonical variate as a measure of Rewarded Learning. The correlations suggest that individuals obtaining high scores on this function tend to make relatively few errors on the task, and also to have slightly elevated impressions of the task, $X1$, and the experimenter, $X2$. We did not attempt to interpret the third function because it will be recalled that the third eigenvalue was not significant.

It should be noted that the sample size in this example is very small, and it is probable that there would be considerable sampling fluctuation in the correlations (and the standardized discriminant function coefficients) that we are interpreting. Much larger sample sizes are usually used when calculating discriminant functions, however, when using them in the context of a multivariate analysis of variance, the structure coefficients are used as a guide to interpretation of the canonical variate.

The important point to remember in all of this is that it is not so much the labels that are applied, but what this analysis of the canonical variates tells you about the results obtained. If we were to focus only on the univariate results, we would conclude that the treatment conditions had an effect only on the number of errors made during learning (i.e., $X3$). But there seems to be more going on than that. It seems likely that the number of errors made is influenced by, or influences, reactions toward the experimenter and/or the task, and these influences are reflected in the multivariate results. It may be that you might choose not to interpret these multivariate results, but they might direct you to conduct further studies to attempt to clarify what they might mean. Alternatively, you may wish to investigate the multivariate effects further.

One possibility is to follow up the multivariate results with further univariate analyses intended to clarify the interpretation. One such analysis you might perform is an analysis of covariance on one of the variables covarying out the effect of one or more of the other variables, thus demonstrating a univariate effect once variation attributable to the other variable(s) is(are) controlled. In this context, such an analysis is referred to as a *step-down analysis,* and it makes the assumption that the variable you choose as the dependent variable is influenced by the one or ones you choose as the covariate(s). A discussion of this is beyond the scope of this chapter, but it shouldn't surprise you to learn that analysis of covariance is one technique often used in multivariate analysis of variance to help clarify the interpretation. If you wish to use this strategy, you are advised to consult textbooks that discuss its use (see, for example, Stevens, 1986: Tabachnick & Fidell, 1989).

Understanding the Reasons for the Results

Rather than considering the multivariate analysis of variance as some form of arithmetic trickery, and the interpretation of canonical variates as arbitrary name calling, you might gain some appreciation of these particular data by considering the original data. Consider the data for $X1$, for example. The means increase from Treatment 1 to 2 to 3, and then decrease at Treatment 4. For $X2$, the pattern is different, decreasing from Treatment 1 to 2, then increasing considerably at Treatment 3, then decreasing slightly. For $X3$, the means decrease fairly steadily from Treatment 1 to 4, while for $X4$, the means for Treatments 1 and 2 are similar; there is a slight increase at Treatment 3, and a return to the previous level at Treatment 4. In short, the patterns of means are all quite different.

It is possible, however, to calculate the correlations among the variables, removing from these correlations any variability associated with the Treatment conditions. This is done by computing the **within cell correlations** (this option is available in **SPSS WINDOWS MANOVA,** though we did not call for it in our example). These correlations are as follows:

	$X1$	$X2$	$X3$	$X4$
$X1$				
$X2$	.78			
$X3$	−.07	.09		
$X4$	−.49	−.54	−.38	

Examination of these correlations will reveal that some of them are not consistent with the pattern of means described above. You will note, for example that although $X1$ and $X2$ correlate quite highly and positively, the pattern of means for these two variables across the four treatment levels is very different. Moreover, $X4$ tends to correlate negatively with both $X1$ and $X2$, and thus, you would expect it to have a pattern that is the opposite of these other variables, but this is not the case. In fact the pattern, though less variable, is comparable to that for $X2$. When the analysis considers the four variables together in the multivariate form, all this information is brought into play, and the net effect is that it is shown that the treatments do appear to have an effect on different combinations of the four variables. This is the essence of the multivariate effect.

OVERVIEW FOR PRESENTING RESULTS

If you are performing a multivariate analysis of variance to control the Type I error, and your intention is to interpret the univariate results, then it is best to use the **SPSS GLM MULTIVARIATE** program. It provides all the results you need, and in addition provides information at both the univariate and multivariate level about the proportions of variance accounted for (eta-squared), as well as the power of the various tests. In the present example, one would state that significant multivariate effects were obtained (Pillai's Trace = 1.396, $F(12,45) = 3.266$, $p<.002$). Since there is a significant effect, this means that one could simply evaluate each univariate F-ratio at the usual alpha level (generally .05). Thus, a researcher would state something to the effect that "Analysis of the univariate effects demonstrated a significant effect for $X3$ ($F(3,16) = 4.870$, $p<.014$)." He/she would then follow this up with post hoc tests of means. In Chapter 3, we recommended the use of the Tukey HSD procedure in such a situation, but we subsequently (Chapters 4, 5, and 6) found that we could make use of a number of other procedures. The same procedures apply here. In fact, **SPSS WINDOWS GLM** also provides post hoc tests of means (though that aspect was not discussed here). To perform such tests, however, *you would select the option **POST HOC** in Step 5 (page 266), or select the relevant options in Step 7 (page 267) after moving the treatment factor (**A**) to **Display Means** and select **compare main effects** in the **GLM Multivariate Options** window shown in this step*.

If you were performing the multivariate analysis of variance in order also to investigate the multivariate effects, then you would want to use the **SPPS WINDOWS MANOVA** program. It does not give information about the power and eta-squared associated with the various tests, but it does provide information necessary to interpret the various canonical variates. This information is particularly useful when dealing with a single factor multivariate analysis of variance. In the present example, you would note that two of the canonical variates were significant. For the first canonical variate, the treatments accounted for 59.6% of the variance. Interpretation of the first canonical variate suggested that it reflected Resultant Positive Affect toward the Experiment, that scores on this canonical variate tended to correlate negatively with attitudes toward the Experimenter, and that it distinguished primarily Treatment 2 (Ridicule) from the other three treatments. That is, those obtaining the Ridicule treatment had less Resultant Positive Affect toward the Experiment than those in the other three treatment conditions. For the second canonical variate, the treatments accounted for 50.4% of the variance. Interpretation of this canonical variate suggested that it tended to reflect Rewarded Learning, that high scores on this variate tended to be associated with few errors in the learning task and positive attitudes toward the experimenter and the task. Examination of the Centroids indicated that it tended to distinguish primarily Treatment 4 (Monetary Reward) from the other three. That is, those in the Monetary Reward condition tended to have lower Rewarded Learning scores than those in the other conditions. Following this, attention could then be directed to a consideration of the univariate effects as discussed in the previous paragraph.

As can be seen, the two approaches to multivariate analysis of variance overlap to a considerable extent. They differ primarily in how they deal with the multivariate effects. In the former case, they are used mostly to control Type I error. In the second, it is assumed that the aggregate scores (the canonical variates, or discriminant functions) have psychological meaning, and thus can be interpreted. These interpretations are not easy to make, as we saw, and sometimes it may be the case that the canonical variates are simply the result of the mathematics, and the complex interplay of the treatments and the dependent variables. If the interpretations are meaningful it should be possible to do follow up research, focussing attention on concepts that are consistent with the aggregate variables. In the context of the present example, this would involve focussing attention on concepts and measures of variables such as Resultant Positive Affect and Rewarded Learning that are something more than the complex aggregate of variables observed in this study. Perhaps the point to be drawn from all of this is that a participant in an experiment can be influenced simultaneously on a number of factors, and attributing effects only to individual variables may provide an incomplete picture. Countering this view is the simplicity of interpreting dependent variables one at a time.

DISCRIMINANT FUNCTION ANALYSIS

The application of multivariate analysis of variance discussed in this chapter is closely linked to a very similar procedure called *discriminant function analysis*. Discriminant Function Analysis can be performed in **SPSS WINDOWS.** This procedure will not be discussed here, but its use is similar to that of GLM. The mathematics underlying multivariate analysis of variance and discriminant function analysis are identical except that in discriminant function analysis, the intent is to use the weighted aggregates to predict the group in which the participant belongs and to count the number of correct identifications. If the proportion of correct identifications is high for each group, then this suggests that you could use the discriminant function with other samples to predict group membership of the participants. That is, the procedure is like multiple regression, except rather than predicting a score on a dependent variable, one is predicting group membership. Moreover, by interpreting the nature of the discriminant functions using the procedures discussed above, one might be able to understand the processes determining group membership.

Consider an example in which a researcher attempts to distinguish between individuals diagnosed as Psychotic, Neurotic or Normal. The underlying hypothesis might be that there are different psychological processes that distinguish between these three groups, and that by administering a battery of tests to large samples of these groups, it might be possible to isolate important causal dimensions. Once these dimensions have been identified, they could be used to identify individuals who potentially belong to one of these different groups. Discriminant Function Analysis could be used in this type of research, though since there are only three groups, it would be possible to isolate only two discriminant functions (obviously, this assumes that there were at least two measures). There are ways to use the data to permit the researcher to identify which group the individual would be assigned to based on the discriminant functions, and then to determine the number of times the prediction is correct and the number of times it is incorrect. This material can then be used to assess how good the model is in predicting group membership. If the hit rate (the number of correct identifications) is high, it could well be that with other samples of individuals one could use the function to classify individuals as Psychotic, Neurotic, or Normal. If cross-validation showed this classification to be reliable (i.e., with a high hit rate), it might prove useful in a diagnostic setting.

In addition to using the data from the discriminant functions to predict group membership, a researcher could also attempt to interpret them using the procedures described above. In this way, the researcher might also identify basic psychological processes that distinguish between the three groups. This type of study isn't without its problems, of course. First, there is the issue that the classification would be better in the sample under investigation than it would be in the cross-validation sample, simply because prediction capitalizes on sampling errors. Second, even though previously defined groups differ, it doesn't necessarily mean that the differences are responsible for group definition. It is nonetheless a useful procedure.

You could, if you wish, use the data in **mandat.dat** (the data we used above with both **GLM** and **MANOVA**) to perform a discriminant function analysis. However, having clicked on Statistics or Analyze (as appropriate) on step 4 (page 266), you would then click on *Classify* in the drop-down menu, and then on *Discriminant* on the side menu. This would take you into the Discriminant Function Analysis, and if you followed the instructions you would obtain the output. The first thing you would note is that virtually all of the statistics are the same as those we have discussed above, though the tables are formatted and labelled differently. For example, the Descriptive Statistics are labelled Group Statistics, but they consist of the same means and standard deviations. The tests of significance of the discriminant functions uses a different statistic (χ^2) than that described on page 275 (where F-ratios were used), and the group centroids look quite different. This latter difference is illusory, however; the differences between the centroids are the same. The major different information that can be produced by *Discriminant* is the classification table. This is shown below:

Classification Results[a]

		A	1.00	2.00	3.00	4.00	Total
				Predicted Group Membership			
Original	Count	1.00	3	1	0	1	5
		2.00	0	5	0	0	5
		3.00	1	0	3	1	5
		4.00	0	0	0	5	5
	%	1.00	60.0	20.0	.0	20.0	100.0
		2.00	.0	100.0	.0	.0	100.0
		3.00	20.0	.0	60.0	20.0	100.0
		4.00	.0	.0	.0	100.0	100.0

[a]80.0% of original grouped cases correctly classified.

This table shows the nature of the predictions and gives an indication of how well the functions predicted group membership. Note accuracy was perfect for groups 2 and 4, but not for groups 1 and 3. Overall, accuracy was 80%. Obviously, there isn't much to be gained by using discriminant function analysis for a small data set such as this, but for larger groups, and more variables, it can be quite informative.

This very brief discussion of discriminant function analysis was not meant to serve as an introduction to the procedure. It was made only to show the similarities between multivariate analysis of variance on the one hand and discriminant function analysis on the other. There are many theoretical and conceptual issues that should be understood before using discriminant function analysis. More detailed descriptions of the technique can be found in Marascuilo and Levin (1983), Stevens (1986) and Tabachnick and Fidell (1989).

Table 1

Basic Parameters

$S = \min\{df_1, p\}$ where: $\min$ = minimum value.

df_1 = the degrees of freedom for the numerator for the corresponding univariate effect.

p = the number of dependent variables.

$m = \dfrac{|p - df_1| - 1}{2}$ where: $|\ |$ = absolute value

$r = \max\{p, df_1\}$ where: $\max$ = maximum value

$n = \dfrac{df_e - p - 1}{2}$ where: df_e = degrees of freedom for the error term for the corresponding univariate analysis.

a = Number of levels of the treatment factor.

N = Total number of subjects in the study.

Pillai's Trace

$$P' = \Sigma \frac{\lambda}{1 + \lambda}$$

$$\text{Approximate } F = \frac{(N - a - p + S)P'}{r(S - P')}$$

$$v_1 = p(a - 1) \quad v_2 = S(df_e - p + S)$$

Hotelling's Trace

$$H = \Sigma\lambda$$

$$\text{Approximate } F = \frac{2(Sn + 1)H}{S^2(2m + S + 1)}$$

$$v_1 = S(2m + p) \quad v_2 = 2(Sn + 1)$$

Wilks' Lambda

$$\Lambda = \pi \frac{1}{1 + \lambda}$$

$$\text{Approximate } F = \frac{v_2(1 - \lambda^{1/b})}{v_1(\lambda^{1/b})}$$

$$v_1 = p(df_1) \quad v_2 = a'b - \frac{(p(df_1))}{2} + 1$$

$$\text{where: } a' = (N - 1) - \frac{(p + a)}{2}$$

$$b = \sqrt{\frac{p^2 df_1^2 - 4}{p^2 + df_1^2 - 5}}$$

Roy's Largest Root

$$L = \frac{\lambda_1}{1 + \lambda_1}$$

Table 2

Basic Parameters

$$S = \min\{3.4\} = 3 \qquad m = \frac{|4 - 3| - 1}{2} = 0$$

$$r = \max\{4, 3\} = 4 \qquad n = \frac{16 - 4 - 1}{2} = 5.5$$

$$a = 4$$
$$N = 20$$

Pillai's Trace

$$p' = \frac{1.472}{2.472} + \frac{1.016}{2.016} + \frac{.422}{1.422} = 1.396$$

$$\text{Approximate } F = \frac{(20 - 4 - 4 + 3)(1.396)}{4(3 - 1.396)} = 3.264$$

$$v_1 = 4(4 - 1) = 12 \quad v_2 = 3(16 - 4 + 3) = 45$$

Hotelling's Trace

$$H = 1.472 + 1.016 + .422 = 2.91$$

$$\text{Approximate } F = \frac{2\{(3)(5.5) + 1\}\, 2.91}{9(2(0) + 3 + 1} = 2.83$$

$$v_1 = 3(2(0) + 4) = 12 \quad v_2 = 2\{(3)(5.5 + 1)\} = 35$$

Wilks' Lambda

$$\Lambda = (.4045307)(.4960317)(.7032348) = .1411$$

$$\text{Approximate } F = \frac{(34.69)(1 - .1411^{.3779644})}{12(.1411^{.3779644})} = 3.169$$

$$v_1 = 4(3) = 12 \quad v_2 = (15)(2.6457513) - \frac{(4(3))}{2} + 1 = 34.69$$

$$\text{where } a' = (20 - 1) - \frac{(4 + 4)}{2} = 15$$

$$b = \sqrt{\frac{(16)(9) - 4}{16 + 9 - 4}} = 2.6457513$$

Roy's Largest Root

$$L = \frac{1.472}{1 + 1.472} = .5955$$

Appendix Tables—Sampling Distributions

Table A   The Standard Normal Distribution

z	Area: m to z	Area: q Smaller	Ordinate
.00	.00000	.50000	.3989
.05	.01994	.48006	.3984
.10	.03983	.46017	.3970
.15	.05962	.44038	.3945
.20	.07926	.42074	.3910
.25	.09871	.40129	.3867
.30	.11791	.38209	.3814
.35	.13683	.36317	.3752
.40	.15542	.34458	.3683
.45	.17364	.32636	.3605
.50	.19146	.30854	.3521
.55	.20884	.29116	.3429
.60	.22575	.27425	.3332
.65	.24215	.25785	.3230
.70	.25804	.24196	.3123
.75	.27337	.22663	.3011
.80	.28814	.21186	.2897
.85	.30234	.19766	.2780
.90	.31594	.18406	.2661
.95	.32894	.17106	.2541
1.00	.34134	.15866	.2420
1.05	.35314	.14686	.2299
1.10	.36433	.13567	.2179
1.15	.37493	.12507	.2059
1.20	.38493	.11507	.1942
1.25	.39435	.10565	.1826
1.30	.40320	.09680	.1714
1.35	.41149	.08851	.1604
1.40	.41924	.08076	.1497
1.45	.42647	.07353	.1394
1.50	.43319	.06681	.1295
1.55	.43943	.06057	.1200
1.60	.44520	.05480	.1109
1.65	.45053	.04947	.1023
1.70	.45543	.04457	.0940
1.75	.45994	.04006	.0863
1.80	.46407	.03593	.0790
1.85	.46784	.03216	.0721

Table A from pages 502 and 503 of *Psychological Statistics,* 4th ed. by Quinn McNemar, 1969, John Wiley and Sons, Inc.

Table A   The Standard Normal Distribution (*continued*)

z	Area: *m* to *z*	Area: *q* Smaller	Ordinate
1.90	.47128	.02872	.0656
1.95	.47441	.02559	.0596
2.00	.47725	.02275	.0540
2.05	.47982	.02018	.0488
2.10	.48214	.01786	.0440
2.15	.48422	.01578	.0396
2.20	.48610	.01390	.0355
2.25	.48778	.01222	.0317
2.30	.48928	.01072	.0283
2.35	.49061	.00939	.0252
2.40	.49180	.00820	.0224
2.45	.49286	.00714	.0198
2.50	.49379	.00621	.0175
2.55	.49461	.00539	.0154
2.60	.49534	.00466	.0136
2.65	.49598	.00402	.0119
2.70	.49653	.00347	.0104
2.75	.49702	.00298	.0091
2.80	.49744	.00256	.0079
2.85	.49781	.00219	.0069
2.90	.49813	.00187	.0060
2.95	.49841	.00159	.0051
3.00	.49865	.00135	.0044
3.25	.49942	.00058	.0020
3.50	.49977	.00023	.0009
3.75	.49991	.00009	.0004
4.00	.49997	.00003	.0001

Table A from pages 502 and 503 of *Psychological Statistics,* 4th ed. by Quinn McNemar, 1969, John Wiley and Sons, Inc.

Table B   Distribution of t*

df	$P = .1$	.05	.02	.01	.001
1	6.314	12.706	31.821	63.657	636.619
2	2.920	4.303	6.965	9.925	31.598
3	2.353	3.182	4.541	5.841	12.941
4	2.132	2.776	3.747	4.604	8.610
5	2.015	2.571	3.365	4.032	6.859
6	1.943	2.447	3.143	3.707	5.959
7	1.895	2.365	2.998	3.499	5.405
8	1.860	2.306	2,896	3.355	5.041
9	1.833	2.262	2.821	3.250	4.781
10	1.812	2.228	2.764	3.169	4.587
11	1.796	2.201	2.718	3.106	4.437
12	1.782	2.179	2.681	3.055	4.318
13	1.771	2.160	2.650	3.012	4.221
14	1.761	2.145	2.624	2.977	4.140
15	1.753	2.131	2.602	2.947	4.073
16	1.746	2.120	2.583	2.921	4.015
17	1.740	2.110	2.567	2.898	3.965
18	1.734	2.101	2.552	2.878	3.922
19	1.729	2.093	2.539	2.861	3.883
20	1.725	2.086	2.528	2.845	3.850
21	1.721	2.080	2.518	2.831	3.819
22	1.717	2.074	2.508	2.819	3.792
23	1.714	2.069	2.500	2.807	3.767
24	1.711	2.064	2.492	2.797	3.745
25	1.708	2.060	2.485	2.787	3.725
26	1.706	2.056	2.479	2.779	3.707
27	1.703	2.052	2.473	2.771	3.690
28	1.701	2.048	2.467	2.763	3.674
29	1.699	2.045	2.462	2.756	3.659
30	1.697	2.042	2.457	2.750	3.646
40	1.684	2.021	2.423	2.704	3.551
60	1.671	2.000	2.390	2.660	3.460
120	1.658	1.980	2.358	2.617	3.373
∞	1.645	1.960	2.326	2.576	3.291

*Table B is abridged from Table III of Fisher and Yates: *Statistical Tables for Biological, Agricultural and Medical Research,* Oliver and Boyd, Ltd., Edinburgh, by permission of the authors and publishers. © 1963 R. A. Fisher and F. Yates. Reprinted by permission of Addison Wesley Longman Limited. Reprinted by permission of Pearson Education Limited.

Table C   **Table of F for .05 (roman), .01 (*italic*), and .001 (bold face) levels of significance***

n_2 \ n_1	1	2	3	4	5	6	8	12	24	∞
1	161	200	216	225	230	234	239	244	249	254
	4052	*4999*	*5403*	*5625*	*5724*	*5859*	*5981*	*6106*	*6234*	*6366*
	405284	**500000**	**540379**	**562500**	**576405**	**585937**	**598144**	**610667**	**623497**	**636619**
2	18.51	19.00	19.16	19.25	19.30	19.33	19.37	19.41	19.45	19.50
	98.49	*99.01*	*99.17*	*99.25*	*99.30*	*99.33*	*99.36*	*99.42*	*99.46*	*99.50*
	998.5	**999.0**	**999.2**	**999.2**	**999.3**	**999.3**	**999.4**	**999.4**	**999.5**	**999.5**
3	10.13	9.55	9.28	9.12	9.01	8.94	8.84	8.74	8.64	8.53
	34.12	*30.81*	*29.46*	*28.71*	*28.24*	*27.91*	*27.49*	*27.05*	*26.60*	*26.12*
	167.5	**148.5**	**141.1**	**137.1**	**134.6**	**132.8**	**130.6**	**128.3**	**125.9**	**123.5**
4	7.71	6.94	6.59	6.39	6.26	6.16	6.04	5.91	5.77	5.63
	21.20	*18.00*	*16.69*	*15.98*	*15.52*	*15.21*	*14.80*	*14.37*	*13.93*	*13.46*
	74.14	**61.25**	**56.18**	**53.44**	**51.71**	**50.53**	**49.00**	**47.41**	**45.77**	**44.05**
5	6.61	5.79	5.41	5.19	5.05	4.95	4.82	4.68	4.53	4.36
	16.26	*13.27*	*12.06*	*11.39*	*10.97*	*10.67*	*10.27*	*9.89*	*9.47*	*9.02*
	47.04	**36.61**	**33.20**	**31.09**	**29.75**	**28.84**	**27.64**	**26.42**	**25.14**	**23.78**
6	5.99	5.14	4.76	4.53	4.39	4.28	4.15	4.00	3.84	3.67
	13.74	*10.92*	*9.78*	*9.15*	*8.75*	*8.47*	*8.10*	*7.72*	*7.31*	*6.88*
	35.51	**27.00**	**23.70**	**21.90**	**20.81**	**20.03**	**19.03**	**17.99**	**16.89**	**15.75**
7	5.59	4.74	4.35	4.12	3.97	3.87	3.73	3.57	3.41	3.23
	12.25	*9.55*	*8.45*	*7.85*	*7.46*	*7.19*	*6.84*	*6.47*	*6.07*	*5.65*
	29.22	**21.69**	**18.77**	**17.19**	**16.21**	**15.52**	**14.63**	**13.71**	**12.73**	**11.69**
8	5.32	4.46	4.07	3.84	3.69	3.58	3.44	3.28	3.12	2.93
	11.26	*8.65*	*7.59*	*7.01*	*6.63*	*6.37*	*6.03*	*5.67*	*5.28*	*4.86*
	25.42	**18.49**	**15.83**	**14.39**	**13.49**	**12.86**	**12.04**	**11.19**	**10.30**	**9.34**
9	5.12	4.26	3.86	3.63	3.48	3.37	3.23	3.07	2.90	2.71
	10.56	*8.02*	*6.99*	*6.42*	*6.06*	*5.80*	*5.47*	*5.11*	*4.73*	*4.31*
	22.86	**16.39**	**13.90**	**12.56**	**11.71**	**11.13**	**10.37**	**9.57**	**8.72**	**7.81**
10	4.96	4.10	3.71	3.48	3.33	3.22	3.07	2.91	2.74	2.54
	10.04	*7.56*	*6.55*	*5.99*	*5.64*	*5.39*	*5.06*	*4.71*	*4.33*	*3.91*
	21.04	**14.91**	**12.55**	**11.28**	**10.48**	**9.92**	**9.20**	**8.45**	**7.64**	**6.76**
11	4.84	3.98	3.59	3.36	3.20	3.09	2.95	2.79	2.61	2.40
	9.65	*7.20*	*6.22*	*5.67*	*5.32*	*5.07*	*4.74*	*4.40*	*4.02*	*3.60*
	19.69	**13.81**	**11.56**	**10.35**	**9.58**	**9.05**	**8.35**	**7.63**	**6.85**	**6.00**
12	4.75	3.88	3.49	3.26	3.11	3.00	2.85	2.69	2.50	2.30
	9.33	*6.93*	*5.95*	*5.41*	*5.06*	*4.82*	*4.50*	*4.16*	*3.78*	*3.36*
	18.64	**12.97**	**10.80**	**9.63**	**8.89**	**8.38**	**7.71**	**7.00**	**6.25**	**5.42**

*Table C is reprinted, in rearranged form, from Table V of Fisher and Yates: *Statistical Tables for Biological, Agricultural and Medical Research*, Oliver and Boyd, Ltd., Edinburgh, by permission of the authors and publishers. © 1963 R. A. Fisher and F. Yates. Reprinted by permission of Addison Wesley Longman Limited. Reprinted by permission of Pearson Education Limited.

Table C Table of F for .05 (roman), .01 (*italic*), and .001 (bold face) levels of significance* (*continued*)

n_2 \ n_1	1	2	3	4	5	6	8	12	24	∞
13	4.67	3.80	3.41	3.18	3.02	2.92	2.77	2.60	2.42	2.21
	9.07	*6.70*	*5.74*	*5.20*	*4.86*	*4.62*	*4.30*	*3.96*	*3.59*	*3.16*
	17.81	**12.31**	**10.21**	**9.07**	**8.35**	**7.86**	**7.21**	**6.52**	**5.78**	**4.97**
14	4.60	3.74	3.34	3.11	2.96	2.85	2.70	2.53	2.35	2.13
	8.86	*6.51*	*5.56*	*5.03*	*4.69*	*4.46*	*4.14*	*3.80*	*3.43*	*3.00*
	17.14	**11.78**	**9.73**	**8.62**	**7.92**	**7.43**	**6.80**	**6.13**	**5.41**	**4.60**
15	4.54	3.68	3.29	3.06	2.90	2.79	2.64	2.48	2.29	2.07
	8.68	*6.36*	*5.42*	*4.89*	*4.56*	*4.32*	*4.00*	*3.67*	*3.29*	*2.87*
	16.59	**11.34**	**9.34**	**8.25**	**7.57**	**7.09**	**6.47**	**5.81**	**5.10**	**4.31**
16	4.49	3.63	3.24	3.01	2.85	2.74	2.59	2.42	2.24	2.01
	8.53	*6.23*	*5.29*	*4.77*	*4.44*	*4.20*	*3.89*	*3.55*	*3.18*	*2.75*
	16.12	**10.97**	**9.00**	**7.94**	**7.27**	**6.81**	**6.19**	**5.55**	**4.85**	**4.06**
17	4.45	3.59	3.20	2.96	2.81	2.70	2.55	2.38	2.19	1.96
	8.40	*6.11*	*5.18*	*4.67*	*4.34*	*4.10*	*3.79*	*3.45*	*3.08*	*2.65*
	15.72	**10.66**	**8.73**	**7.68**	**7.02**	**6.56**	**5.96**	**5.32**	**4.63**	**3.85**
18	4.41	3.55	3.16	2.93	2.77	2.66	2.51	2.34	2.15	1.92
	8.28	*6.01*	*5.09*	*4.58*	*4.25*	*4.01*	*3.71*	*3.37*	*3.00*	*2.57*
	15.38	**10.39**	**8.49**	**7.46**	**6.81**	**6.35**	**5.76**	**5.13**	**4.45**	**3.67**
19	4.38	3.52	3.13	2.90	2.74	2.63	2.48	2.31	2.11	1.88
	8.18	*5.93*	*5.01*	*4.50*	*4.17*	*3.94*	*3.63*	*3.30*	*2.92*	*2.49*
	15.08	**10.16**	**8.28**	**7.26**	**6.61**	**6.18**	**5.59**	**4.97**	**4.29**	**3.52**
20	4.35	3.49	3.10	2.87	2.71	2.60	2.45	2.28	2.08	1.84
	8.10	*5.85*	*4.94*	*4.43*	*4.10*	*3.87*	*3.56*	*3.23*	*2.86*	*2.42*
	14.82	**9.95**	**8.10**	**7.10**	**6.46**	**6.02**	**5.44**	**4.82**	**4.15**	**3.38**
21	4.32	3.47	3.07	2.84	2.68	2.57	2.42	2.25	2.05	1.81
	8.02	*5.78*	*4.87*	*4.37*	*4.04*	*3.81*	*3.51*	*3.17*	*2.80*	*2.36*
	14.59	**9.77**	**7.94**	**6.95**	**6.32**	**5.88**	**5.31**	**4.70**	**4.03**	**3.26**
22	4.30	3.44	3.05	2.82	2.66	2.55	2.40	2.23	2.03	1.78
	7.94	*5.72*	*4.82*	*4.31*	*3.99*	*3.76*	*3.45*	*3.12*	*2.75*	*2.31*
	14.38	**9.61**	**7.80**	**6.81**	**6.19**	**5.76**	**5.19**	**4.58**	**3.92**	**3.15**
23	4.28	3.42	3.03	2.80	2.64	2.53	2.38	2.20	2.00	1.76
	7.88	*5.66*	*4.76*	*4.26*	*3.94*	*3.71*	*3.41*	*3.07*	*2.70*	*2.26*
	14.19	**9.47**	**7.67**	**6.69**	**6.08**	**5.65**	**5.09**	**4.48**	**3.82**	**3.05**
24	4.26	3.40	3.01	2.78	2.62	2.51	2.36	2.18	1.98	1.73
	7.82	*5.61*	*4.72*	*4.22*	*3.90*	*3.67*	*3.36*	*3.03*	*2.66*	*2.21*
	14.03	**9.34**	**7.55**	**6.59**	**5.98**	**5.55**	**4.99**	**4.39**	**3.74**	**2.97**

*Table C is reprinted, in rearranged form, from Table V of Fisher and Yates: *Statistical Tables for Biological, Agricultural and Medical Research*, Oliver and Boyd, Ltd., Edinburgh, by permission of the authors and publishers. © 1963 R. A. Fisher and F. Yates. Reprinted by permission of Addison Wesley Longman Limited. Reprinted by permission of Pearson Education Limited.

Table C   Table of F for .05 (roman), .01 (*italic*), and .001 (bold face) levels of significance* (*continued*)

n_2 \ n_1	1	2	3	4	5	6	8	12	24	∞
25	4.24	3.38	2.99	2.76	2.60	2.49	2.34	2.16	1.96	1.71
	7.77	*5.57*	*4.68*	*4.18*	*3.86*	*3.63*	*3.32*	*2.99*	*2.62*	*2.17*
	13.88	**9.22**	**7.45**	**6.49**	**5.88**	**5.46**	**4.91**	**4.31**	**3.66**	**2.89**
26	4.22	3.37	2.98	2.74	2.59	2.47	2.32	2.15	1.95	1.69
	7.72	*5.53*	*4.64*	*4.14*	*3.82*	*3.59*	*3.29*	*2.96*	*2.58*	*2.13*
	13.74	**9.12**	**7.36**	**6.41**	**5.80**	**5.38**	**4.83**	**4.24**	**3.59**	**2.82**
27	4.21	3.35	2.96	2.73	2.57	2.46	2.30	2.13	1.93	1.67
	7.68	*5.49*	*4.60*	*4.11*	*3.78*	*3.56*	*3.26*	*2.93*	*2.55*	*2.10*
	13.61	**9.02**	**7.27**	**6.33**	**5.73**	**5.31**	**4.76**	**4.17**	**3.52**	**2.75**
28	4.20	3.34	2.95	2.71	2.56	2.44	2.29	2.12	1.91	1.65
	7.64	*5.45*	*4.57*	*4.07*	*3.75*	*3.53*	*3.23*	*2.90*	*2.52*	*2.06*
	13.50	**8.93**	**7.19**	**6.25**	**5.66**	**5.24**	**4.69**	**4.11**	**3.46**	**2.70**
29	4.18	3.33	2.93	2.70	2.54	2.43	2.28	2.10	1.90	1.64
	7.60	*5.42*	*4.54*	*4.04*	*3.73*	*3.50*	*3.20*	*2.87*	*2.49*	*2.03*
	13.39	**8.85**	**7.12**	**6.19**	**5.59**	**5.18**	**4.64**	**4.05**	**3.41**	**2.64**
30	4.17	3.32	2.92	2.69	2.53	2.42	2.27	2.09	1.89	1.62
	7.56	*5.39*	*4.51*	*4.02*	*3.70*	*3.47*	*3.17*	*2.84*	*2.47*	*2.01*
	13.29	**8.77**	**7.05**	**6.12**	**5.53**	**5.12**	**4.58**	**4.00**	**3.36**	**2.59**
40	4.08	3.23	2.84	2.61	2.45	2.34	2.18	2.00	1.79	1.51
	7.31	*5.18*	*4.31*	*3.83*	*3.51*	*3.29*	*2.99*	*2.66*	*2.29*	*1.80*
	12.61	**8.25**	**6.60**	**5.70**	**5.13**	**4.73**	**4.21**	**3.64**	**3.01**	**2.23**
60	4.00	3.15	2.76	2.52	2.37	2.25	2.10	1.92	1.70	1.39
	7.08	*4.98*	*4.13*	*3.65*	*3.34*	*3.12*	*2.82*	*2.50*	*2.12*	*1.60*
	11.97	**7.76**	**6.17**	**5.31**	**4.76**	**4.37**	**3.87**	**3.31**	**2.69**	**1.90**
120	3.92	3.07	2.68	2.45	2.29	2.17	2.02	1.83	1.61	1.25
	6.85	*4.79*	*3.95*	*3.48*	*3.17*	*2.96*	*2.66*	*2.34*	*1.95*	*1.38*
	11.38	**7.31**	**5.79**	**4.95**	**4.42**	**4.04**	**3.55**	**3.02**	**2.40**	**1.56**
∞	3.84	2.99	2.60	2.37	2.21	2.09	1.94	1.75	1.52	1.00
	6.64	*4.60*	*3.78*	*3.32*	*3.02*	*2.80*	*2.51*	*2.18*	*1.79*	*1.00*
	10.83	**6.91**	**5.42**	**4.62**	**4.10**	**3.74**	**3.27**	**2.74**	**2.13**	**1.00**

*Table C is reprinted, in rearranged form, from Table V of Fisher and Yates: *Statistical Tables for Biological, Agricultural and Medical Research,* Oliver and Boyd, Ltd., Edinburgh, by permission of the authors and publishers. © 1963 R. A. Fisher and F. Yates. Reprinted by permission of Addison Wesley Longman Limited. Reprinted by permission of Pearson Education Limited.

Table D Percentage Points of the Studentized Range

Error df	α	Number of Means (p) or Number of Steps Between Ordered Means (r)									
		2	3	4	5	6	7	8	9	10	11
2	.05	6.08	8.33	9.80	10.9	11.7	12.4	13.0	13.5	14.0	14.4
	.01	14.0	19.0	22.3	24.7	26.6	28.2	29.5	30.7	31.7	32.6
3	.05	4.50	5.91	6.82	7.50	8.04	8.48	8.85	9.18	9.46	9.72
	.01	8.26	10.6	12.2	13.3	14.2	15.0	15.6	16.2	16.7	17.8
4	.05	3.93	5.04	5.76	6.29	6.71	7.05	7.35	7.60	7.83	8.03
	.01	6.51	8.12	9.17	9.96	10.6	11.1	11.5	11.9	12.3	12.6
5	.05	3.64	4.60	5.22	5.67	6.03	6.33	6.58	6.80	6.99	7.17
	.01	5.70	6.98	7.80	8.42	8.91	9.32	9.67	9.97	10.24	10.48
6	.05	3.46	4.34	4.90	5.30	5.63	5.90	6.12	6.32	6.49	6.65
	.01	5.24	6.33	7.03	7.56	7.97	8.32	8.61	8.87	9.10	9.30
7	.05	3.34	4.16	4.68	5.06	5.36	5.61	5.82	6.00	6.16	6.30
	.01	4.95	5.92	6.54	7.01	7.37	7.68	7.94	8.17	8.37	8.55
8	.05	3.26	4.04	4.53	4.89	5.17	5.40	5.60	5.77	5.92	6.05
	.01	4.75	5.64	6.20	6.62	6.96	7.24	7.47	7.68	7.86	8.03
9	.05	3.20	3.95	4.41	4.76	5.02	5.24	5.43	5.59	5.74	5.87
	.01	4.60	5.43	5.96	6.35	6.66	6.91	7.13	7.33	7.49	7.65
10	.05	3.15	3.88	4.33	4.65	4.91	5.12	5.30	5.46	5.60	5.72
	.01	4.48	5.27	5.77	6.14	6.43	6.67	6.87	7.05	7.21	7.36
11	.05	3.11	3.82	4.26	4.57	4.82	5.03	5.20	5.35	5.49	5.61
	.01	4.39	5.15	5.62	5.97	6.25	6.48	6.67	6.84	6.99	7.13
12	.05	3.08	3.77	4.20	4.51	4.75	4.95	5.12	5.27	5.39	5.51
	.01	4.32	5.05	5.50	5.84	6.10	6.32	6.51	6.67	6.81	6.94
13	.05	3.06	3.73	4.15	4.45	4.69	4.88	5.05	5.19	5.32	5.43
	.01	4.26	4.96	5.40	5.73	5.98	6.19	6.37	6.53	6.67	6.79
14	.05	3.03	3.70	4.11	4.41	4.64	4.83	4.99	5.13	5.25	5.36
	.01	4.21	4.89	5.32	5.63	5.88	6.08	6.26	6.41	6.54	6.66
15	.05	3.01	3.67	4.08	4.37	4.59	4.78	4.94	5.08	5.20	5.31
	.01	4.17	4.84	5.25	5.56	5.80	5.99	6.16	6.31	6.44	6.55
16	.05	3.00	3.65	4.05	4.33	4.56	4.74	4.90	5.03	5.15	5.26
	.01	4.13	4.79	5.19	5.49	5.72	5.92	6.08	6.22	6.35	6.46
17	.05	2.98	3.63	4.02	4.30	4.52	4.70	4.86	4.99	5.11	5.21
	.01	4.10	4.74	5.14	5.43	5.66	5.85	6.01	6.15	6.27	6.38
18	.05	2.97	3.61	4.00	4.28	4.49	4.67	4.82	4.96	5.07	5.17
	.01	4.07	4.70	5.09	5.38	5.60	5.79	5.94	6.08	6.20	6.31
19	.05	2.96	3.59	3.98	4.25	4.47	4.65	4.79	4.92	5.04	5.14
	.01	4.05	4.67	5.05	5.33	5.55	5.73	5.89	6.02	6.14	6.25
20	.05	2.95	3.58	3.96	4.23	4.45	4.62	4.77	4.90	5.01	5.11
	.01	4.02	4.64	5.02	5.29	5.51	5.69	5.84	5.97	6.00	6.19
24	.05	2.92	3.53	3.90	4.17	4.37	4.54	4.68	4.81	4.92	5.01
	.01	3.96	4.55	4.91	5.17	5.37	5.54	5.69	5.81	5.92	6.02
30	.05	2.89	3.49	3.85	4.10	4.30	4.46	4.60	4.72	4.82	4.92
	.01	3.89	4.45	4.80	5.05	5.24	5.40	5.54	5.65	5.76	5.85
40	.05	2.86	3.44	3.79	4.04	4.23	4.39	4.52	4.63	4.73	4.82
	.01	3.82	4.37	4.70	4.93	5.11	5.26	5.39	5.50	5.60	5.69
60	.05	2.83	3.40	3.74	3.98	4.16	4.31	4.44	4.55	4.65	4.73
	.01	3.76	4.28	4.59	4.82	4.99	5.13	5.25	5.36	5.45	5.53
120	.05	2.80	3.36	3.68	3.92	4.10	4.24	4.36	4.47	4.56	4.64
	.01	3.70	4.20	4.50	4.71	4.87	5.01	5.12	5.21	5.30	5.37
∞	.05	2.77	3.31	3.63	3.86	4.03	4.17	4.29	4.39	4.47	4.55
	.01	3.64	4.12	4.40	4.60	4.76	4.88	4.99	5.08	5.16	5.23

Table D is abridged from Table 29 in *Biometrika Tables for Statisticians,* vol 1, 2nd ed. New York Cambridge, 1958. Edited by E. S. Pearson and R. O. Hartley. Reproduced with the kind permission of the editors and trustees of *Biometrika.*

Table D   Percentage Points of the Studentized Range (*continued*)

Number of Means (p) or Number of Steps Between Ordered Means (r)

12	13	14	15	16	17	18	19	20	α	Error df
14.7	15.1	15.4	15.7	15.9	16.1	16.4	16.6	16.8	.05	2
33.4	34.1	34.8	35.4	36.0	36.5	37.0	37.5	37.9	.01	
9.72	10.2	10.3	10.5	10.7	10.8	11.0	11.1	11.2	.05	3
17.5	17.9	18.2	18.5	18.8	19.1	19.3	19.5	19.8	.01	
8.21	8.37	8.52	8.66	8.79	8.91	9.03	9.13	9.23	.05	4
12.8	13.1	13.3	13.5	13.7	13.9	14.1	14.2	14.4	.01	
7.32	7.47	7.60	7.72	7.83	7.93	8.03	8.12	8.21	.05	5
10.70	10.89	11.08	11.24	11.40	11.55	11.68	11.81	11.93	.01	
6.79	6.92	7.03	7.14	7.24	7.34	7.43	7.51	7.59	.05	6
9.48	9.65	9.81	9.95	10.08	10.21	10.32	10.43	10.54	.01	
6.43	6.55	6.66	6.76	6.85	6.94	7.02	7.10	7.17	.05	7
8.71	8.86	9.00	9.12	9.24	9.35	9.46	9.55	9.65	.01	
6.18	6.29	6.39	6.48	6.57	6.65	6.73	6.80	6.87	.05	8
8.18	8.31	8.44	8.55	8.66	8.76	8.85	8.94	9.03	.01	
5.98	6.09	6.19	6.28	6.36	6.44	6.51	6.58	6.64	.05	9
7.78	7.91	8.03	8.13	8.23	8.33	8.41	8.49	8.57	.01	
5.83	5.93	6.03	6.11	6.19	6.27	6.34	6.40	6.47	.05	10
7.49	7.60	7.71	7.81	7.91	7.99	8.08	8.15	8.23	.01	
5.71	5.81	5.90	5.98	6.06	6.13	6.20	6.27	6.33	.05	11
7.25	7.36	7.46	7.56	7.65	7.73	7.81	7.88	7.95	.01	
5.61	5.71	5.80	5.88	5.95	6.02	6.09	6.15	6.21	.05	12
7.06	7.17	7.26	7.36	7.44	7.52	7.59	7.66	7.73	.01	
5.53	5.63	5.71	5.79	5.86	5.93	5.99	6.05	6.11	.05	13
6.90	7.01	7.10	7.19	7.27	7.35	7.42	7.48	7.55	.01	
5.46	5.55	5.64	5.71	5.79	5.85	5.91	5.97	6.03	.05	14
6.77	6.87	6.96	7.05	7.13	7.20	7.27	7.33	7.39	.01	
5.40	5.49	5.57	5.65	5.72	5.78	5.85	5.90	5.96	.05	15
6.66	6.76	6.84	6.93	7.00	7.07	7.14	7.20	7.26	.01	
5.35	5.44	5.52	5.59	5.66	5.73	5.79	5.84	5.90	.05	16
6.56	6.66	6.74	6.82	6.90	6.97	7.03	7.09	7.15	.01	
5.31	5.39	5.47	5.54	5.61	5.67	5.73	5.79	5.84	.05	17
6.48	6.57	6.66	6.73	6.81	6.87	6.94	7.00	7.05	.01	
5.27	5.35	5.43	5.50	5.57	5.63	5.69	5.74	5.79	.05	18
6.41	6.50	6.58	6.65	6.73	6.79	6.85	6.91	6.97	.01	
5.23	5.31	5.39	5.46	5.53	5.59	5.65	5.70	5.75	.05	19
6.34	6.43	6.51	6.58	6.65	6.72	6.78	6.84	6.89	.01	
5.20	5.28	5.36	5.43	5.49	5.55	5.61	5.66	5.71	.05	20
6.28	6.37	6.45	6.52	6.59	6.65	6.71	6.77	6.82	.01	
5.10	5.18	5.25	5.32	5.38	5.44	5.49	5.55	5.59	.05	24
6.11	6.19	6.26	6.33	6.39	6.45	6.51	6.56	6.61	.01	
5.00	5.08	5.15	5.21	5.27	5.33	5.38	5.43	5.47	.05	30
5.93	6.01	6.08	6.14	6.20	6.26	6.31	6.36	6.41	.01	
4.90	4.98	5.04	5.11	5.16	5.22	5.27	5.31	5.36	.05	40
5.76	5.83	5.90	5.96	6.02	6.07	6.12	6.16	6.21	.01	
4.81	4.88	4.94	5.00	5.06	5.11	5.15	5.20	5.24	.05	60
5.60	5.67	5.73	5.78	5.84	5.89	5.93	5.97	6.01	.01	
4.71	4.78	4.84	4.90	4.95	5.00	5.04	5.09	5.13	.05	120
5.44	5.50	5.56	5.61	5.66	5.71	5.75	5.79	5.83	.01	
4.62	4.68	4.74	4.80	4.85	4.89	4.93	4.97	5.01	.05	∞
5.29	5.35	5.40	5.45	5.49	5.54	5.57	5.61	5.65	.01	

**Table E   Distribution of χ^2*

n	$P = .99$	.98	.95	.90	.80	.70	.50
1	.00016	.00063	.0039	.016	.064	.15	.46
2	.02	.04	.10	.21	.45	.71	1.39
3	.12	.18	.35	.58	1.00	1.42	2.37
4	.30	.43	.71	1.06	1.65	2.20	3.36
5	.55	.75	1.14	1.61	2.34	3.00	4.35
6	.87	1.13	1.64	2.20	3.07	3.83	5.35
7	1.24	1.56	2.17	2.83	3.82	4.67	6.35
8	1.65	2.03	2.73	3.49	4.59	5.53	7.34
9	2.09	2.53	3.32	4.17	5.38	6.39	8.34
10	2.56	3.06	3.94	4.86	6.18	7.27	9.34
11	3.05	3.61	4.58	5.58	6.99	8.15	10.34
12	3.57	4.18	5.23	6.30	7.81	9.03	11.34
13	4.11	4.76	5.89	7.04	8.63	9.93	12.34
14	4.66	5.37	6.57	7.79	9.47	10.82	13.34
15	5.23	5.98	7.26	8.55	10.31	11.72	14.34
16	5.81	6.61	7.96	9.31	11.15	12.62	15.34
17	6.41	7.26	8.67	10.08	12.00	13.53	16.34
18	7.02	7.91	9.39	10.86	12.86	14.44	17.34
19	7.63	8.57	10.12	11.65	13.72	15.35	18.34
20	8.26	9.24	10.85	12.44	14.58	16.27	19.34
21	8.90	9.92	11.59	13.24	15.44	17.18	20.34
22	9.54	10.60	12.34	14.04	16.31	18.10	21.34
23	10.20	11.29	13.09	14.85	17.19	19.02	22.34
24	10.86	11.99	13.85	15.66	18.06	19.94	23.34
25	11.52	12.70	14.61	16.47	18.94	20.87	24.34
26	12.20	13.41	15.38	17.29	19.82	21.79	25.34
27	12.88	14.12	16.15	18.11	20.70	22.72	26.34
28	13.56	14.85	16.93	18.94	21.59	23.65	27.34
29	14.26	15.57	17.71	19.77	22.48	24.58	28.34
30	14.95	16.31	18.49	20.60	23.36	25.51	29.34

*Table E is abridged from Table IV of Fisher and Yates: *Statistical Tables for Biological, Agricultural and Medical Research.* Oliver and Boyd, Ltd., Edinburgh, by permission of the authors and publishers. © 1963 R. A. Fisher and F. Yates. Reprinted by permission of Addison Wesley Longman Limited. Reprinted by permission of Pearson Education Limited.

Table E Distribution of χ^2* (*continued*)

n	.30	.20	.10	.05	.02	.01	.001
1	1.07	1.64	2.71	3.84	5.41	6.64	10.83
2	2.41	3.22	4.60	5.99	7.82	9.21	13.82
3	3.66	4.64	6.25	7.82	9.84	11.34	16.27
4	4.88	5.99	7.78	9.49	11.67	13.28	18.46
5	6.06	7.29	9.24	11.07	13.39	15.09	20.52
6	7.23	8.56	10.64	12.59	15.03	16.81	22.46
7	8.38	9.80	12.02	14.07	16.62	18.48	24.32
8	9.52	11.03	13.36	15.51	18.17	20.09	26.12
9	10.66	12.24	14.68	16.92	19.68	21.67	27.88
10	11.78	13.44	15.99	18.31	21.16	23.21	29.59
11	12.90	14.63	17.28	19.68	22.62	24.72	31.26
12	14.01	15.81	18.55	21.03	24.05	26.22	32.91
13	15.12	16.98	19.81	22.36	25.47	27.69	34.53
14	16.22	18.15	21.06	23.68	26.87	29.14	36.12
15	17.32	19.31	22.31	25.00	28.26	30.58	37.70
16	18.42	20.46	23.54	26.30	29.63	32.00	39.25
17	19.51	21.62	24.77	27.59	31.00	33.41	40.79
18	20.60	22.76	25.99	28.87	32.35	34.80	42.31
19	21.69	23.90	27.20	30.14	33.69	36.19	43.82
20	22.78	25.04	28.41	31.41	35.02	37.57	45.32
21	23.86	26.17	29.62	32.67	36.34	38.93	46.80
22	24.94	27.30	30.81	33.92	37.66	40.29	48.27
23	26.02	28.43	32.01	35.17	38.97	41.64	49.73
24	27.10	29.55	33.20	36.42	40.27	42.98	51.18
25	28.17	30.68	34.38	37.65	41.57	44.31	52.62
26	29.25	31.80	35.56	38.88	42.86	45.64	54.05
27	30.32	32.91	36.74	40.11	44.14	46.96	55.48
28	31.39	34.03	37.92	41.34	45.42	48.28	56.89
29	32.46	35.14	39.09	42.56	46.69	49.59	58.30
30	33.53	36.25	40.26	43.77	47.96	50.89	59.70

*Table E is abridged from Table IV of Fisher and Yates: *Statistical Tables for Biological, Agricultural and Medical Research.* Oliver and Boyd, Ltd., Edinburgh, by permission of the authors and publishers. © 1963 R. A. Fisher and F. Yates. Reprinted by permission of Addison Wesley Longman Limited. Reprinted by permission of Pearson Education Limited.

References

Agresti, A. (1996). *An introduction to categorical data analysis.* New York: John Wiley & Sons.

Babington-Smith, B. (1950). On some difficulties encountered in the use of factorial designs and analysis of variance with psychological experiments. *British Journal of Psychology, 40,* 250–268.

Baron, R. M., & Kenny, D. A. (1986). The moderator-mediator variable distinction in social psychological research: Conceptual, strategic, and statistical considerations. *Journal of Personality and Social Psychology, 51,* 1173–1182.

Baxter, B. (1942). A study of reaction time using factorial design. *Journal of Experimental Psychology, 31,* 430–437.

Beasley, T. M., & Schumacker, R. E. (1995). Multiple regression approach to analyzing contingency tables: Post hoc and planned comparison procedures. *The Journal of Experimental Education, 64,* 79–93.

Bliss, C. I. (1967). *Statistics in biology.* Vol. 1. NY: McGraw Hill.

Box, G. E. P. (1950). Problems in the analysis of growth and wear curves. *Biometrics, 6,* 362–389.

Box, G. E. P. (1954). Some theorems in quadratic forms applied in the study of analysis of variance problems: II. Effects of inequality of variance and covariance between errors in the two-way classification. *Annals of Mathematical Statistics, 35,* 484–498.

Browne, M. W. (1975). Predictive validity of a linear regression equation. *British Journal of Mathematical and Statistical Psychology, 28,* 79–87.

Carroll, J. B. (1953). An analytic solution for approximating simple structure in factor analysis. *Psychometrika, 18,* 23–38.

Carroll, J. B. (1957). Biquartimin criterion for rotation to oblique simple structure in factor analysis. *Science, 126,* 1114–1115.

Cattell, R. B. (1966). The Scree test for the Number of Factors. *Multivariate behavioral research, 1,* 245–276.

Cattell, R. B. (1978). *The scientific use of factor analysis in behavioral and life sciences.* NY: Plenum Press.

Cochran, W. G. (1952). The chi-square test of goodness of fit. *Annals of Mathematical Statistics, 23,* 315–345.

Cochran, W. G. & Cox, G. M. (1957) *Experimental designs.* NY: Wiley.

Cohen, J. (1968). Multiple regression as a general data-analytic system. *Psychological Bulletin, 70,* 426–443.

Cohen, J. (1978). Partialed products are interactions; partialed powers are curve components. *Psychological Bulletin, 85,* 858–866.

Cohen, J. (1988). *Statistical power analysis for the behavioral sciences.* Hillsdale, NJ: Lawrence Erlbaum.

Cohen, J., & Cohen, P. (1975). *Applied multiple regression/correlation analysis for the behavioral sciences.* NY: Erlbaum.

Collier, R. O., Baker, F. B., Mandeville, G. K., & Hayes, T. F. (1967). Estimates of test size for several test procedures based on conventional variance ratios in the repeated measures design. *Psychometrika, 32,* 339–353.

Comrey, A. L. (1973). *A first course in factor analysis.* NY: Academic Press.

Cowles, M. (1989). *Statistics in psychology: An historical perspective.* Hillsdale, NJ: Lawrence Erlbaum.

Delucchi, K. L. (1993). On the use and misuse of Chi-square. In G. Keren & C. Lewis (eds.). *A handbook for data analysis in the behavioral sciences: Statistical issues.* Hillsdale, NJ: Lawrence Erlbaum.

Dunn, O. J., & Clark, V. A. (1969). Correlation coefficients measured on the same individuals. *Journal of the American Statistical Association. 64,* 366–377.

Edwards, A.E. (1950). *Experimental Design in Psychological Research.* NY: Rinehart.

Edwards, A. E. (1985). *Experimental design in psychological research.* NY: HarperCollins.

Ferguson, G. A. (1966). *Statistical analysis in psychology and education* (2nd ed.). NY: McGraw Hill.

Ferguson, G. A. (1981). *Statistical analysis in psychology and education.* NY: McGraw Hill.

Fisher, R. A. (1915). Frequency distribution of values of the correlation coefficient in samples from an indefinitely large population. *Biometrika, 10,* 507–521.

Fisher, R. A. (1925a). Applications of "Student's" distribution. *Metron, 5,* 90–104.

Fisher, R. A. (1925b). *Statistical methods for research workers.* London: Oliver & Boyd.

Fisher, R. A. (1935). *The design of experiments.* London: Oliver & Boyd.

Fisher, R. A., & MacKenzie, W. A. (1923). Studies in crop variation. II. The manurial response of different potato varieties. *Journal of Agricultural Science, 13,* 311–320.

Freund, J. E. (1974). *Modern Elementary Statistics* (4th ed.). Englewood Cliffs, NJ: Prentice Hall.

Galton, F. (1877). Typical laws of heredity. *Proceedings of the Royal Institution of Great Britain, 8,* 282–301.

Galton, F. (1885). Regression towards mediocrity in hereditary stature. *Journal of the Anthropological Institute of Great Britain and Ireland, 15,* 246–263.

Galton, F. (1889). *Natural inheritance.* London: Macmillan

Garrett, H. E. (1940). Variability in learning under massed and spaced practice. *Journal of Experimental Psychology, 26,* 547–567.

Garrett, H. E., & Zubin, J. (1943). The analysis of variance in psychological research. *Psychological Bulletin, 40,* 233–267.

Geisser, S., & Greenhouse, S. W. (1958). An extension of Box's results on the use of the F distribution in multivariate analysis. *The Annals of Mathematical Statistics, 29,* 885–891.

Gilliland, A. R. & Humphreys, D. W. (1943). Age, sex, method, and interval as variables in time estimation. *Journal of Genetic Psychology, 63,* 123–130.

Glass, G. V., Peckham, P. D., & Sanders, J. R. (1972). Consequences of failure to meet assumptions underlying the fixed effects analysis of variance and covariance. *Review of Educational Research. 42,* 237–288.

Greenhouse, S. W. & Geisser, S. (1959). On methods in the analysis of profile data. *Psychometrika, 55,* 431–433.

Guadagnoli, E. & Velicer, W. F. (1988). Relation of sample size to the stability of component patterns. *Psychological Bulletin, 103,* 265–275.

Guilford, J. P. (1931). The predictions of affective values. *American Journal of Psychology, 44,* 467–478.

Haberman, S. J. (1973). The analysis of residuals in cross-classified tables. *Biometrics, 29,* 205–222.

Herzberg, P. A. (1969). The parameters of cross validation, *Psychometrika,* Monograph Supplement No. 16.

Horst, P., & Edwards, A. L. (1982) Analysis of nonorthogonal designs: The 2_k-factorial experiment. *Psychological Bulletin. 91,* 190–192.

Hotelling, H. (1931). The generalization of "Student's" ratio. *Annals of Mathematical Statistics, 2,* 360–378.

Hotelling, H. (1940). The selection of variates for use in prediction with some comments on the general problem of nuisance parameters. *Annals of Mathematical Statistics, 11,* 271–283.

Hummel, T. J., & Sligo, J. (1971). Empirical comparison of univariate and multivariate analysis of variance procedures. *Psychological Bulletin, 76,* 49–57.

Humphreys, L. G. (1943). The strength of the Thorndikian response as a function of the number of practice trials. *Journal of Comparative Psychology. 35,* 101–110.

Huynh, H., & Feldt, L. S. (1976). Estimation of the Box correction for degrees of freedom from sample data in randomized block and split-plot designs. *Journal of Educational Statistics, 1,* 69–82.

Jöreskog, K. G. (1969). A general approach to confirmatory maximum likelihood factor analysis. *Psychometrika, 34,* 183–202.

Kaiser, H. F. (1958). The varimax criterion for analytic rotation in factor analysis. *Psychometrika, 23,* 187–200.

Kaiser, H. F. (1960). The application of electronic computers to factor analysis. *Educational and Psychological Measurement, 20,* 141–151.

Kenny, D. A. (1979). *Correlation and causality.* NY: John Wiley.

Kirk, R. E. (1982). *Experimental design: Procedures for the behavioral sciences* (2nd ed.). Pacific Grove, CA: Brooks/Cole.

Kirk, R. E. (1995). *Experimental design: Procedures for the behavioral sciences.* (3rd ed.). Pacific Grove, CA: Brooks/Cole.

Knapp, T. (1978). Canonical correlation analysis: A general parametric significance-testing system. *Psychological Bulletin, 85,* 410–416.

Kogan, L. S. (1953). Variance designs in psychological research. *Psychological Bulletin, 50,* 1–40.

Levene, H. (1960). Robust tests for equality of variances. In I. Olkins (ed.) *Contributions to probability and statistics.* Stanford, CA: Stanford University Press.

Lewis, C. (1993). Analyzing means from repeated measures data. In G. Keren & C. Lewis (Eds.) *A handbook for data analysis in the behavioral sciences: Statistical issues.* Hillsdale, NJ: Lawrence Erlbaum.

Lewis, D. & Burke, C. J. (1949). The use and misuse of the Chi-square test. *Psychological Bulletin, 46,* 433–489.

Lindquist, E. F. (1953). *Design and analysis of experiments in psychology and education.* Boston: Houghton Mifflin.

Lovie, A. D. (1979). The analysis of variance in experimental psychology: 1934–1945. *British Journal of Mathematical and Statistical Psychology, 32,* 151–178.

Lovie, A. D. (1981). On the early history of ANOVA in the analysis of repeated measure designs in psychology. *British Journal of Mathematical and Statistical Psychology, 34,* 1–15.

MacDonald, P. L. & Gardner, R. C. (in press) Type I error rate comparisons of post hoc procedures for I x J Chi-square tables. Educational and Psychological Measurement

Macdonell, W. R. (1901). On criminal anthropometry and the identification of criminals. *Biometrika, 1,* 177–227.

MacIntyre, P. D. (1990). Issues and recommendations in the use of factor analysis. *The Western Journal of Graduate Research, 2,* 59–73.

Marascuilo, L. A., & Levin, J. R. (1983). *Multivariate statistics in the social sciences: A researcher's guide.* Monterey, CA: Brooks/Cole

Mauchly, J. W. (1940). Significance test for sphericity of a normal n-variate distribution. *Annals of Mathematical Statistics, 11,* 204–209.

McNemar, Q. (1969). *Psychological statistics* (4th ed.). NY: Wiley.

Meng, X.-L., Rosenthal, R., & Rubin, D. B. (1992). Comparing correlated correlation coefficients. *Psychological Bulletin. 111,* 172–175.

Milligan, G. W., Wong, D. S., & Thompson, P. A. (1987). Robustness properties of non-orthogonal analysis of variance. *Psychological Bulletin, 101,* 464–470.

Montgomery, D. C. (1984). *Design and analysis of experiments* (2nd ed.). NY: John Wiley.

Morrison, D. F. (1967). *Multivariate statistical methods.* NY: McGraw Hill.

Mulaik, S. A. (1972). *The foundations of factor analysis.* NY: McGraw-Hill.

Myers, J. L. & Well, A. D. (1991). *Research design and statistical analysis.* NY: HarperCollins.

Neufeld, R. W. J., & Gardner, R. C. (1990). Data aggregation in evaluating psychological constructs: Multivariate and logical deductive considerations. *Journal of Mathematical Psychology, 34,* 276–296.

Newman, D. (1939). The distribution of the range in samples from a normal population expressed in terms of an independent estimate of standard deviation. *Biometrika, 31,* 20–30.

Norusis, M. J. (1991). *The SPSS guide to data analysis for SPSS/PC+.* (2nd ed.). Chicago: SPSS Inc.

Nunnally, J. C. (1978). *Psychometric theory* (2nd ed.). NY: McGraw-Hill.

O'Brien, R. G., & Kaiser, M. K. (1985). MANOVA method for analysing repeated measures designs: An extensive primer. *Psychological Bulletin, 97,* 316–333.

Olson, C. L. (1976). On choosing a test statistic in MANOVA. *Psychological Bulletin, 83,* 579–586.

Overall, J. E., & Spiegel, D. K. (1969). Concerning least squares analysis of experimental data. *Psychological Bulletin, 72,* 311–322.

Pearson, K. (1896). Mathematical contributions to the theory of evolution. III. Regression, heredity, and panmixia. *Philosophical Transactions of the Royal Society, A, 187,* 253–318.

Pearson, K. (1900). On the criterion that a given system of deviations from the probable in the case of a correlated system of variables is such that it can be reasonably supposed to have arisen from random sampling. *Philosophical Magazine, 50,* 157–175.

Pearson, K. (1901). On lines and planes of closest fit to systems of points in space. *Philosophical Magazine, 6,* 559–572.

Pearson, K. (1904). Mathematical contributions to the theory of evolution. XII. On the theory of contingency and its relation to association and normal correlation, *Draper's Company Research Memoirs, Biometric Series I.*

Pearson, K. (1911). On the probability that two independent distributions of frequency are really samples from the same population. *Biometrika, 8,* 250–254.

Pedhazur, E. J. (1982). *Multiple regression in behavioral research: Explanation and prediction.* NY: Holt, Rinehart & Winston.

Pedhazur, E. J. & Schmelkin, L. P. (1991). Measurement, design, and analysis: An integrated approach. Hillsdale, NJ: Lawrence Erlbaum.

Rao, C. R. (1952). *Advanced statistical methods in biometric research.* NY: Wiley.

Reitz, W. (1934). Statistical techniques for the study of institutional differences. *Journal of Experimental Education, 3,* 11–24.

Rubin-Rabson, G. (1937). The influence of analytical pre-study in memorizing piano music. *Archives of Psychology, 31* (No. 220).

Rucci, A. J., & Tweney, R. D. (1980). Analysis of variance and the "second discipline" of scientific psychology: A historical account. *Psychological Bulletin, 87,* 166–184.

Satterthwaite, F. E. (1946). An approximate distribution of estimates of variance components. *Biometrics Bulletin, 2,* 110–114.

Shen, E. (1940). Experimental design and statistical treatment in educational research. *Journal of Experimental Education, 8,* 346–353.

Snedecor, G. W. (1934). *Calculation and interpretation of the analysis of variance and covariance.* Ames, Iowa: Collegiate Press.

Snedecor, G. W. (1937). *Statistical methods.* Ames, IA: Collegiate Press.

Snedecor, G. W. (1946). *Statistical methods.* Ames, IA: Iowa State College Press.

Spearman, C. (1904). General intelligence, objectively determined and measured. *American Journal of Psychology,15,* 201–293.

Spearman, C. (1927). *The abilities of man.* NY: Macmillan.

Spinner, B., & Gabriel, R. M. (1981). Factorial analysis of variance with unequal cell frequencies. *Canadian Psychology, 22,* 260–270.

SPSS Inc. Reports. (1986). *SPSS statistical algorithms.* Chicago: SPSS Inc.

Stevens, J. (1986). *Applied multivariate statistics for the social sciences.* Hillsdale, NJ: Lawrence Erlbaum.

Stevens, J. (1996). Applied multivariate statistics for the social sciences (3rd ed.). Hillsdale, NJ: Lawrence Erlbaum.

"Student" (1908a). The probable error of a mean. *Biometrika, 6,*1–25.

"Student" (1908b). Probable error of a correlation coefficient. *Biometrika, 6,* 302–310.

"Student" (1923). On testing varieties of cereals. *Biometrika, 15,* 271–293.

"Student" (1927). Errors of routine analysis. *Biometrika, 19,* 151–164.

Tabachnick, B. G., & Fidell, L. S. (1989). *Using multivariate statistics.* (2nd ed.). NY: Harper & Row.

Thomson, G. H. (1956). *The factorial analysis of human ability.* Boston: Houghton Mifflin.

Thurstone, L. L. (1947). *Multiple factor analysis.* Chicago: University of Chicago Press.

Tippett, L. H. C. (1925). On the extreme individuals and the range of samples taken from a normal population. *Biometrika, 17,* 364–387.

Tukey, J. W. (1953). The problem with multiple comparisons. Unpublished manuscript. Princeton University.

Vernon, P. E. (1961). *The structure of human abilities* (2nd ed.). London: Methuen.

Welch, B. L. (1938). The significance of the difference between two means when the population variances are unequal. *Biometrika, 29,* 350–362.

Wherry, R. J. (1931). A new formula for predicting the shrinkage of the coefficient of multiple correlation. *Annals of Mathematical Statistics, 2,* 440–457.

Wilks, S.S. (1932). Certain generalizations in ANOVA. *Biometrika, 24,* 471–474.

Wilkinson, L. (1999). Statistical Methods in Psychology Journals: Guidelines and Explanations. *American Psychologist, 54,* 594–604.

Winne, P. H. (1983). Distortions of construct validity in multiple regression analysis. *Canadian Journal of Behavioural Science, 15,* 187–202.

Yates, F. (1934). Tests of significance for 2 X 2 contingency tables. *Journal of the Royal Statistical Society, Series A, 147,* 426.

Yule, G. U. (1897). On the theory of correlation. *Journal of the Royal Statistical Society, 60,* 812–854.

Yule, G. U. (1907). On the theory of correlation for any number of variables treated by a new system of notation. *Proceedings of the Royal Society, Series A, 79,* 182–193.

Author Index

Sanders, J. R., 62, 86
Satterthwaite, F. E., 151
Schmelkin, L. P., 242, 244
Schumacker, R. E., 168
Shen, E., 40
Sligo, J., 262–64
Snedecor, G. W., 65, 129, 262
Spearman, C., 237
Spiegel, D. K., 88, 103, 266
Spinner, B., 104
SPSS Inc. Reports, 35
Stevens, J., 207, 218, 242, 244, 262, 279–81, 284
"Student," 40, 41, 65, 73, 79, 181

Tabachnick, B. G., 207, 218, 222, 240, 262–64, 280, 281, 284
Thomson, G. H., 237
Thompson, P. A., 86, 95
Thurstone, L. L., 238, 245
Tippett, L. H. C., 73
Tukey, J. W., 72–74, 97, 98, 100, 101, 123
Tweney, R. D., 41, 65, 113

Velicer, W. F., 243
Vernon, P. E., 238

Welch, B. L., 43

Well, A. D., 60, 63, 104, 107, 122, 129, 141
Wherry, R. J., 205, 218, 225
Wilks, S. S., 113, 122, 261, 262, 270
Wilkinson, L., 2
Winne, P. H., 209, 212
Wong, D. S., 86, 95

Yates, F., 157, 159
Yule, G. U., 205

Zubin, J., 114

Subject Index

8's ~75 Outliers = 7

Sw v. Re   1117 vs 1097   [20 secs]

incon v. con   1153 vs 1065   [88 secs)

12's   outliers = 7

Sw v. Re   937 vs 868 [69]

incon vs con   968 vs 837 [131]

20s   outliers - 15

Sw vs Re   645 vs 600   [45 secs]

incon vs co-   673 vs 567   [106 secs]

	Sw In	Sw Con	Re In	Re Con
			1148	1057
8	1167	1077	938	810
	1014	877		
12			653	549
	705	592		
20				